Undergraduate Texts in Mathematics

Joel Franklin

Methods of
Mathematical Economics

Linear and Nonlinear Programming,
Fixed-Point Theorems

Springer-Verlag

New York Heidelberg Berlin

Joel Franklin
Department of Applied Mathematics
California Institute of Technology
Pasadena, CA 91125
USA

Editorial Board

AMS Subject Classification (1980): 90-01

With 38 Illustrations.

Library of Congress Cataloging in Publication Data

Franklin, Joel N
   Methods of mathematical economics.

   (Undergraduate texts in mathematics)
   Includes index.
   1. Linear programming.   2. Nonlinear programming.
3. Fixed point theory.   4. Economics, Mathematical.
I. Title
QA402.5.F73   519.7'2   79-27342

Printed in the United States of America.

9 8 7 6 5 4 3 2 1

ISBN 0-387-90481-6 Springer-Verlag New York
ISBN 3-540-90481-6 Springer-Verlag Berlin Heidelberg

To the memory of

Jan van der Corput
distinguished mathematician, inspiring teacher
–a friend I cannot find again.

Preface

In 1924 the firm of Julius Springer published the first volume of *Methods of Mathematical Physics* by Richard Courant and David Hilbert. In the preface, Courant says this:

> Since the seventeenth century, physical intuition has served as a vital source for mathematical problems and methods. Recent trends and fashions have, however, weakened the connection between mathematics and physics; mathematicians, turning away from the roots of mathematics in intuition, have concentrated on refinement and emphasized the postulational side of mathematics, and at times have overlooked the unity of their science with physics and other fields. In many cases, physicists have ceased to appreciate the attitudes of mathematicians. This rift is unquestionably a serious threat to science as a whole; the broad stream of scientific development may split into smaller and smaller rivulets and dry out. It seems therefore important to direct our efforts toward reuniting divergent trends by clarifying the common features and interconnections of many distinct and diverse scientific facts. Only thus can the student attain some mastery of the material and the basis be prepared for further organic development of research.
>
> The present work is designed to serve this purpose for the field of mathematical physics. . . . Completeness is not attempted, but it is hoped that access to a rich and important field will be facilitated by the book.

When I was a student, the book of Courant and Hilbert was my bible. Not in a thousand years could anything I wrote rival a book written by Courant, inspired by the teaching of Hilbert. But if imitation is the sincerest form of flattery, I may be forgiven for imitating Courant–Hilbert.

This book relates to economics as Courant–Hilbert related to physics. Courant–Hilbert is not about physics, and this book is not about economics; both books are about mathematics. Each book presents some topics associated with a single field of application; neither book aims for completeness.

Though I hope some economists will read it, this book is mainly meant to be a text for mathematics students. It is written for undergraduates and first-year graduate students. The part on linear programming could easily be taught to sophomores, and the rest of the book is not much harder.

When I was a student, it was fashionable to give courses called "Elementary Mathematics from a Higher Point of View." That always seemed to me the precise opposite of what was needed. What *I* needed was a few courses on higher mathematics from an elementary point of view.

For instance, I wanted to understand the Brouwer fixed-point theorem. That meant I had to take a course on topology, which was quite difficult and time-consuming. The Brouwer theorem seemed to me a priceless jewel guarded by a dragon called topology. Whenever I got near the jewel, the dragon would breathe fire on me. It was frustrating. The statement of Brouwer's theorem was so simple. Why was the proof so hard? (I never did take the course in topology.)

Later, as a post-doctoral fellow at the Courant Institute, I attended lectures on nonlinear partial differential equations by Louis Nirenberg. He made everything depend on some marvelous theorems of Leray and Schauder. I was eager to learn them. What did I need to know first? The Brouwer fixed-point theorem, of course. There it was again. No way. It was becoming an obsession.

A decade later, my colleague Adriano Garsia taught me his easy proof of the Brouwer theorem. I give it to you now in this book; it has never before appeared in print. I give you also Milnor's astonishing proof, which appeared in a journal in late 1978. Milnor's proof is almost too easy to believe.

You may be surprised to see the Schauder theorem here, too. Doesn't that require your students to have a background in functional analysis?

Not really. I give them the Banach space of continuous functions with the maximum norm. That takes five minutes to explain; maybe ten. That's enough functional analysis to start with. Later, if they ever take a course on functional analysis, they'll have no trouble extending what they know to general Banach spaces. Schauder's theorem is one of the very great achievements of science. It is a principal tool of modern nonlinear analysis, as one sees, for instance, in the work of Felix Browder and his associates. So great a result, so useful a tool, should be available to all mathematics students with an absolute minimum of preparation.

In this preface I'm talking to you, my colleague, who will teach the course. In all the rest of the book I talk directly to the student. I've tried to make the writing plain, direct, and readable.

Pasadena, California   Joel Franklin

Contents

Linear Programming 1

1 Introduction to Linear Programming

I first heard about linear programming around 1958. I had just come to Caltech as an associate professor. I was making a trip to New York with my boss, Professor Gilbert McCann, who was the director of Caltech's new computing center. We were making a survey of large industrial computer installations to find out what were the principal industrial uses of computers. One of the companies we planned to visit was the Mobil Oil Corporation.

When we arrived at Mobil, a secretary told us that we would be meeting with Dr. Albert Sokolov*.

Good heavens, I thought, that can't be my old friend Al Sokolov from NYU, can it? Al and I had been post-doctoral fellows at the Courant Institute in New York University. I remembered him as a quiet fellow, with a pleasant personality and a deep knowledge of mathematics.

After a short wait, another secretary came to take McCann and me to Dr. Sokolov's office. This was a long trip. We went through many corridors and passed by many lesser offices before we arrived at the office of Dr. Sokolov.

Sokolov's office seemed about the size of the Rose Bowl. In the distance, behind a large desk, we saw Dr. Sokolov himself. After a long walk over thick carpeting, we seated ourselves in front of his desk. It *was* Al.

"Al," I said, "you've come up in the world."

"Oh, it's nothing . . . nothing, really," he said.

The shy manner was the same; only the surroundings were different. At NYU Al and I had worked in small dusty offices with no air conditioning.

---

* "Albert Sokolov" is not his real name.

After all, we were scholars; we were expected to be poor. But somehow Al had not lived up to that expectation.

We had a nice chat about computers at Mobil. The company had a huge new computing center. I knew it must have cost millions of dollars. Was it worth it? I asked him:

"Al, you've got a huge installation here, millions of dollars worth. I know oil companies have a lot of money, but they don't like to waste it, either. How long will it take the company to pay off your investment in computers?"

He thought for a moment, apparently making a rough mental calculation. Then he answered:

"We paid it off in about two weeks."

"That's amazing," I said. "What kind of problems do you do with this computer?"

"Mainly linear programming."

Al explained at length. Using linear programming, they were able to make optimal production decisions that had formerly been made—not so well—by vice presidents. The result was a great gain for the company. Other big oil companies were doing the same; it was very good for business. It was also good for the consumer, who was getting more of what he wanted at less cost.

Let me tell you what linear programming is about and show you a few examples.

Linear programming is about *linear inequalities*. As you know, a linear equation is something like this:

$$3x_1 - 4x_2 + 9x_3 = 7.$$

Well then, a linear inequality is something like this:

$$3x_1 - 4x_2 + 9x_3 \leqslant 7.$$

Linear algebra is the study of systems of linear equations, and linear programming is the study of systems of linear inequalities.

In real linear algebra, all the constants and all the unknowns (variables) are supposed *real*—positive, negative, or zero. The number of equations and the number of unknowns are supposed finite. Likewise, in linear programming all quantities are real and all systems are finite.

Linear programming is more general than real linear algebra. You see, any real linear equation can be rewritten as two linear inequalities. For instance, the equation $x_1 - 2x_2 = 3$ can be rewritten as the pair of inequalities $x_1 - 2x_2 \leqslant 3$, $x_1 - 2x_2 \geqslant 3$.

That simple remark proves the importance of linear programming. You already know how important linear algebra is. Nobody could make a complete list of the applications of real linear algebra. Well, real linear algebra is just a special case of linear programming. But the converse is false: you can't rewrite the linear inequality $x_1 - 2x_2 \leqslant 3$ as a system of linear equations.

A linear programming problem has three parts:

(i) a finite collection of linear inequalities or equations in a finite number of unknowns $x_1, \ldots, x_n$;
(ii) sign constraints $x_i \geqslant 0$ on same subset of the unknowns—possibly all or none of them;
(iii) a linear function to be minimized or maximized.

A solution $x_1, \ldots, x_n$ of the first two conditions is called *feasible*; a solution to all three conditions is called *optimal*. As you will see, the first two conditions alone usually have infinitely many feasible solutions; but the three conditions together usually have only one optimal solution.

EXAMPLE 1. Investment management. In 1972 Alfred Broaddus wrote an article for the Monthly Review of the Federal Reserve Bank of Richmond. It was called *Linear Programming: A New Approach to Bank Portfolio Management*.

Broaddus wanted to explain linear programming to bankers. During the 1960's, the Bankers Trust Company had developed a complex linear programming model to help the managers reach their investment decisions. The model had proved useful, and so other bankers got interested.

To explain the idea, Broaddus used a much simplified example, which I will show you now.

Suppose the bank has 100 million dollars. Part of this money will be put into loans (L), and part into securities (S). Loans earn high interest. Securities earn lower interest, but they have the advantage of liquidity: at any time, they can be sold at market value.

In Broaddus's example, money loaned out earns 10%; money put into securities earns 5%. Let L and S be the amounts of money in loans and securities. Then the total rate of return is $0.10L + 0.05S$. The bank wants to maximize this rate subject to certain constraints.

Sign constraints. We must have

$$L \geqslant 0 \quad \text{and} \quad S \geqslant 0. \tag{1}$$

Total-funds constraint. Assuming that the total amount available for investment is 100 (in millions of dollars), we must have

$$L + S \leqslant 100. \tag{2}$$

Liquidity constraint. For various reasons (Federal Reserve requirements, etc.), the bank wishes to keep at least 25% of its invested funds liquid. This means $S \geqslant 0.25(L + S)$, *or*

$$L - 3S \leqslant 0. \tag{3}$$

Loan-balance constraint. The bank has certain big customers it never wants to disappoint. If they want loans, they shall have loans. The bank expects its prime customers to ask for loans totaling $30 million, and so L must be at least that big:

$$L \geqslant 30. \tag{4}$$

Those are all the constraints. If L and S satisfy all four constraints, then L and S make up a *feasible* portfolio. If L and S are feasible, and if

$$0.10L + 0.05S = \text{maximum}, \tag{5}$$

then L and S make up an *optimal* portfolio. Thus, an optimal portfolio maximizes the total rate of return subject to the constraints.

We can solve the bank's problem by drawing a picture. In the plane with Cartesian coordinates L and S, the inequality $L \geqslant 0$ stands for the right half-plane; the inequality $S \geqslant 0$ stands for the upper half-plane. The combined constraint (1) stands for the intersection of these two half-planes, namely, the first quadrant. The second constraint ($L + S \leqslant 100$) stands for the half-plane below the line $L + S = 100$. The third constraint ($L - 3S \leqslant 0$) stands for the half-plane above the line $L - 3S = 0$. The last constraint ($L \geqslant 30$) stands for the half-plane to the right of the line $L = 30$.

The feasible points (L,S) must satisfy all the constraints. That means they must lie in *all* of the corresponding half-planes. Then they must lie in the intersection of all these half-planes. This intersection is the triangle in Figure 1. This triangle gives the feasible solutions (L,S).

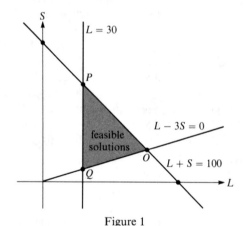

Figure 1

Which point in the triangle is optimal? To find out, we draw the lines of constant return:

$$0.10L + 0.05S = \text{constant}.$$

These are the lines $2L + S = \text{constant}$. On each of these lines all points (L,S) give the same total rate of return. These lines all have slope -2, and so they are parallel to each other.

Look at the feasible triangle in Figure 1. Draw the line with slope -2 through the vertex Q; do the same for the vertex P and for the vertex O. This gives three parallel lines, with the least return on the line through Q and the greatest return on the line through O. All other points of the triangle have intermediate returns. *The point O is the optimal solution.*

As a check, look at the Cartesian coordinates (L,S) for the vertices:

$$Q = (30,10), \quad P = (30,70), \quad O = (75,25).$$

The respective rates of return $(0.10L + 0.05S)$ are

$$3.5 < 6.5 < 8.75.$$

Thus, the optimal portfolio has $L = 75$, $S = 25$, and it produces the annual rate of return \$8.75 million.

EXAMPLE 2. The diet problem. In 1945 George Stigler published a paper called "The Cost of Subsistence." This was no mere mathematical exercise; it appeared in the Journal of Farm Economics. It presented a basic economic problem of world food supply: What is the minimum cost of a nutritionally adequate diet?

Suppose we label the available foods $1, 2, \ldots, n$. A daily *diet* for a single individual is a set of components $x_1 \geqslant 0, x_2 \geqslant 0, \ldots, x_n \geqslant 0$. Thus, x_3 would be the amount of the third food in the daily diet of one individual.

If one gram (or other unit) of food j costs c_j, then the component x_j costs $c_j x_j$. The total cost of the diet is $\sum c_j x_j$. That is what we'd like to minimize.

An adequate diet must provide at least the minimum daily requirements of certain nutrients—calories, various vitamins, protein, fat, carbohydrate, crude fiber, certain amino acids, minerals, etc. The available foods are known to contain the required nutrients in various amounts.

Let a_{ij} be the amount of nutrient i in one gram of food j. Then the component x_j contains the amount $a_{ij}x_j$ of nutrient i. The total amount of nutrient i provided by the diet $x_1, \ldots, x_n$ is the sum $a_{i1}x_1 + \cdots + a_{in}x_n$.

Let b_i be the minimum daily requirement of nutrient i ($i = 1, \ldots, m$). Then an adequate diet x must satisfy these linear inequalities:

$$a_{i1}x_1 + a_{i2}x_2 + \cdots + a_{in}x_n \geqslant b_i \qquad (i = 1, \ldots, m) \tag{6}$$
$$x_1 \geqslant 0, x_2 \geqslant 0, \ldots, x_n \geqslant 0.$$

Under those constraints we wish to minimize the cost:

$$c_1x_1 + c_2x_2 + \cdots + c_nx_n = \text{minimum}. \tag{7}$$

The diet problem is a perfect example of the standard minimum problem of linear programming. In 1945, when Stigler's paper appeared, there was no good computer algorithm for solving large linear programs. In 1945 there were no good computers, period.

Linear programming is a child of the computer age. A theoretical result was published in 1902 by Julius Farkas, but he couldn't have dreamed how important his theorem would become. After all, the computations were impossible. The Farkas theorem was just another beautiful curiosity of pure mathematics. Then came the computer—and with it, the simplex method of George Dantzig. The simplex method does for linear programming what

Gauss's method of elimination does for linear algebra: it gives you a way to compute the answer. Dantzig's method appeared in 1951, and suddenly linear programming sprang to life.

EXAMPLE 3. The transportation problem. In this example the unknowns x_{ij} will have two subscripts. But that doesn't matter; we will still be looking for a finite number of unknowns satisfying linear inequalities and sign constraints.

Suppose oil is produced at certain *plants* in different locations—Arabia, Venezuela, Mexico, Alaska, ...; let s_i be the supply of oil at plant i. And suppose oil is required at certain *markets*—New York, Tokyo, London, ...; let d_j be the amount demanded at market j. We assume the total supply is enough to meet the total demand: $\sum s_i \geqslant \sum d_j$.

Let c_{ij} be the shipping cost per barrel for shipping from plant i to market j. Let x_{ij} be the number of barrels shipped from plant i to market j. Then the total shipping cost is $\sum\sum c_{ij}x_{ij}$. We wish to minimize the total shipping cost subject to the supply and demand constraints.

Let's number the plants $i = 1, \ldots, m$, the markets $j = 1, \ldots, n$. The total amount shipped out of plant i cannot exceed the supply s_i:

$$\sum_{j=1}^{n} x_{ij} \leqslant s_i \qquad (i = 1, \ldots, m).$$

The total amount shipped into market j must at least meet the demand d_j:

$$\sum_{i=1}^{m} x_{ij} \geqslant d_j \qquad (j = 1, \ldots, n).$$

All amounts x_{ij} must be $\geqslant 0$. We wish to minimize the total shipping cost:

$$\sum_{i=1}^{m} \sum_{j=1}^{n} c_{ij}x_{ij} = \text{minimum}.$$

The transportation problem has practical value and theoretical importance. Before long, you will know how to solve it.

EXAMPLE 4. Maximum return from resources. Suppose an oil company has supplies $s_1, \ldots, s_m$ of various crude products (resources). In the refineries, the crude products can be used to make various refined products. The company will be able to sell the refined products at current unit prices $p_1, \ldots, p_n$. The problem is to use the available crude products to make the collection of refined products that will maximize the total selling price.

Suppose that one unit of refined product j requires the amount a_{ij} of crude product i. Suppose we will make the amount x_j of refined product j; then x_j uses $a_{ij}x_j$ of crude i. Summing over all $j = 1, \ldots, n$, we get the total use of crude i, and this must be $\leqslant s_i$, which is the available supply:

$$a_{i1}x_1 + a_{i2}x_2 + \cdots + a_{in}x_n \leqslant s_i \qquad (i = 1, \ldots, m).$$

We require all $x_j \geqslant 0$, and we want to maximize the total selling price:

$$p_1 x_1 + p_2 x_2 + \cdots + p_n x_n = \text{maximum}.$$

Example 4 is standard maximum problem of linear programming. Before long, you will know how to solve it—it is easier than the transportation problem.

Example 4 assumes that the unit market prices p_j are independent of the produced quantities x_j. That is a good assumption for a single company, but a bad assumption for the economy of a whole nation. As the economists would say, it is a good assumption for *micro*-economics, but a bad assumption for *macro*-economics. That is typical for linear economic models. In all applied mathematics, as a rule, linear models are adequate for small variations, but inadequate for large variations. Linear programming is a good way to manage an oil refinery, but a bad way to manage a country.

EXAMPLE 5. *Astronomy and Astrophysics* is the name of the scientific journal in which, in 1972, Harvard astronomer S. M. Faber published a paper called "Quadratic Programming Applied to the Problem of Galaxy Population Synthesis." Got that?

Well, you and I may not understand astrophysics, but we can understand Dr. Faber's problem. She wanted to make a least-squares calculation. She'd taken a lot of data, and she wanted to find out the numbers of stars in various galaxies.

When she made the calculation, some of the galaxy populations came out negative. Bad. Galaxy populations are never negative.

So she asked herself: What if I make a least-squares calculation with the constraint that the unknowns must be nonnegative?

Now her problem looked something like this:

$$\sum_{i=1}^{m} (a_{i1} x_1 + \cdots + a_{in} x_n - b_i)^2 = \text{minimum}$$

for $x_1 \geqslant 0, \cdots, x_n \geqslant 0$. (Here m is bigger than n: m is the number of data points; n is the number of galaxies studied.)

Without the sign constraints $(x_j \geqslant 0)$ Faber's problem would be an example of classical least squares. Gauss gave the solution:

$$x = (A^T A)^{-1} A^T b.$$

But with the sign constraints the problem is an example of *quadratic programming*.

Quadratic programming is *non*linear programming. You have no right to hope that a problem in quadratic programming can be solved by the simplex method of *linear* programming. But it can; Philip Wolfe showed how.

Wolfe's article appeared in the economics journal *Econometrica*. Quadratic programming appeared as a method of mathematical economics, but now it comes to the service of science. It makes short work of Dr. Faber's problem on galaxy populations. Using Wolfe's method, the computations are about as quick as the classical computations of Gauss.

And they are much more general. I didn't tell you the full story about Faber's problem. In addition to the sign constraints $(x_j \geqslant 0)$, she wants to require a bunch of other constraints, which look like this:

$$\alpha_i \leqslant c_{i1}x_1 + \cdots + c_{in}x_n \leqslant \beta_i \qquad (i = 1, \ldots, k).$$

No problem. Wolfe's method can handle those, too. You'll be surprised to learn how easy it is.

In general, linear programming has shown a surprising ability to handle *non*linear problems. A marvelous example is the problem of Chebyshev approximation.

EXAMPLE 6. Chebyshev approximation. In his *Introduction to Numerical Analysis*, Edward Stiefel shows how linear programming can be used to solve this problem:

We are given an over-determined system of linear equations

$$a_{i1}x_1 + a_{i2}x_2 + \cdots + a_{in}x_n = b_i \qquad (i = 1, \ldots, m).$$

We have many more equations than unknowns x_j; we cannot expect to solve the equations exactly.

Unavoidably, there will be errors:

$$\varepsilon_i = b_i - (a_{i1}x_1 + \cdots + a_{in}x_n) \qquad (i = 1, \ldots, m).$$

The errors ε_i will depend on our choice of the numbers x_j. Let us define the maximum absolute error:

$$\mu \equiv \max(|\varepsilon_1|, |\varepsilon_2|, \ldots, |\varepsilon_m|).$$

Problem. *Choose the x_j so as to make μ as small as possible.*

This problem appears in many contexts. In engineering it's just what you want for safety calculations. The worst error is the only one that counts. That's the one that breaks the bridge or blows up the nuclear reactor. In numerical analysis the worst error is often the best measure of the error of a subroutine.

The theory of Chebyshev approximation was well known; there were plenty of existence-and-uniqueness theorems. But no one knew how to compute the answers. Then, around 1960, comes Edward Stiefel, who says in effect:

Look here, the maximum absolute error μ satisfies

$$-\mu \leqslant \varepsilon_i \leqslant \mu \qquad (i = 1, \ldots, m).$$

In other words, μ satisfies these inequalities:

$$-\mu \leqslant b_i - a_{i1}x_1 - \cdots - a_{in}x_n \leqslant \mu \qquad (i = 1, \ldots, m).$$

The problem is to choose $x_1, \ldots, x_m$ so that μ can be as small as possible.

Define the new unknown $x_0 = \mu$. Then this is the problem: Find numbers $x_0, x_1, \ldots, x_n$ satisfying the linear inequalities

$$x_0 + a_{i1}x_1 + \cdots + a_{in}x_n \geqslant b_i$$
$$(i = 1, \ldots, m)$$
$$x_0 - a_{i1}x_1 - \cdots - a_{in}x_n \geqslant -b_i,$$

with

$$x_0 = \text{minimum}.$$

That is a problem in linear programming; you can compute the answers by the simplex method.

Now let's get to work.

Appendix: Vectors, Matrices, and Linear Algebra

I assume you already have some experience with sets of linear equations. I'm not going to teach you linear algebra here—that is a basic subject that deserves a separate course. Anyway, for this book you need only a small part of linear algebra. What you will need to know I will summarize now.

In this book all numbers are *real* (positive, negative, or zero); we won't need complex numbers. Real numbers will sometimes be called *scalars*.

A *vector* $\mathbf{x}$ is a finite, ordered collection of real numbers $x_1, \ldots, x_n$. In other words, $\mathbf{x}$ is a real-valued function (x_i) defined on a finite set of integers $i = 1, \ldots, n$. The numbers x_i are called the *components* of $\mathbf{x}$.

If $\mathbf{x}$ and $\mathbf{y}$ both have n components, then their *inner product* is

$$\mathbf{x} \cdot \mathbf{y} = x_1 y_1 + x_2 y_2 + \cdots + x_n y_n.$$

The Euclidian length of $\mathbf{x}$ is

$$|\mathbf{x}| = \sqrt{(\mathbf{x} \cdot \mathbf{x})} = \sqrt{(x_1^2 + \cdots + x_n^2)}.$$

A vector $\mathbf{x}$ (in boldface) can be represented by a *column* vector x (not in boldface) or by a *row* vector x^T. For instance, if $\mathbf{x}$ has the two components $x_1 = 7$ and $x_2 = 9$, then $\mathbf{x}$ can be represented by the column vector

$$x = \begin{bmatrix} 7 \\ 9 \end{bmatrix}$$

or by the row vector $x^T = [7,9]$. A column vector is a matrix with only one column; a row vector is a matrix with only one row.

An $m \times n$ *matrix* A is a rectangular array of numbers a_{ij} with m rows $(i = 1, \ldots, m)$ and n columns $(j = 1, \ldots, n)$. For example, if $m = 2$ and $n = 3$, we have the matrix

$$A = \begin{bmatrix} 9 & -4 & 0 \\ \sqrt{2} & \pi & 1 \end{bmatrix}.$$

Here $a_{22} = \pi$, $a_{13} = 0$.

The *transpose* of this matrix is

$$A^T = \begin{bmatrix} 9 & \sqrt{2} \\ -4 & \pi \\ 0 & 1 \end{bmatrix}.$$

In general, if $A = (a_{ij})$, then $A^T = (b_{ij})$ with $b_{ij} = a_{ji}$ $(i = 1, \ldots, m; j = 1, \ldots, n)$.

The *system of linear equations*

$$\sum_{j=1}^{n} a_{ij} x_j = b_i \qquad (i = 1, \ldots, m)$$

may be written in the compact form $Ax = b$, where A is a matrix, and where x and b are column vectors.

If A has components a_{ij}, then λA has components λa_{ij}.

If A and B are both matrices with m rows and n columns, then $A + B$ is the matrix with components $c_{ij} = a_{ij} + b_{ij}$.

If A is a $p \times q$ matrix and B is a $q \times r$ matrix, then AB is a $p \times r$ matrix with components

$$c_{ij} = \sum_{k=1}^{q} a_{ik} b_{kj}.$$

For example, if x^T is the 1×2 matrix $[7,9]$, then

$$x^T x = (130), \quad \text{but } xx^T = \begin{bmatrix} 49 & 63 \\ 63 & 81 \end{bmatrix}.$$

The matrix product is associative, but not generally commutative:

$$(XY)Z = X(YZ), \quad \text{but } XY \neq YX \text{ (usually)}.$$

If the vectors $x^1, \ldots, x^k$ all have n components, then a *linear combination* of them is a vector

$$y = c_1 x^1 + \cdots + c_k x^k$$

with components

$$y_i = \sum_{j=1}^{k} c_j x_i^{(j)}.$$

For example, using column vectors, we have

$$\begin{bmatrix} -5 \\ -1 \end{bmatrix} = 7 \begin{bmatrix} 1 \\ 2 \end{bmatrix} - 3 \begin{bmatrix} 4 \\ 5 \end{bmatrix}.$$

The vectors $x^1, \ldots, x^k$ are called *linearly independent* if no one of them is a linear combination of the others. That means

$$\sum_{j=1}^{k} c_j x^j = 0 \qquad \text{only if } all \ c_j = 0.$$

The vectors x with n components constitute the real, n-dimensional vector space R^n.

A *linear subspace* of R^n is subset L that contains all the linear combinations of all of its points. The vectors

$$b^1, \ldots, b^d$$

are a *basis* for L if they are linearly independent and if they *span* L, so that

$$L = \{y : y = c_1 b^1 + \cdots + c_d b^d\}.$$

A theorem says that every basis for L has the same number of vectors. That number, d, is called the *dimension* of L. If L is a linear subspace of R^n, then L has a dimension d in the range $0 \leqslant d \leqslant n$. We say $d = 0$ if L consists of the single vector $x = 0$.

Rank of a matrix. Let A be an $m \times n$ matrix. If A has r independent columns, but doesn't have $r + 1$ independent columns, then we say rank $A = r$.

A theorem says rank $A = $ rank A^T.

If A is an $n \times n$ matrix, then the equation $Ax = b$ has a unique solution x for every b in R^n if and only if A has independent columns (rank $A = n$).

If A is an $m \times n$ matrix, and if b lies in R^m, then the equation $Ax = b$ has some solution x in R^n if and only if the rank of A is not increased by adjoining to A the vector b as a new column. For example, the equation

$$\begin{bmatrix} 1 & 2 & 3 \\ 2 & 4 & 6 \end{bmatrix} x = \begin{bmatrix} 4 \\ 8 \end{bmatrix}$$

has a solution because

$$\text{rank} \begin{bmatrix} 1 & 2 & 3 \\ 2 & 4 & 6 \end{bmatrix} = \text{rank} \begin{bmatrix} 1 & 2 & 3 & 4 \\ 2 & 4 & 6 & 8 \end{bmatrix}.$$

(Both ranks equal 1.)

Notation. For linear programming I use column vectors x and row vectors x^T. Subscripts denote different components x_i of a single vector x, but superscripts denote different vectors x^i.

For nonlinear programming and for the fixed-point theorems I denote vectors by boldface letters x. Thus, $f(x)$ is a vector-valued function of a vector, but $g(x)$ (with g not in boldface) denotes a scalar-valued (real-valued) function of a vector.

I denote matrices by capital letters, and I don't use bold-face for matrices.

In the discussion of the Schauder theorem, the boldface vector notation **x** is used for points in Banach space. I do this to distinguish points of the space from real constants. For instance, if **x** stands for the cosine function $\cos t$ and **y** stands for the sine function $\sin t$, then $a\mathbf{x} + b\mathbf{y}$ stands for some linear combination like

$$a\mathbf{x} + b\mathbf{y} = \sqrt{2} \cos t - 8.9 \sin t.$$

Here it is natural to think of **x** and **y** as generalized vectors.

2 Linear Programs and Their Duals

A *linear program* (or *linear programming problem*) looks like this: First, there is a set of linear equations or inequalities. Second, there are sign constraints $x_j \geqslant 0$ on some or all of the unknowns. Third, there is a linear form to be minimized or maximized.

EXAMPLE 1. Solve these equations:

$$\begin{aligned} x_1 - 2x_2 + x_3 &= 4 \\ -x_1 + 3x_2 &= 5. \end{aligned} \tag{1}$$

Require the unknowns to satisfy the sign constraints

$$x_1 \geqslant 0, \quad x_2 \geqslant 0, \quad x_3 \geqslant 0. \tag{2}$$

A vector x that satisfies conditions (1) and (2) is called a *feasible solution*. Look for an *optimal solution* x, which makes

$$x_1 + 2x_2 + 3x_3 = \text{minimum}. \tag{3}$$

This is an example of a *canonical minimum problem*, which is the main form of linear programming used in computer solution. In general, a canonical minimum problem looks like this:

$$\begin{aligned} Ax &= b \\ x &\geqslant 0 \qquad \text{(meaning } all \text{ components } x_i \geqslant 0) \\ c^T x &= \text{min}. \end{aligned}$$

In our example, we have the matrix

$$A = \begin{bmatrix} 1 & -2 & 1 \\ -1 & 3 & 0 \end{bmatrix}. \tag{4}$$

The unknown vector x is

$$x = \begin{bmatrix} x_1 \\ x_2 \\ x_3 \end{bmatrix}. \tag{5}$$

The given *requirement vector* is

$$b = \begin{bmatrix} 4 \\ 5 \end{bmatrix}. \tag{6}$$

The *cost vector* is

$$c^T = [1,2,3]. \tag{7}$$

EXAMPLE 2. Solve these inequalities:

$$
\begin{aligned}
y_1 - y_2 &\leqslant 1 \\
-2y_1 + 3y_2 &\leqslant 2 \\
y_1 &\leqslant 3.
\end{aligned} \tag{8}
$$

The unknowns y_1, y_2 may be any real numbers—here there are no sign constraints. A vector y that satisfies the inequalities (4) is called a *feasible solution*. Look for an *optimal solution* y, which also satisfies

$$4y_1 + 5y_2 = \text{maximum}. \tag{9}$$

This program looks different from the first. In the first program there were *equations* (1); here there are *inequalities* (8). In the first program there were *sign constraints*; here there are none. The first program was a *minimum problem* (3); this one is a *maximum problem* (9).

We can state this problem using matrices and vectors. Here we have the unknown vector

$$y^T = [y_1, y_2]. \tag{10}$$

The inequalities become

$$y^T A \leqslant c^T, \tag{8}$$

and the maximum condition is

$$y^T b = \text{maximum}. \tag{9}$$

As it happens, the matrix A and the vectors b and c^T came from the preceding example; they were defined in formulas (4), (6), and (7). But here they appear in different ways. Before, A was multiplied on the right by the unknown column x; now A is multiplied on the left by the unknown row y^T. Before, b was a requirement vector; now it is a price vector. Before, c was a cost vector; now it is a requirement vector.

The program

$$y^T A \leqslant c^T, \quad y^T b = \text{max}. \tag{11}$$

is called the *dual* of the program

$$Ax = b, \quad x \geqslant 0, \quad c^T x = \text{min}. \tag{12}$$

You're going to be hearing a lot about duals and the *duality principle*. I won't give you the full story now, but here is a sample:
The two optimal values are equal:

$$\boxed{\min c^T x \text{ for primal} = \max y^T b \text{ for dual}} \tag{13}$$

But more of that later. Now we are just handling some matters of form.

EXAMPLE 3. Solve these inequalities:

$$
\begin{aligned}
x_1 - 2x_2 + x_3 &\geqslant 4 \\
-x_1 + 3x_2 \qquad &\geqslant 5
\end{aligned}
\tag{14}
$$

with the sign constraints

$$x_1 \geqslant 0, \quad x_2 \geqslant 0, \quad x_3 \geqslant 0. \tag{15}$$

Look for an optimal solution satisfying

$$x_1 + 2x_2 + 3x_3 = \text{minimum}. \tag{16}$$

This is the same as Example 1 except that the equations have been replaced by inequalities. With the matrix and vectors of Example 1, our new program has this form:

$$Ax \geqslant b, \quad x \geqslant 0, \quad c^T x = \min. \tag{17}$$

A vector x satisfying $Ax \geqslant b$, $x \geqslant 0$ is called a *feasible solution*; a feasible solution that minimizes $c^T x$ is called an *optimal solution*.

(We never speak of an "optimal solution" unless it is also feasible. Strictly speaking, we shouldn't say "optimal solution" at all, but just "solution", since a linear programming problem is a problem of optimization. But the redundant phrase *optimal solution* is common usage, and we will follow it.)

A program with the form (17) is called a *standard* minimum problem. Its *dual* has the following form:

$$y^T A \leqslant c^T, \quad y \geqslant 0, \quad y^T b = \max. \tag{18}$$

This is the same as the dual (11) except that now we have the sign constraints $y \geqslant 0$.

The general linear program and its dual. The *primal* problem looks like this: We require certain *inequalities* and *equations*:

$$
\begin{aligned}
\sum_{j=1}^{n} a_{ij} x_j &\geqslant b_i \qquad \text{for } i \text{ in } I_1 \\
&= b_i \qquad \text{for } i \text{ in } I_2,
\end{aligned}
\tag{19}
$$

where I_1 and I_2 are disjoint sets of integers whose union is the set

$$I = I_1 \cup I_2 = \{1,2,\ldots,m\}. \tag{20}$$

We require certain *sign constraints*:

$$x_j \geqslant 0 \qquad \text{for } j \text{ in } J_1, \tag{21}$$

where J_1 is a specified subset of indices

$$J_1 \subset J = \{1,2,\ldots,n\}. \tag{22}$$

(If J_1 is empty, there are no sign constraints; if $J_1 = J$, we require *all* $x_j \geqslant 0$.)
A *feasible solution* x solves (19) and (21); an *optimal solution* x is a feasible
solution minimizing a given linear form:

$$\sum_{j=1}^{n} c_j x_j = \text{minimum}. \tag{23}$$

The corresponding *dual* problem looks like this: We look for a vector y
with component $y_1,\ldots,y_m$. We require

$$\sum_{i=1}^{m} y_i a_{ij} \leqslant c_j \qquad \text{for } j \text{ in } J_1 \tag{24}$$
$$= c_j \qquad \text{for } j \text{ in } J_2,$$

where J_1 is the subset mentioned in (22), and where J_2 is the complement
$J_2 = J - J_1$. For sign constraints, we require

$$y_i \geqslant 0 \qquad \text{for } i \text{ in } I_1. \tag{25}$$

For optimality we require

$$\sum_{i=1}^{m} y_i b_i = \text{maximum}. \tag{26}$$

EXAMPLE 4. Look back at Example 1 and its dual, Example 2. What are the
index sets? They are

$$I = \{1,2\}; \quad J = \{1,2,3\}$$
$$I_1 = \varnothing, \quad I_2 = I; \quad J_1 = J, \quad J_2 = \varnothing,$$

where $\varnothing$ stands for the empty set. Now Example 1 becomes a case of the
general primal, and Example 2 becomes a case of the general dual.

EXAMPLE 5. Look back at Example 3. The index sets are

$$I = \{1,2\}; \quad J = \{1,2,3\}$$
$$I_1 = I, \quad I_2 = \varnothing; \quad J_1 = J, \quad J_2 = \varnothing.$$

The next example will show how to handle inequalities and sign constraints that go the wrong way.

EXAMPLE 6. Let us try to state the following linear program as a general minimum problem:

$$
\begin{aligned}
x_1 - 2x_2 + x_3 &\leqslant 4 \\
-x_1 + 3x_2 \quad\;\; &\geqslant 5 \\
x_1 + \quad\quad x_3 &= 10 \\
x_1 \geqslant 0,\; x_3 &\leqslant 0 \\
x_1 + 2x_2 + 3x_3 &= \text{maximum.}
\end{aligned}
$$

The first inequality goes the wrong way, so we multiply it by -1, which gives

$$
-x_1 + 2x_2 - x_3 \geqslant 4.
$$

The constraint $x_3 \leqslant 0$ goes the wrong way, so we define the new unknown $x_3' = -x_3 \geqslant 0$. Finally, we change the maximum problem into a minimum problem by multiplying the thing to be optimized by -1.

The result of all this is the following restatement of the original maximum problem:

$$
\begin{aligned}
-x_1 + 2x_2 + x_3' &\geqslant -4 \\
-x_1 + 3x_2 \quad\;\; &\geqslant 5 \\
x_1 \quad\quad - x_3' &= 10 \\
x_1 \geqslant 0,\; x_3' &\geqslant 0 \\
-x_1 - 2x_2 + 3x_3' &= \text{minimum.}
\end{aligned}
$$

This takes the form of a general minimum problem. The index sets are

$$
I = \{1,2,3\}; \quad J = \{1,2,3\}
$$
$$
I_1 = \{1,2\}, \quad I_2 = \{3\}; \quad J_1 = \{1,3\}, \quad J_2 = \{2\}.
$$

In the last example we restated a maximum problem as a minimum problem. This brings up an interesting general question: *Can we restate the general dual problem as an equivalent problem in primal form?*

Of course we can. Look at the general dual problem (24)–(26). First we restate (24) as follows:

$$
\sum_{i=1}^{m} (-a_{ij})y_i \geqslant -c_j \qquad \text{for } j \text{ in } J_1
$$
$$
= -c_j \qquad \text{for } j \text{ in } J_2. \tag{24'}
$$

We use the sign constraints unchanged:

$$
y_i \geqslant 0 \qquad \text{for } i \text{ in } I_1. \tag{25'}
$$

Finally, we get a *minimum* problem by replacing b by $-b$:

$$\sum_{i=1}^{m} (-b_i)y_i = \text{minimum.} \tag{26'}$$

The dual of the dual is the primal. The last three formulas state the dual in the form of primal. The original primal problem was defined by a matrix A, by vectors b and c, and by index sets I_1 and J_1; this problem appears in formulas (19), (21), and (23). Let's denote this primal problem by

$$P(A;b,c;I_1,J_1). \tag{27}$$

(We don't need to mention the sets I_2 and J_2, since they are just the complements of I_1 and J_1.) Using this notation, we can denote the problem (24'), (25'), (26') by

$$P(-A^T;-c,-b;J_1,I_1). \tag{28}$$

The effect of taking the dual was to replace A by $-A^T$, b by $-c$, c by $-b$, I_1 by J_1, and J_1 by I_1.

EXAMPLE 7. Suppose the primal is the canonical minimum problem

$$Ax = b, \quad x \geqslant 0, \quad c^T x = \text{min.} \tag{29}$$

Using the notation (27), we can denote this problem by $P(A;b,c;\varnothing,J)$, where $\varnothing$ is the null set and $J = \{1, \ldots ,n\}$. Let us now form the new primal (28). Calling the new unknown y, we get the new primal $P(-A^T;c,b;J,\varnothing)$:

$$-A^T y \geqslant -c, \quad -b^T y = \text{min.} \tag{30}$$

Sure enough, this is equivalent to

$$y^T A \leqslant c^T, \quad y^T b = \text{max,} \tag{31}$$

which is the dual of the original primal.

In general, if P is the primal and DP is its dual, we have found

$$DP(A;b,c;I_1,J_1) = P(-A^T;-c,-b;J_1,I_1). \tag{32}$$

In other words, the dual of the primal is the new primal obtained from these interchanges:

$$A \leftrightarrow -A^T; b \leftrightarrow c; I_1 \leftrightarrow J_1. \tag{33}$$

If you apply these interchanges *twice*, you get back where you started. For instance, if you take minus the transpose twice, you get back the original matrix. Thus, if we apply the operator D twice, we get

$$\begin{aligned} D \cdot DP(A;b,c;I_1,J_1) &= DP(-A^T;-c,-b;J_1,I_1) \\ &= P(A;b,c;I_1,J_1). \end{aligned} \tag{34}$$

In other words, *the dual of the dual is the primal.*

The general problem in canonical form. The canonical minimum problem is

$$Ax = b, \quad x \geqslant 0, \quad c^T x = \min. \tag{35}$$

Here there are no inequalities ($I_1 = \varnothing$), and we require all $x_j \geqslant 0$ ($J_1 = J$). This is the problem $P(A;b,c;\varnothing,J)$. It looks less general than the general problem $P(A;b,c;I_1,J_1)$, which may require some inequalities—

$$\sum_{j=1}^n a_{ij} x_j \geqslant b_i \qquad (i \in I_1), \tag{36}$$

and which may leave some unknowns free—

$$-\infty < x_j < \infty \qquad (j \in J_2). \tag{37}$$

But we can put the general problem in canonical form. All we have to do is define some new unknowns.

For every inequality (36) we define the *slack variable* $z_i \geqslant 0$, and we write (36) as an *equation*:

$$\sum_{j=1}^n a_{ij} x_j - z_i = b_i \qquad (i \in I_1). \tag{36'}$$

And for every free x_j we write

$$x_j = u_j - v_j \qquad (j \in J_2), \tag{37'}$$

requiring $u_j \geqslant 0$ and $v_j \geqslant 0$. This depends on the deep truth that every real number is the difference of two positive numbers. Now we have a problem with all equations and with all unknowns $\geqslant 0$; the general problem has become canonical.

EXAMPLE 8. Here is a general problem:

$$\begin{aligned}
x_1 + 2x_2 &\geqslant 3 \\
4x_1 + 5x_2 &= 6 \\
x_1 \geqslant 0, \quad -\infty &< x_2 < \infty, \\
7x_1 + 8x_2 &= \min.
\end{aligned} \tag{38}$$

This is equivalent to the canonical problem

$$\begin{aligned}
x_1 + 2u_2 - 2v_2 - z_1 &= 3 \\
4x_1 + 5u_2 - 5v_2 &= 6 \\
x_1 \geqslant 0, \quad u_2 \geqslant 0, \quad v_2 \geqslant 0, \quad z_1 &\geqslant 0 \\
7x_1 + 8u_2 - 8v_2 &= \min.
\end{aligned} \tag{38'}$$

Later we'll spend a long time discussing computer methods for linear program in canonical form. Now you understand why these methods will apply to linear programs of every form.

I haven't yet shown you why the dual is so important, but as you will see before long, duality is the heart of linear programming.

PROBLEMS

1. State this problem as a canonical minimum problem:

$$3x_1 - 4x_2 \geq 0$$
$$5x_1 + 2x_3 \leq 0$$
$$6x_2 + 7x_3 = 0$$
$$x_1 \geq 0, \quad x_3 \geq 0; \quad x_2 = \max.$$

2. State the dual of Problem 1.

3. State Problem 1 as a standard minimum problem.

4. State the dual of the problem in Example 6.

5. Consider the linear system

$$Ax = b, \quad x \geq 0,$$

   with *nothing* to be optimized. Show how to state this system as a canonical minimum problem by the right choice for the cost vector c.

6. State the linear system $Ax = b$ as a canonical minimum problem. What is the dual program?

7. Solve this linear program graphically:

$$3x_1 + 4x_2 \leq 12$$
$$5x_1 + 2x_2 \leq 10$$
$$x \geq 0; \quad x_1 + x_2 = \max.$$

8. State the dual of Problem 7 and solve it graphically. Verify that the maximum for the primal equals the minimum for the dual.

9. A Chebyshev minimum problem (see Section 1): State the following problem as a linear program:

$$|3x_1 + 4x_2 - 7| \leq \varepsilon$$

$$|2x_1 + 3x_2 - 5| \leq \varepsilon$$
$$|-x_1 + 4x_2 - 9| \leq \varepsilon$$
$$\varepsilon = \min.$$

10. State the dual of Problem 9.

11. Consider the system of *strict* inequalities

$$\sum_{j=1}^{n} a_{ij}x_j > 0 \qquad (i = 1, \ldots, m).$$

   Show how this system is equivalent to the following:

$$\sum_{j=1}^{n} a_{ij}u_j \geq 1 \qquad (i = 1, \ldots, m).$$

12. Solve this problem:
$$3x_1 + 4x_2 \leqslant 12$$
$$4x_1 + 5x_2 \leqslant 20$$
$$x \geqslant 0; \quad 5x_1 + 6x_2 = \max.$$

13. State and solve the dual of Problem 12. Verify the equality of the primal and dual optima.

14. State the following problem as a linear program:
$$5 \cdot |3x_1 + 4x_2 - 7| + 2 \cdot |2x_1 + 3x_2 - 5| + 8 \cdot |-x_1 + 4x_2 - 9| = \min.$$

15. Find the dual program for Problem 14.

16. Find the dual of this linear program:
$$-d \leqslant Ax - b \leqslant d$$
$$x \geqslant 0; \quad c^T x = \min.$$

3 How the Dual Indicates Optimality

You've seen that every linear programming problem can be put in *canonical form*:

$$Ax = b, \quad x \geqslant 0 \tag{1}$$

$$c^T x = \text{minimum}. \tag{2}$$

If a vector x satisfies (1), it's called a *feasible* solution; if it satisfies (1) and (2), it's called an *optimal* solution.

Some linear programs have no feasible solution. For example, this one has none:

$$x_1 = -1, \quad x_1 \geqslant 0; \quad 3x_1 = \min. \tag{3}$$

Some linear programs have feasible solutions but no optimal solution. Look at this:

$$x_1 - x_2 = 0, \quad x \geqslant 0; \quad -2x_1 = \min. \tag{4}$$

If we set $x_1 = x_2 = \lambda$ and let $\lambda \to +\infty$, we can drive the cost down to $-\infty (-2\lambda \to -\infty)$. Since no single feasible solution produces minimum cost, we say there is no optimal solution.

If an optimal solution exists, it need not be unique. Look at this program:

$$x_1 + x_2 = 1, \quad x \geqslant 0; \quad x_1 + x_2 = \min. \tag{5}$$

Here all x are optimal on the segment connecting (1,0) with (0,1).

Mathematicians love pathological cases, and you have just seen three. The *normal* case is this: A linear program has many feasible solutions, and one of them is the unique optimal solution. Here is a normal example:

EXAMPLE 1.

$$2x_1 + x_2 - x_3 = 4, \quad x \geqslant 0, \tag{6}$$

$$3x_1 + 5x_2 = \text{minimum}. \tag{7}$$

If you regard x_3 as a slack variable, the requirement (6) becomes an inequality in 2 dimensions:

$$2x_1 + x_2 \geqslant 4, \quad x \geqslant 0. \tag{6'}$$

The feasible solutions (x_1, x_2) appear in Figure 1. The slack x_3 doesn't appear in Figure 1, but it equals $2x_1 + x_2 - 4 \geqslant 0$.

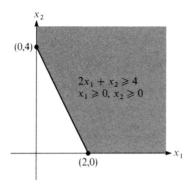

Figure 1

Figure 1 shows infinitely many feasible solutions. Where is the optimal solution?

The lines of constant cost are the lines

$$3x_1 + 5x_2 = \text{constant}.$$

A few of these lines appear in Figure 2. Now I want you to imagine Figure 2 superimposed on Figure 1. Can you see which feasible solution has the least cost?

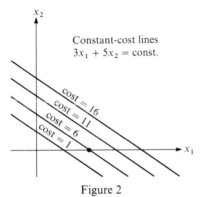

Figure 2

It is the unique optimal solution

$$(x_1,x_2) = (2,0).$$

At this point one of the constant-cost lines just touches the feasible set. The line that does this is labeled cost = 6 in Figure 2. None of the lower-cost lines hits the feasible set. Using the slack x_3, we get the unique optimal solution

$$(x_1,x_2,x_3) = (2,0,0). \tag{8}$$

The minimum cost equals 6.

   This example is typical, and you can learn a lot from it. Note that the optimal vector (8) has only *one* non-zero component. The matrix A in (6) consists of only *one* row:

$$A = [2,1,-1]. \tag{9}$$

The vector (8) is called a *basic* optimal solution; it has r non-zero components as A has r independent rows. We'll discuss basic solutions later.
   In this simple example, you could draw pictures and visualize the answer. If the matrix A had been a 10×30 matrix instead of a 1×3 matrix, you would have had a hard time drawing and visualizing. What we need is an analytic technique.
   How about calculus? After all, our problem is a constrained minimum problem. Isn't that what Lagrange multipliers are for?
   In calculus, we learned how to solve constrained minimum problems. Suppose we have one constraint and three unknowns:

$$\varphi(x_1,x_2,x_3) = \text{min.}; \quad \psi(x_1,x_2,x_3) = \text{const.}$$

The method was to form the Lagrange function $\varphi - \lambda\psi$ and set the derivatives equal to zero:

$$\frac{\partial}{\partial x_j}[\varphi(x_1,x_2,x_3) - \lambda\psi(x_1,x_2,x_3)] = 0 \qquad (j = 1,2,3).$$

But Example 1 *is* a constrained minimum problem:

$$2x_1 + x_2 - x_3 = 4; \quad 3x_1 + 5x_2 = \text{min.}$$

Let's form the Lagrange equations for this example:

$$3 - 2\lambda = 0$$
$$5 - \lambda = 0$$
$$\lambda = 0.$$

Evidently, the Lagrange multiplier must equal $\frac{3}{2}$, 5, *and* 0.
   What went wrong? If you look back at (6), you see we have sign constraints $x_j \geqslant 0$. In 3 dimensions, the points x that satisfy the full constraint (6) constitute the intersection of a plane with the orthant $x \geqslant 0$. The unique

optimal point (2,0,0) lies on the *boundary*. And now we remember: Calculus works when the optimal point lies in the *interior*.

If you want a simple example, try this one: Minimize the single function $3x + 5$ for $x \geqslant 0$. Setting the derivative equal to zero, we get the equation $3 = 0$, which we don't believe.

In general, calculus fails in linear programming because the optimal x occurs on the boundary of the feasible set. To compute the optimal x, we shall need a numerical method; but first we need an answer to this question: *How can we know an optimal solution when we see one?* We need a sufficient condition for x to be an optimal solution of the linear program

$$Ax = b, \quad x \geqslant 0, \quad c^T x = \min. \tag{10}$$

Bounds from the dual. The dual program is

$$y^T A \leqslant c^T, \quad y^T b = \max. \tag{11}$$

If x is *any* feasible solution for the primal, and if y is *any* feasible solution of the dual, then

$$y^T Ax = y^T(Ax) = y^T b \tag{12}$$

and

$$y^T Ax = (y^T A)x \leqslant c^T x. \tag{13}$$

Thus, $c^T x \geqslant y^T b$.

EXAMPLE 2. The dual of Example 1 is the program

$$y_1[2,1,-1] \leqslant [3,5,0]; \quad 4y_1 = \max. \tag{14}$$

Pick any feasible solution for the dual, say $y_1 = 1$. Then $y^T b = 4$, and we conclude

$$c^T x \geqslant 4 \qquad \text{for all feasible } x. \tag{15}$$

Indeed, we know that is true because we found min $c^T x = 6$.

In general, any y that is feasible for the dual gives a lower bound for the required minimum value of $c^T x$ for the primal.

Now suppose we find a pair of feasible solutions $\hat{x}$ and $\hat{y}$ that produce *equality*:

$$c^T \hat{x} = \hat{y}^T b. \tag{16}$$

Then we are in luck. As you will now see, $\hat{x}$ *must then be optimal for the primal.* And by the way, $\hat{y}$ is optimal for the dual.

Proof? Easy. Let x be any competing feasible solution of the primal. Then we know $c^T x \geqslant \hat{y}^T b$ because $\hat{y}$ is feasible for the dual. Now the assumption of equality (16) implies

$$c^T x \geqslant \hat{y}^T b = c^T \hat{x}, \tag{17}$$

and this must hold for *every* feasible x. In short, $\hat{x}$ minimizes $c^T x$ over all feasible x.

Similarly, for every y that is feasible for the dual, the equality (16) implies

$$y^T b \leqslant c^T \hat{x} = \hat{y}^T b. \tag{18}$$

Done.

EXAMPLE 3. Suppose we had chosen $\hat{y}_1 = \frac{3}{2}$ instead of $y_1 = 1$ in Example 2. This would give

$$\hat{y}^T b = (\tfrac{3}{2}) \cdot (4) = 6.$$

Example 2 is the dual of Example 1. If we call $\hat{x}$ the feasible solution of the primal with components $2, 0, 0$, we get

$$c^T \hat{x} = 3\hat{x}_1 + 5\hat{x}_2 + 0\hat{x}_3 = 6.$$

Since $\hat{y}^T b = c^T \hat{x}$, we conclude that $\hat{x}$ is optimal for the primal, and $\hat{y}$ is optimal for the dual.

In general, as we have proved, *the equality $\hat{y}^T b = c^T \hat{x}$ is a sufficient condition for optimality.*

Is it also a *necessary* condition? If $\hat{x}$ is optimal for the primal, must there be some $\hat{y}$ feasible for the dual satisfying $\hat{y}^T b = c^T \hat{x}$? The answer is *yes*, but that is harder to prove. That is the *duality theorem*, which we will prove later.

The equilibrium theorem. If x is feasible for the primal, it satisfies

$$\sum_{j=1}^{n} a_{ij} x_j = b_i \qquad (i = 1, \ldots, m) \tag{19}$$

$$x_j \geqslant 0 \qquad (j = 1, \ldots, n). \tag{20}$$

(With no loss of generality, we consider linear programming in the canonical form.) If y is feasible for the dual, it satisfies

$$\sum_{i=1}^{m} y_i a_{ij} \leqslant c_j \qquad (i = 1, \ldots, m). \tag{21}$$

We have found a condition for optimality:

$$\sum_{i=1}^{m} y_i b_i = \sum_{j=1}^{n} c_j x_j. \tag{22}$$

How does this equality happen? The answer appears in the following theorem.

Theorem 1. *Let x be feasible for the primal canonical program, and let y be feasible for the dual. Then*

$$y^T b \leqslant c^T x. \tag{23}$$

Equality occurs if and only if the equilibrium condition holds:

$$\boxed{\sum_{i=1}^{m} y_i a_{ij} = c_j \quad \text{if} \quad x_j > 0} \tag{24}$$

This says, if the jth component of x is *positive*, then the jth dual inequality (21) must be achieved as an *equation*.

PROOF. By the sign constraints (20) and by the dual inequalities (21), we have

$$\sum_{j=1}^{n} x_j \left(c_j - \sum_{i=1}^{m} y_i a_{ij} \right) \geq 0, \tag{25}$$

and now the primal equations (19) give

$$\sum_{j=1}^{n} x_j c_j = \sum_{i=1}^{m} y_i b_i \geq 0, \tag{26}$$

which is the required inequality $x^T c - y^T b \geq 0$.

Equality occurs iff equality occurs in (25). In the sum (25) *each* term is ≥ 0; the component x_j is ≥ 0 by (20), and the factor $(\ldots)$ is ≥ 0 by (21). Therefore, the sum equals zero only if every single term equals zero, which means this: If x_j is positive, its factor $(c_j - \sum_i y_i a_{ij})$ must be zero. That is the equilibrium condition (24). $\qquad\square$

EXAMPLE 4. In Example 3 we have the feasible pair

$$x = \begin{bmatrix} 2 \\ 0 \\ 0 \end{bmatrix}, \quad y = (\tfrac{3}{2}).$$

Here the component x_1 is positive, and we have the corresponding equilibrium equation

$$y_1 a_{11} = (\tfrac{3}{2})(2) = 3 = c_1.$$

At once, we conclude x and y are optimal. (By the way, according to (14), the other two dual inequalities are

$$y_1 \cdot 1 \leq 5, \quad y_1 \cdot (-1) \leq 0,$$

and they are both satisfied strictly.)

EXAMPLE 5. Let's take a harder example—one that we couldn't solve by drawing pictures. Here's the primal:

$$5x_1 - 6x_2 + 4x_3 - 2x_4 = 0$$
$$x_1 - x_2 + 6x_3 + 9x_4 = 16$$
$$x \geq 0$$
$$x_1 + 5x_2 + 2x_3 + 13x_4 = \text{minimum}.$$

Here we have 2 equations in 4 unknowns. We can try to solve the equations with just 2 non-zero components. For instance, let's use x_2 and x_3. This gives the numbers

$$x_2 = 2, \quad x_3 = 3,$$

Good luck: they turned out positive. Setting $x_1 = x_4 = 0$, we have a feasible solution x for the primal.

Is x optimal? That's easy to check. The dual inequalities are

$$5y_1 + y_2 \leqslant 1$$
$$-6y_1 - y_2 \leqslant 5$$
$$4y_1 + 6y_2 \leqslant 2$$
$$-2y_1 + 9y_2 \leqslant 13.$$

Since our primal x has positive second and third components, the equilibrium condition requires that the second and third dual inequalities be satisfied as equations. The unique solution of these two equations is

$$y_1 = -1, \quad y_2 = 1.$$

The negative number y_1 doesn't bother us, since the dual problem has no sign constraints. But *we must always verify that our equilibrium solution y satisfies the* other *dual inequalities.* In this example, we must verify the first and fourth inequalities:

$$5y_1 + y_2 \leqslant 1, \quad -2y_1 + 9y_2 \leqslant 13.$$

Again we have good luck. We have verified that our equilibrium solution y solves *all* the dual inequalities. Now the equilibrium theorem says $c^T x = y^T b$, and so x is optimal for the primal and y is optimal for the dual.

Example 5 was not as contrived as you might think. The solution x was what we will call a *basic* solution. As you will see, if a canonical program has any feasible solution, it has a *basic* feasible solution; and if it has any optimal solution, it has a *basic* optimal solution.

PROBLEMS

1. Draw the set of feasible solutions to this problem:

$$x_1 + 2x_2 \leqslant 4, \quad x \geqslant 0, \quad c_1 x_1 + c_2 x_2 = \text{max.}$$

2. For Problem 1, locate *all* the optimal solutions for these values of (c_1, c_2): $(2,1)$; $(1,3)$; $(50,100)$; $(-1,0)$; $(0,-1)$; $(-6,-7)$.

3. For the following primal, write the dual and use it to find one or two lower bounds for the primal value:

$$\begin{bmatrix} 1 & 2 & 3 \\ 6 & 5 & 4 \end{bmatrix} x = \begin{bmatrix} 1 \\ 2 \end{bmatrix}, \quad x \geqslant 0, \quad x_1 + x_2 + x_3 = \text{min.}$$

4. Consider this problem:

$$2 \leqslant x_1 + 2x_2 + 9x_3 \leqslant 7, \quad x \geqslant 0,$$
$$-7x_1 + 9x_2 + 16x_3 = \text{max.}$$

Write the dual, and get an upper bound for the primal maximum.

5. Consider this problem:

$$2 \leqslant x_1 + 2x_2 + 9x_3 \leqslant 7, \quad x \geqslant 0,$$
$$-7x_1 + 9x_2 + 16x_3 = \min.$$

Write the dual, and get a lower bound for the primal minimum.

6. Write the *equilibrium* conditions for Problem 3.

7. Find the optimal solution for Problem 3 as follows: Compute the feasible solutions with only two positive components; then check the equilibrium conditions.

8. Write the program in Problem 4 as a canonical minimum problem. What are the equilibrium conditions?

4 Basic Solutions

We define a basic solution x as follows. Suppose x solves $Ax = b$. If $x \neq 0$, then x has some non-zero components, say $x_\alpha, x_\beta, \ldots$. Then we can write Ax as a linear combination of the corresponding columns of A:

$$Ax = x_\alpha a^\alpha + x_\beta a^\beta + \cdots = b. \tag{1}$$

The solution x is said to *depend* on the columns $a^\alpha, a^\beta, \ldots$ *If the columns $a^\alpha, a^\beta, \ldots$ are linearly independent, then x is called a basic solution.*

This covers the usual case, $b \neq 0$. For the case $b = 0$ we define the basic solution $x = 0$. (In this case x depends on the null subset of columns of A.)

Remember that vectors $a^\alpha, a^\beta, \ldots$ are called *linearly independent* iff the equation

$$\theta_\alpha a^\alpha + \theta_\beta a^\beta + \cdots = 0 \tag{2}$$

implies that *all* the coefficients $\theta_\alpha, \theta_\beta, \ldots$ are zero. Equivalently, the vectors $a^\alpha, a^\beta, \ldots$ are independent iff none of them is a linear combination of the others.

EXAMPLE 1. Define the matrix

$$A = \begin{bmatrix} 1 & -1 & -1 \\ 1 & 2 & -3 \end{bmatrix}. \tag{3}$$

We label the columns a^1, a^2, a^3. The three columns are dependent, because they all lie in a 2-dimensional space. But every *two* of the columns are independent. For example, these two columns are independent:

$$a^2 = \begin{bmatrix} -1 \\ 2 \end{bmatrix}, \quad a^3 = \begin{bmatrix} -1 \\ -3 \end{bmatrix}.$$

EXAMPLE 2. For the matrix (3) let's compute *all* the basic solutions of

$$\begin{bmatrix} 1 & -1 & -1 \\ 1 & 2 & -3 \end{bmatrix} \begin{bmatrix} x_1 \\ x_2 \\ x_3 \end{bmatrix} = \begin{bmatrix} 0 \\ 1 \end{bmatrix}. \tag{4}$$

First, there's a basic solution that depends on columns a^1 and a^2. We get this solution by solving

$$\begin{bmatrix} 1 & -1 \\ 1 & 2 \end{bmatrix} \begin{bmatrix} x_1 \\ x_2 \end{bmatrix} = \begin{bmatrix} 0 \\ 1 \end{bmatrix}.$$

We compute $x_1 = \frac{1}{3}$, $x_2 = \frac{1}{3}$. Setting $x_3 = 0$, we get a basic solution of (4):

$$x = \begin{bmatrix} \frac{1}{3} \\ \frac{1}{3} \\ 0 \end{bmatrix}. \tag{5}$$

Next, there's a basic solution that depends on columns a^1 and a^3. We get it by solving

$$\begin{bmatrix} 1 & -1 \\ 1 & -3 \end{bmatrix} \begin{bmatrix} x_1 \\ x_3 \end{bmatrix} = \begin{bmatrix} 0 \\ 1 \end{bmatrix},$$

obtaining $x_1 = -\frac{1}{2}$, $x_3 = -\frac{1}{2}$. This gives another basic solution of (4):

$$x' = \begin{bmatrix} -\frac{1}{2} \\ 0 \\ -\frac{1}{2} \end{bmatrix}. \tag{6}$$

In the same way, we compute the third basic solution of (4):

$$x'' = \begin{bmatrix} 0 \\ \frac{1}{5} \\ -\frac{1}{5} \end{bmatrix}, \tag{7}$$

which depends on the independent columns a^2, a^3.

There are no other basic solutions. Why? Because the only other sets of *independent* columns consist of only *one* column or of the null set, and none of these sets spans a solution.

But there are millions of *non-basic* solutions. All of them have the form

$$\theta_1 x + \theta_2 x' + \theta_3 x'', \tag{8}$$

where $\theta_1 + \theta_2 + \theta_3 = 1$, where x, x', x'' are the three basic solutions; for then

$$A(\theta_1 x + \theta_2 x' + \theta_3 x'') = \theta_1 b + \theta_2 b + \theta_3 b = b.$$

For instance, here is a non-basic solution:

$$18x - 12x' - 5x'' = \begin{bmatrix} 12 \\ 5 \\ 7 \end{bmatrix}.$$

Plug it into (4) and you'll see that it works. It is non-basic because it depends on the dependent columns a^1, a^2, a^3.

If you want a more exotic example, take $\pi x + ex' + (1 - \pi - e)x''$.

You get the idea: If the matrix A has more columns than rows, the equation $Ax = b$ typically has infinitely many solutions x. But A has only a *finite* number of subsets of independent columns, and so *the equation $Ax = b$ has only a finite number of basic solutions.*

You'll see this is just what we need for linear programming: it cuts down the number of possibilities from infinity to a finite number.

Theorem. *Consider the canonical linear program*

$$Ax = b, \quad x \geqslant 0, \quad c^T x = \min. \tag{9}$$

First, if there is any feasible solution, then there is a basic feasible solution. Second, if there is any optimal solution, then there is a basic optimal solution.

PROOF. First, suppose there is any feasible solution. Let x be a feasible solution with the *fewest* positive components (if there is more than one such feasible solution, pick any one of them).

If x has no positive components, then $x = 0$, and x is basic by definition. Otherwise, let $x_\alpha, x_\beta, \ldots$ be the positive components. We will prove that the columns $a^\alpha, a^\beta, \ldots$ are independent.

Suppose they are dependent. Then there is a linear combination

$$\theta_\alpha a^\alpha + \theta_\beta a^\beta + \cdots = 0, \tag{10}$$

where at least one of the coefficients, say θ_α, is non-zero. We may assume θ_α is positive, for otherwise we make it positive by multiplying the equation (10) by -1.

We have assumed

$$Ax = x_\alpha a^\alpha + x_\beta a^\beta + \cdots = b, \tag{11}$$

where $x_\alpha > 0, x_\beta > 0, \ldots$. Form the equation (11) $- \lambda \cdot$ (10):

$$(x_\alpha - \lambda\theta_\alpha)a^\alpha + (x_\beta - \lambda\theta_\beta)a^\beta + \cdots = b. \tag{12}$$

If λ is not too big, we still have a feasible solution, with components

$$x_\alpha - \lambda\theta_\alpha \geqslant 0, \quad x_\beta - \lambda\theta_\beta \geqslant 0, \ldots. \tag{13}$$

But if λ is too big, we no longer have a feasible solution, since we get a negative component

$$x_\alpha - \lambda\theta_\alpha < 0 \quad \text{if} \quad \lambda > x_\alpha/\theta_\alpha.$$

Choose λ as large as you can, keeping all components $\geqslant 0$ in (13). If θ_i is $\leqslant 0$, then $x_i - \lambda\theta_i$ remains positive for all $\lambda \geqslant 0$; but if θ_i is > 0, we must require $\lambda \leqslant x_i/\theta_i$. Since λ must be $\leqslant$ *all* these quotients, we choose

$$\lambda = \min\{x_i/\theta_i : x_i > 0 \text{ and } \theta_i > 0\}. \tag{14}$$

If the minimum quotient occurs for $i = \mu$, then $x_\mu - \lambda\theta_\mu = 0$ in (13). Now the identity (12) shows that we have found a new feasible solution that has *fewer* positive components than x has; the new μth component is zero whereas the old μth component x_μ was positive. This contradicts our assumption that x was a feasible solution with the fewest possible positive components. Therefore, the columns $a^\alpha, a^\beta, \ldots$ couldn't have been dependent, as in (10).

Conclusion: *the feasible solution x is basic*. That finishes the first half of the proof; the second half goes much the same way:

Assume x is an *optimal* solution of the canonical linear program (9). Some optimal solutions may have more positive components than others; assume our optimal x has the fewest possible positive components. We will show that x is basic.

If $x = 0$, then x is basic by definition. If $x \neq 0$, call the positive components $x_\alpha, x_\beta, \ldots$. Again we must prove that the matrix columns $a^\alpha, a^\beta, \ldots$ are independent. We will show that if they are dependent, then we can construct a new optimal solution with fewer positive components.

Suppose $a^\alpha, a^\beta, \ldots$ are dependent. Let

$$\theta_\alpha a^\alpha + \theta_\beta a^\beta + \cdots = 0, \tag{15}$$

where we may assume some coefficient is positive, say $\theta_\alpha > 0$. Then we assert

$$\theta_\alpha c_\alpha + \theta_\beta c_\beta + \cdots = 0, \tag{16}$$

where c is the given cost vector.

Proof of (16): We know $Ax = b$, which says

$$x_\alpha a^\alpha + x_\beta a^\beta + \cdots = b. \tag{17}$$

Form the equation (17) $- \lambda \cdot$ (15):

$$(x_\alpha - \lambda\theta_\alpha)a^\alpha + (x_\beta - \lambda\theta_\beta)a^\beta + \cdots = b. \tag{18}$$

Since $x_\alpha > 0$, $x_\beta > 0, \ldots$, we have

$$x_\alpha - \lambda\theta_\alpha \geq 0, \quad x_\beta - \lambda\theta_\beta \geq 0, \ldots \tag{19}$$

for small $|\lambda|$; then the components (19) give a new feasible solution. The *new cost* is

$$c_\alpha(x_\alpha - \lambda\theta_\alpha) + c_\beta(x_\beta - \lambda\theta_\beta) + \cdots = \text{old cost} - \lambda(\theta_\alpha c_\alpha + \theta_\beta c_\beta + \cdots). \tag{20}$$

If (16) were false, we could decrease the cost by letting λ be some small positive or negative number. Then x would not be optimal. Contradiction; (16) is now proved.

Let λ start at zero and slowly increase. As long as the new components (19) remain ≥ 0, they give a new *optimal* solution, since (16) implies new cost = old cost in (20).

Assuming $\theta_\alpha > 0$, we see that the component $x_\alpha - \lambda\theta_\alpha$ becomes negative if λ is too big. Take λ as large as possible, keeping *all* the new components

(19) $\geqslant 0$; set

$$\lambda = \min\{x_i/\theta_i\colon x_i > 0 \text{ and } \theta_i > 0\}. \tag{21}$$

If the minimum quotient occurs for $i = \mu$, then $x_\mu - \lambda\theta_\mu = 0$ in (19), and so the new optimal solution has fewer positive components than the old optimal solution x. This contradicts our assumption.

Conclusion: the columns $a^\alpha, a^\beta, \ldots$ are independent, and so *the optimal solution x is basic*. This finishes the proof of the theorem on basic solutions. $\square$

Armed with this theorem, we are ready to attack the problem of numerical computation.

PROBLEMS

1. For the matrix in formula (3) there are 6 non-empty sets of independent columns. What are they?

2. Let

$$A = \begin{bmatrix} 1 & 0 & -1 & 0 & -1 \\ 1 & 0 & 2 & 0 & -3 \end{bmatrix}.$$

What are the non-empty subsets of independent columns?

3. For the matrix in Problem 2 find *all* the basic solutions of

$$Ax = \begin{bmatrix} 0 \\ 1 \end{bmatrix}.$$

Using the basic solutions, represent the non-basic solutions. (See Example 1.)

4. Find all the basic solutions of

$$\begin{bmatrix} 1 & 2 & 3 \\ 4 & 5 & 6 \\ 7 & 8 & 9 \end{bmatrix} x = \begin{bmatrix} 0 \\ 3 \\ 6 \end{bmatrix}.$$

5. Find all the basic solutions of

$$\begin{bmatrix} 1 & 2 & 3 \\ 4 & 5 & 6 \\ 7 & 0 & 1 \end{bmatrix} x = \begin{bmatrix} 0 \\ 3 \\ 6 \end{bmatrix}.$$

Why do Problems 4 and 5 have different numbers of basic solutions?

6. Consider the equation

$$\begin{bmatrix} 1 & 0 & -1 \\ 1 & 1 & 1 \end{bmatrix} x = b, \quad x \geqslant 0.$$

Find all the basic feasible solutions x for these values of b:

$$\begin{bmatrix} 2 \\ 0 \end{bmatrix}; \begin{bmatrix} 3 \\ 3 \end{bmatrix}; \begin{bmatrix} 3 \\ 6 \end{bmatrix}; \begin{bmatrix} 0 \\ 7 \end{bmatrix}; \begin{bmatrix} -2 \\ 4 \end{bmatrix}; \begin{bmatrix} -5 \\ -5 \end{bmatrix}; \begin{bmatrix} -7 \\ 0 \end{bmatrix}.$$

Draw a picture of the set of all b if x is feasible.

7. Find the optimal basic solution x for

$$\begin{bmatrix} 1 & 0 & -1 \\ 1 & 1 & 1 \end{bmatrix} x = \begin{bmatrix} 0 \\ 7 \end{bmatrix}, \quad x \geqslant 0, \quad x_2 - x_3 = \min.$$

8. Same as last problem, but now require $x_1 + x_3 = \min.$

9. Write the standard program

$$\begin{bmatrix} 1 & 2 \\ 3 & 4 \end{bmatrix} x \geqslant \begin{bmatrix} 6 \\ 5 \end{bmatrix}, \quad x \geqslant 0, \quad x_1 + x_2 = \min.$$

   in canonical form by introducing two slack variables x_3 and x_4. Find all the basic feasible solutions; find the basic optimal solution. (The new matrix will have four columns. Draw them as vectors in the plane, and draw the vector with components 6,5.)

10. Find all feasible solutions x for

$$\begin{bmatrix} 1 & -1 & -1 \\ 0 & 1 & -1 \end{bmatrix} x = \begin{bmatrix} 0 \\ 0 \end{bmatrix}, \quad x \geqslant 0.$$

    Which feasible solution is basic?

11. Prove or disprove this assertion: Let $x^1, \ldots, x^N$ be all the basic feasible solutions of $Ax = b$, $x \geqslant 0$; then x is a feasible solution *if* it is a convex combination

$$x = \theta_1 x^1 + \cdots + \theta_N x^N \qquad (\theta_i \geqslant 0, \sum \theta_i = 1).$$

12. Prove or disprove the converse of the preceding assertion (using *only if* instead of *if*).

13. Let A be an $m \times n$ matrix with $m \leqslant n$. Suppose at most r columns of A are independent (A has rank $\leqslant r$). At most how many basic solutions can $Ax = b$ have if b is fixed?

5 The Idea of the Simplex Method

Most computer algorithms for linear programming come from the simplex method of George Dantzig. Because the applications of linear programming are so numerous and important, we will later discuss several simplex algorithms. But now I just want to give you the idea of the method, the bare bones; we'll put the flesh on later.

We take the linear programming problem in canonical form:

$$Ax = b, \quad x \geqslant 0, \quad c^T x = \min. \tag{1}$$

We'll make a couple of simplifying assumptions, which are almost always satisfied.

Assumptions of non-degeneracy. Let A have m rows and n columns; we have fewer equations than unknowns, so we have $m < n$.

(i) We assume that the m *rows* of A are linearly independent. From linear algebra, we know this is equivalent to assuming that A has m independent *columns*. (Usually A will have *several* sets of m independent columns.)

(ii) We assume that b is *not* a linear combination of *fewer* than m columns of A. In other words, if

$$Ax = x_1 a^1 + x_2 a^2 + \cdots + x_n a^n = b, \qquad (2)$$

we must know that *at least* m of the components x_j are non-zero.

The first assumption implies that the equation $Ax = b$ has a solution x for every b. That is because the columns of A span the whole m-dimensional space in which the vector b lies.

If assumption (i) is false, the m rows of A are dependent, which means that the m equations $\sum a_{ij} x_j = b_i$ are dependent or, worse, inconsistent. For instance, if

$$A = \begin{bmatrix} 1 & 2 & 3 \\ 2 & 4 & 6 \end{bmatrix}, \qquad (3)$$

its rows are dependent. Then $Ax = b$ gives the equations

$$x_1 + 2x_2 + 3x_3 = b_1$$
$$2x_1 + 4x_2 + 6x_3 = b_2,$$

which are dependent if $b_2 = 2b_1$, or inconsistent if $b_2 \neq 2b_1$.

In practice, if equations are dependent, one or more of them should be erased. If the equations are inconsistent, they should be forgotten—or at least reconsidered.

What does the assumption (ii) mean?

EXAMPLE 1. Look at this:

$$\begin{bmatrix} 1 & 2 & 3 \\ 2 & 4 & 1 \end{bmatrix} \begin{bmatrix} x_1 \\ x_2 \\ x_3 \end{bmatrix} = \begin{bmatrix} 6 \\ 2 \end{bmatrix}. \qquad (4)$$

Here the matrix A has independent rows, so assumption (i) is OK. But assumption (ii) is false here, because the vector b on the right is a multiple of just *one* column:

$$2a^3 = 2 \begin{bmatrix} 3 \\ 1 \end{bmatrix} = \begin{bmatrix} 6 \\ 2 \end{bmatrix} = b, \qquad (5)$$

while A has *two* rows.

This kind of problem creates an annoying technical difficulty for the simplex method. But please note how fragile it is: the slightest perturbation will destroy it. Suppose b is replaced by

$$b' = \begin{bmatrix} 6 + \delta \\ 2 + \varepsilon \end{bmatrix}, \qquad (6)$$

where δ and ε are small errors; for instance, δ and ε could be digital-computer roundoff errors, or they could be data-measurement errors. Then the slightly perturbed vector b' satisfies assumption (ii)—unless by some incredible bad luck δ equals 3ε.

This example is typical. *If assumption* (ii) *is not satisfied then a random perturbation of the vector b satisfies assumption* (ii) *almost surely.* (In fact, the degenerate vectors b lie in the finite union of the linear subspaces spanned by subsets of $m - 1$ columns of A; all these subspaces have dimensions less than m, and so a random perturbation of b in m dimensions almost surely lies outside their union.)

And so we will make the two assumptions of non-degeneracy. Now the simplex method works without a hitch. The method has two phases:

Phase I finds a first basic feasible solution of $Ax = b$, $x \geqslant 0$. Or if the problem has no feasible solution, Phase I proves that fact.

Phase II starts with a first basic feasible solution and ends with a basic optimal solution. Or if the problem has no optimal solution, Phase II proves that fact, and it shows you how to construct feasible solutions x that drive the cost $x^T c$ down to minus infinity.

Both phases work in finite numbers of steps. We get exact answers, except for the inevitable computer roundoff errors. We shall not have to rely on infinite convergent sequences; a finite number of steps will give a precise answer. The simplex method plays the same role in linear programming that Gaussian elimination plays in linear algebra.

How to do Phase I. Assume you already know how to do Phase II; then I can show you how to do Phase I. Let's write out the equations:

$$\sum_{j=1}^{n} a_{ij}x_j = b_i \qquad (i = 1, \ldots, m). \tag{7}$$

We are looking for a feasible solution, x, with m positive components. *We assume all* b_i *are positive*; if any b_i is negative, multiply the ith equation by -1.

We can state Phase I as a minimum problem for which we already have a first basic feasible solution. We state this problem:

$$\sum_{j=1}^{n} a_{ij}x_j + z_i = b_i \qquad (i = 1, \ldots, m)$$
$$x_1 \geqslant 0, \ldots, x_n \geqslant 0, \quad z_1 \geqslant 0, \ldots, z_m \geqslant 0 \tag{8}$$
$$z_1 + \cdots + z_m = \text{minimum}.$$

This is a canonical minimum problem with m equations and $n + m$ unknowns. We assume this problem is non-degenerate.

Here is a first basic solution:

$$x_j = 0 \quad (j = 1, \ldots, n); \qquad z_i = b_i \quad (i = 1, \ldots, m). \tag{9}$$

This is a basic solution; it contains only m positive components. The matrix in the preliminary problem (8) has the $n + m$ columns $a^1, \ldots, a^n, e^1, \ldots, e^m$; the first n columns come from A, and the last m columns come from the $m \times m$ identity matrix. Using composite matrices and vectors, we could write (8) in the form

$$[A \quad I]\begin{bmatrix} x \\ z \end{bmatrix} = b$$
$$x \geqslant 0, \quad z \geqslant 0, \quad \textstyle\sum z_i = \min. \tag{8'}$$

Our basic feasible solution (9) depends on the m independent columns $e^1, \ldots, e^m$. The cost of this solution is $\sum z_i = \sum b_i > 0$.

Now carry out a Phase II calculation on the preliminary minimum problem (8). When you're done, there are two possibilities:

Case 1: $\min \sum z_i = 0$. In this case the final z equals zero, and so the basic optimal solution of the preliminary problem satisfies

$$Ax = b, \quad x \geqslant 0. \tag{10}$$

Then x is a basic feasible solution of the original problem.

Case 2: $\min \sum z_i > 0$. In this case the original has no feasible solution. For if x were a feasible solution of the original problem, then x along with $z = 0$ would give a *zero*-cost solution of the preliminary problem (8).

EXAMPLE 2. Suppose the original feasibility problem is

$$-x_1 - 2x_2 = 3, \quad x_1 \geqslant 0, \quad x_2 \geqslant 0. \tag{11}$$

Then the preliminary minimum problem is

$$-x_1 - 2x_2 + z_1 = 3$$
$$x_1 \geqslant 0, \quad x_2 \geqslant 0, \quad z_1 \geqslant 0 \tag{12}$$
$$z_1 = \text{minimum.}$$

The unique solution of this problem is $x_1 = 0$, $x_2 = 0$, $z_1 = 3$. Since the preliminary minimum cost is positive, the original problem (11) has no feasible solution.

EXAMPLE 3. Suppose the original feasibility problem is

$$x_1 + 2x_2 = 3, \quad x_1 \geqslant 0, \quad x_2 \geqslant 0. \tag{13}$$

Then the preliminary minimum problem is

$$x_1 + 2x_2 + z_1 = 3$$
$$x_1 \geqslant 0, \quad x_2 \geqslant 0, \quad z_1 \geqslant 0 \tag{14}$$
$$z_1 = \text{minimum.}$$

The first feasible solution is $x_1 = 0$, $x_2 = 0$, $z_1 = 3$; a basic optimal solution is $x_1 = 3$, $x_2 = 0$, $z_3 = 0$. This gives a feasible solution for (13).

Before we discuss Phase II, I want to prove something that we'll need:

Lemma on Non-Degeneracy. *Assume this problem is non-degenerate:*

$$Ax = b, \quad x \geqslant 0, \quad x^T c = \min,$$

where A has m rows. Then x is a basic feasible solution iff x is a feasible solution with exactly *m positive components.*

PROOF. If x is a basic feasible solution, it cannot have more than m positive components; for then it would depend on a dependent subset of columns of A. Nor can x have fewer than m positive components; for then b would be a linear combination of fewer than m columns of A. This would violate assumption (ii).

Conversely, if x is any feasible solution with exactly m positive components, we can show that x must be basic. For instance, suppose $x_1 > 0, \ldots, x_m > 0$ and $x_j = 0$ for $j > m$. Then

$$Ax = x_1 a^1 + \cdots + x_m a^m = b.$$

Suppose the columns $a^1, \ldots, a^m$ were dependent:

$$\theta_1 a^1 + \cdots + \theta_m a^m = 0,$$

with some $\theta_i > 0$. Then

$$(x_1 - \lambda \theta_1)a^1 + \cdots + (x_m - \lambda \theta_m)a^m = b,$$

and we could make one or more coefficients zero by setting

$$\lambda = \min\{x_i/\theta_i : \theta_i > 0\}.$$

Then b would be a combination of fewer than m columns of A. This violates assumption (ii); therefore the columns $a^1, \ldots, a^m$ are independent, and the feasible solution x is basic.   □

How to do Phase II. Let x be a given basic feasible solution of the non-degenerate canonical program

$$Ax = b, \quad x \geqslant 0, \quad c^T x = \min.$$

Using the equilibrium equations (discussed in the last section), we will find out if x is optimal.

Let B be the set of indices j for which x_j is positive:

$$B = \{j : x_j > 0\}. \tag{16}$$

We will call B *the basis.* If A has m rows, then the set B contains m members, and so we write $|B| = m$.

The basic solution x depends on the columns a^j for j in the basis B, that is, for $x_j > 0$. We may also call these columns *the basis,* which is a slight misuse of language that will cause no trouble.

The m columns in the basis constitute a matrix M with m columns and m rows. This, too, we will call *the basis* when we feel like it; it would be better to call it the *basic matrix*. Since its columns are independent, the square matrix M has an inverse.

EXAMPLE 4. Consider

$$\begin{bmatrix} 1 & 2 & 3 \\ 4 & 5 & 6 \end{bmatrix} x = \begin{bmatrix} 4 \\ 10 \end{bmatrix}. \tag{17}$$

Suppose our given basic solution is $x^T = [1,0,1]$. Then $x_1 > 0$ and $x_3 > 0$, so the basis is

$$B = \{1,3\}. \tag{18}$$

The set B has two members: $|B| = 2$. The solution x depends on the basis columns (the first and third), which constitute the basis matrix

$$M = \begin{bmatrix} 1 & 3 \\ 4 & 6 \end{bmatrix}. \tag{19}$$

We won't use the symbol B to designate the basis matrix; the symbol B will always designate the index set.

Back to the general case. We have

$$\sum_B x_j a^j = b, \tag{20}$$

where we sum over j in B. Since the basis columns constitute an invertible matrix M, we can solve the m equilibrium equations

$$y^T a^j = c_j \qquad (j \in B). \tag{21}$$

Using the matrix M, we could write (21) in the form

$$y^T M = \hat{c}^T, \tag{22}$$

where the vector $\hat{c}$ has the m components c_j for $j \in B$. The unique solution is

$$y^T = \hat{c}^T M^{-1}. \tag{23}$$

We now have two possibilities:

Case 1. Suppose the equilibrium solution y is feasible for the dual. Then, as you saw in the last section, x is optimal for the primal problem (15); and by the way, y is optimal for the dual problem

$$y^T A \leqslant c^T, \quad y^T b = \max, \tag{24}$$

with $y^T b = c^T x$.

How shall we know if y is feasible for the dual? That is easy. Feasibility in (24) means $y^T A \leqslant c^T$; written out, this says

$$y^T a^j \leqslant c_j \qquad (j = 1, \ldots, n). \tag{25}$$

By the equilibrium equations (21), these inequalities are satisfied as equations for j in B. So all we have to do is take the inner products of y with the $n - m$ non-basic columns a^j and check the inequalities (25) for $j \notin B$.

Suppose the check fails. Then we are in

Case 2. Suppose, for some non-basic $j = s$,

$$y^T a^s > c_s. \tag{26}$$

Then the equilibrium solution y is infeasible for the dual, and we have proved nothing.

You will now see that the wrong-way inequality (26) is telling us something: *we can reduce our cost by bringing a^s into the basis.* Here's how we do it:

We first express the non-basic column a^s as a combination of the current basic columns:

$$a^s = \sum_B t_j a^j. \tag{27}$$

In terms of the basis matrix, this says

$$a^s = Mt, \quad \text{or} \quad t = M^{-1} a^s. \tag{28}$$

If we multiply equation (27) by λ and add the result to equation (20), we get

$$\lambda a^s + \sum_B (x_j - \lambda t_j) a^j = b. \tag{29}$$

If λ is *positive* and small, all the $m + 1$ coefficients in (29) are positive, so we have a new feasible solution of the primal. The *new cost* is

$$\lambda c_s + \sum_B (x_j - \lambda t_j) c_j, \tag{30}$$

whereas the *old cost* was

$$x^T c = \sum_B x_j c_j. \tag{31}$$

Subtracting the new from the old, we get

$$\text{old cost} - \text{new cost} = \lambda(z_s - c_s), \tag{32}$$

where we define

$$z_s = \sum_B t_j c_j. \tag{33}$$

Remember, λ must be positive because it is the coefficient of a^s. Equation (32) says we reduce our cost if

$$z_s - c_s > 0. \tag{34}$$

But this inequality does hold in Case 2. Proof: The definition (33) says $z_s = \hat{c}^T t$; the equilibrium condition (22) says $\hat{c}^T = y^T M$. Therefore,

$$z_s = \hat{c}^T t = y^T M t.$$

But (28) says $Mt = a^s$, and so

$$z_s = y^T a^s, \tag{35}$$

where y is the equilibrium solution. Now we recall that the wrong-way inequality $y^T a^s > c_s$ defines Case 2, and so we do have $z_s - c_s > 0$.

The new solution. According to (32), the bigger we make λ, the more we reduce the cost; so we will make λ as big as we can. According to (29), if B is the current basis, then λ must satisfy these limitations:

$$\lambda \geqslant 0, \quad x_j - \lambda t_j \geqslant 0 \qquad \text{for } j \text{ in } B, \tag{36}$$

so that the new solution will be feasible. Now we see that Case 2 has two sub-cases:

Case 2a. Suppose all t_j are $\leqslant 0$, where (27) defines the t_j. Then (36) says we can make λ as large as we wish. Now (32) says we can drive the cost to minus infinity by making $\lambda \to \infty$. In this sub-case there is no optimal solution x to the original problem. Now the computation stops; equation (29) shows how to construct a non-basic solution $x(\lambda)$ with arbitrarily low cost.

Case 2b. Suppose at least one t_j is >0. Then (36) says that the biggest value we can choose for λ is

$$\lambda^* = \min\{x_j/t_j : t_j > 0\}. \tag{37}$$

Any bigger value would produce a negative coefficient in (29).

If the minimum (37) is achieved for $j = p$, then the coefficient of a^p becomes zero in the equation (29). *Therefore p is unique*, for if more than one coefficient became zero in (29), then b could be represented as a linear combination of fewer than m columns of A. That would violate non-degeneracy assumption (ii).

So, if we choose the biggest admissible value λ^*, exactly one coefficient becomes zero in the representation

$$\lambda^* a^s + \sum_{j \in B} (x_j - \lambda^* t_j) a^j = b. \tag{38}$$

Now the lemma on non-degeneracy implies that this equation defines a new basis:

$$B' = \{s\} + B - \{p\}, \tag{39}$$

formed by adding the index s to B and removing the unique index p.

Now we can write (38) in the form

$$\sum_{j \in B'} x'_j a^j = b, \tag{40}$$

where the new coefficients are the m positive numbers

$$x'_s = \lambda^*, \quad x'_j = x_j - \lambda^* t_j \qquad (j \in B, j \neq p). \tag{41}$$

Non-degeneracy implies that all m coefficients x'_j are positive and that the m columns a^j are independent for j in the new basis B'.

Thus, in Case 2b, we compute a *new basic feasible solution* x'. Doing so, we *lower* the cost by the *positive* amount $\lambda^*(z_s - c_s)$. We now go back to the beginning of Phase II, using the new x' instead of the old x. This ends the description of Phase II.

The computation has to stop after a finite number of iterations. Here's why:

If we ever find that we are in Case 1, we stop because we have proved that our basic feasible solution is optimal.

If we find we are in Case 2a, we stop because we have found that no optimal solution exists.

If we find we are in Case 2b, we compute a new *basic* solution x' with *lower cost*. Therefore, we can only go through Case 2b a finite number of times. That is because the matrix A has only a finite number of times. That is because the matrix A has only a finite number of subsets of m columns, and so the equation $Ax = b$ has only a finite number of basic solutions. Now suppose we pass through Case 2b many times, with a succession of basic solutions $x^1, x^2, x^3, \ldots$ Since the cost *decreases* with each new basic solution, we have

$$c^T x^1 > c^T x^2 > c^T x^3 > \cdots. \tag{42}$$

Therefore, all our basic solutions $x^1, x^2, \ldots$ are *different*; and so the number of these solutions is *finite*.

And so the number of iterations is finite.

Using non-degeneracy, we proved that cycling is impossible: we never return to a former basic solution in Case 2b. In a degenerate problem, in practice cycling is unlikely, and luck will usually bring us through. But cycling is possible in degenerate cases; this was proved in 1951 by A. J. Hoffman. Later we'll discuss the lexicographic simplex method, which makes cycling impossible in every case.

Now let me give you some examples of Phase II calculations.

EXAMPLE 5. Consider this problem:

$$\begin{bmatrix} 1 & 2 & -3 \\ 4 & 5 & -9 \end{bmatrix} \begin{bmatrix} x_1 \\ x_2 \\ x_3 \end{bmatrix} = \begin{bmatrix} 4 \\ 13 \end{bmatrix}$$

$$x \geq 0$$

$$x_1 + x_2 - 3x_3 = \min.$$

We start with the basic feasible solution

$$x_1 = 2, \quad x_2 = 1, \quad x_3 = 0$$

Here the basis matrix and its inverse are

$$M = \begin{bmatrix} 1 & 2 \\ 4 & 5 \end{bmatrix}, \quad M^{-1} = \frac{1}{3} \begin{bmatrix} -5 & 2 \\ 4 & -1 \end{bmatrix}.$$

If we compute $M^{-1}a^{(3)}$, we get

$$\begin{bmatrix} t_1 \\ t_2 \end{bmatrix} = \frac{1}{3}\begin{bmatrix} -5 & 2 \\ 4 & -1 \end{bmatrix}\begin{bmatrix} -3 \\ -9 \end{bmatrix} = \begin{bmatrix} -1 \\ -1 \end{bmatrix}.$$

To find out if we can decrease the cost by bringing in a^3, we compute

$$z_3 - c_3 = t_1 c_1 + t_2 c_2 - c_3 = -1 - 1 + 3 = 1 > 0.$$

Since $z_3 - c_3$ is positive, we should bring in a^3. We are in Case 2.

But look: Both t_j are $\leqslant 0$. Therefore we are in Case 2a. There is no limit to how much a^3 we can bring in, and we can drive the cost to minus infinity. Here we have

$$\lambda a^3 + (2 - \lambda t_1)a^1 + (1 - \lambda t_2)a^2 = b,$$

with $t_1 = t_2 = -1$, and so we get the family of non-basic feasible solutions

$$x(\lambda) = \begin{bmatrix} 2 + \lambda \\ 1 + \lambda \\ \lambda \end{bmatrix}.$$

The new cost is

$$c^T x = 3 - \lambda,$$

which goes to $-\infty$ as $\lambda \to +\infty$.

EXAMPLE 6. Look at this problem:

$$\begin{bmatrix} 1 & 2 & 3 \\ 4 & 5 & 6 \end{bmatrix} x = \begin{bmatrix} 3 \\ 9 \end{bmatrix}$$

$$x \geqslant 0$$

$$3x_1 + 3x_2 + 2x_3 = \min.$$

I give you the basic feasible solution

$$x_1 = 1, \quad x_2 = 1, \quad x_3 = 0.$$

You take it from there.

You first form the basis matrix and its inverse:

$$M = \begin{bmatrix} 1 & 2 \\ 4 & 5 \end{bmatrix}, \quad M^{-1} = \frac{1}{3}\begin{bmatrix} -5 & 2 \\ 4 & -1 \end{bmatrix}.$$

Then you compute

$$M^{-1}a^{(3)} = \begin{bmatrix} t_1 \\ t_2 \end{bmatrix} = \begin{bmatrix} -1 \\ 2 \end{bmatrix}.$$

Next you compute

$$z_3 - c_3 = (-3 + 6) - 2 = 1 > 0.$$

Since this is positive, you decide to bring in a^3. Since one of the t_j is positive, you are in Case 2b.

How much a^3 can you bring in? You have

$$\lambda a^3 + (x_1 - \lambda t_1)a^1 + (x_2 - \lambda t_2)a^2 = b,$$

where $t_1 = -1$ and $t_2 = +2$. Therefore you make λ equal

$$\lambda^* = x_2/t_2 = \tfrac{1}{2},$$

obtaining the new basic solution

$$x'_1 = \tfrac{3}{2}, \quad x'_2 = 0, \quad x'_3 = \tfrac{1}{2}.$$

You have lowered the cost by this amount:

$$\text{old cost} - \text{new cost} = \lambda^*(z_3 - c_3) = \tfrac{1}{2}.$$

In fact, the old cost was 6; the new cost is $\tfrac{5}{2}$.

EXAMPLE 7. We continue the last example, starting with the computed basic feasible solution

$$x_1 = \tfrac{3}{2}, \quad x_2 = 0, \quad x_3 = \tfrac{1}{2}.$$

Now the basis is $B = \{1,3\}$. The basis matrix and its inverse are

$$M = \begin{bmatrix} 1 & 3 \\ 4 & 6 \end{bmatrix}, \quad M^{-1} = \frac{1}{6}\begin{bmatrix} -6 & 3 \\ 4 & -1 \end{bmatrix}.$$

Applying M^{-1} to the non-basic column, a^3, we get

$$M^{-1}a^2 = \begin{bmatrix} t_1 \\ t_3 \end{bmatrix} = \begin{bmatrix} \tfrac{1}{2} \\ \tfrac{1}{2} \end{bmatrix},$$

from which we compute

$$z_2 - c_2 = t_1 c_1 + t_3 c_3 - c_2 = \tfrac{5}{2} - 3 < 0.$$

Since $z_s - c_s$ is $\leqslant 0$ for *all* non-basic s (in this example there is only one), we are in Case 1. We are done: our basic feasible solution is optimal.

The last two examples are typical: we iterate Case 2b until we end in Case 1. The Case 2a seldom occurs, because costs seldom go to minus infinity.

For large problems, like those in the petroleum industry, it would take a lot of computer time if we had to invert a new basis matrix M with each new iteration. As I'll show you later, when we discuss numerical methods, you won't have to do that. You can go from one iteration to the next and get the new inverse M^{-1} very quickly; that's what happens in the revised simplex algorithm and in the dual simplex tableau algorithm. In one version of the tableau algorithm no inverse M^{-1} is computed; we go from basis to basis with no explicit use of any inverse matrix.

But now let's return to the theory, which tells us what all the numbers mean.

Reference

George B. Dantzig, *Linear Programming and Extensions*, Princeton University Press, 1963.

PROBLEMS

1. Consider the system $Ax = b$ where

$$A = \begin{bmatrix} 1 & 2 & 3 \\ 3 & 6 & 9 \end{bmatrix}.$$

For which vectors b is the system redundant? For which is it inconsistent?

2. Consider the system

$$\begin{bmatrix} 1 & 2 & 3 \\ 9 & 6 & 3 \end{bmatrix} x = b.$$

Which vectors b *fail* to satisfy the assumption (ii)? Draw these vectors in the plane.

3. In Phase *I*, in formula (8) we required all $b_i > 0$. Why is Phase I degenerate if some $b_i = 0$?

4. By direct observation, find the three basic solutions of

$$\begin{bmatrix} 1 & 0 & -1 \\ 1 & 1 & 0 \end{bmatrix} x = \begin{bmatrix} -1 \\ 1 \end{bmatrix}, \quad x \geqslant 0,$$

and note which two of the basic solutions are feasible. As an exercise, *compute* one of the basic feasible solutions by a Phase I calculation. (Remember to multiply the first equation by -1; then start with $x_1 = x_2 = x_3 = 0$, $z_1 = z_2 = 1$.)

5. Continuing the last problem, use a Phase II calculation to compute the basic solution minimizing $x_1 + x_2 + x_3$.

6. Apply Phase I to this program:

$$x_2 + 2x_3 = 3$$
$$x_1 + 2x_2 + 3x_3 = 4, \qquad x \geqslant 0.$$

What does Phase I tell you?

7. Apply the simplex method to this program:

$$\begin{bmatrix} 2 & 1 & -1 \\ 1 & -2 & 2 \end{bmatrix} x = \begin{bmatrix} 1 \\ 1 \end{bmatrix}, \quad x \geqslant 0,$$

$$x_1 - x_2 = \min.$$

Find a feasible solution with cost $x_1 - x_2 = -10^{99}$.

8. Starting with the basic solution that depends on the first two columns, apply Phase II to this program:

$$\begin{bmatrix} -1 & 2 & 3 \\ 2 & 3 & 1 \end{bmatrix} x = \begin{bmatrix} 1 \\ 5 \end{bmatrix}, \quad x \geqslant 0, \quad x_2 = \min.$$

9. Choose the number ω so that the following program has a solution. Then write down the optimal solution,

$$\begin{bmatrix} -1 & 2 & 3 \\ 2 & 3 & 1 \\ -5 & -4 & 1 \end{bmatrix} x = \begin{bmatrix} 1 \\ 5 \\ \omega \end{bmatrix}, \quad x \geqslant 0, \quad x_2 = \min.$$

10. Look at this program:

$$\begin{bmatrix} 1 & 1 & 2 \\ 2 & 1 & 1 \end{bmatrix} x = \begin{bmatrix} 3 + \varepsilon \\ 3 \end{bmatrix}, \quad x \geqslant 0, \quad x_2 = \min.$$

The program is degenerate if $\varepsilon = 0$. Solve the program for small $\varepsilon > 0$, and take the limit as $\varepsilon \to 0$.

6 Separating Planes for Convex Sets

To prove the duality theorem, I will use a standard theorem in the repertoire of every professional mathematician. If you know it already, you should skip this section or just look it over quickly.

I'll make the presentation brief. All we'll need for the duality theorem is the following Theorem 1. Much later, when we discuss nonlinear programming, we'll use Theorem 3.

Definition of convex set. Let C be a set in the real Euclidean N-dimensional space. The set C is called *convex* if it contains the line segment connecting every pair of its points. In other words, if C contains x and y, then C should contain all the points

$$(1 - \theta)x + \theta y \qquad (0 \leqslant \theta \leqslant 1).$$

(If C consists of only one point, we call C convex.)

Definition of closed set. The set F is called *closed* if it contains all its limit points. In other words, if all the points $x^1, x^2, x^3, \ldots$ lie in F, and if

$$x^{(k)} \to x^0 \quad \text{as} \quad k \to \infty,$$

then x^0 should lie in F. (Here superscripts denote different points; subscripts will denote different coordinates.)

EXAMPLE. In 2 dimensions, the half-plane $3x_1 - 5x_2 < 7$ is convex but not closed.

EXAMPLE. The half-plane $3x_1 - 5x_2 \leqslant 7$ is convex *and* closed.

EXAMPLE. The annulus $1 \leqslant |x| \leqslant 2$ is closed but not convex.

EXAMPLE. In N dimensions, a *convex polytope* can be generated by any finite set of points $x^1, \ldots, x^p$. The polytope

$$\langle x^1, \ldots, x^p \rangle$$

consists of all the convex combinations

$$x = \theta_1 x^1 + \theta_2 x^2 + \cdots + \theta_p x^p$$

where

$$\theta_1 + \cdots + \theta_p = 1, \quad \text{with all } \theta_j \geqslant 0.$$

Every convex polytope is convex and closed.

Lemma. *Let C be a closed convex set that does not contain the origin $x = 0$. Then C contains a nearest point x^0, with*

$$|x^0| = \min\{|x|: x \in C\} > 0$$

(The assumption that C is convex is superfluous but useful. The assumption that C is closed is necessary, as you see from this example: The convex set $x_1 > 5$ contains no point that minimizes the distance to the origin.)

PROOF. Let δ be the greatest lower bound of $|x|$ for all x in C:

$$\delta = \inf\{|x|: x \in C\}.$$

Let $x^1, x^2, \ldots$ be a sequence of points in C such that

$$|x^k| \to \delta \quad \text{as} \quad k \to \infty. \tag{1}$$

Then we can use convexity to prove that x^k converges to the required nearest point x^0.

We use the parallelogram law of vector algebra:

$$|x^p - x^q|^2 + |x^p + x^q|^2 = 2|x^p|^2 + 2|x^q|^2. \tag{2}$$

By convexity, the midpoint $\frac{1}{2}(x^p + x^q)$ must lie in C, and so we have

$$\left|\tfrac{1}{2}(x^p + x^q)\right| \geqslant \delta.$$

Now (2) gives

$$|x^p - x^q|^2 + (2\delta)^2 \leqslant 2|x^p|^2 + 2|x^q|^2. \tag{3}$$

As p and q tend to infinity, the right-hand side goes to $4\delta^2$, by (1). Now (3) implies

$$\overline{\lim_{p,q \to \infty}} \ |x^p - x^q|^2 + 4\delta^2 \leqslant 4\delta^2,$$

which says $x^p - x^q \to 0$, and so the sequence x^k has a limit: $x^k \to x^0$. Since C is closed, the limit x^0 lies in C.

Since $|x^k| \to \delta$, we find $|x^0| = \delta$. And so C does contain a point x^0 that minimizes the distance to the origin.

Definition of separating plane. The equation of a plane in R^N (real N-dimensional space) is

$$a^T x + \beta = 0 \tag{4}$$

provided that the constant vector a is non-zero. This plane is said to *separate* the sets S_1 and S_2 if

$$a^T x + \beta \geqslant 0 \qquad \text{for all } x \text{ in } S_1$$
$$a^T x + \beta \leqslant 0 \qquad \text{for all } x \text{ in } S_2. \tag{5}$$

In the lenient definition (5), equalities may occur, so that the sets S_1 and S_2 may have some points *on* the plane; the two sets may even have some points in common. But if both inequalities are *strict*, this can't happen. Then

$$a^T x + \beta > 0 \qquad \text{for all } x \text{ in } S_1$$
$$a^T x + \beta < 0 \qquad \text{for all } x \text{ in } S_2. \tag{6}$$

In this case we say the plane *strictly* separates the two sets.

Even if the two sets are disjoint, they need not have a separating plane. An example appears in Figure 1.

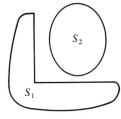

Figure 1

But if both disjoint sets are convex, there must be a separating plane, as we will prove. A typical example appears in Figure 2.

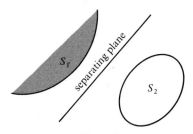

Figure 2

The main theorem is Theorem 1, in which one set is convex and closed while the other set is a single point. In this case we get strict separation, which is what we'll later use to prove the duality theorem of linear programming.

Theorem 1. *Let C be a closed convex set. Suppose the point b lies outside C. Then there is a plane that strictly separates C from b.*

PROOF. With no loss of generality, suppose $b = 0$; if $b \neq 0$, make a preliminary change of coordinates $x' = x - b$.

According to the lemma, C contains a point x^0 that minimizes $|x|$:

$$0 < |x^0| = \delta \leqslant |x| \qquad \text{for all } x \text{ in } C. \tag{7}$$

Let u be the unit vector that points from the origin to the nearest point on C:

$$u = \delta^{-1} x^0. \tag{8}$$

Let m be the midpoint $\frac{1}{2}x^0$. Define the plane

$$u^T(x - m) = 0. \tag{9}$$

(In formula (4) this makes $a = u$, $\beta = -u^T m$.) We will now prove that this plane strictly separates C from the origin, as in Figure 3.

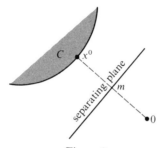

Figure 3.

For $x = 0$ we have

$$u^T(x - m) = u^T(-\tfrac{1}{2}x^0) = -\tfrac{1}{2}\delta < 0. \tag{10}$$

But for all x in C we will prove

$$u^T(x - m) \geqslant \tfrac{1}{2}\delta > 0. \tag{11}$$

If x lies in C, then so does the convex combination $(1 - \theta)x^0 + \theta x$. Therefore we have

$$|x^0|^2 \leqslant |(1 - \theta)x^0 + \theta x|^2 \qquad (0 \leqslant \theta \leqslant 1).$$

Expanding the right-hand side, we get

$$|x^0|^2 \leqslant |x^0|^2 + 2\theta(x^0)^T(x - x^0) + \theta^2|x - x^0|^2,$$

and

$$0 \leqslant 2\theta(x^0)^T(x - x^0) + O(\theta^2) \qquad (0 \leqslant \theta \leqslant 1).$$

If you divide by $\theta > 0$ and let $\theta \to +0$, you deduce

$$0 \leqslant (x^0)^T(x - x^0) \qquad \text{for all } x \text{ in } C. \tag{12}$$

But $x^0 = \delta u$, and $x^0 = 2m$; therefore (12) says

$$0 \leqslant (\delta u)^T(x - m - m).$$

Dividing by $\delta > 0$, we get

$$0 \leqslant u^T(x - m) - u^T m,$$

which proves (11), since $u^T m = \delta/2$.

And so the theorem is proved. Note the crucial role played by the assumption that C is closed: if a point b is not in a closed set, then the set contains a point x^0 that is nearest to b, and the distance δ is positive. If C isn't closed, we can't say that.

You now know all you'll need for linear programming. I suggest you skip the rest of this section until you need it for nonlinear programming.

Lemma. *In R^N, let S be any set of points. Then S contains a denumerable subset that is dense in S.*

PROOF. Let's prove it for $N = 1$. Consider all the open intervals I that have rational endpoints:

$$\frac{a}{b} < x < \frac{c}{d} \, (a,b,c,d = \text{integers}).$$

If S contains a point in I, pick exactly one such point:

$$\frac{a}{b} < x(a,b,c,d) < \frac{c}{d}.$$

These points are denumerable, and they constitute a subset $S' \subset S$. The subset S' is dense in S, because every point x_0 in S is the limit of rational numbers a/b from below and of rational numbers c/d from above, and so

$$x(a,b,c,d) \to x_0.$$

For dimensions $N > 1$ the proof is the same; but now, instead of the intervals I, we must use the N-dimensional rectangles whose vertices have rational coordinates. $\qquad\qquad\qquad\qquad\qquad\qquad\qquad\qquad\qquad\qquad\qquad\square$

In the next theorem, we'll assume C is convex but not necessarily closed. Then we still get a separating plane, but the separation may not be strict.

EXAMPLE. For $N = 2$ the open right half-plane $x_1 > 0$ as a convex set that doesn't contain the origin $x = 0$. There is no nearest point x^0, and the distance δ equals zero. The separating plane is the vertical axis $x_1 = 0$.

Theorem 2. *Let C be any convex set that does not contain the origin $x = 0$. Then there is a separating plane (5) with*

$$a^T x + \beta \geqslant 0 \quad \text{in} \quad C, \qquad a^T x + \beta = \beta \leqslant 0 \quad \text{for} \quad x = 0, \qquad (13)$$

where the constant vector a is non-zero.

PROOF. By the lemma, we can choose a denumerable set of points $x^1, x^2, \ldots$ that lie in S and that are dense in S. Using the first p points, we form the convex polytope

$$C_p = \langle x^1, x^2, \ldots, x^p \rangle. \tag{14}$$

Then

$$C_1 \subset C_2 \subset C_3 \subset \cdots \subset C; \tag{15}$$

and as $p \to \infty$, every point in C is the limit of points in C_p.

The convex polytope C_p is a subset of C, so C_p doesn't contain the origin $x = 0$. Since C_p is closed, we can use Theorem 1. By formulas (10) and (11), we have

$$u = u^p, \quad m = m^p, \quad \delta = \delta_p$$

such that

$$(u^p)^T(x - m^p) = -\tfrac{1}{2}\delta_p < 0 \quad (x = 0)$$
$$\geqslant \tfrac{1}{2}\delta_p > 0 \quad (x \in C_p) \tag{16}$$

Here u^p is a unit vector; δ_p is the distance from the origin to C_p; and

$$m^p = (\delta_p/2)u^p. \tag{17}$$

If x lies in C_q, the lower inequality (16) holds for all $p \geqslant q$.

The inclusions (15) imply $\delta_1 \geqslant \delta_2 \geqslant \ldots$, and so the positive numbers δ_p tend to a limit $\delta_0 \geqslant 0$. The unit vectors u^p need not converge, but they must have a convergent subsequence, whose limit is some unit vector u^0 (see Problem 20). Now the last two formulas imply, in the limit as $p \to \infty$,

$$(u^0)^T(x - m^0) \leqslant 0 \quad \text{for} \quad x = 0$$
$$\geqslant 0 \quad \text{for} \quad x \in C_q. \tag{18}$$

For each q, the second inequality holds for all x in C_q. Since every x in C is the limit of points in C_q as $q \to \infty$, the second inequality (18) holds for all x in C. This completes the proof.

It is now surprisingly easy to prove that there is a separating plane for every disjoint pair of convex sets. (In Theorems 1 and 2 one of the pair was a single point.)

Theorem 3. Let C_1 and C_2 be disjoint convex sets in R^N. Then there is a separating plane (5).

PROOF. Form the set of all differences:

$$C = C_1 - C_2 = \{x - y : x \in C_1, y \in C_2\}. \tag{19}$$

Since C_1 and C_2 are disjoint, we have $x \neq y$, and so C doesn't contain the origin $z = 0$.

The set C is convex. For if z and z' lie in C, then we have

$$z = x - y \quad \text{and} \quad z' = x' - y',$$

and so
$$(1 - \theta)z + \theta z' = x'' - y'', \tag{20}$$

where
$$\begin{array}{l} x'' = (1 - \theta)x + \theta x' \in C \\ y'' = (1 - \theta)y + \theta y' \in C' \end{array} \qquad (0 \leqslant \theta \leqslant 1).$$

Therefore, the convex combination (20) also lies in C.

Now we apply Theorem 2 to the convex set C. From (13), we have
$$a^T z + \beta \geqslant 0 \qquad \text{for all } z \text{ in } C, \tag{21}$$

with $\beta \leqslant 0$ and $a \neq 0$.

What does this say about C_1 and C_2? It says
$$a^T(x - y) + \beta \geqslant 0 \quad \text{with} \quad \beta \leqslant 0,$$
and so
$$a^T x \geqslant a^T y \qquad \text{for all } x \in C_1, y \in C_2. \tag{22}$$

Therefore, for x in C_1 and y in C_2,
$$\inf a^T x \geqslant \sup a^T y. \tag{23}$$

Now set γ equal to either the *inf* or the *sup* in (23)—or to any number between. Then *both* of these inequalities hold:
$$\begin{array}{ll} a^T x - \gamma \geqslant 0 & \text{for all } x \text{ in } C_1 \\ a^T y - \gamma \leqslant 0 & \text{for all } y \text{ in } C_2. \end{array} \tag{24}$$

And so we have found a separating plane.

PROBLEMS

1. Show that the half-plane $3x_1 - 5x_2 < 7$ is convex but not closed.

2. Show that the half-plane $3x_1 - 5x_2 \leqslant 7$ is convex *and* closed.

3. Show that the annulus $1 \leqslant |x| \leqslant 2$ is closed but not convex.

4. Prove that every convex polytope is convex and closed.

5. Let C be the closed disk
$$(x_1 + 3)^2 + (x_2 - 4)^2 \leqslant 1.$$

   Using the notation of the proof of Theorem 1, do these things:
   (i) Evaluate the distance δ to the point $b = 0$.
   (ii) Find the coordinates of x^0, of u, and of m.
   (iii) Write the equation of the separating plane (9).

6. For the last problem find the equations of all the planes (lines) that strictly separate the disk from the origin.

7. Let C be the unbounded, closed, convex set
$$\{x: x \in R^2, x \leqslant 0, x_1 x_2 \geqslant 1\}.$$

(This is the convex hull of one branch of a hyperbola.) Do the three things that Problem 5 asks for.

8. Let F be the closed set

$$\{x: x \in R^2, x_2 \geqslant 1 - |x_1|\}.$$

Show that F is not convex. Find the *two* points in F that are nearest to the origin (at distance $\delta = \frac{1}{2}\sqrt{2}$). Let $x^1, x^2, \ldots$ be a sequence in F such that $|x^k| \to \delta$. Show that the sequence x^k may diverge.

*9. The Bolzano-Weierstrass theorem says every bounded sequence has a bounded sequence (see Problem 20). Deduce that the sequence x^k in Problem 8 must have a convergent subsequence. Show that the limit lies in F and minimizes the distance to the origin.

10. Let S be the set of irrational numbers. Show that the nonzero rational multiples of $\sqrt{2}$ are a denumerable dense subset of S.

11. In the plane, let C_1 be the open disk

$$C_1 = \{x: (x_1 + 3)^2 + (x_2 - 4)^2 < 1\},$$

and let C_2 be the closed disk

$$C_2 = \{x: x_1^2 + x_2^2 \leqslant 16\}.$$

Show that these convex sets are disjoint, but that the distance between them is $\delta = 0$. Find the separating plane (line). Is the separation strict?

12. In the plane, let C_1 and C_2 be the disjoint sets

$$C_1 = \{x: x_1 > 0, x_1 x_2 \geqslant 1\},$$
$$C_2 = \{x: x_1 < 0, x_1 x_2 \leqslant -1\}.$$

Show that both sets are convex and closed. Find the difference set C. Observe that C is convex, but show that C is not closed. What is the distance δ between C_1 and C_2? What is the separating plane? Is the separation strict?

*13. Let C_1 and C_2 be convex, disjoint, and closed; let C_1 be bounded. Then prove that the distance between the sets is positive, and prove there is a strictly separating plane.

14. Let S by any set in R^N. Let C consist of all convex combinations

$$\theta_1 x^1 + \cdots + \theta_n x^n \qquad \text{with } \theta_i \geqslant 0, \ \sum \theta_i = 1, \ x^i \in S.$$

The set C is called the *convex hull* of S. Prove that C is convex.

*15. Let C be the convex hull just defined for a set S in R^N. Prove that C consists of all convex combinations of n points in S where *it suffices to take* $n \leqslant N + 1$. (For example, if S lies in the plane R^2, then C consists of the convex combinations of all subsets of three or fewer points.) For the proof, use the theorem on basic solutions.

*16. (Continuation). Show that the convex hull of a set S is the intersection of *all* the convex sets that include S.

17. In the plane, let S be any closed polygon that is not convex. Show that the convex hull has greater area, but has smaller perimeter.

*18. In R^N, if a closed half-space $a^T x + \beta \geq 0$ includes the set S, show that the half-space includes the convex hull of S. Deduce that two sets in R^N have a separating plane if and only if their convex hulls have a separating plane.

*19. Generalize Problem 9: Let F be any non-empty closed set in R^N; let b lie outside F. Prove that F contains a nearest point to b.

*20. Prove the Bolzano-Weirstrass theorem as follows: First look at R^1. Let x_i ($i = 1$, $2, \ldots$) lie between a_0 and b_0. Let $m_0 = \frac{1}{2}(a_0 + b_0)$. Show that infinitely many x_i lie in $[a_0, m_0]$. or ininitely many lie in $[m_0, b_0]$; accordingly let $[a_1, b_1]$ be one of those two intervals. Similarly define $[a_n, b_n]$. Show that $a_n{\uparrow}, b_n{\downarrow}, b_n - a_n \to 0$. Show that there is a convergent subsequence x_n^*, where $a_n \leq x_n^* \leq b_n$. Extend the result to R^N by looking at the N coordinates separately, taking subsequences of subsequences.

7 Finite Cones and the Farkas Alternative

We have considered linear programming in the canonical form

$$Ax = b, \quad x \geq 0 \tag{1}$$
$$c^T x = \text{minimum.} \tag{2}$$

We defined the *feasible solutions* as the vectors x satisfying (1). An optimal solution is a feasible solution with minimum cost $c^T x$.

A feasible solution x may not exist; that depends on the matrix A and on the vector b. We will now give a geometric meaning to the condition of feasibility (1).

Let A be an $m \times n$ matrix. Define the set of all linear combinations of the columns of A with coefficients $x_j \geq 0$:

$$C = \{x_1 a^1 + x_2 a^2 + \cdots + x_n a^n : \text{all } x_j \geq 0\}. \tag{3}$$

The set C is called the *finite cone* generated by the finite collection of vectors $a^1, a^2, \ldots, a^n$. In terms of the matrix A and of vectors $x \geq 0$, the definition (3) says

$$C = \{Ax : x \geq 0\}. \tag{4}$$

This gives a geometric meaning to feasibility: *The equation $Ax = b$ has a solution $x \geq 0$ if and only if b lies in the finite cone C.*

EXAMPLE 1. Consider the equation $Ax = b$ for $x \geq 0$, where A is the matrix

$$A = \begin{bmatrix} 2 & 0 & -1 \\ 1 & 1 & 2 \end{bmatrix}. \tag{5}$$

For this matrix the finite cone C is the shaded set in Figure 1.

A feasible solution $x \geq 0$ exists iff b lies in the cone C. For instance, if $b = (1,0)^T$, then b lies outside the cone, so no feasible solution x exists. But

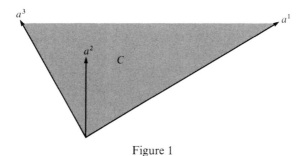

Figure 1

if $b = [-9,63]^T$, then b lies in the shaded region between a^2 and a^3, so a feasible solution x does exist. (The 3-dimensional vectors x don't appear in Figure 1; only the 2-dimensional vectors Ax appear.)

The cone in Figure 1 is generated by the three columns of A. The same cone is generated by just the first and third columns. It could not be generated by the first and second columns or by the second and third.

EXAMPLE 2. Let A be the matrix

$$A = \begin{bmatrix} 2 & 1 & -3 \\ -1 & 3 & -2 \end{bmatrix}. \tag{6}$$

The columns of this matrix appear in Figure 2.

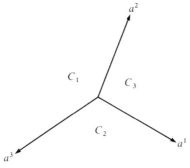

Figure 2

What finite cone C do these three columns generate? They generate the whole plane. Therefore, every equation $Ax = b$ has a feasible solution $x \geqslant 0$.

Again each pair of columns is independent, but this time no single pair generates the whole cone C. The pair a^1, a^2 generates a sub-cone that we will call a *basic cone*; so does the pair a^2, a^3; and so does the pair a^3, a^1. *The full cone C is the union of the basic cones.* In Figure 2 we see

$$C = C_1 \cup C_2 \cup C_3.$$

Does that sound familiar? It is nothing but a geometrical restatement of our theorem on basic feasible solutions. Let me explain:

Definition. If the vectors $v^1, \ldots, v^k$ are independent, then we call their finite cone a *basic cone*:

$$\{p_1 v^1 + \cdots + p_k v^k : \text{all } p_j \geqslant 0\}. \tag{7}$$

Theorem on Basic Cones. *Let* $a^1, \ldots, a^n$ *generate the finite cone* C. *Let* $C_1, \ldots, C_q$ *be the basic cones generated by the subsets of independent vectors* a^j. *Then* C *is the union of the basic cones:*

$$C = C_1 \cup C_2 \cup \cdots \cup C_q. \tag{8}$$

PROOF. Let A be the matrix with columns $a^1, \ldots, a^n$. The cone C consists of the vectors $b = Ax$ with $x \geqslant 0$. In other words, $Ax = b$ has a feasible solution $x \geqslant 0$ iff b lies in C.

By the theorem on basic solutions (Section 4), if the equation $Ax = b$ has a feasible solution $x \geqslant 0$, then the equation has a *basic* feasible solution:

$$b = \sum_{j \in B} x'_j a^j, \tag{9}$$

where the columns a^j are independent for $j \in B$, with all $x'_j \geqslant 0$.

The subset of columns $\{a^j\}$ ($j \in B$) generates one of the basic cones C_k in the union (8). And so the full cone C consists of those vectors b that lie in one or more of the basic cones C_k.   □

To prove the duality theorem of linear programming, we shall use the strict separating-plane theorem for convex sets. But first we must prove that finite cones are convex and closed.

Lemma. *Every finite cone is convex and closed.*

PROOF. Convexity is easy. Let C be generated by the columns of A, so C is the set of points Ax with $x \geqslant 0$. Let Ax^1 and Ax^2 be two points in C. Then

$$(1 - \theta)Ax^1 + \theta Ax^2 = A((1 - \theta)x^1 + \theta x^2),$$

where the vector in parentheses is $\geqslant 0$ if $0 \leqslant \theta \leqslant 1$. Therefore, C is convex.

Closedness is harder. First look at one of the basic cones C_k in the union (8). Let's show that each C_k is closed.

Let $b^1, b^2, \ldots$ lie in C_k, and suppose

$$b^N \to b^* \quad \text{as} \quad N \to \infty. \tag{10}$$

We want to show that b^* lies in C_k. Using the formula (9), we write

$$b^N = \sum_{j \in B} x_{Nj} a^j \quad (N = 1, 2, \ldots), \tag{11}$$

where the independent columns $\{a^j\}$ ($j \in B$) generate the basic cone C_k.

By linear independence, we know

$$\sum_B u_j a^j \neq 0 \quad \text{if some } u_j \neq 0.$$

Letting u lie on the unit sphere $|u| = 1$, we get a positive lower bound

$$\left| \sum_B u_j a^j \right| \geq \varepsilon > 0 \quad \text{if} \quad \sum_B u_j^2 = 1. \tag{12}$$

Now by homogeneity we deduce

$$\left| \sum_B v_j a^j \right| \geq \varepsilon \rho \quad \text{if} \quad \sum_B v_j^2 = \rho^2. \tag{13}$$

(This result would be false if the vectors a^j were dependent.)

Since we assume the b^N converge in (11), we know that $b^N - b^M \to 0$ as N and M go to infinity. Then

$$b^N - b^M = \sum_{j \in B} (x_{Nj} - x_{Mj}) a^j \to 0 \quad \text{as} \quad N, M \to \infty. \tag{14}$$

Now set $x_{Nj} - x_{Mj} = v_j$ in (13). Then (13) says

$$|b^N - b^M| \geq \varepsilon \rho_{NM} \quad \text{if} \quad \sum_{j \in B} (x_{Nj} - x_{Mj})^2 = \rho_{NM}^2.$$

Dividing by $\varepsilon > 0$, we find that $\rho_{NM} \to 0$ as $N \to \infty$ and $M \to \infty$. Therefore, for each $j \in B$ there is a limit

$$\lim_{N \to \infty} x_{Nj} = x_j^* \geq 0. \tag{15}$$

Using these limits in (11), we get

$$b^* = \sum_B x_j^* a^j,$$

which shows that the limit b^* lies in C_k. This proves that each basic cone C_k is closed.

It follows that the union C is closed. For suppose b^N in C and suppose $b^N \to b^*$ as $N \to \infty$. Since the number of basic cones C_j is finite, an infinite subsequence of the convergent sequence b^N must lie in some single basic cone C_k. Since the basic cone C_k is closed, the limit b^* must lie in C_k. But C_k lies in C, and so the limit b^* lies in C. $\qquad \square$

Now comes the great theorem of Julius Farkas: *the alternative of linear programming*. This plays the same role in linear programming that the Fredholm alternative plays in linear algebra. By the way, we'll show that the Farkas alternative immediately implies the Fredholm alternative. But most important for us is this: *The Farkas theorem gives the duality theorem of linear programming.* That you will see in the next section.

Farkas proved his theorem in 1902. Just for fun, I looked up his paper in the old journal where it was published. His proof is long and tedious;

I never could quite understand it. As you know, the first proof of a great theorem is often long and tedious, like the first trip into a new territory. But we no longer go from the east coast to the west by covered wagon, and we need not prove Farkas's theorem by Farkas's method. We will use the separating-plane theorem (Theorem 1 of the last section).

The Farkas Alternative. *Either the equation*

(i) $Ax = b$ *has a solution* $x \geqslant 0$

or (*exclusive*)

(ii) $y^T A \geqslant 0$, $y^T b < 0$ *has a solution* y.

(Here the *or* is exclusive, meaning that one case must occur but both cases cannot occur.)

PROOF. Both cases cannot occur, for if $y^T A \geqslant 0$ and $x \geqslant 0$, then $y^T A x \geqslant 0$, which says $y^T b \geqslant 0$, and so (ii) is false.

It remains to show that one of the two cases must occur. Let us suppose (i) is false and prove that then (ii) must be true.

If (i) is false then the point b lies outside the finite cone C generated by the columns of the matrix A. As we have proved, the cone C is convex and closed. Therefore, there is a plane that *strictly* separates C from b:

$$a^T z + \beta > 0 \qquad \text{for } z \text{ in } C \tag{16}$$
$$a^T z + \beta < 0 \qquad \text{for } z = b \tag{17}$$

In (16) set $z = A(\lambda x)$ where x is any fixed vector $\geqslant 0$, and where λ is positive. This gives

$$a^T A(\lambda x) + \beta > 0 \qquad \text{for } x \geqslant 0, \lambda > 0.$$

Dividing by λ and letting $\lambda \to +\infty$, we get

$$a^T A x \geqslant 0 \quad \text{for} \quad x \geqslant 0.$$

Since this holds for *all* $x \geqslant 0$, we deduce

$$a^T A \geqslant 0. \tag{18}$$

Since the origin lies in C, we may set $z = 0$ in (16); this shows $\beta > 0$. Now (17) says

$$a^T b = -\beta < 0. \tag{19}$$

Done. All you do now is set $y = a$, and the last two formulas give Farkas's case (ii).   □

EXAMPLE 3. As in Example 1, define

$$A = \begin{bmatrix} 2 & 0 & -1 \\ 1 & 1 & 2 \end{bmatrix}, \, b = \begin{bmatrix} 1 \\ 0 \end{bmatrix}. \tag{20}$$

As we saw, the equation $Ax = b$ has no solution $x \geqslant 0$. In other words, Farkas (i) is false.

To get a vector y for Farkas (ii), look at Figure 1. Insert the vector b, which points from the origin to the right. We want a vector y with a negative projection on b but with non-negative projections on all three of the a^j. If you look at the figure, you'll see that the vector y must point somewhere between a^2 and a^3. For instance, this will do:

$$y^T = [-1,10].$$

Now we verify $y^T A \geqslant 0$, $y^T b < 0$:

$$y^T A = [8,10,21], \quad y^T b = -1.$$

EXAMPLE 4. *The Fredholm alternative of linear algebra.* Consider the assertion

$$Ax = b \text{ has a solution } x. \tag{1^0}$$

This assertion may be true or false, depending on the given A and b. Let's state this assertion as a Farkas case (i) and get the alternative Farkas case (ii).

Our assertion is not yet in the form (i), because it contains no sign constraint $x \geqslant 0$. So we use an old trick of linear programming: we set the unconstrained $x = u - v$ and require $u \geqslant 0$ and $v \geqslant 0$. Now (1^0) becomes

$$A(u - v) = b \quad \text{has a solution } u \geqslant 0, v \geqslant 0. \tag{1^0}$$

In partioned form, this says

$$[A, -A]\begin{bmatrix} u \\ v \end{bmatrix} = b \quad \text{has a solution} \geqslant 0. \tag{1^0}$$

Now we do have a Farkas case (i). What is the Farkas alternative? It is this

$$y^T[A, -A] \geqslant 0, \quad y^T b < 0 \quad \text{has a solution } y. \tag{ii}$$

If we unpack the first inequality, we find

$$y^T A \geqslant 0 \quad \text{and} \quad y^T(-A) \geqslant 0,$$

which means simply $y^T A = 0$. Now (ii) says

$$y^T A = 0, \quad y^T b < 0 \quad \text{has a solution } y. \tag{ii}$$

Here the sign of $y^T b$ is irrelevant, since we can replace y by $-y$. Thus (ii) says this:

$$y^T A = 0, \quad y^T b \neq 0 \quad \text{has a solution } y. \tag{2^0}$$

In other words, *either* we can solve $Ax = b$ *or* (exclusive) we can find a vector y that is orthogonal to all columns of A but not orthogonal to b. The alternative cases (1^0) and (2^0) constitute the Fredholm alternative of linear algebra, which Fredholm used in his theory of linear integral equations.

EXAMPLE 5. *Steady states of Markov processes.* Suppose that a particle can be in any one of states numbered $1, 2, \ldots, n$ (think of a Mexican jumping bean that can be in any one of n cups). If the particle is in state j, let p_{ij} be the probability of a transition (a jump) to state i. We require $p_{ij} \geqslant 0$ and

$$\sum_{i=1}^{n} p_{ij} = 1 \quad (j = 1, 2, \ldots, n). \tag{21}$$

At a certain instant, let x_j equal the probability that the particle is in state j. Then

$$x_j \geqslant 0 \quad \text{and} \quad \sum_{j=1}^{n} x_j = 1. \tag{22}$$

The vector $x = (x_1, \ldots, x_n)^T$ is called the probability state vector, or just *state vector*.

After a transition the particle will lie in state i with probability

$$y_i = p_{i1}x_1 + p_{i2}x_2 + \cdots + p_{in}x_n \quad (i = 1, \ldots, n). \tag{23}$$

Evidently, all y_i are $\geqslant 0$, and the equations (21) and (22) guarantee $\sum y_i = 1$. By (23) the new state vector y is related to the old state vector x by the equation $y = Px$, where P is the Markov matrix of transition probabilities.

A *steady state* is a state vector x that goes to itself:

$$x = Px, \quad x \geqslant 0, \quad \sum x_i = 1.$$

For instance, if P is symmetric, we have the steady state

$$x = \left(\frac{1}{n}, \frac{1}{n}, \ldots, \frac{1}{n}\right)^T,$$

for then, if $i = 1, \ldots, n$,

$$\sum_{j=1}^{n} p_{ij}x_j = \frac{1}{n} \sum_{j} p_{ij} = \frac{1}{n} \sum_{j} p_{ji} = \frac{1}{n}.$$

But if the Markov matrix P is not symmetric, it is not so easy to prove there is a steady state.

Farkas's theorem implies that every Markov matrix P has a steady state. Here's how:

We will express the steady-state condition as a Farkas case (i). Let A be the matrix whose first n rows and columns are the square matrix $P - I$, and let the $n + 1$st row of A consist of 1's:

$$A = \begin{bmatrix} P - I \\ u^T \end{bmatrix} \quad \text{with} \quad u^T = [1, 1, \ldots, 1]. \tag{24}$$

Thus, A has $n + 1$ rows and n columns. Then the Markov matrix P has a steady state x iff

$$Ax = b \quad \text{has a solution } x \geqslant 0, \tag{i}$$

where b is the vector

$$b_1 = 0, \ldots, b_n = 0; \quad b_{n+1} = 1. \tag{25}$$

Condition (i) just says this:

$$\begin{aligned}(P - I)x &= 0 \\ u^T x &= 1\end{aligned} \quad \text{has a solution } x \geqslant 0.$$

What is the Farkas alternative? It is this:

$$y^T A \geqslant 0, \quad y^T b < 0 \qquad \text{has a solution } y. \tag{ii}$$

Here y must have $n + 1$ components. If we set

$$y^T = [z_1, \ldots, z_n, -\lambda] = [z^T, -\lambda],$$

then (24) gives

$$y^T A = [z^T, -\lambda]\begin{bmatrix} P - I \\ u^T \end{bmatrix} = z^T(P - I) - \lambda u^T,$$

while (25) gives $y^T b = -\lambda$. Now (ii) says

$$z^T(P - I) \geqslant \lambda u^T, \quad \lambda > 0 \qquad \text{has a solution } z, \lambda. \tag{ii}$$

If z and λ satisfy (ii), then

$$\sum_{i=1}^{n} z_i p_{ij} - z_j \geqslant \lambda > 0 \qquad (j = 1, \ldots, n). \tag{26}$$

Let $z_m = \max z_i$. Then (21) implies

$$\sum_{i=1}^{m} z_i p_{ij} \leqslant \max z_i = z_m \qquad (j = 1, \ldots, n).$$

Setting j equal to the special index m, we find

$$\sum_{i=1}^{m} z_i p_{im} - z_m \leqslant 0.$$

Setting $j = m$ in (26), we get a contradiction; so Farkas (ii) is false.

Therefore, Farkas (i) is true: *every Markov matrix has a steady state.*

I've given you this important application to probability theory to make a point: the Farkas theorem has tremendous power, and its use should not be confined to linear programming.

Reference

J. Farkas, Über die Theorie der einfachen Ungleichungen, J. Reine Angew. Math, Vol. 124 (1902) pp. 1–24.

PROBLEMS

1. If A is the matrix

$$A = \begin{bmatrix} 4 & 1 & -2 \\ 1 & 0 & 5 \end{bmatrix},$$

   draw the cone $C = \{Ax: x \geqslant 0\}$.

2. If A is the matrix in Problem 1, draw the cone C_{12} generated by columns 1 and 2. Also draw the other *five* cones generated by non-empty linearly independent subsets of columns. Observe that the union of all six basic cones is the cone C in Problem 1. (Note: Some of these cones are proper subsets of some others)

3. Let A be the matrix

$$A = \begin{bmatrix} 1 & 2 & 3 \\ 4 & 5 & 6 \\ 7 & 8 & 9 \end{bmatrix}.$$

   Which subsets of columns generate basic cones?

4. In the last matrix, change just *one* component. *Now* which subsets of columns generate basic cones?

5. Prove or disprove this assertion: Let $f(x)$ be a continuous function; let $C = \{f(x): x \geqslant 0\}$. Then C is closed. (Hint: In R^1, look at $f(x) = 1/(1 + x)$ for $x \geqslant 0$.)

6. In general, prove that the union of a *finite* number of closed sets is closed. Do you need the word *finite*?

7. If the $m \times n$ matrix A has rank r, at most how many basic cones are generated by non-empty subsets of columns?

9. For which b does the system

$$Ax \equiv \begin{bmatrix} 4 & 1 & -2 \\ 1 & 0 & 5 \end{bmatrix} x = b$$

   have a solution $x \geqslant 0$?

10. In the preceding problem let the vector b take these four values:

$$\begin{bmatrix} 1 \\ 1 \end{bmatrix}, \quad \begin{bmatrix} -2 \\ 3 \end{bmatrix}, \quad \begin{bmatrix} -1 \\ 6 \end{bmatrix}, \quad \begin{bmatrix} 1 \\ -7 \end{bmatrix}.$$

   For two of these vectors b, find vectors y satisfying

$$y^T A \geqslant 0, \quad y^T b = -99.$$

11. By introducing slacks, prove this: Either

$$Ax \leqslant b \qquad \text{has a solution } x \geqslant 0$$

   or (exclusive)

$$y^T A \geqslant 0, \quad y^T b < 0 \qquad \text{has a solution } y \geqslant 0.$$

12. Note that $Ax = 0$, $x \geqslant 0$ has a *nonzero* solution x iff

$$Ax = 0, \quad e^T x = 1 \qquad \text{has a solution } x \geqslant 0,$$

where $e^T = (1,1,\ldots,1)$. Prove that the Farkas alternative is:

$$y^T A > 0 \qquad \text{has a solution.}$$

13. Find the Farkas alternative of this assertion: The system

$$\begin{bmatrix} 1 & 2 & 3 \\ 4 & 5 & 6 \\ 7 & 8 & 9 \end{bmatrix} x = b$$

has a solution x with $x_1 \geqslant 0$ and $x_3 \geqslant 0$. (Hint: Set $x_2 = u_2 - v_2$, with $u_2 \geqslant 0$, $v_2 \geqslant 0$.)

*14. Find the Farkas alternative of this assertion: There exist vectors x and y satisfying

$$Ax \leqslant b \qquad y^T A \geqslant c^T$$
$$x \geqslant 0 \qquad\qquad y \geqslant 0$$
$$c^T x \geqslant y^T b.$$

(The answer appears in the next section. Method: Use composite matrices and composite vectors.)

15. Let A be defined as in Problem 13. Find the Fredholm alternative of this assertion: The system $Ax = b$ has a solution x.

*16. Let P be the Markov matrix

$$P = \frac{1}{9} \begin{bmatrix} 1 & 2 & 5 \\ 0 & 3 & 4 \\ 8 & 4 & 0 \end{bmatrix}.$$

Find the *steady state* x.

*17. Let P and Q be Markov matrices with the same dimensions. Show that PQ and QP are Markov matrices with state vectors x and y satisfying $Qx = y$, $Py = x$.

*18. In the plane, draw the cone C generated by the *infinite* sequence of vectors

$$a^j = \begin{pmatrix} j \\ 1 \end{pmatrix} \qquad (j = 1, 2, 3, \ldots),$$

Is the cone C closed? Let $b = (1,0)^T$. Is b in C? If not, is there a point in C that is nearest to b? Let A be the $2 \times \infty$ matrix with the columns a^j. Does $Ax = b$ have a solution $x \geqslant 0$? Is there a vector y satisfying $y^T A \geqslant 0$, $y^T b < 0$? Does the Farkas alternative hold in infinite dimensions?

19. A *cone* in R^N is a set C such that if $x \in C$, then $\lambda x \in C$ for all scalars $\lambda \geqslant 0$. A *finite* cone satisfies the definition (3). Define a cone in R^3 that isn't a finite cone.

20. Let C be a cone in R^N. Definite the set

$$C^* = \{ y: y^T x \leqslant 0 \text{ for all } x \in C \}.$$

Show that C^* is a *cone* in R^N. The cone C^* is called the *dual* of the cone C.

21. In the plane, let the cone C consist of $x = 0$ and of all points $x > 0$. Is C a finite cone? Show that C^* consists of all $x \leqslant 0$. Define the dual of the dual: $C^{**} = (C^*)^*$. For this example show that C^{**} consists of all $x \geqslant 0$. Note that C^{**} is bigger than C. In general, prove $C^{**} \supset C$ for cones in R^N. Give an example where $C^{**} = C$.

22. Use the Farkas theorem to prove $C^{**} = C$ if C is a *finite* cone.

*23. If C is a *finite* cone, prove that the dual cone C^* is also a *finite* cone.

8 The Duality Principle

We'll begin with an easy consequence of the Farkas theorem.

Lemma. *Either*

$$Ax \leqslant b \qquad \text{has a solution } x \geqslant 0 \tag{i}$$

or (exclusive)

$$y^T A \geqslant 0, \quad y^T b < 0 \qquad \text{has a solution } y \geqslant 0. \tag{ii}$$

PROOF. As usual, we express inequalities as equations by introducing slack variables $z_i \geqslant 0$. Using the vector z, we can write $Ax \leqslant b$ as $Ax + z = b$. Then the alternative (i) takes the form

$$[A,I]\begin{bmatrix} x \\ z \end{bmatrix} = b \qquad \text{has a solution} \quad \begin{bmatrix} x \\ z \end{bmatrix} \geqslant 0. \tag{i}$$

Now the Farkas theorem says (i) is true *or* (exclusive)

$$y^T[A,I] \geqslant 0, \quad y^T b < 0 \qquad \text{has a solution } y. \tag{ii}$$

Since $y^T[A,I] = [y^T A, y^T]$, the proof is done.

Now we can derive the duality principle. For convenience, we'll use the standard form of linear programming. As you know, this entails no loss of generality, because every linear programming problem can be put in standard form.

Duality Theorem. *We consider the primal problem*

$$Ax \geqslant b, \quad x \geqslant 0, \quad c^T x = \min.$$

and its dual,

$$y^T A \leqslant c^T, \quad y \geqslant 0, \quad y^T b = \max.$$

Then exactly one of these four cases occurs:

1. The normal case: Both the primal and the dual have optimal solutions, and the two optimal values are equal:

$$\min c^T x = \max y^T b. \tag{1}$$

2. The primal has no feasible solution x, but the dual has feasible solutions y with

$$y^T b \to +\infty. \tag{2}$$

3. The dual has no feasible solution y, but the primal has feasible solutions x with

$$c^T x \to -\infty. \tag{3}$$

4. Neither the primal nor the dual has a feasible solution. (Examples of all four cases appear after the proof.)

PROOF. We will find the four cases by straightforward use of our lemma. All we have to do is write the normal case (1) in the form of a Farkas alternative (i). Then we'll look at the Farkas alternative (ii) and see what it says.

NOTATION. We will use a compound matrix $\hat{A}$ and compound vectors $\hat{x}, \hat{y}, \hat{b}$ in place of A, x, y, b in the lemma.

To use our lemma, we want to write the normal case as a collection of inequalities to be solved by non-negative unknowns. First we write

$$(-A)x \leqslant -b, \quad x \geqslant 0, \tag{4}$$

which says x is feasible for the primal. Then we write

$$A^T y \leqslant c, \quad y \geqslant 0, \tag{5}$$

which says y is feasible for the dual.

Finally, we write the *inequality*

$$c^T x - b^T y \leqslant 0 \tag{6}$$

to express the *equation* $c^T x = y^T b$. In fact, the strict inequality $(<)$ is impossible in (6), since all feasible x and y satisfy

$$c^T x \geqslant y^T b, \tag{7}$$

as we proved before. Therefore, the inequality (6) can hold only as an equation. Then, as we proved, x is optimal for the primal and y is optimal for the dual.

To use the form (i) of our lemma, we will express the inequalities (4), (5), (6) with a compound matrix

$$\hat{A} = \begin{bmatrix} -A & O \\ O & A^T \\ c^T & -b \end{bmatrix} \tag{8}$$

If A has m rows and n columns, then the compounded matrix $\hat{A}$ has $m + n + 1$ rows and $n + m$ columns. We'll also need the compound vectors

$$\hat{x} = \begin{bmatrix} x \\ y \end{bmatrix}, \quad \hat{b} = \begin{bmatrix} -b \\ c \\ 0 \end{bmatrix}.$$

The first vector has $n + m$ components; the second has $m + n + 1$. Now we can express (4), (5), (6) as follows:

$$\hat{A}\hat{x} \leqslant \hat{b} \qquad \text{has a solution } \hat{x} \geqslant 0. \tag{i}$$

What is the Farkas alternative (ii)? It is this:

$$\hat{y}^T\hat{A} \geqslant 0, \quad \hat{y}^T\hat{b} < 0 \qquad \text{has a solution } \hat{y} \geqslant 0. \tag{ii}$$

We'll express this with a compound vector $\hat{y}$. If you look at the definition of $\hat{A}$, you see that it's partitioned into three sets of rows. So we'll partition $\hat{y}^T$ like this:

$$\hat{y}^T = [v^T, u^T, \lambda]. \tag{10}$$

Here v has m components, u has n, and λ has one. Then (ii) says that the following system is solvable:

$$[v^T, u^T, \lambda] \begin{bmatrix} -A & O \\ O & A^T \\ c^T & -b^T \end{bmatrix} \geqslant 0$$

$$[v^T, u^T, \lambda] \begin{bmatrix} -b \\ c \\ 0 \end{bmatrix} < 0$$

$$[v^T, u^T, \lambda] \geqslant 0.$$

Now let's unpack and see what we've got. This is what we've found for Farkas (ii):

$$v^T(-A) + \lambda c^T \geqslant 0, \quad u^T A^T - \lambda b^T \geqslant 0, \quad v^T(-b) + u^T c < 0$$
$$v \geqslant u, \quad u \geqslant 0, \quad \lambda \geqslant 0.$$

This says:

$$Au \geqslant \lambda b \qquad v^T A \leqslant \lambda c^T \qquad c^T u < v^T b \tag{ii}$$
$$\text{has a solution } u \geqslant 0, v \geqslant 0, \lambda \geqslant 0.$$

What does this imply? It looks like a primal-dual pair. Indeed, if λ is positive, then u/λ is feasible for the primal, and v/λ is feasible for the dual, and their values satisfy

$$c^T(u/\lambda) < (v/\lambda)^T b. \tag{11}$$

But that is impossible. For every primal-dual feasible pair, the primal value must be $\geqslant$ the dual value in (11). *Therefore* (ii) *implies* $\lambda = 0$.

Now (ii) is reduced to this:

$$Au \geqslant 0, \quad v^T A \leqslant 0, \quad c^T u < v^T b \tag{ii}$$
$$\text{has a solution } u \geqslant 0, \quad v \geqslant 0.$$

The inequality $c^T u < v^T b$ implies

$$c^T u < 0 \quad \text{or} \quad 0 < v^T b \quad \text{(or both)}. \tag{12}$$

First suppose $c^T u < 0$. Then the dual has no feasible solution y. For if

$$y^T A \leqslant c^T, \quad y \geqslant 0$$

and if, by (ii),

$$Au \geqslant 0, \quad u \geqslant 0,$$

then we could deduce

$$0 \leqslant y^T (Au) \leqslant c^T u.$$

If the primal also has no feasible solution, then we have Case 4. But if the primal has a feasible solution x, then

$$A(x + \lambda u) \geqslant b, \quad x + \lambda u \geqslant 0 \quad \text{if} \quad \lambda \geqslant 0$$

and

$$c^T (x + \lambda u) = c^T x + \lambda(c^T u) \rightarrow -\infty \quad \text{as} \quad \lambda \rightarrow \infty.$$

Then we have Case 3.

Second, suppose $0 < v^T b$ in (12). Then the primal has no feasible solution x. For if

$$Ax \geqslant b, \quad x \geqslant 0$$

and if, by (ii),

$$v^T A \leqslant 0, \quad v \geqslant 0,$$

then we could deduce

$$0 \geqslant (v^T A)x \geqslant v^T b.$$

If the dual also has no feasible solution, then we have Case 4. But if the dual has a feasible solution y, then

$$(y + \lambda v)^T A \leqslant c^T, \quad y + \lambda v \geqslant 0 \quad \text{if} \quad \lambda \geqslant 0$$

and

$$(y + \lambda v)^T b = y^T b + \lambda(v^T b) \rightarrow \infty \quad \text{as} \quad \lambda \rightarrow \infty.$$

Then we have Case 2.

This completes the proof of the duality theorem. Let me summarize the argument: Unless we have the normal Case 1, the lemma implies there are vectors u and v satisfying

$$Au \geqslant 0, \quad u \geqslant 0, \quad v^T A \leqslant 0, \quad v \geqslant 0,$$

with

$$c^T u < 0 \quad \text{or} \quad 0 < v^T b \text{ (or both)}.$$

The inequality $c^T u < 0$ implies we have Case 4 or Case 3; the inequality $0 < v^T b$ implies we have Case 4 or 2. Thus, either we have the normal Case 1 or we have one of the other three cases. Since the four cases are mutually exclusive, exactly one of them occurs.

EXAMPLE 1. Here is an example of the normal case:

$$x_1 + 2x_2 \geqslant 1; \quad x \geqslant 0; \quad 3x_1 + 4x_2 = \min.$$
$$y_1 \leqslant 3, \quad 2y_1 \leqslant 4; \quad y_1 \geqslant 0; \quad y_1 = \max.$$

Both optimal values equal 2.

EXAMPLE 2. Here the primal has no feasible solution, while the dual has optimal value $+\infty$:

$$-x_1 - 2x_2 \geqslant 1; \quad x \geqslant 0; \quad 3x_1 + 4x_2 = \min.$$
$$-y_1 \leqslant 3, \quad -2y_1 \leqslant 4; \quad y_1 \geqslant 0; \quad y_1 = \max.$$

EXAMPLE 3. Here is the reverse of the last example:

$$x_1 \geqslant -3, \quad 2x_1 \geqslant -4; \quad x_1 \geqslant 0; \quad -x_1 = \min.$$
$$y_1 + 2y_2 \leqslant -1; \quad y \geqslant 0; \quad -3y_1 - 4y_2 = \max.$$

The primal has minimum cost $-\infty$; the dual has no feasible solution.

EXAMPLE 4. Here there is no feasible x and no feasible y:

$$x_1 \geqslant 2, \quad -3x_2 \geqslant 4; \quad x \geqslant 0; \quad -5x_1 - 6x_2 = \min.$$
$$y_1 \leqslant -5, \quad -3y_2 \leqslant -6; \quad y \geqslant 0; \quad 2y_1 + 4y_2 = \max.$$

Using the duality theorem, we can prove the full equilibrium theorem. Before, we proved the easy half of it. We will revert to linear programming in the canonical form because that's the form we use in computation.

Equilibrium theorem. *The feasible solution x is optimal for*

$$Ax = b, \quad x \geqslant 0, \quad c^T x = \min. \tag{13}$$

if and only if there exists a vector y satisfying

$$\sum_{i=1}^{m} y_i a_{ij} \leqslant c_j \qquad (j = 1, \ldots, n) \tag{14}$$

with equality for all j for which x_j is positive. (Here A is the matrix with components a_{ij}, as usual.)

PROOF. Before, we proved only the "if" part. But now we have the duality theorem, and we know that the primal (13) has an optimal solution x only in Case 1. In that case there exists a vector y that is optimal for the dual:

$$y^T A \leqslant c^T, \quad y^T b = \max.$$

And the two optimal values are equal: $c^T x = y^T b$.
     Then we have

$$0 = c^T x - y^T b = (c^T - y^T A)x,$$

which says

$$0 = \sum_{j=1}^{n} \left(c_j - \sum_{i=1}^{m} y_i a_{ij} \right) x_j. \tag{15}$$

For feasible x we have $x_j \geqslant 0$; for feasible y every factor $(\ldots)$ in (15) is also $\geqslant 0$. So equation (16) implies that the factors $(\ldots)$ equal zero for all j for which x_j is positive. $\square$

We used the equilibrium equations and the dual vector y in our discussion of the simplex method. You may now think that the dual vector y has no meaning, though it can be useful. In the next section, you'll see that the optimal dual vector y does have meaning: *the component y_i is a shadow cost.* If the requirement b_i changes by δb_i, and if the basis doesn't change, then the minimum cost changes by y_i times δb_i. In applications like those in petroleum industry, this information is valuable because the data b_i are seldom exact.

PROBLEMS

1. Guess the optimal solution of this problem:

$$\begin{bmatrix} 1 & 2 & 3 \\ 2 & 3 & 4 \end{bmatrix} x = \begin{bmatrix} 5 \\ 7 \end{bmatrix}, \quad x \geqslant 0, \quad 2x_1 + x_2 + x_3 = \min.$$

Then solve the two equilibrium equations for the optimal dual vector (y_1, y_2); verify the equilibrium inequality (daul feasibility). For this example, identify the compound matrix $\hat{A}$ and the compound vectors $\hat{x}, \hat{b}$. Verify the inequality $\hat{A}\hat{x} \leqslant \hat{b}$.

2. Verify the duality principle for the degenerate canonical program

$$\begin{bmatrix} 1 & 2 & 3 \\ 2 & 3 & 4 \end{bmatrix} x = \begin{bmatrix} 4 \\ 6 \end{bmatrix}, \quad x \geqslant 0, \quad x_1 + x_3 = \min.$$

3. Let A be the matrix

$$A = \begin{bmatrix} 1 & 0 & -1 \\ 0 & 1 & 0 \end{bmatrix}.$$

Consider all the canonical minimum problems $Ax = b$, $x \geqslant 0$, $c^T x = \min.$ Identify those pairs of vectors b, c that produce each of the four cases in the duality theorem.

4. Let A be the matrix

$$A = \begin{bmatrix} 1 & -1 & 0 \\ 1 & 1 & -1 \end{bmatrix}.$$

Now do as in Problem 3.

5. Obtain an equilibrium theorem for the *standard* linear program

$$Ax \geqslant b, \quad x \geqslant 0, \quad c^T x = \min.$$

(Introduce slack variables and use the canonical form.)

6. Verify the equilibrium theorem for the degenerate program in Problem 3.

7. Find equilibrium conditions for the Chebyshev approximation problem

$$-x_0 \leqslant \sum_{j=1}^{n} a_{ij} x_j - b_i \leqslant x_0 \quad (i = 1, \dots, m)$$

$$x_0 = \min.$$

*8. Refer to the discussion of the idea of the simplex method. Use the simplex method to prove the duality theorem for *nondegenerate* canonical minimum problems. Does this proof work for degenerate problems? (Does the proof in the text work for degenerate problems? Yes!)

9 Perturbations and Parametric Programming

In applications, data are seldom exact, so it's important to know how the solution changes if the data change a little.

Of course, one way to find out is to do the whole computation over and over for various proposed sets of data. If the problem is big, and if each computation takes hours of computer time, this process is slow and very expensive. What's worse, you may get no insight—just pages and pages of numbers.

What you want to know is this: What is the effect of each input on the minimum cost? Which of the inputs affect the cost most?

Now I'll show you how the *dual* vector answers these questions. And so you'll see why the dual vector is cherished by oil-company vice presidents and not just by mathematicians.

As you know, by the simplex method we solve the linear programming problem in canonical form:

$$Ax = b, \quad x \geqslant 0, \quad c^T x = \min. \tag{1}$$

We assume that the problem is non-degenerate.

At each stage of the simplex method, we use a vector y that solves the equilibrium equations,

$$y^T a^j = c_j \quad (j \in B), \tag{2}$$

where B is the current basis. We stop when the equilibrium vector y is feasible for the dual program:

$$y^T a^j \leqslant c_j \quad \text{for all } j = 1, \ldots, n. \tag{3}$$

When this happens, x is optimal for the primal (1); and by the way, y is optimal for the dual:

$$y^T A \leqslant c^T, \quad y^T b = \max, \tag{4}$$

with

$$\min. \text{cost} = c^T x = y^T b. \tag{5}$$

Question: *What happens to the minimum cost if the requirement vector b changes by a small perturbation δb?*

Answer: *The minimum cost changes by this amount:*

$$\delta \text{ cost} = y^T(\delta b) = y_1 \delta b_1 + y_2 \delta b_2 + \cdots + y_m \delta b_m. \tag{6}$$

In applied mathematics, perturbation theory usually gives answers that are approximate—correct to first order. But I have a surprise for you: Formula (6) is exact.

This gives meaning to the dual vector y. The component y_i is the *shadow cost* of the ith requirement: if the ith requirement changes by δb_i, then the minimum cost changes by exactly δb_i time y_i—provided $|\delta b|$ isn't too big.

This beautiful result follows from the equilibrium theorem. For suppose b changes by δb; then we can solve the system

$$\sum_{j \in B} (x_j + \delta x_j)a^j = b + \delta b \tag{7}$$

for the m unknowns $x_j + \delta x_j$ $(j \in B)$. This is a non-singular linear system of m equations in m unknowns; the matrix of the system is the invertible basis matrix M whose m columns are the a^j for j in B.

By non-degeneracy, we have $x_j > 0$ for the basic components $(j \in B)$ of the original basic optimal solution x. Therefore, we have

$$x_j + \delta x_j > 0 \quad \text{for} \quad j \in B \tag{8}$$

provided $|\delta b|$ is small enough. That's because the m components (8) constitute the vector $M^{-1}(b + \delta b)$, as you see by multiplying (7) by the inverse of the basis matrix. Therefore,

$$(\delta x_j)_{j \in B} = M^{-1}\delta b, \tag{9}$$

so all the numbers δx_j tend to zero as the perturbation vector δb tends to zero.

Thus, the numbers $x_j + \delta x_j$ are all positive for $j \in B$, and they give a basic *feasible* solution for the primal problem (1) with b perturbed by δb. But is this solution *optimal*?

Yes. You see, the old optimal dual vector y still solves the equilibrium and feasibility conditions:

$$y^T a^j = c_j \, (j \in B); \quad y^T a^j \leqslant c_j \, (j = 1, \ldots, n). \tag{10}$$

After all, c hasn't changed and B hasn't changed—B is still the index set where the primal feasible components are positive. That's all we need to know. The equilibrium theorem says that the new basic feasible solution $x + \delta x$ is *optimal*; and by the way, the old optimal dual vector y remains optimal.

All right. It seems almost too easy. Let's look back. What made the proof work? Just one thing: the perturbed basic components $x_j + \delta x_j$ had to remain $\geqslant 0$; as long as the data perturbation δb was small enough to guarantee that, the proof went through.

Ah, you say, but what if δb doesn't remain small enough to guarantee that? What then?

Then the optimal basis B has to change, and our pretty formula (6) doesn't work any more, and you have to go to the computer for another run.

For large perturbations δb, or for degenerate problems, I'll give you a theorem on what is called *parametric programming*. We consider two requirement vectors, b^0 and b^1. We introduce the parameter θ and draw the line segment

$$b(\theta) = (1 - \theta)b^0 + \theta b^1 \quad (0 \leqslant \theta \leqslant 1),$$

If you keep the matrix A and the cost vector c fixed, then the family of vectors $b(\theta)$ generates a family of linear programs:

$$Ax = (1 - \theta)b^0 + \theta b^1 \qquad (0 \leqslant \theta \leqslant 1)$$
$$x \geqslant 0, \quad c^T x = \min. \equiv \mu(\theta). \tag{11}$$

The question is this: *How does the minimum cost $\mu(\theta)$ behave as a function of the parameter θ?*

You'll see that $\mu(\theta)$ behaves like the function in Figure 1: *it is continuous, convex, and piecewise linear.* This doesn't give you numerical results as our small-perturbation formula (6) did, but it does give you a general, qualitative understanding.

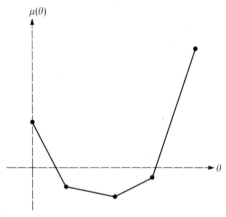

Figure 1

This reminds me of a comment by the famous electrical engineer John R. Pierce. Speaking of Shannon's information theory, he said: "What some of us attained was perhaps wisdom rather than knowledge."

Theorem. *Suppose that the linear program* (11) *has optimal solutions x^0 and x^1 for $\theta = 0$ and $\theta = 1$, respectively. Then the program has an optimal solution for every intermediate value, $0 < \theta < 1$. The minimum cost $\mu(\theta)$ is continuous, convex, and piecewise linear for $0 \leqslant \theta \leqslant 1$.*

PROOF. Please note that the theorem does not assume nondegeneracy. Nor does it assume that optimal solutions exist for $0 < \theta < 1$; we have to prove that.

We'll use the dual program:

$$y^T A \leqslant c^T, \quad y^T[(1 - \theta)b^0 + \theta b^1] = \max. \tag{12}$$

Note that the dual feasibility condition $(y^T A \leqslant c^T)$ is independent of the parameter θ; so if y is feasible for $\theta = 0$, then y is feasible for all θ.

But we assume that the primal problem has an optimal solution x^0 for $\theta = 0$. Then the dual has a solution $y = y^0$ that is optimal for $\theta = 0$; so y^0 is feasible for $0 \leqslant \theta \leqslant 1$.

We'll now show that the primal problem has *feasible* solutions for $0 \leqslant \theta \leqslant 1$. Here they are:

$$\bar{x} = (1 - \theta)x^0 + \theta x^1 \qquad (0 \leqslant \theta \leqslant 1). \qquad (13)$$

Here x^0 is the given optimal solution for $b = b^0$, and x^1 is optimal for $b = b^1$. Then the vector $\bar{x}$ satisfies

$$\bar{x} \geqslant 0, \quad A\bar{x} = (1 - \theta)b^0 + \theta b^1. \qquad (14)$$

In general, $\bar{x}$ is not optimal, but it is feasible.

For each θ in $0 \leqslant \theta \leqslant 1$, we've found a pair of vectors ($\bar{x}$ and y^0) that are feasible for the primal and the dual. Now the duality theorem tells us this: For each θ, we have the normal case—*optimal solutions exist for the primal and dual problems, and they have a common value,*

$$\mu(\theta) = \min c^T x = \max y^T b. \qquad (15)$$

Now we'll show that $\mu(\theta)$ looks like Figure 1. We'll prove this: *For each θ, $\mu(\theta)$ is the maximum of a finite number of linear functions*:

$$\mu(\theta) = \max[\lambda_1(\theta), \lambda_2(\theta), \ldots, \lambda_N(\theta)], \qquad (16)$$

where each $\lambda_k(\theta)$ has the form

$$\lambda_k(\theta) = \alpha_k + \beta_k \theta \qquad (0 \leqslant \theta \leqslant 1). \qquad (17)$$

(In Figure 1 I've drawn $\mu(\theta)$ as the maximum of four linear functions.)

We'll use the theorem on basic optimal solutions. First, we write the dual (12) as a canonical minimum problem. We write the unconstrained vector y as the difference $u - v$, with $u \geqslant 0$ and $v \geqslant 0$; and we introduce the slack vector $z \geqslant 0$. Then (12) becomes the canonical minimum problem

$$A^T(u - v) + z = c; \quad u \geqslant 0, \quad v \geqslant 0, \quad z \geqslant 0$$
$$-[(1 - \theta)b^0 + \theta b^1]^T(u - v) = -\mu(\theta) = \min. \qquad (18)$$

We've proved that the equivalent problem (12) has an optimal solution; therefore, the canonical problem (18) has a *basic* optimal solution. But there is only a *finite* number of basic feasible solutions:

$$\{u^k, v^k, z^k\} \qquad (k = 1, \ldots, N). \qquad (19)$$

Each feasible solution is a triple of vectors $\{u, v, z\}$, and the feasible solutions are independent of θ because A and c are independent of θ.

For each θ, to minimize the cost $-\mu(\theta)$ in (18), we pick the best of the N basic feasible solutions. This gives

$$-\mu(\theta) = \min_{1 \leqslant k \leqslant N} \{-[(1 - \theta)b^0 + \theta b^1]^T(u^k - v^k)\}.$$

Multiplying this by -1, we get

$$\mu(\theta) = \max_{1 \leqslant k \leqslant N} \{\alpha_k + \beta_k \theta\}, \tag{20}$$

where, if $y^k = u^k - v^k$,

$$\alpha_k = (b^0)^T y^k, \quad \beta_k = (b^1 - b^0)^T y^k.$$

This proves the asserted formula (16), which implies that $\mu(\theta)$ is continuous and piecewise linear. (It is continuous because it is the maximum of a finite number of continuous functions.)

It remains to prove $\mu(\theta)$ is convex:

$$\mu((1 - \tau)\theta_1 + \tau\theta_2) \leqslant (1 - \tau)\mu(\theta_1) + \tau\mu(\theta_2) \qquad (0 \leqslant \tau \leqslant 1). \tag{21}$$

To prove this, suppose $\theta = (1 - \tau)\theta_1 + \tau\theta_2$, and suppose

$$\mu(\theta) = \lambda_m(\theta) = \max_{1 \leqslant k \leqslant N} \lambda_k(\theta). \tag{22}$$

Here the maximinzing index m depends on θ. If θ stays fixed, the linear function λ_m satisfies

$$\lambda_m(\theta) = \lambda_m((1 - \tau)\theta_1 + \tau\theta_2) = (1 - \tau)\lambda_m(\theta_1) + \tau\lambda_m(\theta_2). \tag{23}$$

But

$$\lambda_m(\theta_1) \leqslant \max_k \lambda_k(\theta_1) = \mu(\theta_1),$$

and similarly, $\lambda_m(\theta_2) \leqslant \mu(\theta_2)$. Therefore, (23) gives

$$\lambda_m(\theta) \leqslant (1 - \tau)\mu(\theta_1) + \tau\mu(\theta_2).$$

Since $\lambda_m(\theta)$ equals $\mu(\theta)$, this function is convex.

Perturbations of the cost vector. In the canonical problem (1), suppose we perturb the cost vector c. What is the effect on the minimum cost?

Let x be a basic optimal solution belonging to the cost vector c. Let $x_j > 0$ for $j \in B$, and assume the problem is non-degenerate.

The equilibrium and feasibility conditions are

$$y^T a^j = c_j \qquad \text{for } j \text{ in } B \tag{24}$$

$$y^T a^s \leqslant c_s \qquad \text{for } s \text{ not in } B. \tag{25}$$

Usually the inequalities (25) will be strict inequalities ($<$). Assuming this, let c become $c + \delta c$, and let $y + \delta y$ solve the non-singular linear system

$$(y + \delta y)^T a^j = c_j + \delta c_j \qquad \text{for } j \text{ in } B. \tag{24'}$$

If δc is small, then δy must be small; so we must have

$$(y + \delta y)^T a^s < c_s \qquad \text{for } s \text{ not in } B, \tag{25'}$$

provided the strict inequalities ($<$) hold in (25).

Then we assert this: *x remains an optimal basic solution for the perturbed primal, and the perturbed minimum cost is just* $(c + \delta c)^T x$.

PROOF. Since A and b do not change, x remains feasible for the perturbed primal problem. Since $x_j > 0$ for j in B, formulas (24') and (25') provide new equilibrium conditions when c becomes $c + \delta c$. Therefore, x remains optimal.

The preceding analysis fails if the inequalities (25) are not strict, or if the problem is degenerate, or if δc is large. Then, as before, we can use parametric programming.

Before, we perturbed the requirement vector; now, instead, we are perturbing the cost vector. But in principle, that can't make any difference. We can always restate a linear programming problem so that the primal becomes a dual and the dual becomes a primal. Then the cost vector becomes a requirement vector, and *vice versa*. And now we can apply our theorem on parametric programming.

Before we analyze more complicated perturbations, we'll need a theorem that guarantees uniqueness for the optimal solution vector.

Uniqueness Theorem. *Let A be an $m \times n$ matrix. Let x^0 be a basic optimal solution for the canonical program*

$$Ax = b, \quad x \geqslant 0, \quad c^T x = \min. \tag{26}$$

Let $x_j > 0$ for $j \in B$; let $x_s = 0$ for $s \in B'$. Let an optimal dual vector y^0 satisfy the conditions

$$y^T a^j = c_j \, (j \in B), \quad y^T a^s < c_s \, (s \in B'), \tag{27}$$

with strict inequalities for the non-basic indices $s \in B'$. Then x^0 is the unique optimal solution of the primal, and y^0 is the unique optimal solution of the dual.

PROOF. Suppose x^1 is another optimal solution for the primal (we don't assume x^1 is a basic solution). Let $x^1 - x^0 = v$. Then $Av = Ax^1 - Ax^0 = 0$, and $v_s = x_s^1$ for $s \in B'$; so

$$Av = 0, \quad \text{with } v_s \geqslant 0 \quad \text{for} \quad s \in B'. \tag{28}$$

Therefore,

$$0 = y^T Av = \sum_{j \in B} (y^T a^j) v_j + \sum_{s \in B'} (y^T a^s) v_s,$$

or

$$0 = \sum_B c_j v_j + \sum_{B'} (y^T a^s) v_s. \tag{29}$$

If $v \neq 0$, then $v_s \neq 0$ for some $s \in B'$, because $Av = 0$ implies $v = 0$ if v depends only on B. But if, for $s \in B'$,

$$v_s \geqslant 0 \qquad \text{with some } v_s \neq 0,$$

then the strict inequalities $y^T a^s < c_s$ imply

$$\sum_{B'} (y^T a^s) v_s < \sum_{B'} c_s v_s.$$

Now (29) implies

$$0 < \sum_B c_j v_j + \sum_{B'} c_s v_s,$$

or

$$0 < c^T v = c^T(x^1 - x^0),$$

so x^1 could not be optimal.

Now we know that x^0 is the unique optimal solution of the primal. Then every optimal dual solution y must satisfy the equilibrium equations

$$y^T a^j = c_j \qquad (j \in B), \tag{30}$$

as we proved in the Equilibrium Theorem. Since the vectors a^j are assumed independent for $j \in B$, the equations (30) have a unique solution, namely $y = y^0$. So y^0 is the unique optimal solution of the dual problem,

$$y^T A \leqslant c^T, \quad y^T b = \max. \tag{31}$$

This uniqueness theorem is useful because its assumptions are usually correct. Usually the problem is non-degenerate, and usually the non-basic dual inequalities hold strictly. Now, making these assumptions, we can obtain a complete first-order perturbation theory, covering simultaneous perturbations of b, c, and the matrix A.

First, I want to make a remark on perturbations of the matrix, $A \to A + \delta A$: Now we cannot expect the first-order perturbation formula to be exact.

To see this, let A be an ordinary square, invertible matrix M, and consider the non-singular linear system

$$Mv = b,$$

with solution $v = M^{-1}b$. Let M become $M + \delta M$, and let's get a first-order perturbation formula for the solution.

The perturbed solution, $v + \delta v$, satisfies the exact equation

$$(M + \delta M)(v + \delta v) = b, \tag{32}$$

or

$$Mv + (\delta M)v + M(\delta v) + (\delta M)(\delta v) = b.$$

Since $Mv = b$, we may cancel those terms, obtaining

$$(\delta M)v + M(\delta v) + (\delta M)(\delta v) = 0. \tag{33}$$

The product $(\delta M)(\delta v)$ is a second-order term: it is the product of two small quantities. If we neglect the second-order term, we can solve for δv:

$$\delta v \cong - M^{-1}(\delta M)v. \tag{34}$$

This is the first-order perturbation formula by δv. It is inexact because we neglected the second-order term in the exact formula (33).

EXAMPLE 1. Let $\alpha, \beta, \gamma, \delta$ be small. Let

$$\begin{bmatrix} 1 + \alpha & 2 + \beta \\ 3 + \gamma & 4 + \delta \end{bmatrix} (v + \delta v) = \begin{bmatrix} 5 \\ 6 \end{bmatrix}$$

Then to first order the perturbation δv satisfies

$$\delta v \cong \frac{1}{2} \begin{bmatrix} 4 & -2 \\ -3 & 1 \end{bmatrix} \begin{bmatrix} \alpha & \beta \\ \gamma & \delta \end{bmatrix} \begin{bmatrix} 5 \\ 6 \end{bmatrix}.$$

Now let's go from linear algebra to linear programming. In the next example, you'll see we have to be careful: *the minimum cost may depend discontinuously on the matrix A*

EXAMPLE 2. For small $\varepsilon > 0$, consider the canonical problem

$$(1 + \varepsilon)^{-1} x_1 - (1 - \varepsilon) x_2 = 1$$
$$x_1 - x_2 = 1$$
$$x \geqslant 0, \quad x_1 = \min$$

For $\varepsilon \neq 0$, the two equations have the unique solution

$$x_1 = 1 + \varepsilon^{-1}, \quad x_2 = \varepsilon^{-1},$$

and so the minimum cost is $1 + \varepsilon^{-1}$, which tends to ∞ as $\varepsilon \to 0$. But if $\varepsilon = 0$, the two equations both say $x_1 - x_2 = 1$, and the minimum cost for $x \geqslant 0$ is $x_1 = 1$. And so the solution x and the minimum cost depend discontinuously on the matrix.

Regular perturbation theory. In the last example, the limiting problem was degenerate. *Now assume*, instead, *that the canonical problem*

$$Ax = b, \quad x \geqslant 0, \quad c^T x = \min.$$

is non-degenerate, and assume that x^0 and y^0 satisfy the conditions of our uniqueness theorem. Let A, b, and c have small perturbations $\delta A, \delta b$, and δc. Then we can derive formulas for the first order perturbations $\delta x, \delta y$, and $\delta \mu$ (where $\mu = c^T x = y^T b$).

Let M be the basis matrix, whose columns are the basic columns a^j for $j \in B$. We assume $x_j^0 > 0$ for $j \in B$, $x_s^0 = 0$ for $s \in B'$. The perturbation δA induces a perturbation of the basis matrix:

$$\delta M = (\delta a^j)_{j \in B}.$$

For small perturbations δA, the matrix $M + \delta M$ remains non-singular, since its determinant remains non-zero.

The vector x^0 has n components; m of them are positive, and $n - m$ of them are zero. We now define the compressed vector $\hat{x}$ consisting of just the m positive components of x^0. Thus, we have

$$Ax^0 = \sum_{j \in B} x_j^0 a^j = M\hat{x} = b. \tag{35}$$

Similarly, we define the vector

$$\hat{c} = (c_j)_{j \in B}.$$

Then we can write the m equilibrium equations, $y^T a^j = c_j \ (j \in B)$, in the simple form

$$y^T M = \hat{c}^T. \tag{36}$$

For regular perturbations the basis B stays fixed. Then these are the *exact* equations that determine $\delta\hat{x}$, δy, and $\delta\mu$:

$$(M + \delta M)(\hat{x} + \delta\hat{x}) = b + \delta b, \tag{37}$$

$$(y^0 + \delta y)^T(M + \delta M) = (\hat{c} + \delta\hat{c})^T, \tag{38}$$

$$\mu + \delta\mu = (\hat{c} + \delta\hat{c})^T(\hat{x} + \delta\hat{x})$$
$$= (y^0 + \delta y)^T(b + \delta b) \tag{39}$$

(Notation: In all these formulas, if v is a vector with components v_j for $j = 1, 2, \ldots, n$, then $\hat{v}$ is the vector with just the components v_j for j in the basic index set B.)

Since M has an inverse, all these equations are solvable if δM is small enough. And since we've assumed the *strict* inequalities

$$(y^0)^T a^s < c_s \qquad (s \in B'),$$

we must obtain

$$(y^0 + \delta y)^T a^s < c_s + \delta c_s \qquad (s \in B')$$

for small perturbations. Then the basis B does not change, and the exact solutions

$$\hat{x} + \delta\hat{x}, \quad y^0 + \delta y, \quad \mu + \delta\mu$$

give the new optimal primal and dual vectors and the new minimum cost; that follows from the equilibrium theorem.

To get first-order approximations, we drop the second-order terms in the exact equations. After cancellations, we get

$$(\delta M)\hat{x} + M(\delta\hat{x}) \cong \delta b \tag{37.1}$$

$$(\delta y)^T M + (y^0)^T M \cong (\delta\hat{c})^T \tag{38.1}$$

$$\delta\mu \cong \hat{c}^T \delta\hat{x} + (\delta\hat{c})^T \hat{x}$$
$$\cong (y^0)^T \delta b + (\delta y)^T b \tag{39.1}$$

If we solve for $\delta\hat{x}$ and δy, we get

$$\boxed{\begin{aligned} \delta\hat{x} &\cong M^{-1}[\delta b - (\delta M)\hat{x}] \\ (\delta y)^T &\cong [(\delta\hat{c})^T - (y^0)^T(\delta M)]M^{-1} \end{aligned}} \tag{40}$$

and now (39.1) gives $\delta\mu$.

Finally, let's find the first-order perturbation of the inverse basis matrix. Let $M^{-1} = U$. Suppose M becomes $M + \delta M$. Then U becomes $U + \delta U$, where

$$(M + \delta M)(U + \delta U) = I.$$

To first-order, this gives

$$MU + (\delta M)U + M(\delta U) \cong I.$$

If we cancel MU and I, we can solve for δU:

$$\delta U \cong -M^{-1}(\delta M)U$$

or

$$\boxed{\delta U \cong -U(\delta M)U.} \tag{41}$$

EXAMPLE 3. Consider the canonical program

$$\begin{bmatrix} 1 & 2 & 3 \\ 4 & 5 & 6 \end{bmatrix} x = \begin{bmatrix} 5 \\ 14 \end{bmatrix} (Ax = b)$$

$$x \geq 0, \quad x_2 = \min. \qquad (\mu = c^T x = \min.)$$

This is a solution: $x_1 = 2$, $x_2 = 0$, $x_3 = 1$. Here we have

$$B = \{1,3\}, \quad \hat{x} = \begin{bmatrix} 2 \\ 1 \end{bmatrix}, \quad \hat{c}^T = [0,0] = [c_1, c_3].$$

$$M = \begin{bmatrix} 1 & 3 \\ 4 & 6 \end{bmatrix}, \quad M^{-1} = U = -\frac{1}{6}\begin{bmatrix} 6 & -3 \\ -4 & 1 \end{bmatrix},$$

$$(y^0)^T = \hat{c}^T M^{-1} = [0,0].$$

Note the strict inequality for the non-basic index $s = 2$:

$$(y^0)^T a^2 = 0 < c_2 = 1.$$

This inequality shows we can use regular-perturbation theory. Given small perturbations δA, δb, δc, we know the basis doesn't change, and we have formulas for $\delta \hat{x}$, δy, $\delta \mu$, and δU.

For instance, since $\hat{c} = 0$, formula (39.1) gives the cost perturbation

$$\delta \mu \cong (\delta \hat{c})^T \hat{x} = 2\delta c_1 + \delta c_3.$$

Reference

J. R. Pierce, The early days of information theory, IEEE Transactions on Information Theory, Vol. IT-19 (1973) pp. 3–8.

PROBLEMS

1. Let $x(\theta)$ be optimal for

$$\begin{bmatrix} 1 & 2 & 3 \\ 4 & 5 & 6 \end{bmatrix} x = (1 - \theta)\begin{bmatrix} 1 \\ 3 \end{bmatrix} + \theta\begin{bmatrix} 4 \\ 9 \end{bmatrix}, \quad x \geq 0,$$

$$[3,3,5]x = \min. \equiv \mu(\theta).$$

Let $y(\theta)$ be optimal for the dual. Show that $x(0) = [\frac{1}{3},\frac{1}{3},0]^T$, and find $y(0)$. Using formula (6), find $\mu(\theta)$ for small θ.

2. In the preceding program, solve for $x(\theta)$ and $y(\theta)$ for $0 \leqslant \theta \leqslant 1$, and draw the graph of $\mu(\theta)$. For which θ is $x(\theta)$ not unique? As θ increases from zero, where does the perturbation formula (6) fail? Where is $\mu'(\theta)$ discontinuous?

3. Let $x(\theta)$ be optimal for

$$\begin{bmatrix} 1 & 2 & 3 \\ 4 & 5 & 6 \end{bmatrix} x = \begin{bmatrix} 1 \\ 3 \end{bmatrix}, \quad x \geqslant 0,$$

$$[3,3,4 - 2\theta]x = \min. \equiv \mu(\theta)$$

Let $y(\theta)$ be optimal for the dual. For $0 \leqslant \theta \leqslant 1$ find $x(\theta)$ and $y(\theta)$, and draw the graph of $\mu(\theta)$. For which θ is $x(\theta)$ not unique? For which θ is $\mu'(\theta)$ discontinuous?

4. Consider the canonical minimum problem

$$\begin{bmatrix} 1 & 0 & 2 & 4 \\ 1 & 5 & 7 & 1 \\ 2 & 0 & 1 & 1 \end{bmatrix} x = \begin{bmatrix} 7 \\ 9 \\ 4 \end{bmatrix}, \quad x \geqslant 0,$$

$$[2,19,6,-2]x = \min.$$

(The large cost component $c_2 = 19$ makes one guess $x_2 = 0$.) Compute the optimal x and the optimal dual y; verify that $c^T x = y^T b = 6$. Compute the new optimal cost if the requirement vector b changes to

$$b + \delta b = \begin{bmatrix} 7.003 \\ 8.999 \\ 4.002 \end{bmatrix}.$$

(Do not compute the new optimal x.)

5. In Example 1 set $\alpha = \varepsilon$, $\beta = -\varepsilon$, $\gamma = 2\varepsilon$, $\delta = 3\varepsilon$ where $\varepsilon = 0.01$. Compute the exact value of δv and compare it with the first-order perturbation.

6. Let M^{-1} exist, and for small $|\varepsilon|$ let

$$(M + \varepsilon P)(v + \varepsilon v^{(1)} + \varepsilon^2 v^{(2)} + \cdots) = b.$$

If v is known, show how to compute the vectors $v^{(1)}, v^{(2)}, \ldots$ recursively, assuming the power series converges.

*7. (Continuation.) If M^{-1} exists, show that the determinant of $M + \varepsilon P$ is a polynomial in ε that is nonzero for $\varepsilon = 0$. Deduce that the vector $(M + \varepsilon P)^{-1}b$ has components that are analytic functions of ε for small $|\varepsilon|$, so that a convergent power series $\Sigma \varepsilon^k v^{(k)}$ does exist.

8. Using the first-order perturbation formula, compute an approximate inverse for the matrix.

$$\begin{bmatrix} 0.999 & 2.001 \\ 2.998 & 3.002 \end{bmatrix}.$$

9. In Example 3, use the perturbations

$$\delta A = \varepsilon \begin{bmatrix} 5 & -1 & 7 \\ -2 & 0 & 3 \end{bmatrix}, \quad \delta b = \varepsilon \begin{bmatrix} 1 \\ -2 \end{bmatrix},$$

$$\delta c^T = \varepsilon[2, -5, 7],$$

where $\varepsilon = 10^{-4}$. To first order, compute δx, δy, $\delta \mu$, and δU.

10 The Simplex Tableau Algorithm

Previously, I explained to you the idea of the simplex method—what it does and why it works. Now we'll get into the details of an algorithm you might use for a general computer code.

Let A be an $m \times n$ matrix with $m \leq n$; assume the rows are linearly independent. Consider the canonical linear program

$$Ax = b, \quad x \geq 0, \quad c^T x = \min. \tag{1}$$

If we assume that b is a linear combination of no fewer than m columns of A, then the problem is what we called *non-degenerate*.

Suppose we start a Phase II calculation. We have a basic feasible solution x, and we want to compute a new basic feasible solution x' with lower cost. To get a first basic feasible solution, we had to perform a Phase I calculation. As I showed you, Phase I calculations are just special Phase II calculations, so they do not require a different algorithm.

Suppose our given basic feasible solution x depends on the m columns a^j for $j = j_1, \ldots, j_m$. Then we have

$$x_j > 0 \quad \text{for} \quad j \in B; \quad B = \{j_1, \ldots, j_m\}. \tag{2}$$

Let me call the basic vectors

$$v^i = a^{j_i} \quad (i = 1, \ldots, m). \tag{3}$$

Then $v^1, \ldots, v^m$ are the columns of the current basis matrix M.

We now express all the columns of A in terms of the basic columns:

$$a^j = t_{1j}v^1 + t_{2j}v^2 + \cdots + t_{mj}v^m \quad (j = 1, \ldots, n), \tag{4}$$

and similarly we can write

$$b = t_{10}v^1 + t_{20}v^2 + \cdots + t_{m0}v^m. \tag{5}$$

This gives the *simplex tableau*

$$(t_{ij})\, i = 1, \ldots, m; \quad j = 1, \ldots, n, 0. \tag{6}$$

EXAMPLE 1. Let

$$A = \begin{bmatrix} 2 & 3 & 5 \\ 3 & 4 & 7 \end{bmatrix}, \quad b = \begin{bmatrix} 9 \\ 13 \end{bmatrix}. \tag{7}$$

Let the current basis vectors be the third and the first columns of A: $v^1 = a^3$, $v^2 = a^1$. Then this is the tableau:

	a^1	a^2	a^3	b
a^3	0	1	1	1
a^1	1	-1	0	2

The second column, for instance, says

$$a^3 - a^1 = a^2. \tag{8}$$

The last column says

$$a^3 + 2a^1 = b. \tag{9}$$

This gives the components of a basic solution: $x_3 = 1$, $x_1 = 2$, $x_2 = 0$. If you look at the matrix A and the vector b defined in (7), you can verify formulas (8) and (9).

The extended simplex tableau. For some purposes, it's convenient to extend the tableau by expressing the natural unit vectors $e^1, \ldots, e^m$ in terms of the current basis:

$$e^j = \sum_{i=1}^{m} u_{ij} v^i \qquad (j = 1, \ldots, m). \tag{10}$$

This extends the tableau like this:

	a^1	$\cdots$	a^n	b	e^1	$\cdots$	e^m
v^1	t_{11}	$\cdots$	t_{1n}	t_{10}	u_{11}	$\cdots$	u_{1m}
.		$\cdots$	.	.	.	$\cdots$	.
v^m	t_{m1}	$\cdots$	t_{mn}	t_{m0}	u_{m1}	$\cdots$	u_{mm}

$$\tag{11}$$

Since the natural unit vectors e^j are the columns of the identity matrix, I, and since the basis vectors v^i are the columns of the basis matrix, M, the equations (10) can be written as the matrix equation

$$I = MU, \tag{12}$$

where U is the $m \times m$ matrix (u_{ij}). Thus, U is the inverse of the current basis matrix, M.

Similarly, the original tableau equations, (4) and (5), can be written as the matrix equation

$$[A,b] = MT \tag{13}$$

where $T = (t_{ij})$ $(i = 1, \ldots, m; j = 1, \ldots, n, 0)$. And since $U = M^{-1}$, the extended tableau equals

$$[T; U] = M^{-1}[A,b;I], \tag{14}$$

EXAMPLE 2. In Example 1 the basis matrix is

$$M = [a^3, a^1] = \begin{bmatrix} 5 & 2 \\ 7 & 3 \end{bmatrix}.$$

Therefore,

$$U = M^{-1} = \begin{bmatrix} 3 & -2 \\ -7 & 5 \end{bmatrix} = (u_{ij}).$$

This gives the extended tableau

	a^1	a^2	a^3	b	e^1	e^2
a^3	0	1	1	1	3	-2
a^1	1	-1	0	2	-7	5

$$(15)$$

The first part expresses all the columns of A in terms of the current basis; the second part gives the positive components of the current basic solution; and the last part gives the inverse of the current basis matrix.

Changing the basis. Suppose we are given a simplex tableau (11), with a current basis $v^1, \ldots, v^m$. The basic vectors v^i are certain columns of A.

Suppose a^s isn't in the current basis, and we've decided to bring it into the basis. We want to replace one of the current basic vectors by a^s. How do we do this? How do we get the new tableau? And most important: How can we be sure that the new basic solution will be feasible?

We assume that the current basic solution is feasible:

$$t_{i0} > 0 \qquad (i = 1, \ldots, m). \tag{16}$$

Thus, the current basic feasible solution x satisfies

$$Ax = \sum_{j=1}^{n} x_j a^j = \sum_{j \in B} x_j a^j = \sum_{i=1}^{m} t_{i0} v^i = b, \tag{17}$$

and so the t_{i0} are just the positive components of x.

Let the *new* tableau have the components

$$t'_{ij} \qquad (i = 1, \ldots, m; j = 1, \ldots, n, 0), \tag{18}$$

$$u'_{ij} \qquad (i, j = 1, \ldots, m). \tag{19}$$

Suppose we replace the current basic vector v^r by the vector a^s, leaving the other basic vectors v^i unchanged. Then the new basic solution x' will have non-zero components

$$t'_{i0} \qquad (i = 1, \ldots, m). \tag{20}$$

If x' is to be feasible, *the components t'_{i0} must be positive*. This requirement will decide the choice of v^r.

Let's express a^s in terms of the current basis:

$$a^s = t_{1s} v^1 + \cdots + t_{rs} v^r + \cdots + t_{ms} v^m. \tag{21}$$

The basic vectors $v^1, \ldots, v^r, \ldots, v^m$ are required to be linearly independent. *If a^s replaces v^r in the basis, we must require $t_{rs} \neq 0$; for if $t_{rs} = 0$, equation (21) shows that the new basis would be dependent.*

If $t_{rs} \neq 0$, we can express v^r in terms of the *new* basis:

$$v^r = t_{rs}^{-1} \left(a^s - \sum_{\substack{i=1 \\ i \neq r}}^{m} t_{is} v^i \right) \tag{22}$$

Therefore, if we can express something in terms of $v^1, \ldots, v^r, \ldots, v^m$, we can surely express it in terms of $v^1, \ldots, a^s, \ldots, v^m$. Therefore, the new set really is a basis for the vector space R^m. The new basis is

$$(v^1)' = v^1, \ldots, (v^r)' = a^s, \ldots, (v^m)' = v^m. \tag{23}$$

Let's get the new tableau. The coefficients t'_{ij} must satisfy

$$a^j = t'_{1j}(v^1)' + \cdots + t'_{rj}(v^r)' + \cdots + t'_{mj}(v^m)',$$

which means

$$a^j = t'_{rj} a^s + \sum_{\substack{i=1 \\ i \neq r}}^{m} t'_{ij} v^i. \tag{24}$$

This uniquely defines the coefficients because the new basis consists of independent vectors.

In terms of the *old* basis, we had

$$a^j = t_{rj} v^r + \sum_{i \neq r} t_{ij} v^i. \tag{25}$$

Now, for the old vector v^r I want you to insert the representation (22), which express v^r in terms of the new basis. This is what you get:

$$a^j = t_{rj} t_{rs}^{-1} \left(a^s - \sum_{i \neq r} t_{is} v^i \right) + \sum_{i \neq r} t_{ij} v^i. \tag{26}$$

This represents a^j in terms of the *new* basis. The coefficient of a^s is

$$\boxed{t'_{rj} = t_{rj}/t_{rs},} \tag{27}$$

and for $i \neq r$ the coefficient of v^i is:

$$\boxed{t'_{ij} = t_{ij} - (t_{is}/t_{rs}) t_{rj} \qquad (i \neq r),} \tag{28}$$

These are the formulas for the new tableau.

For the extended tableau, we also want new coefficients u'_{ij}. This is no problem if we regard the natural unit vectors e^j as columns of an extended matrix $[A,I]$—indeed, this is exactly what we do in Phase I calculations. Then we may regard

$$e^1 = a^{n+1}, \quad e^2 = a^{n+2}, \ldots, e^m = a^{n+m}, \tag{29}$$

and so we may define

$$u_{ij} = t_{i,n+j} \qquad (i,j = 1, \ldots, m). \tag{30}$$

Replacing j by $n + j$ in formulas (27), (28), we get

$$u'_{rj} = u_{rj}/t_{rs} \tag{31}$$

$$u'_{ij} = u_{ij} - (t_{is}/t_{rs})u_{rj} \qquad (i \neq r). \tag{32}$$

These complicated formulas have a simple meaning. If we replace v^r by a^s, let's call row r of the old tableau *the pivot row*, and call column s the *pivot column*. Call t_{rs} the *pivot element*.

The transformation formulas (27) and (31) say this: *Divide the pivot row by the pivot element.*

The formulas (28) and (32) say this: If $i \neq r$, define the multiplier $\theta_i = t_{is}/t_{rs}$. *To transform row i, subtract from it θ_i times the pivot row.*

In summary, for the pivot row r,

$$\text{new row } r = (\text{old row } r)/t_{rs}; \tag{33}$$

for row $i \neq r$,

$$\text{new row } i = (\text{old row } i) - \theta_i (\text{old row } r). \tag{34}$$

The multiplier θ_i has a simple interpretation. In the new tableau, we shall have $(v^r)' = a^s$, and so column s of the new tableau will have rth component $t'_{rs} = 1$ and will have ith component $t'_{is} = 0$ if $i \neq r$. Therefore, in formula (34) θ_i *must be the unique multiplier that makes* $t'_{is} = 0$. Indeed, if we set $j = s$ in (28), we get

$$t'_{is} = t_{is} - (t_{is}/t_{rs})t_{rs} = 0 \qquad (i \neq r),$$

where $(t_{is}/t_{rs}) = \theta_i$.

How to choose the pivot row. Given the pivot column s, there is only one possible choice for the pivot row r, as you will now see. Remember, we assume that our problem is non-degenerate.

For the current basic feasible solution, we have the positive components $t_{i0}(i = 1, \ldots, m)$. The new basic components will be, by (27) and (28),

$$t'_{r0} = t_{r0}/t_{rs}$$

$$t'_{i0} = t_{i0} - (t_{is}/t_{rs})t_{r0} \qquad (i \neq r).$$

Since t'_{r0} must be positive, we must require $t_{rs} > 0$—*the pivot element must be positive.*

Since t'_{i0} must be positive for $i \neq r$, we must have

$$t_{i0} - (t_{is}/t_{rs})t_{r0} > 0 \qquad \text{for } i \neq r. \tag{35}$$

All four t's in this formula are positive except possibly t_{is}. If t_{is} is $\leqslant 0$, the inequality (27) is true; if t_{is} is positive, the inequality is true iff

$$t_{r0}/t_{rs} < t_{i0}/t_{is} \qquad (i \neq r, t_{is} > 0). \tag{36}$$

Thus, r satisfies

$$t_{r0}/t_{rs} = \min\{t_{i0}/t_{is}: t_{is} > 0, i = 1, \ldots, m\}. \tag{37}$$

This minimization uniquely determines r. For if the minimimum occurred for $i = r$ and for $i = \rho$, then we should have

$$t_{r0}/t_{rs} = t_{\rho0}/t_{\rho s},$$

which would violate the strict inequality (36) if $\rho \neq r$.

EXAMPLE 3. In the tableau (15) in Example 2, the current basic vectors are a^3 and a^1. Suppose we want to bring a^2 into the basis. To get a new feasible solution, we require $t_{rs} > 0$; and for $s = 2$, this implies $r = 1$, since $t_{12} = 1$ and $t_{22} = -1$. Thus, a^2 will replace $v^1 = a^3$ in the basis.

To get the new tableau, we divide the pivot row by the pivot element $t_{12} = 1$, which leaves the first row unchanged. We than add the first row to the second, producing $t'_{22} = 0$. The result is this tableau:

	a^1	a^2	a^3	b	e^1	e^2
a^2	0	1	1	1	3	-2
a^1	1	0	1	3	-4	3

$$\tag{38}$$

Note that the new solution components (below b) are positive.

EXAMPLE 4. In the last example, only one component of the pivot column was positive. Now suppose the pivot column is

$$t^{(s)} = \begin{bmatrix} 3 \\ -1 \\ 5 \end{bmatrix}.$$

Now there are two possibilities for the choice of r, since the pivot column has two positive components. Which one shall we choose?

To decide that, we have to look at the solution column. Suppose the solution column is

$$t^{(0)} = \begin{bmatrix} 4 \\ 1 \\ 2 \end{bmatrix}.$$

Dividing by $t_{is} > 0$, we form the ratios $\frac{4}{3}$ and $\frac{2}{5}$. Since the second ratio is smaller, we decide that the divisor 5 will be the pivot element, and so $r = 3$ will be the pivot row.

How to choose the pivot column. Before we choose the pivot row, we must choose the pivot column. We will choose the pivot column s to lower the cost if that is possible.

The old cost is

$$c^T x = \sum_{j \in B} c_j \hat{x}_j = \hat{c}_1 t_{10} + \cdots + \hat{c}_m t_{m0}. \tag{39}$$

Here the notation $\hat{c}_i$ stands for the unit cost of the basic vector v^i. If $v^i = a^{j_i}$, then $\hat{c}_i = c_{j_i}$. Similarly, the tableau element t_{i0} equals $\hat{x}_i = x_{j_i}$ for the current solution x.

If we decide to choose the pivot column s, what will the new cost be?

In order to introduce the amount λa^s into the solution, we add λ times the equation

$$a^s - \sum_{i=1}^m t_{is} v^i = 0 \tag{40}$$

to the equation

$$\sum_{i=1}^m t_{i0} v^i = Ax = b, \tag{41}$$

If all coefficients remain positive, we get a new feasible solution $x(\lambda)$, with

$$\lambda a^s + \sum_{i=1}^m (t_{i0} - \lambda t_{is}) v^i = Ax(\lambda) = b. \tag{42}$$

The new cost equals

$$\lambda c_s + \sum_{i=1}^m (t_{i0} - \lambda t_{is}) \hat{c}_i. \tag{43}$$

In this expression,

$$\sum_{i=0}^m t_{i0} \hat{c}_i = \text{old cost}; \quad \sum_{i=1}^m t_{is} \hat{c}_i \equiv z_s. \tag{44}$$

Therefore, (43) implies

$$\text{new cost} = \text{old cost} - \lambda(z_s - c_s). \tag{45}$$

And so it pays to bring in a^s iff $z_s - c_s > 0$.

As you see from (42), if all t_{is} are $\leqslant 0$ in the pivot column, we can let $\lambda \to +\infty$ and still $x(\lambda)$ will be a feasible solution. (This is called Case 2a in "The Idea of the Simplex Method.") If $z_s - c_s > 0$ and all t_{is} are $\leqslant 0$, the computation should stop, because now we know how to drive the cost to minus infinity. The computer should print out all the coefficients in formulas (42)–(45).

If $z_s - c_s > 0$ and if some $t_{is} > 0$, we are in what we called Case 2b. If several indices s satisfy this condition, we may choose any of them—for instance, we may choose the one that maximizes $z_s - c_s$. Having chosen the pivot column s, we choose the pivot row r by formula (37). We then form a new tableau by the rules (33), (34).

This decreases the cost by $\lambda^*(z_s - c_s)$, where λ^* is the coefficient of a^s in the new basic solution. Since $a^s = (v^r)'$, we have

$$\lambda^* = t'_{r0} = t_{r0}/t_{rs}.$$

If we call the old cost z_0 and call the new cost z_0', we have

$$z_0' = z_0 - \left(\frac{z_s - c_s}{t_{rs}}\right) t_{r0}. \tag{46}$$

The criterion row. So far, we've defined the extended tableau

$$[T;U] = M^{-1}[A,b;I], \tag{47}$$

where M is the current basis matrix. This tableau has m rows and $n + 1 + m$ columns. The tableau lacks certain information that we want, and we will put that information in a row at the bottom:

$$z_1 - c_1, \ldots, z_n - c_n, z_0; \quad y_1, \ldots, y_m. \tag{48}$$

This is the *criterion row*.

The first n components have the form

$$z_j - c_j = \sum_{i=1}^{m} t_{ij}\hat{c}_i - c_j \quad (j = 1, \ldots, n). \tag{49}$$

If a^j is in the current basis, then we shall have $z_j - c_j = 0$; for if $a^j = v^k$, then $t_{ij} = 1$ for $i = k$ and $t_{ij} = 0$ for $i \neq k$, and $\hat{c}_k = c_j$. If a^j is not in the current basis, we know that j is a candidate for pivot column if $z_j - c_j > 0$. But if all $z_j - c_j$ are ≤ 0, then the current basic feasible solution is optimal, as we proved in our previous discussion of the idea of the method.

The next component in the criterion row is the current cost:

$$z_0 = \sum_{i=1}^{m} t_{i0}\hat{c}_i = \hat{c}^T \hat{x} = c^T x. \tag{50}$$

The last m components in the criterion row are defined as follows:

$$y_j = \sum_{i=1}^{m} u_{ij}\hat{c}_i \quad (j = 1, \ldots, m). \tag{51}$$

Here $(u_{ij}) = U$ is the inverse of the basis matrix; U makes up the last part of the extended tableau (47).

The meaning of y^T: The definition (51) says

$$y^T = \hat{c}^T U,$$

or

$$y^T M = \hat{c}^T,$$

or

$$y^T a^k = c_k \quad \text{if} \quad k \in B. \tag{52}$$

Thus, y^T is the *equilibrium solution.* At the last stage all $z_j - c_j$ are ≤ 0, and then y^T will be the optimal solution of the dual problem:

$$y^T A \leq c^T, \quad y^T b = \max. \tag{53}$$

Then y^T will satisfy

$$y^T a^j = z_j \lessgtr c_j, \quad \text{with "=" if } j \in B. \tag{54}$$

(Again please refer to "The Idea of the Simplex Method.")
    When we append the criterion row, the tableau looks like this:

t_{11}	$\cdots$	t_{1n}	t_{10}	u_{11}	$\cdots$	u_{1m}
.	$\cdots$	.	.	.	$\cdots$	.
t_{m1}	$\cdots$	t_{mn}	t_{m0}	u_{m1}	$\cdots$	u_{mm}
$z_1 - c_1$	$\cdots$	$z_m - c_m$	z_0	y_1	$\cdots$	y_m

$$(55)$$

Now I'm going to show you the most surprising thing about the simplex tableau algorithm: *The criterion row transforms like all the other non-pivot rows.*
    In other words, I assert this: For some θ_0,

$$\text{new criterion row} = \text{old criterion row} - \theta_0 \text{ (pivot row)}. \tag{56}$$

Since a^s is entering the basis, we must have $z'_s - c_s = 0$ in the new tableau. If formula (56) is right, then

$$z'_s - c_s = z_s - c_s - \theta_0 \cdot t_{rs},$$

and so we must have

$$\theta_0 = (z_s - c_s)/t_{rs}. \tag{57}$$

PROOF OF (56). I have to prove three things:

$$z'_j - c_j = z_j - c_j - \theta_0 t_{rj} \quad (j = 1, \ldots, n) \tag{i}$$
$$z'_0 = z_0 - \theta_0 t_{r0} \tag{ii}$$
$$y'_j = y_j - \theta_0 u_{rj} \quad (j = 1, \ldots, m). \tag{iii}$$

First, I use the definition for the new tableau:

$$z'_j = \sum_{i=1}^{m} t'_{ij} \hat{c}_i$$

$$= \sum_{i \neq r} (t_{ij} - t_{is} t_{rj}/t_{rs}) \hat{c}_i + (t_{rj}/t_{rs}) c_s.$$

In the last sum, I may *include* the term for $i = r$, since it is zero. Then I get

$$z'_j = \sum_{i=1}^{m} t_{ij} c_i - (t_{rj}/t_{rs}) \left(\sum_{i=1}^{m} t_{is} c_i - c_s \right)$$

$$= z_j - (t_{rj}/t_{rs})(z_s - c_s)$$

$$= z_j - \theta_0 t_{rj} \quad (j = 1, \ldots, n)$$

That proves (i).

Second, I recall the cost-transformation formula (46), which we proved before. Formula (ii) merely restates (46).

Third, for the new tableau,

$$y'_j = \sum_{i=1}^{m} \hat{c}'_i u'_{ij}$$

$$= \sum_{\substack{i=1 \\ i \neq r}}^{m} \hat{c}_i(u_{ij} - u_{rj}t_{is}/t_{rs}) + c_s u_{rj}/t_{rs}.$$

Including the zero term for $i = r$, I get

$$y'_j = \sum_{i=1}^{m} \hat{c}_i u_{ij} - (u_{rj}/t_{rs})\left(\sum_{i=1}^{m} \hat{c}_i t_{is} - c_s\right)$$

$$= y_j - (u_{rj}/t_{rs})(z_s - c_s)$$

$$= y_j - \theta_0 u_{rj} \qquad (j = 1, \ldots, m).$$

That proves (iii) and ends the proof of the transformation formula for the criterion row.

You now have the complete description of the simplex-tableau algorithm. It is hard to understand, but easy to use. Most people who use it don't understand it, but I hope you won't be one of those.

Let's use the algorithm to solve a numerical problem. Let's solve

$$Ax = b, \quad x \geqslant 0, \quad c^T x = \min,$$

where

$$A = \begin{bmatrix} 1 & 2 & 3 \\ 4 & 5 & 6 \end{bmatrix}, \quad b = \begin{bmatrix} 5 \\ 13 \end{bmatrix}, \quad c^T = [7,1,1]. \qquad (58)$$

First we'll do Phase I, then Phase II.

EXAMPLE 5. We want to solve

$$\begin{bmatrix} 1 & 2 & 3 & 1 & 0 \\ 4 & 5 & 6 & 0 & 1 \end{bmatrix} \cdot \begin{bmatrix} x_1 \\ x_2 \\ x_3 \\ s_1 \\ s_2 \end{bmatrix} = \begin{bmatrix} 5 \\ 13 \end{bmatrix} \qquad (59)$$

The first basic feasible solution is $s_1 = 5$, $s_2 = 13$, $x = 0$. This is the first tableau:

	a^1	a^2	a^3	e^1	e^2	b
e^1	1	2	3	1	0	5
e^2	4	5	6	0	1	13
	5	7	9	0	0	18

In Phase I calculations we don't bother to use the extended tableau, since the natural unit vectors e^j are columns of the matrix.

Please note the criterion row at the bottom. In the Phase I calculation the cost vector is

$$c^T = [0,0,0,1,1].$$

It is *not* the vector c^T given in (58); in Phase II (Example 6) we'll switch back to the definition (58). Using the Phase I definition of c^T, you can see how the first criterion row was calculated. Note particularly the zeros under e^1 and e^2.

The biggest $z_j - c_j$ is 9. It occurs for $j = 3$, so we'll bring a^3 into the basis. This gives the pivot column $s = 3$. (We might, instead, have chosen $s = 1$ or 2.)

To choose the pivot row r, we form the two ratios $\frac{5}{3}, \frac{13}{6}$. The first is smaller, so we must choose $r = 1$. This makes the pivot element $t_{13} = 3$. Please draw a circle around it.

After you use the elimination rules, this is what you get for the second tableau:

	a^1	a^2	a^3	e^1	e^2	b
a^3	$\frac{1}{3}$	$\frac{2}{3}$	1	$\frac{1}{3}$	0	$\frac{5}{3}$
e^2	2	1	0	-2	1	3
	2	1	0	-3	0	3

The biggest $z_j - c_j$ is 2. It occurs for $j = 1$, so we'll set $s = 1$ and bring a^1 into the basis.

To choose r, we form the ratios

$$\left(\tfrac{5}{3}\right) \div \left(\tfrac{1}{3}\right) \quad \text{and} \quad 3 \div 2.$$

The second is smaller, so we must choose $r = 2$. Draw a circle around the new pivot element, $t_{21} = 2$.

As before, you divide the pivot row by the pivot element, and you subtract multiples of the pivot row from the other row so as to get zeros in the rest of the pivot column. This is what you get:

	a^1	a^2	a^3	e^1	e^2	b
a^3	0	$\frac{1}{2}$	1	$\frac{2}{3}$	$-\frac{1}{6}$	$\frac{7}{6}$
a^1	1	$\frac{1}{2}$	0	-1	$\frac{1}{2}$	$\frac{3}{2}$
	0	0	0	-1	-1	0

(60)

Now all five criterion elements $z_j - c_j$ are $\leqslant 0$. Therefore, you have an optimal solution. The last column says

$$x_3 = \tfrac{7}{6}, \quad x_1 = \tfrac{3}{2}, \quad \text{cost} = 0.$$

Please verify that these numbers do solve the problem (59).

EXAMPLE 6. Now we are ready to do a Phase II calculation for the problem (58).

In Example 5, we did the Phase I calculation, which gave us the first basic feasible solution for Phase II. As you will now see, Phase I ends with the initial tableau for Phase II—except that *we must re-calculate the criterion row*. Then we shall get this tableau:

	a^1	a^2	a^3	b	e^1	e^2
a^3	0	$\frac{1}{2}$	1	$\frac{7}{6}$	$\frac{2}{3}$	$-\frac{1}{6}$
a^1	1	$\frac{1}{2}$	0	$\frac{3}{2}$	-1	$\frac{1}{2}$
	0	3	0	$\frac{35}{3}$	$-\frac{19}{3}$	$-\frac{10}{3}$

(61)

Please carefully compare this tableau with the final tableau (60) for Phase I.

The first thing you notice is this: The two columns labeled e^1 and e^2 have been moved to the right of the solution column (labeled b). That is merely a matter of convention; it is customary but unnecessary. Except for this transposition, the numbers in the first two rows are the same in the two tableaus.

But the criterion rows are entirely different in the two tableaus. That always happens when we go from Phase I to Phase II. Why? Because the cost vectors are different. In Phase I the cost vector was

$$c^T = [0,0,0,1,1]. \tag{62}$$

This was an artificial cost vector that was contrived to give positive costs to the slack variables s_1, s_2. When we drove the slack variables out of the basis, we got the final Phase I cost zero. Then the solution column gave a first basic feasible solution x for Phase II.

Now we will use the original, given cost vector

$$c^T = [7,1,1].$$

As you see, this has nothing to do with the artificial Phase I cost vector (62). It doesn't even have the same number of components. That is because we no longer use the slack variables $s_1 s_2$; they are gone forever.

So where does the new criterion row come from? It comes from the new basic costs ($c_3 = 1$ and $c_1 = 7$) and from the upper part of the tableau. I'll compute three of the six criterion-row components for you:

$$z_2 - c_2 = (\tfrac{1}{2}) \cdot 1 + (\tfrac{1}{2}) \cdot 7 - 1 = 3$$
$$z_0 = (\tfrac{7}{6}) \cdot 1 + (\tfrac{3}{2}) \cdot 7 = \tfrac{35}{3}$$
$$y_1 = (\tfrac{2}{3}) \cdot 1 + (-1) \cdot 7 = -\tfrac{19}{3}.$$

You can do the other three.

The last two criterion components are y_1 and y_2. At each stage in Phase II, they solve the equilibrium equations. At the end, they will give the optimal dual vector y^T. As you know from our discussion of perturbations, the optimal dual components y_i are the shadow costs, and they provide very useful information. But if you don't think you'll need them, you don't have to compute them. *In the Phase II calculation, the last part of the tableau is optional.* If you won't be using the basis inverse (u_{ij}) or the shadow costs y_j, then don't compute them.

Now let's do Phase II, starting with the tableau (61). The only positive $z_j - c_j$ is $z_2 - c_2 = 3$. Therefore, the pivot column is $s = 2$.

To choose the pivot row, we form the ratios

$$(\tfrac{7}{6}) \div (\tfrac{1}{2}) = \tfrac{7}{3} \quad \text{and} \quad (\tfrac{3}{2}) \div (\tfrac{1}{2}) = 3.$$

The first is smaller, so we must choose the pivot row $r = 1$. Draw a circle around the pivot element $t_{rs} = t_{12} = \tfrac{1}{2}$. We're going to replace $v^1 = a^3$ by a^2 in the basis. Using the transformation rules, we get this tableau:

	a^1	a^2	a^3	b	e^1	e^2
a^2	0	1	2	$\tfrac{7}{3}$	$\tfrac{4}{3}$	$-\tfrac{1}{3}$
a^1	1	0	-1	$\tfrac{1}{3}$	$-\tfrac{5}{3}$	$\tfrac{1}{3}$
	0	0	-6	$\tfrac{14}{3}$	$-\tfrac{31}{3}$	$\tfrac{13}{3}$

(63)

Now we have all $z_j - c_j \leq 0$ $(j = 1, 2, 3)$. That means we're done. The optimal basic feasible solution x has the positive components

$$x_2 = \tfrac{7}{3}, \quad x_1 = \tfrac{1}{3}. \tag{64}$$

The minimum cost is

$$c^T x = z_0 = \tfrac{14}{3}. \tag{65}$$

The optimal dual components (the shadow costs) are

$$y_1 = -\tfrac{31}{3}, \quad y_2 = \tfrac{13}{3}. \tag{66}$$

Please check these conditions:

$$Ax = b, \quad x \geqslant 0, \quad y^T A \leqslant c^T, \quad c^T x = y^T b, \tag{67}$$

where A, b, and c are defined in the original problem (58). Then you'll believe all we've done.

References

1. G. B. Dantzig: Programming in a Linear Structure, *Econometrica*, Vol. 17, pp. 73–74, 1949.
2. G. B. Dantzig, Maximization of Linear Functions of Variables Subject to Linear Inequalities, in T. C. Koopmans (editor) *Activity Analysis of Production and Allocation*, pp. 339–347, Wiley, 1951.

PROBLEMS

1. In Example 1 replace b by $(1,1)^T$. Let the current basis be $v^1 = a^2$ and $v^2 = a^1$. Express a^3 and b as linear combinations of the basis, and write the tableau. Write the current basic solution x. Write the basis matrix M and its inverse U. Write the extended tableau. Verify equation (14).

2. Here is an extended tableau:

	a^1	a^2	a^3	b	e^1	e^2
v^1	4	0	1	6	-3	-8
v^2	7	1	0	-1	2	5

Identify v^1 and v^2 as columns of A. Find numerical values for M, U, A, b, T, x. Verify equation (13).

3. Start with the tableau in Problem 2. Let $c^T = (1,2,3)$. Compute $z_1, z_2, z_3, z_0, y_1, y_2$; then write the criterion row (48).

4. Start with the tableau in Problem 2. Let $c^T = (9,1,-1)$. Compute the criterion row. Answer: $(-6,0,0,-7,5,13)$. Now use the transformation rules to replace a^3 by a^1 in the basis; write the new extended tableau with criterion row.

5. Define

$$A = \begin{bmatrix} 2 & 3 & 1 \\ 5 & 6 & 4 \end{bmatrix}, \quad b = \begin{bmatrix} 2 \\ 7 \end{bmatrix}.$$

Do a Phase I calculation to get a basic feasible solution of $Ax = b$, $x \geqslant 0$.

6. Define A and b as in Problem 5. Set $v^1 = a^3$, $v^2 = a^1$; and start with the basic feasible solution $x^0 = \frac{1}{3}(1,0,4)^T$. Let $c^T = (5,3,1)$. Do a Phase II calculation to get optimal primal and dual vectors for $Ax = b$, $x \geqslant 0$, $c^Tx = \min$. Answer: The optimal primal vector is $\frac{1}{6}(0,1,9)^T$. Finally, check that $c^Tx = y^Tb$.

7. For small $\varepsilon \neq 0$ let $x(\varepsilon)$ solve

$$\begin{bmatrix} 2 & 3 & 1 \\ 5 & 6 & 4 \end{bmatrix} x = \begin{bmatrix} 2+\varepsilon \\ 5 \end{bmatrix}, \quad x \geqslant 0, \quad 5x_1 + x_2 = \min.$$

What happens to the optimal primal and dual vectors as $\varepsilon \to 0$? (Note: The problem is degenerate for $\varepsilon = 0$.) Use the equilibrium theorem to check optimality in the limit.

8. Do a Phase I calculation for

$$\begin{bmatrix} 2 & 3 & 1 \\ 5 & 6 & 4 \end{bmatrix} x = \begin{bmatrix} 1 \\ 5 \end{bmatrix}, \quad x \geqslant 0.$$

What does Phase I tell you?

9. Do a Phase II calculation for

$$\begin{bmatrix} 2 & -3 & 1 \\ 5 & -6 & 4 \end{bmatrix} x = \begin{bmatrix} 2 \\ 7 \end{bmatrix}, \quad x \geqslant 0, \quad x_1 - x_2 - x_3 = \min.$$

Start with $x^0 = \frac{1}{3}[1,0,4]^T$. What does Phase II tell you? Compute a feasible solution with cost -10^{10}.

11 The Revised Simplex Algorithm

Around 1954, Dantzig and his colleagues found a way to make the simplex algorithm more efficient.

You remember that the simplex tableau had three groups of columns: first, the columns labeled $a^1, \ldots, a^n$; second, the single columns labeled b; third, the columns labeled $e^1, \ldots, e^m$. Now you'll see this: *You don't need to compute the first group of columns.* All you need from the first n columns is the pivot column, but you can compute that single column when you need it. Let me explain.

This is the problem, as usual:

$$Ax = b, \quad x \geqslant 0, \quad c^T x = \min. \tag{1}$$

Here A is an $m \times n$ matrix, which is given along with the vectors b and c. We'll assume the problem is non-degenerate.

First, we store the matrix (a_{ij}) and the vectors (b_i) and (c_j) in the computer memory. We will never change these numbers, but we'll need them to compute the other numbers.

At each stage, we'll start with these numbers from the simplex tableau:

$$\begin{array}{|c|ccc|}
\hline
t_{10} & u_{11} & \cdots & u_{1m} \\
\cdot & \cdot & \cdots & \cdot \\
t_{m0} & u_{m1} & \cdots & u_{mm} \\
\hline
z_0 & y_1 & \cdots & y_m \\
\hline
\end{array} \tag{2}$$

And we'll also start with a list of the basic indices:

$$\{j_1, \ldots, j_m\}. \tag{3}$$

At each stage, we'll modify the numbers in (2) and (3).

The numbers mean precisely what they meant in the last section. The t_{i0} give a current basic solution; the u_{ij} give the inverse of the current basis; z_0 gives the current cost; the y_j solve the equilibrium equations. All these numbers are given at the beginning of Phase I, namely,

$$t_{i0} = b_i, \quad u_{ij} = \delta_{ij}, \quad z_0 = \sum b_i, \quad y_i = 1. \tag{4}$$

The numbers z_0 and y_j must be re-computed at the beginning of Phase II, namely,

$$z_0 = \sum_{i=1}^{m} t_{i0}\hat{c}_i, \quad y_j = \sum_{i=1}^{m} u_{ij}\hat{c}_i, \tag{5}$$

where $\hat{c}_i = c_{j_i}$.

Keep in mind, we'll be doing exactly what we did in the simplex-tableau algorithm—with one exception: we won't compute all the t_{ij} and $z_j - c_j$.

So, how do we modify the abbreviated tableau? Pick one non-basic index j. Compute the number

$$z_j = \sum_{i=1}^{m} y_i a_{ij}. \tag{6}$$

(This formula is discussed in "The Idea of the Simplex Method.") If z_j satisfies $z_j > c_j$, set $j = s$; this will be the index of the pivot column. But if $z_j \leqslant c_j$, try some other non-basic index j.

If $z_j \leqslant c_j$ for *all* non-basic indices j, you're done. Then you have the optimal basic solution, with the positive components

$$\hat{x}_i = x_{j_i} = t_{i0} \qquad (i = 1, \ldots, m). \tag{7}$$

The minimum cost is z_0, and the optimal dual vector is y^T.

Suppose, instead, you've computed z_j by formula (6), and you've found $z_j > c_j$. Then, setting $j = s$, you proceed as follows.

First you compute the pivot column of the simplex tableau:

$$t_{is} = \sum_{k=1}^{m} u_{ik} a_{ks} \qquad (i = 1, \ldots, m). \tag{8}$$

If all t_{is} are $\leqslant 0$, you're in Case 2a; you can drive the cost to minus infinity by setting

$$x(\lambda) = \lambda a^s + \sum_{i=1}^{m} (t_{i0} - \lambda t_{is}) v^i$$

$$\text{cost} = c^T x(\lambda) = c^T x(0) - \lambda(z_s - c_s), \quad \lambda \to \infty. \tag{9}$$

If, instead, some t_{is} are > 0, you pick the pivot row r by the old formula:

$$t_{r0}/t_{rs} = \min\{t_{i0}/t_{is}: t_{is} > 0\}. \tag{10}$$

This is what we called Case 2b. Now you should modify the tableau by the old transformation rules with one exception: you don't compute the first n columns; you compute only the last $1 + m$ columns.

Here are the rules:

$$\text{new row } r = (\text{old row } r)/t_{rs}; \tag{11}$$

and for $i \neq r$,

$$\text{new row } i = (\text{old row } i) - \theta_i \cdot (\text{old row } r), \tag{12}$$

where

$$\theta_i = t_{is}/t_{rs} \qquad (i \neq r; i = 1, \ldots, m)$$
$$\theta_0 = (z_s - c_s)/t_{rs}. \tag{13}$$

Finally you should replace the old basic index j_r by s.

Now you've got your new abbreviated tableau (2) and your new basis (3). Now you can continue. As you know, the algorithm must succeed after only a finite number of tableau modifications.

EXAMPLE. I want to re-do the last example of the preceding section. Please compare the two calculations to see how to use the short tableau.

The problem is $Ax = b$, $x \geq 0$, $c^T x = $ min., where

$$A = \begin{bmatrix} 1 & 2 & 3 \\ 4 & 5 & 6 \end{bmatrix}, \quad b = \begin{bmatrix} 5 \\ 13 \end{bmatrix}, \quad c^T = [7,1,1].$$

We're doing a Phase II calculation. We start with the short tableau

$\frac{7}{6}$	$\frac{2}{3}$	$-\frac{1}{6}$
$\frac{3}{2}$	-1	$\frac{1}{2}$
$\frac{35}{13}$	$-\frac{19}{3}$	$\frac{10}{3}$

and with the basis $\{3,1\}$, meaning that a^3 and a^1 are the current basic vectors.

The only non-basic column is a^2. We compute

$$z_2 = y^T a^2 = (-\tfrac{19}{3}) \cdot 2 + (\tfrac{10}{3}) \cdot 5 = 4.$$

Here y^T came from the tableau, while a^2 came from permanent storage. Since $c_2 = 1$, we have $z_2 - c_2 = 3 > 0$, so the pivot column is $s = 2$.

Now we have to compute the pivot tableau column:

$$\begin{bmatrix} t_{12} \\ t_{22} \end{bmatrix} = Ua^2 = \begin{bmatrix} \tfrac{2}{3} & -\tfrac{1}{6} \\ -1 & \tfrac{1}{2} \end{bmatrix} \begin{bmatrix} 2 \\ 5 \end{bmatrix} = \begin{bmatrix} \tfrac{1}{2} \\ \tfrac{1}{2} \end{bmatrix}.$$

To get the pivot row r, we compute the ratios t_{i0}/t_{is} for $t_{is} > 0$:

$$t_{10}/t_{12} = \tfrac{7}{6} \div \tfrac{1}{2}, \quad t_{20}/t_{22} = \tfrac{3}{2} \div \tfrac{1}{2}.$$

The first is smaller, so $r = 1$. Now we draw a circle around the pivot element $t_{12} = \tfrac{1}{2}$.

Now I'll write the pivot column next to the old short tableau:

$\frac{1}{2}$	$\frac{7}{6}$	$\frac{2}{3}$	$-\frac{1}{6}$
$\frac{1}{2}$	$\frac{3}{2}$	-1	$\frac{1}{2}$
3	$\frac{35}{3}$	$-\frac{19}{3}$	$\frac{10}{3}$

The transformation rules require us to apply the elementary row operations that convert the pivot column to $[1,0,0]^T$. If we do so, we get the new short tableau:

$\frac{7}{3}$	$\frac{4}{3}$	$-\frac{1}{3}$
$\frac{1}{3}$	$-\frac{5}{3}$	$\frac{1}{3}$
$\frac{14}{3}$	$-\frac{31}{3}$	$\frac{13}{3}$

Finally we must replace $j_1 = 3$ by $s = 2$ to obtain the new basis $\{2,1\}$.

Now start over with the new tableau. The only non-basic column is $j = 3$. Therefore, we compute

$$z_3 = y^T a^3 = \left[-\tfrac{31}{3}, \tfrac{13}{3}\right]\left[\begin{smallmatrix}3\\6\end{smallmatrix}\right] = -5.$$

Then we find $z_3 - c_3 = -5 - 1 = -6 < 0$. That means we're done.

From the last tableau and basis, we get

$$x_2 = \tfrac{7}{3}, \quad x_1 = \tfrac{1}{3}; \quad y_1 = \tfrac{31}{3}, \quad y_2 = \tfrac{13}{3};$$

and there we have the optimal primal and dual solutions. From the tableau, we also get the final cost $z_0 = \tfrac{14}{3}$. This completes the example.

I told you that the revised simplex algorithm was more efficient than the full simplex tableau algorithm, but that isn't always true. In Phase II, using the original simplex tableau algorithm, you don't have to compute U and y^T if you don't want to; using the revised algorithm, you have to compute U and y^T at every stage.

Another advantage of the original algorithm is this: You compute the *full* array $z_1 - c_1, \ldots, z_n - c_n$; by the elimination rule, this computations is quick and accurate. Having the full array $z_j - c_j$, you don't have to pick the first positive one; you can pick the largest $z_j - c_j$ to give the pivot column $j = s$. Usually this gives a greater cost reduction, since the single-stage cost reduction equals the product $(t_{r0}/t_{rs}) \cdot (z_s - c_s)$.

The factor t_{r0}/t_{rs} is unknown until you know the pivot row r, which is a function of the pivot columns s. If you wished, you could pick s to maximize the product (t_{r0}/t_{rs}) times $z_s - c_s$. That would maximize the single-stage cost reduction, but it would require extra computation.

As for storage, the revised algorithm requires the original matrix A in permanent storage; the original algorithm does not.

Both algorithms are, for most cases, excellent. In general, you may use either one with confidence. The simplex method has been called the most important numerical method invented in the twentieth century. When you think of all its applications, it is hard to disagree with that assessment.

Reference

G. B. Dantzig, A. Orden, and P. Wolfe: Generalized Simplex Method for Minimizing a Linear Form under Linear Inequality Restraints, *Pacific J. Math.* Vol. 5 (1955) pp. 183–195.

PROBLEMS

1. Consider the problem

$$\begin{bmatrix} 1 & 2 & 3 \\ 4 & 5 & 6 \end{bmatrix} x = \begin{bmatrix} 3 \\ 9 \end{bmatrix}, \quad x \geqslant 0, \quad x_2 + x_3 = \min.$$

Start with the feasible solution $x^0 = (1,1,0)^T$. Compute optimal primal and dual solutions by the revised simplex algorithm.

2. Consider the problem

$$\begin{bmatrix} 1 & 2 & 3 & 1 & 0 \\ 4 & 5 & 6 & 0 & 1 \end{bmatrix} x = \begin{bmatrix} 3 \\ 9 \end{bmatrix}, \quad x \geqslant 0, \quad x_4 + x_5 = \min.$$

Start with the feasible solution $x^0 = [0,0,0,3,9]^T$. Compute an optimal solution by the revised simplex algorithm. (This is a Phase I calculation for Problem 1.)

3. Apply the revised simplex algorithm to

$$\begin{bmatrix} 1 & 2 & 3 \\ 4 & 5 & 6 \end{bmatrix} x = \begin{bmatrix} 3 \\ 5 \end{bmatrix}, \quad x \geqslant 0, \quad x_2 + x_3 = \min.$$

(First introduce slacks for Phase I.)

4. Apply the revised simplex algorithm to

$$\begin{bmatrix} 1 & -2 & 3 \\ 4 & -5 & 6 \end{bmatrix} x = \begin{bmatrix} 3 \\ 9 \end{bmatrix}, \quad x \geqslant 0, \quad x_1 - x_2 = \min.$$

5. Solve by the revised simplex algorithm:

$$\begin{bmatrix} 5 & 2 & 1 \\ 2 & 3 & 8 \end{bmatrix} x = \begin{bmatrix} 7 \\ 5 \end{bmatrix}, \quad x \geqslant 0, \quad x_2 + x_3 = \min.$$

First use Phase I to get a basic feasible solution. Then use Phase II to get optimal primal and dual solutions. (Answer: The minimum cost equals $\frac{11}{38}$.)

12 A Simplex Algorithm for Degenerate Problems

We've discussed the simplex method for non-degenerate linear programming problems. I showed you two practical algorithms—simplex tableau and revised simplex. Now I'd like to show you how to make the method work even for degenerate problems.

This will be a theoretical discussion. As I explained before, degeneracy is a fragile condition—the slightest round-off error will usually produce a nondegenerate problem. In practice, the best thing to do about the possibility of degeneracy is to ignore it. Still, I want to show you the *lexicographic simplex algorithm* because the mathematics is fascinating.

We are given an mxn matrix A along with vectors b and c. This is the problem:

$$Ax = b, \quad x \geqslant 0, \quad c^T x = \min. \tag{1}$$

We have called this problem *non-degenerate* if
  i) rank $A = m$, and
  ii) b is a linear combination of no fewer than m columns of A.
Otherwise the problem is called *degenerate*.

Always we assume $m \leqslant n$. If condition (i) is false, then the linear system $Ax = b$ is either inconsistent or redundant. If it's inconsistent, then the problem has no solution, and that's that. But if the system $Ax = b$ is consistent and redundant, then some of the equations should be eliminated. If A has rank $r < m$, then $m - r$ redundant equations should be eliminated, leaving a system $\bar{A}x = \bar{b}$, where the matrix $\bar{A}$ consists of r independent rows of A. Now the problem (1) is equivalent to

$$\bar{A}x = \bar{b}, \quad x \geqslant 0, \quad c^T x = \text{min.}, \tag{2}$$

in which condition (i) is satisfied. So from now on we'll assume condition (i) holds.

Suppose condition (ii) fails. Then there can be a basic feasible solution x with fewer than m positive components. Why should this make trouble for the simplex method?

Because now *cycling is possible*. If some basic solution component t_{r0} equals zero in the simplex tableau, and if $z_s - c_s > 0$ with $t_{rs} > 0$, then surely

$$0 = t_{r0}/t_{rs} = \min\{t_{i0}/t_{is} : t_{is} > 0\}, \tag{3}$$

since all the competing quotients are $\geqslant 0$. So, if s is the pivot column, then r may be the pivot row. If now a^s replaces v^r in the basis, then the cost decreases by *zero*:

$$\text{new cost} = \text{old cost} - \frac{t_{r0}}{t_{rs}}(z_s - c_s) = \text{old cost} - 0. \tag{4}$$

Since the cost doesn't decrease, we can't be sure that we get a new basic solution at each stage of the simplex method. Thus, if the cost stayed the same at three successive stages, we might start with a basic solution x^1, go to a new basic solution x^2, and then go back to x^1. Then the process would cycle forever, and the method would fail.

To get around this, we'll introduce *lexicographic ordering*. We'll order vectors the way we order words in a dictionary.

Let's use the symbol "G.T." to stand for "is lexicographically greater than." Then, for instance, we have

$$lot \text{ G.T.} \quad log \text{ G.T.} \quad lie \text{ G.T.} \quad got. \tag{5}$$

Thus, *log* comes after *lie* in the dictionary.

If we use the numbers $1, \ldots, 26$ instead of the letters $a, \ldots, z$, the example (5) becomes

$$(11,15,20)\text{G.T.} \ (11,15,7)\text{G.T.} \ (11,9,5)\text{G.T.} \ (7,15,20).$$

You see the idea. Let the vector $\mathbf{a}$ have real components $a_0, a_1, \ldots, a_m$; let $\mathbf{b}$ have real components $b_0, b_1, \ldots, b_m$. Then we'll write $\mathbf{a}$ G.T. $\mathbf{b}$ to mean this: *For some $j = 0, \ldots, m$,*

$$a_j > b_j, \quad \text{while } a_i = b_i \quad \text{for all} \quad i < j. \tag{6}$$

You have enough experience with dictionaries to accept without proof this assertion: *The relation* G.T. *establishes a complete ordering of the real vector space* R^N. In other words, for every **a** and **b** in the space of real vectors with N components, either **a** G.T. **b** or **b** G.T. **a** or **a** = **b**; and if **a** G.T. **b** and **b** G.T. **c**, then **a** G.T. **c**.

EXAMPLE 1. Let the components of the vectors **a** and **b** be the coefficients of two polynomials in ε:

$$p(\varepsilon) = a_0 + a_1\varepsilon + \cdots + a_m\varepsilon^m$$
$$q(\varepsilon) = b_0 + b_1\varepsilon + \cdots + b_m\varepsilon^m.$$

Suppose $p(\varepsilon) > q(\varepsilon)$ for all sufficiently small $\varepsilon > 0$; then **a** G.T. **b**. Conversely, if **a** G.T. **b**, then $p(\varepsilon) > q(\varepsilon)$ for small $\varepsilon > 0$.

Now we'll apply lexicographic ordering to linear programming. Consider the canonical program (1). Suppose condition (i) holds, but suppose condition (ii) fails. Without loss of generality, assume all $b_i \geqslant 0$ (if any b_i is negative, multiply the ith equation by -1).

We will use the revised simplex tableau:

$$
\begin{array}{|c|ccc|}
\hline
t_{10} & u_{11} & \cdots & u_{1m} \\
\cdot & \cdot & \cdots & \cdot \\
t_{m0} & u_{m1} & \cdots & u_{mm} \\
\hline
z_0 & y_1 & \cdots & y_m \\
\hline
\end{array}
\tag{7}
$$

Here (u_{ij}) is the inverse of the current basis; the vector (y_i) solves the equilibrium equations; z_0 is the current cost; and (t_{i0}) gives the current basic feasible solution, that is,

$$x_{j_i} = t_{i0} \quad \text{where} \quad B = \{j_1, \ldots, j_m\}. \tag{8}$$

Since we allow degeneracy, we may not assume all $t_{i0} > 0$; we may only assume all $t_{i0} \geqslant 0$.

The tableau (7) has $m + 1$ rows, each with $1 + m$ components. Call the first row **t**(1), call the second **t**(2), ..., and call the mth row **t**(m); call the last row **w**. *We will require that all of the first m rows be lexicographically positive*:

$$\boxed{\mathbf{t}(i) \equiv [t_{i0}, u_{i1}, \ldots, u_{im}] \text{ G.T. } \mathbf{0}.} \tag{9}$$

This relaxes the requirement $t_{i0} > 0$. Now we only require $t_{i0} \geqslant 0$; but if $t_{i0} = 0$, we require the first non-zero component of the ith row of U to be positive. Please note that this requirement is met at the beginning of Phase I; for then we have $t_{i0} = b_i \geqslant 0$ and $U = I$.

The last row is the generalized cost:

$$\mathbf{w} = [z_0, y_1, \ldots, y_m] \tag{10}$$

When we change the basis, we will get a new tableau, with a new cost row $\mathbf{w}'$. *We will require*

$$\boxed{\mathbf{w} \text{ G.T. } \mathbf{w}'.} \tag{11}$$

This relaxes the requirement $z_0 > z'_0$. But it is enough for our purpose: *it prevents cycling.* The argument is the same as before. As we go from basis to basis, we get a succession of decreasing cost vectors:

$$\mathbf{w} \text{ G.T. } \mathbf{w}' \text{ G.T. } \cdots \text{ G.T. } \mathbf{w}^{(p)}. \tag{12}$$

Since no two of these cost vectors are equal, no two of the bases are equal.

Here's how we do all this. Just as before, we compute

$$z_j - c_j = y^T a^j - c_j \tag{13}$$

for j not in the basis. If all these numbers are $\leqslant 0$, we know that the current basic feasible solution is optimal. But if $z_s - c_s > 0$, we know the current solution is not optimal, and we may choose the pivot column s.

Exactly as before, we compute the pivot tableau column. We already have the last component, $z_s - c_s$; the first m components are

$$t_{is} = \sum_{k=1}^{m} u_{ik} a_{ks} \qquad (i = 1, \ldots, m).$$

As before, if all t_{is} are $\leqslant 0$, we can drive the cost to minus infinity (Case 2a). So suppose some $t_{is} > 0$ (Case 2b).

Now watch this. We're going to choose the pivot row r. Up to now, the algorithm has been identical to the revised simplex method, but now there will be a subtle difference. We will choose r by this rule:

$$\mathbf{t}(r)/t_{rs} = \min\{\mathbf{t}(i)/t_{is} : t_{is} > 0\}. \tag{14}$$

By "min" here we mean the *lexicographic minimum,* which is the minimum vector according to the ordering "G.T."

The lexicographic minimum (14) is unique. For otherwise there would be two rows, say r and ρ, such that

$$\mathbf{t}(r)/t_{rs} = \mathbf{t}(\rho)/t_{\rho s}, \text{ with } r \neq \rho.$$

Then the two rows $\mathbf{t}(r)$ and $\mathbf{t}(\rho)$ would be proportional (dependent). Now look at the last m components of the two vectors; they would have to be proportional. Thus, rows r and ρ of U would be proportional. Then det $U = 0$. But that is impossible for any inverse matrix, because *all* inverse matrices have non-zero determinants.

So the lexicographic minimum (14) uniquely determines the pivot row r. This amounts to a tie-breaking rule in case $t_{r0}/t_{rs} = t_{\rho 0}/t_{\rho s}$. Now the computation proceeds exactly as before, giving a new tableau, with components $t'_{i0}, u'_{ij}, z'_0, y'_j$. We must now prove these two assertions:

$$\mathbf{t}'(i) \text{ G.T. } \mathbf{0} \qquad (i = 1, \ldots, m), \tag{15}$$

$$\mathbf{w} \text{ G.T. } \mathbf{w}'. \tag{16}$$

Proof that $\mathbf{t}'(i)$ G.T. $\mathbf{0}$. By the usual simplex rule, we compute the new row r as follows:

$$\mathbf{t}'(r) = \mathbf{t}(r)/t_{rs}.$$

This is G.T. $\mathbf{0}$ by induction, since we assume $\mathbf{t}(r)$ G.T. $\mathbf{0}$ in the old tableau. As usual, the pivot element t_{rs} is positive.

For $i \neq r$, the simplex rule gives

$$\mathbf{t}'(i) = \mathbf{t}(i) - (t_{is}/t_{rs})\mathbf{t}(r).$$

If t_{is} is $\leqslant 0$, this gives $\mathbf{t}'(i)$ G.T. $\mathbf{0}$ because $\mathbf{t}(i)$ G.T. $\mathbf{0}$ and $\mathbf{t}(r)$ G.T. $\mathbf{0}$. If t_{is} is > 0, then the unique minimization (14) implies

$$\mathbf{t}'(i) = t_{is}\big[\mathbf{t}(i)/t_{is} - \mathbf{t}(r)/t_{rs}\big] \text{ G.T. } \mathbf{0}.$$

Proof that $\mathbf{w}$ G.T. $\mathbf{w}'$. It remains only to prove that the generalized cost decreases lexicographically. By the usual simplex rule, we compute the new last row:

$$\mathbf{w}' = \mathbf{w} - \theta_0 \mathbf{t}(r),$$

with $\theta_0 = (z_s - c_s)/t_{rs} > 0$. By induction, we assume $\mathbf{t}(r)$ G.T. $\mathbf{0}$ in the old tableau. Therefore,

$$\mathbf{w} - \mathbf{w}' = \theta_0 \mathbf{t}(r) \text{ G.T. } \mathbf{0},$$

and so we have $\mathbf{w}$ G.T. $\mathbf{w}'$. This completes the proof that the lexicographic simplex algorithm succeeds even for degenerate problems.

EXAMPLE 2. I want you to see a simple example of the tie-breaking rule for choosing the pivot row. Suppose, at some stage, the pivot column and the revised simplex tableau look like this:

1	0	1	-1	3
1	0	0	5	7
1	3	-6	2	1
1	5	-1	9	2

Here you see all $t_{is} = 1$ and even $z_s - c_s = 1$.

Next you see the solution column $(t_{i0}), z_0$. Here we have some solution components $t_{i0} = 0$; that would be impossible in a non-degenerate problem. But note:

$$\mathbf{t}(1) = [0,1,-1,3] \text{ G.T. } \mathbf{0}$$

and also $\mathbf{t}(2)$ G.T. $\mathbf{0}$, even though $t_{10} = t_{20} = 0$.

The last three columns give the matrix U on top and the vector y^T below.

Since all three t_{is} are positive, we have three candidates for pivot row. By the old scheme, we compute the three ratios

$$t_{i0}/t_{is} = 0, 0, 3 \qquad \text{for } i = 1, 2, 3.$$

Here rows $i = 1$ and 2 produce a tie for the minimum. But look at this:

$$\mathbf{t}(1)/t_{1s} = [0, 1, -1, 3],$$
$$\mathbf{t}(2)/t_{2s} = [0, 0, 5, 7].$$

Since the first vector is G.T. the second, we break the tie by choosing the pivot row $r = 2$.

Since the whole pivot column consists of 1's, we compute the new tableau by just subtracting the pivot row from the other rows. This gives the new bottom row

$$\mathbf{w'} = \boxed{5 \mid -1 \quad 4 \quad -5} \ .$$

This is the new generalized cost. Its first component is $z'_0 = 5$.

The old generalized cost was

$$\mathbf{w} = \boxed{5 \mid -1 \quad 9 \quad 2} \ ,$$

also with first component $z_0 = 5$. Note that $\mathbf{w}$ G.T. $\mathbf{w'}$ while $z_0 = z'_0$: the generalized cost decreases while the scalar cost stays the same.

Finally, I'd like to make some short remarks on the connection of the lexicographic algorithm with perturbations and with the duality theorem.

Perturbations. If you look back at Example 1, you can see what we've done in terms of perturbations. Suppose we replace the original requirement vector b by a family of vectors

$$b(\varepsilon) = b + \varepsilon e^1 + \cdots + \varepsilon^m e^m \qquad (0 < \varepsilon \ll 1),$$

where $e^1, \ldots, e^m$ are the columns of I. Now consider the family of problems

$$Ax = b(\varepsilon), \quad x \geqslant 0, \quad c^T x = \min. \tag{17}$$

If rank $A = m$, you can show that these problems are non-degenerate for all sufficiently small $\varepsilon > 0$, even though the limiting problem with $\varepsilon = 0$ is degenerate (see Problem 9). Since the perturbed problems (17) are non-degenerate, you can solve them with the original simplex method. The effect of the perturbations is to translate the common ordering ">" into the lexicographic ordering "G.T."

The duality theorem. By using the separating-plane theorem for convex sets, we proved this: *If the primal problem (1) has an optimal solution x^0, then the dual problem,*

$$y^T A \leqslant c^T, \quad y^T b = \max, \tag{18}$$

has an optimal solution y^0, *with*

$$c^T x^0 = (y^0)^T b. \tag{19}$$

As we just showed, the lexicographic simplex method works even for degenerate problems (1). If a optimal solution exists, this algorithm computes a basic optimal solution x^0 in a finite number of steps. At the last stage, the vector y satisfies

$$\begin{aligned} y^T a^j &= c_j & \text{for } j \text{ in the basis} \\ y^T a^k &= z_k \leqslant c_k & \text{for } k \text{ not in the basis.} \end{aligned} \tag{20}$$

It follows that y is an optimal dual solution y^0 satisfiying the cost equality (19). Thus, the lexicographic algorithm gives an independent, purely algebraic proof of the duality principle.

References

1. Dantzig, G. B., A. Orden, and P. Wolfe: Generalized Simplex Method for Minimizing a Linear Form under Linear Inequality Restraints, *Pacific J. Math.* Vol. 5, pp. 183–195, 1955.
2. Charnes, A.: Optimality and Degeneracy in Linear Programming, *Econometrica*, Vol. 20, pp. 160–170, 1952.

PROBLEMS

1. For the vector space R^N, prove:
   (i) **a** G.T. **b** or **b** G.T. **a** or **a** = **b**;
   (ii) if **a** G.T. **b** and **b** G.T. **c**, then **a** G.T. **c**.

2. In the plane R^2 draw pictures illustrating the two assertions in Problem 1.

3. For Example 1 prove that **a** G.T. **b** if and only if $p(\varepsilon) > q(\varepsilon)$ in some interval $0 < \varepsilon < \varepsilon_0$. What is the largest possible value of ε_0 if $\mathbf{a} = (5, -7, 1)$ and $\mathbf{b} = (5, -9, 7)$?

4. Show that the following problem is degenerate for $\varepsilon = 0$, but is nondegenerate for small $\varepsilon > 0$:

$$\begin{bmatrix} 1 & 2 & 3 \\ 4 & 5 & 6 \end{bmatrix} x = \begin{bmatrix} 2 \\ 5 \end{bmatrix} + \varepsilon \begin{bmatrix} 1 \\ 0 \end{bmatrix} + \varepsilon^2 \begin{bmatrix} 0 \\ 1 \end{bmatrix}.$$

5. Solve by the lexicographic simplex algorithm:

$$\begin{bmatrix} 1 & 2 & 3 \\ 4 & 5 & 6 \end{bmatrix} x = \begin{bmatrix} 2 \\ 5 \end{bmatrix}, \quad x \geqslant 0, \quad x_2 = \min.$$

Start with the feasible solution $x^0 = (0,1,0)^T$.

6. Solve by the lexicographic simplex algorithm:

$$\begin{bmatrix} 1 & -2 & 3 & 1 & 0 \\ 4 & 5 & 6 & 0 & 1 \end{bmatrix} x = \begin{bmatrix} 0 \\ 2 \end{bmatrix}, \quad x \geqslant 0, \quad x_4 + x_5 = \min.$$

(This is a Phase I calculation that is degenerate because **b** has a zero component.)

7. The text says "... all inverse matrices have nonzero determinants." Why is that so?

8. In Example 2 change the component u_{21} from 0 to 1. Now use the lexicographic algorithm to compute the next tableau.

*9. Prove the assertion after formula (17) as follows. Let M be a basis matrix whose columns are m independent columns of A. Look at the vector $\hat{x}(\varepsilon) = M^{-1}b(\varepsilon)$. If M^{-1} has columns $u^1, \ldots, u^m$, show that

$$\hat{x}(\varepsilon) = q + \varepsilon u^1 + \varepsilon^2 u^2 + \cdots + \varepsilon^m u^m,$$

where $q = M^{-1}b$. The ith component of $x(\varepsilon)$ is

$$\hat{x}_i(\varepsilon) = q_i + \varepsilon u_{i1} + \varepsilon^2 u_{i2} + \cdots + \varepsilon^m u_{im}.$$

This polynomial cannot be zero for more than m values of ε unless the coefficients $u_{i1}, \ldots, u_{im}$ are all zero, which is impossible. Why? Deduce that the problems $Ax = b(\varepsilon)$ are nondegenerate except for a finite number of ε.

*10. In part, the duality principle says this: *Suppose the primal ($Ax = b, x \geq 0, c^T x = $ min.) has no feasible solution; then either the dual has no feasible solution, or it has feasible solutions y with $b^T y \to +\infty$.* Prove this by the lexicographic algorithm. (Look at the result of a Phase I calculation.)

13 Multiobjective Linear Programming

Often, you would like to optimize several things at once. You want the *best* car at the *lowest* price.

If you were a government regulator, you might want even more. This is what you'd like to require of General Motors: Design a car that maximizes safety, minimizes fuel consumption, minimizes air pollution, and minimizes purchase cost.

As you know, that is impossible.

Nevertheless, decisions will be made, and some decisions are better than others. Multiobjective decisions require compromises, or trade-offs, in which we are forced to compare things that are incommensurable.

What is the dollar value of a single human life? We don't even like to ask the question. And yet we must answer that question if we design an automobile, a house, or a bridge. If you increase the cost a little, you can make it a little safer. If, in your final design, you could have saved one more life by spending x more dollars, you have answered the question: One life is worth x dollars.

If you think life has infinite value, you will keep spending money until no additional expenditure could make the car safer. Then your car would cost more than people would pay for it. So the decision is not entirely yours; in the end, the buyers will decide what they can afford to pay for a car—and so *they* will set a dollar value on their lives.

What is a sensible way to think about these questions? As children, when we learned arithmetic, we were taught not to compare apples and oranges;

as adults, we do it all the time. Every day, we use our own taste, preference, and judgment; and so we make decisions.

As a rule, we have a right to our own taste. But some decisions are just plain stupid. These are decisions that could be improved in some respect without loss in any other respect. For instance, if you can buy the same car at a lower price, it would be stupid not to do so.

Economists call stupid decisions *inefficient*. All the other decisions are *efficient*: they cannot be improved in one respect without being made worse in some other respect.

For instance, if you could buy your Cadillac at a lower price at a different agency, your decision is inefficient; but if the only car you can buy at a lower price is a Chevrolet, your decision is efficient. Your efficient decision may or may not be wise; you will have to decide that for yourself.

Multiobjective linear programming gives a beautiful example of these ideas.

You remember the diet problem: Design a nutritionally adequate diet at minimum cost. There we had a single objective: to minimize the dollar cost. Let us now add this objective: to minimize the number of calories. Here we are trying to design a nutritionally adequate diet for people on a budget who want to lose weight. They know they could lose weight on filet mignon, but they can't afford it.

As before, we have a list of n foods and a list of m nutrients. Let a_{ij} be the amount of nutrient i in food j. For instance, a_{ij} might be the number of units of vitamin B1 in an ounce of wheat germ; or a_{ij} might be the number of grams of protein in an ounce of milk. Let b_i be the minimum daily requirement of nutrient i. Let $x_j \geq 0$ be a possible quantity of food j in the diet. Then we require

$$a_{i1}x_1 + a_{i2}x_2 + \cdots + a_{in}x_n \geq b_i \tag{1}$$

to satisfy the minimum daily requirement of nutrient i. For a nutritionally adequate diet x, we required the inequality (1) for all nutrients $i = 1, \ldots, m$.

For each food j, as before, we have a *dollar cost*; but now we also have a *calorie cost*. For one ounce of food j, let c_{1j} be the dollar cost, and let c_{2j} be the calorie cost. Suppose a diet contains x_j ounces of food j; this will cost $c_{1j}x_j$ dollars and will cost $c_{2j}x_j$ calories. For the diet x, the total dollar cost is $\sum c_{1j}x_j$, and the total calorie cost is $\sum c_{2j}x_j$.

Thus, the cost has two components: dollars and calories. *The cost is a vector*. If C is the matrix with components c_{ij} ($i = 1, 2; j = 1, \ldots, n$), then the cost is the vector Cx.

What makes one feasible diet better than another? Either it is cheaper without being more fattening, or it is leaner without being more expensive. In other words, x is a better diet than x^0 if

$$\sum c_{1j}x_j < \sum c_{1j}x_j^0 \quad \text{and} \quad \sum c_{2j}x_j \leq \sum c_{2j}x_j^0 \tag{2}$$

or if

$$\sum c_{2j}x_j < \sum c_{2j}x_j^0 \quad \text{and} \quad \sum c_{1j}x_j \leq \sum c_{1j}x_j^0. \tag{3}$$

Using the cost matrix C, we can express these inequalities compactly:

$$Cx \leqslant Cx^0 \quad \text{but} \quad Cx \neq Cx^0. \tag{4}$$

Then x is better than x^0, because (2) or (3) must hold. In this case we call the feasible solution x^0 *inefficient*.

If *no* feasible solution x satisfies (4), we call the feasible solution x^0 *efficient*, and we will write

$$Cx^0 = \text{minimum}. \tag{5}$$

(Mathematically, the vector inequality $u \leqslant v$ is *partial* ordering; it is transitive and relexive, but is incomplete. The minimum (5) refers to the partial ordering.)

And now the main question: *How can we compute the efficient solutions of a multiobjective linear program?*

If we use the canonical form, this is the problem:

$$Ax = b, \quad x \geqslant 0, \quad Cx = \text{min.}, \tag{6}$$

where C is now a matrix with more than one row. Again, the feasible solution x^0 is *efficient* (optimal) if *no* feasible solution x satisfies (4).

I will show you this: If x^0 is efficient, then x^0 solves a conventional problem,

$$Ax = b, \quad x \geqslant 0, \quad (w^T C)x = \text{min.}, \tag{7}$$

in which $w^T C$ is a single row; all components of the vector w will be positive. Conversely, if w is any positive vector, and if x^0 is optimal for the conventional problem (7), then x^0 is an efficient solution of the multiobjective linear program (6). This reduces the new problem to an old one that we can solve.

Theorem. *The vector x^0 is an efficient solution of the multiobjective program (6) if and only if there is a vector $w > 0$ for which x^0 is an optimal solution of the single-objective program (7).*

PROOF. First, suppose x^0 is optimal for (7), where $w > 0$. Suppose $Cx \leqslant Cx^0$ but $Cx \neq Cx^0$. Then

$$w^T(Cx - Cx^0) < 0,$$

contradicting the optimality of x^0. Therefore, x^0 is an efficient solution of (6). That was the easy part of the proof.

Now the hard part. Supposing x^0 is efficient for (6), we must construct a vector $w > 0$ for which x^0 is optimal for (7). We can do this by the duality theorem.

Given x^0, we can regard Cx^0 as a constant vector, and we can define the following conventional linear program:

$$
\begin{aligned}
Ax &= b \\
Cx + z &= Cx^0 \\
x \geqslant 0, \quad &z \geqslant 0 \\
\sum z_i &= \text{max.}
\end{aligned}
\tag{8}
$$

This is a canonical maximum problem to be solved for the composite vector x, z.

Here is a feasible solution of (8): $x = x^0$, $z = 0$. I assert this solution is optimal for (8). Otherwise, we must have $\sum z_i > 0$, and then x would satisfy

$$Ax = b, \quad x \geqslant 0, \quad Cx \leqslant Cx^0, \quad Cx \neq Cx^0, \tag{9}$$

which is impossible if x^0 is efficient for (7).

If A has m rows and C has k rows, we can partition an optimal dual vector for (8) as follows:

$$[-y_1, \ldots, -y_m, w_1, \ldots, w_k] = [-y^T, w^T].$$

Then y and w satisfy

$$-y^T A + w^T C \geqslant 0 \tag{10}$$
$$w^T I \geqslant [1, \ldots, 1], \tag{11}$$
$$-y^T b + w^T (Cx^0) = \text{min.} = 0. \tag{12}$$

The dual minimum equals 0 because the primal maximum equals 0 in (8).

From (8), (10), and (12), we have

$$Ax^0 = b, \quad x^0 \geqslant 0; \quad y^T A \leqslant (w^T C)$$
$$(w^T C)x^0 = y^T b. \tag{13}$$

Therefore, x^0 is optimal for the primal problem

$$Ax = b, \quad x \geqslant 0, \quad (w^T C)x^0 = \text{min.}, \tag{14}$$

while y is optimal for the dual problem

$$y^T A \leqslant (w^T C), \quad y^T b = \text{max.} \tag{15}$$

In this primal-dual pair, we regard $w^T C$ as a given row vector; it is the cost vector in the primal (14) and is the requirement vector in the dual (15).

By (14), x^0 solves the conventional program (7); by (11), the weights w_i are all positive. This ends the proof.

The meaning of the weights. Let's go back to the example of the reducing diet. There we had two cost components:

$$\sum_j c_{1j} x_j = \text{total dollars} \tag{16}$$

and

$$\sum_j c_{2j} x_j = \text{total calories.} \tag{17}$$

The condition of feasibility had the form $Ax \geqslant b$, $x \geqslant 0$; as you know, by using slack variables, we could restate this in the canonical form $Ax = b$, $x \geqslant 0$.

According to the theorem, an *efficient* diet must be a feasible diet that minimizes some linear combination of the cost components:

$$w_1 \cdot (\text{total dollars}) + w_2 \cdot (\text{total calories}) = \text{min.}, \tag{18}$$

with *positive* coefficients w_1 and w_2. This just says $w^T(Cx) = \min.$, with $w > 0$.

The weights w_i in (18) can't be dimensionless, because we mustn't add dollars to calories. These would be appropriate dimensions:

$$\text{dimension of } w_1 = 1/\text{dollar}$$
$$\text{dimension of } w_2 = 1/\text{calorie}. \tag{19}$$

For instance, let us prescribe the values

$$w_1 = 300/\text{dollar}, \quad w_2 = 2/\text{calorie}. \tag{20}$$

With this arbitrary choice of the weights, suppose we minimize the dimensionless linear combination (18):

$$(300/\text{dollar}) \cdot (\text{total dollars}) + (2/\text{calorie}) \cdot (\text{total calories}) = \min.$$

You might call this linear combination a *composite dimensionless cost.*

According to this composite cost, adding \$2 to the daily grocery bill is exactly as bad as adding 300 calories to the daily calorie intake. How many dollars is a calorie worth? If 300 calories are worth \$2, then 1 calorie is worth \$0.067.

This shows what the weights mean. *In general, the numerical values of* w_i *and* w_j *assign relative dimensionless costs to units of the ith and jth cost components.* If $w_1 = 300/\text{dollar}$, then 300 is the dimensionless cost of one dollar. If $w_2 = 2/\text{calorie}$, then 2 is the dimensionless cost of one calorie. Thus, if we identify *dimensionless cost* with *relative worth*, we have

$$\frac{\text{worth of one calorie}}{\text{worth of one dollar}} = \frac{2}{300} = 0.067. \tag{21}$$

If our example had concerned traffic safety instead of reducing diets, then traffic deaths would have replaced calories as one component of the multiobjective cost. Then the ratio of weights would have assigned a dollar value to a life.

The range of possible weights. If we prescribe positive weights w_i for the cost components $\sum c_{ij}x_j$, and if we solve the conventional linear program

$$Ax = b, \quad x \geqslant 0, \quad (w^T C)x = \min., \tag{22}$$

then the optimal solution x^0 will be an efficient solution of the multiobjective linear program

$$Ax = b, \quad x \geqslant 0, \quad Cx = \min. \tag{23}$$

Conversely, suppose x^0 solves $Ax = b$, $x \geqslant 0$; and suppose x^0 is an efficient solution of (23). Then we know that x^0 is an optimal solution of (22) for *some* $w > 0$.

As we've seen, the numerical ratios w_i/w_j have meaning: they assign *worth ratios* to the cost components, as in (20), (21). If the efficient solution

x^0 uniquely determined the direction of the weight vector w, then x^0 would uniquely determine the worth ratios w_i/w_j.

But that is usually false; usually, x^0 determines a range of possible weight vectors. Thus, the efficient solution x^0 determines a set Ω such that for every w in Ω, x^0 is optimal for the conventional program (22). Then the worth ratios w_i/w_j will not be fixed, but may vary within certain intervals.

And so, given an efficient solution x^0, we want to determine the full range Ω of possible weight vectors w. Only when we have the full range Ω can we answer this question: *What are the possible relative worths that the efficient solution x^0 assigns to the various cost components?*

Suppose x^0 is optimal for the conventional problem (22). Then there is an optimal dual vector y satisfying

$$y^T A \leqslant w^T C, \quad y^T b \geqslant w^T C x^0. \tag{24}$$

(In the second inequality, strict inequality " $>$ " is impossible; only " $=$ " may occur.) Conversely, the inequalities (24) imply that x^0 is optimal for (22).

With no loss of generality, we may assume $w_i \geqslant 1$ for the dimensionless numerical values of the positive weight components; for if ρ is any positive scalar, replacing w by ρw leaves the problem (22) unchanged. Therefore, w *is a possible weight vector if and only if w and some vector y satisfy the homogeneous inequalities* (24) *and the inhomogenous inequalities*

$$w_i \geqslant 1 \quad (i = 1, \ldots, k). \tag{25}$$

In the real vector space of $m + k$ dimensions, the composite vector $[y^T, w^T]$ ranges over the intersections of $n + 1 + k$ closed half-spaces; the intersection is a closed convex set Γ. If the set Γ is projected into the k-dimensional space belonging to the coordinates $w_1, \ldots, w_k$, the result is a closed convex set Ω. *This set Ω is the range of possible weight vectors w.* Thus, each efficient solution x^0 determines a *set* of weight vectors.

EXAMPLE. Consider the multiobjective program

$$\begin{bmatrix} 1 & 2 & 3 \\ 4 & 5 & 6 \end{bmatrix} x = \begin{bmatrix} 3 \\ 9 \end{bmatrix}, \quad x \geqslant 0,$$

$$\begin{bmatrix} 1 & 2 & 3 \\ 1 & 1 & 0 \\ 3 & 2 & 1 \\ 4 & 2 & 2 \end{bmatrix} x = \min.$$

Here the cost has four components, as the cost matrix has four rows. I've given you only the dimensionless cost matrix; the actual cost matrix would attach a different dimension to each of the four rows.

We observe a feasible solution: $x^0 = [1,1,0]^T$. We now ask two questions: Is x^0 an efficient solution?

If so, what is the set Ω of its possible weight vectors?

Here x^0 is basic as well as feasible, and these are the equilibrium equations belonging to the conventional program with cost vector $w^T C$:

$$[y_1, y_2] \begin{bmatrix} 1 & 2 \\ 4 & 5 \end{bmatrix} = [w^T c^1, w^T c^2], \tag{26}$$

where c^1, c^2, and c^3 are the columns of the cost matrix. By the equilibrium theorem, x^0 is optimal for (22) iff the equilibrium solution y^T satisfies

$$[y_1, y_2] \begin{bmatrix} 3 \\ 6 \end{bmatrix} \leqslant w^T c^3. \tag{27}$$

Let's eliminate y by solving the equilibrium equations (26):

$$[y_1, y_2] = w^T [c^1, c^2] \cdot \frac{1}{3} \begin{bmatrix} -5 & 2 \\ 4 & -1 \end{bmatrix}.$$

Now the inequality (27) becomes

$$w^T [c^1, c^2] \cdot \frac{1}{3} \begin{bmatrix} -5 & 2 \\ 4 & -1 \end{bmatrix} \cdot \begin{bmatrix} 3 \\ 6 \end{bmatrix} \leqslant w^T c^3$$

or

$$w^T [c^1, c^2] \begin{bmatrix} -1 \\ 2 \end{bmatrix} \leqslant w^T c^3$$

or

$$w^T(-c^1 + 2c^2) \leqslant w^T c^3.$$

From the given cost matrix, this becomes

$$3w_1 + w_2 + w_3 \leqslant 3w_1 + w_3 + 2w_4,$$

or $w_2 \leqslant 2w_4$.

Since the inequality $w_2 \leqslant 2w_4$ has a solution $w > 0$, the feasible solution x^0 is efficient.

The set Ω consists of all four-dimensional vectors w satisfying the normalization $w_i \geqslant 1$ ($i = 1, \ldots, 4$) and solving the inequality $w_2 \leqslant 2w_4$.

Interpretation. The normalization $w_i \geqslant 1$ has no significance, since the weight vector w has the same meaning as ρw if ρ is any positive scalar. Therefore, the possible dimensionless weight vectors are simply the vectors satisfying

$$w_2 \leqslant 2w_4, \quad w_i > 0 \quad (i = 1, 2, 3, 4).$$

So the given efficient solution x^0 says nothing about the first and third components of the multiobjective cost. About the second and fourth components it says only this: *one unit of the second component is worth $\leqslant$ two units of the fourth component.*

And so we compare the incommensurable—apples and oranges, dollars and calories, dollars and lives.

Reference

Jared L. Cohon, *Multiobjective Programming and Planning*, Academic Press, 1978.

PROBLEMS

1. Draw the (feasible) solutions x of these inequalities:

$$3x_1 + x_2 \geq 6$$
$$x_1 + x_2 \geq 4$$
$$x_1 + 3x_2 \geq 6, \quad x \geq 0.$$

Suppose the composite cost is

$$Cx = \begin{pmatrix} 5x_1 + x_2 \\ x_1 + 2x_2 \end{pmatrix}.$$

Show graphically that the efficient points x lie on the line segments pq and qr, where

$$p = \begin{bmatrix} 0 \\ 6 \end{bmatrix}, \quad q = \begin{bmatrix} 1 \\ 3 \end{bmatrix}, \quad r = \begin{bmatrix} 3 \\ 1 \end{bmatrix}.$$

2. For Problem 1 find *all* the weight vectors w belonging to *each* of these efficient points x:

$$\begin{bmatrix} 0 \\ 6 \end{bmatrix}, \quad \frac{1}{2}\begin{bmatrix} 1 \\ 9 \end{bmatrix}, \quad \begin{bmatrix} 1 \\ 3 \end{bmatrix}, \quad \begin{bmatrix} 2 \\ 2 \end{bmatrix}, \quad \begin{bmatrix} 3 \\ 1 \end{bmatrix}.$$

(The weight w *belongs* to x if x minimizes $w^T Cx$.)

3. Put Problem 1 in the canonical form (6) by introducing the nonnegative slacks x_3, x_4, x_5. Let x^0 be the efficient point $(1,3,0,0,4)^T$. Now write the conventional program (8) and its dual. Find an optimal dual vector $(-y_1,-y_2,-y_3,w_1,w_2)$, and verify that (w_1,w_2) is a weight vector belonging to x^0.

4. Prove or disprove this assertion: The efficient points of a canonical multiobjective linear program (6) constitute a convex set.

5. Prove or disprove this assertion: If the canonical multiobjective linear program (6) has an efficient point, then it has a *basic* efficient point.

6. In the text *Example* we observed the basic solution $x^0 = (1,1,0)^T$; then we proved it was efficient by finding all its weight vectors. Now do the same thing for the basic solution $x^1 = (\frac{3}{2},0,\frac{1}{2})^T$.

*7. Generalization: Let x^0 be efficient for the multiobjective program $Ax = b$, $x \geq 0$, $Cx = \min$. Assume $x_j^0 > 0$ for $j \in B$, and let the columns a^j ($j \in B$) constitute a nonsingular basis matrix M. Let $\hat{C}$ be the matrix of columns c^j ($j \in B$). Show that the weight vector $w > 0$ belongs to x^0 if and only if

$$w^T(c^k - \hat{C}M^{-1}a^k) \geq 0 \qquad \text{for all } k \text{ not in } B.$$

(Use the equilibrium theorem, where the dual solution y satisfies $y^T M = w^T \hat{C}$.)

8. Find all the efficient points x and all their weight vectors w:

$$\begin{bmatrix} 3 & 1 & -1 & 0 & 0 \\ 1 & 1 & 0 & -1 & 0 \\ 1 & 3 & 0 & 0 & -1 \end{bmatrix} x = \begin{bmatrix} 6 \\ 4 \\ 6 \end{bmatrix}, \quad x \geqslant 0$$

$$\begin{bmatrix} 2 & 4 & 0 & 0 & 0 \\ 1 & 5 & 0 & 0 & 0 \end{bmatrix} x = \min.$$

14 Zero-Sum, Two-Person Games

In 1928, John von Neumann published a paper called (in German) "On the Theory of Social Games." In 1944, he and the economist Oskar Morgenstern extended this work in their famous book *Theory of Games and Economic Behavior*.

Von Neumann proved a theorem on what he called *zero-sum, two-person games*. His proof used the Brouwer fixed-point theorem. Using an idea of George Dantzig, I'll prove this theorem for you by linear programming. Dantzig's proof is better than von Neumann's because it is elementary and because it is constructive—it shows you how to construct a best strategy.

First you have to know what von Neumann meant by a *game*. In *The Ascent of Man*, Jacob Bronowski tells this story:

> I worked with Johnny von Neumann during the Second World War in England. He first talked to me about his Theory of Games in a taxi in London—one of the favourite places in which he liked to talk about mathematics. And I naturally said to him, since I am an enthusiastic chess player, 'You mean, the theory of games like chess.' 'No, no' he said. 'Chess is not a game. Chess is a well-defined form of computation. You may not be able to work out the answers, but in theory there must be a solution, a right procedure in any position. Now real games,' he said, 'are not like that at all. Real life is not like that. Real life consists of bluffing, of little tactics of deception, of asking yourself what is the other man going to think I mean to do. And that is what games are about in my theory.'

EXAMPLE 1. Let's play a game. When I say NOW, you stick out one or two fingers. At the same instant, I will stick out one or two fingers. You try to match me. You win if you do; you lose if you don't. This is a zero-sum, two person game.

It's called *zero-sum* because the total wealth of the players stays fixed. If we bet a penny a game either a penny goes from me to you or a penny goes from you to me; our total wealth stays fixed.

The game is called *two-person* because there are just two sides. In this example there are literally two persons, but in other examples there are two teams, two corporations, two countries, or two alliances.

Let's call you P and me Q. You have two possible *pure strategies* (show one or two fingers), and so have I. This is *your* payoff matrix:

		one Q two	
		finger	fingers
P	one finger	1	-1
	two fingers	-1	1

For instance, the lower left entry means you lose one penny if you show two fingers while I show one finger.

My payoff matrix would just be the negative of yours, since this game is zero-sum, two-person. What I win you lose, and vice versa. For all such games it is only necessary to write down the payoff matrix for one of the players—say for player P.

If you know what I'm going to do, you can win a penny; if I know what you're going to do, I can win a penny. So we say the game has no solution in *pure strategies*.

Mixed strategies. Suppose we play the game many times. Sometimes you show one finger and sometimes two. Suppose you decide ahead of time that you're going to play your two possible pure strategies with probabilities p_1 and p_2, with $p_1 \geqslant 0$, $p_2 \geqslant 0$, $p_1 + p_2 = 1$. Then the vector p is called a *mixed strategy*.

For instance, suppose we've decided to play a series of 100 games next Saturday. On Friday evening you decide, correctly, that your optimal mixed strategy is $p_1 = p_2 = \frac{1}{2}$. You don't have to keep this secret. If you want to, you can call me up and warn me that you've picked the mixed strategy $p_1 = p_2 = \frac{1}{2}$; your warning won't do me any good.

What you do have to keep secret is the decisions on single plays. When we play on Saturday, before each of the 100 games, you turn your back to me and flip a coin so that I can't see how it lands. If it lands heads, you'll show one finger on the next game; if tails, you'll show two fingers. During our series, you'll be showing one finger about 50 times. I, your opponent, know that in advance, but I don't know what you're going to do on any *single* play.

So what can I do to beat you? Nothing. No matter what I do, unless I peek at the coin, your expected payoff is zero.

Whether you call me on Friday or not, I'll pick a mixed strategy for myself. Naturally, I'll pick the mixed strategy $q_1 = q_2 = \frac{1}{2}$, and I'll plan to pick my individual plays by covertly flipping a coin of my own. Now I don't care what you'll do—as long as you don't peek at my coin. No matter what you'll do, your expected payoff can't be greater than zero; in fact, your *expected* payoff per game will be exactly zero.

Zero is the *value* of this game. This is because you can pick a mixed strategy that will make your expected payoff *at least* zero, whatever I do; and I can pick a mixed strategy that make your expected payoff *no more than* zero, whatever you do. *Von Neumann's theorem says every zero-sum, two-person game has a value in mixed strategies.*

To continue Example 1, suppose you had picked a mixed strategy with $p_1 < \frac{1}{2}$. Then I should pick $q_1 = 1$, $q_2 = 0$, which means that I always show one finger. Then you will match me with probability $p_1 < \frac{1}{2}$, and you will not match me with probability $1 - p_1 > \frac{1}{2}$; your expected payoff per game is

$$p_1 \cdot 1 + (1 - p_1) \cdot (-1) = 2p_1 - 1 < 0.$$

For instance, if you had chosen $p_1 = 0.3$, you could expect to lose about 40 cents in 100 games. Similarly, if you had picked $p_1 > \frac{1}{2}$, I should pick $q_1 = 0$, $q_2 = 1$, giving you the expected payoff

$$p_1 \cdot (-1) + (1 - p_1) \cdot 1 = 1 - 2p_1 < 0.$$

Again, this is negative. The only way you can be sure to break even is to choose $p_1 = \frac{1}{2}$.

EXAMPLE 2. Now suppose this is your payoff matrix:

$$\begin{bmatrix} 5 & 3 \\ 3 & 5 \end{bmatrix}.$$

This game is a joy for you to play because you make money whatever you do.

Still, you have a best mixed strategy. Note that the payoff matrix is the sum

$$\begin{bmatrix} 1 & -1 \\ -1 & 1 \end{bmatrix} + \begin{bmatrix} 4 & 4 \\ 4 & 4 \end{bmatrix}.$$

This is the old payoff matrix with this change: 4 has been added to each component. Whatever happened before will happen now, except that your payoff is increased by 4 cents. Therefore, your best mixed strategy is still $p_1 = p_2 = \frac{1}{2}$, and my best strategy is still $q_1 = q_2 = \frac{1}{2}$.

The *value* of this game is 4. That's the value per game to you. If you want to play me a hundred of these games, you should pay me four dollars in advance if you want to be fair.

EXAMPLE 3. Suppose this is the payoff matrix:

$$\begin{bmatrix} 3 & 3 \\ 3 & 3 \end{bmatrix}.$$

Clearly, the value of this game is 3, and every mixed strategy is optimal. In general, *though the value of the game is unique, the optimal mixed strategies might not be unique.*

EXAMPLE 4. Suppose this is the payoff matrix:

$$\begin{bmatrix} 2 & 1 & -1 \\ -1 & -2 & 3 \end{bmatrix}$$

Now you have two options (pure strategies), while I have three. If I know you will play your first option, I will play my third; if I know you'll play your second option, I'll play my second.

What is your best *mixed* strategy? What is mine? What is the value of this game? You don't know.

I couldn't guess, either. Later we'll compute the answers by linear programming. Your best strategy is

$$p_1 = \tfrac{5}{7}, \quad p_2 = \tfrac{2}{7}; \tag{1}$$

my best strategy is

$$q_1 = 0, \quad q_2 = \tfrac{4}{7}, \quad q_3 = \tfrac{3}{7}; \tag{2}$$

the value of the game is $\tfrac{1}{7}$.

So if you play right, you can expect to be about a penny ahead every seven games, and there's no way I can stop you.

General discussion. Let the payoff matrix A have m rows and n columns. We'll call p and q *probability vectors*, or *mixed strategies*, if

$$p \geqslant 0, \quad \sum_{i=1}^{m} p_i = 1; \quad q \geqslant 0, \quad \sum_{j=1}^{n} q_j = 1. \tag{3}$$

The (expected) *payoff* equals

$$\sum_{i=1}^{m} \sum_{j=1}^{n} p_i a_{ij} q_j = p^T A q. \tag{4}$$

We'll say that the game with payoff matrix A has the *value* ω, and we'll call p and q *optimal* mixed strategies, if

$$\sum_{i=1}^{m} p_i a_{ij} \geqslant \omega \qquad (j = 1, \ldots, n) \tag{5}$$

$$\sum_{j=1}^{n} a_{ij} q_j \leqslant \omega \qquad (i = 1, \ldots, m). \tag{6}$$

Meaning: If the first player plays the mixed strategy p, his expected payoff is $\geqslant \omega$, whatever the second player does. Similarly, if the second player plays the mixed strategy q, the expected payoff to the first player is $\leqslant \omega$, whatever the first player does.

EXAMPLE 5. Taking A, p, and q from Example 4, please verify these computations:

$$[\tfrac{5}{7}, \tfrac{2}{7}] \begin{bmatrix} 2 & 1 & -1 \\ -1 & -2 & 3 \end{bmatrix} = [\tfrac{9}{7}, \tfrac{1}{7}, \tfrac{1}{7}] \geqslant \tfrac{1}{7}[1,1,1]$$

$$\begin{bmatrix} 2 & 1 & -1 \\ -1 & -2 & 3 \end{bmatrix} \begin{bmatrix} 0 \\ \tfrac{4}{7} \\ \tfrac{3}{7} \end{bmatrix} = \tfrac{1}{7}\begin{bmatrix} 1 \\ 1 \end{bmatrix}.$$

These are examples of formulas (5) and (6); they prove that $\omega = \frac{1}{7}$ for the game in Example 4.

   Uniqueness of the value. Suppose some mixed strategies p' and q' satisfy

$$\sum_i p'_i a_{ij} \geq \omega', \quad \sum_j a_{ij} q'_j \leq \omega'.$$

Then

$$\sum_j \left(\sum_i p'_i a_{ij} \right) q_j \geq \omega', \quad \sum_i \left(\sum_j a_{ij} q'_j \right) p_i \leq \omega',$$

and now (6) and (5) imply

$$\omega \geq \omega', \quad \omega \leq \omega',$$

or $\omega = \omega'$. So the value, if it exists, is unique.

Theorem (von Neumann). *Let A be any real matrix. Then the zero-sum, two-person game with payoff matrix A has a value ω satisfying (5) and (6) for some mixed strategies p and q.*

PROOF. With no loss of generality, assume all a_{ij} are positive. Otherwise, if $a_{ij} + \alpha$ is positive for all i and j, then (5) and (6) may be replaced by

$$\sum_i p_i(a_{ij} + \alpha) \geq \omega + \alpha, \quad \sum_j (a_{ij} + \alpha)q_j \leq \omega + \alpha.$$

(This is what we did in Example 2, with $\alpha = 4$.)
   Assuming all $a_{ij} > 0$, we will construct a number $\omega > 0$ satisfying (5) and (6). First we define the unknowns

$$u_i = p_i/\omega \ (i = 1, \ldots, m), \quad v_j = q_j/\omega \ (j = 1, \ldots, n). \tag{7}$$

Then (5) and (6) become

$$\sum_{i=1}^m u_i a_{ij} \geq 1 \qquad (j = 1, \ldots, n)$$

$$\sum_{j=1}^n a_{ij} v_j \leq 1 \qquad (i = 1, \ldots, m), \tag{8}$$

with $u \geq 0$, $v \geq 0$, and with

$$\sum_{i=1}^m u_i = \sum_{j=1}^n v_j = \frac{1}{\omega}. \tag{9}$$

   The required vectors u and v must solve the dual linear programs with the requirements (8) and with the objectives

$$\sum_{i=1}^m u_i = \text{minimum}, \quad \sum_{j=1}^n v_j = \text{maximum}. \tag{10}$$

By the duality theorem, these programs do have optimal solutions because they both have feasible solutions. (Since all a_{ij} are positive, a vector u is feasible if all its components are large; the vector $v = 0$ is feasible for the dual.) Again by the duality theorem, optimal vectors u and v do satisfy the equality (9).

Taking ω, u, and v from (9), we see that ω, p, and q satisfy von Neumann's theorem if $p = \omega u$ and $q = \omega v$.

EXAMPLE 6. To illustrate the solution of games by linear programming, let's first consider the payoff matrix in Example 1:

$$A_1 = \begin{bmatrix} 1 & -1 \\ -1 & 1 \end{bmatrix}.$$

To get a matrix with positive components, we can add any number $\alpha > 1$ to all the components. If we use $\alpha = 4$, we get the payoff matrix

$$A = \begin{bmatrix} 5 & 3 \\ 3 & 5 \end{bmatrix},$$

which occurred in Example 2; the new value equals α plus the old value, that is, $\omega = \alpha + \omega_1 = 4 + \omega_1$.

The solution of the dual programs (8), (9), (10) is

$$u^T = [\tfrac{1}{8}, \tfrac{1}{8}], \quad v^T = [\tfrac{1}{8}, \tfrac{1}{8}],$$

$$u_1 + u_2 = v_1 + v_2 = \tfrac{1}{4} = \frac{1}{\omega}.$$

Therefore, $\omega = 4$, and so $\omega_1 = 0$ for the original game. To get the best mixed strategies, we compute

$$p^T = \omega u^T = 4[\tfrac{1}{8}, \tfrac{1}{8}] = [\tfrac{1}{2}, \tfrac{1}{2}]$$

and, similarly, $q^T = \omega v^T = [\tfrac{1}{2}, \tfrac{1}{2}]$.

EXAMPLE 7. Let's solve Example 4 by linear programming. Call the matrix A_1 and the value ω_1. To get a positive matrix A, add $\alpha = 3$ to every component; then

$$A = \begin{bmatrix} 5 & 4 & 2 \\ 2 & 1 & 6 \end{bmatrix}, \tag{11}$$

with value $\omega = 3 + \omega_1$.

This is the linear programming problem for u:

$$u^T A \geqslant [1,1,1], \quad u \geqslant 0; \quad u_1 + u_2 = \text{min.} = \frac{1}{\omega}. \tag{12}$$

If this were a large problem, we would restate it as a canonical minimum problem and solve it by the simplex method. But for this small problem, we'll do better by judgment.

From the original problem, we judge it unlikely that the best strategy for either player is a pure strategy. And so we expect both components of u (or p) to be positive, and we expect at least two components of v (or q) to be positive. If two components of the dual vector v are positive, then two of the primal inequalities (12) must be equalities in an optimal solution.

There are only three possibilities for two primal equalities in (12); let's try to be lucky. (When I prepared this example, I tried the possibilities in the wrong order, but I'll save you the trouble.) Let's solve the second and third primal inequalities as equalities:

$$[u_1,u_2]\begin{bmatrix} 4 & 2 \\ 1 & 6 \end{bmatrix} = [1,1].$$

$$[u_1,u_2] = \tfrac{1}{22}[5,2].$$

Does this satisfy the *first* primal inequality? Yes:

$$[u_1,u_2]\begin{bmatrix} 5 \\ 2 \end{bmatrix} = \frac{29}{22} > 1.$$

If v is optimal for the dual, the equilibrium theorem requires $v_1 = 0$. Let's solve for v_2 and v_3:

$$Av = \begin{bmatrix} 5 & 4 & 2 \\ 2 & 1 & 6 \end{bmatrix}\begin{bmatrix} 0 \\ v_2 \\ v_3 \end{bmatrix} = \begin{bmatrix} 1 \\ 1 \end{bmatrix},$$

and so

$$v_1 = 0, \quad v_2 = \tfrac{4}{22}, \quad v_3 = \tfrac{3}{22}. \tag{13}$$

The equilibrium theorem assures us that u and v are optimal. The common value of their objective functions is

$$u_1 + u_2 = v_1 + v_2 + v_3 = \frac{7}{22} = \frac{1}{\omega}. \tag{14}$$

For the game, the optimal strategies are $p = \omega u$ and $q = \omega v$; so (12), (13), and (14) give

$$p^T = [\tfrac{5}{7}, \tfrac{2}{7}], \quad q^T = [0, \tfrac{4}{7}, \tfrac{3}{7}]. \tag{15}$$

From (14) we have $\omega = \tfrac{22}{7}$, which is the value for the shifted payoff matrix A, but not for the original matrix A_1. After the definition (11), we wrote the equation $\omega = 3 + \omega_1$, and we will now use it to get the value $\omega_1 = \tfrac{1}{7}$.

This is a good example. The value $\tfrac{1}{7}$ and the optimal strategies would be hard to guess. Note that the second player should never play his first option, but should only play his other two options with relative frequencies $4:3$.

You might object that the game of Example 7 is unfair, since it gives an advantage to the first player. That is irrelevant for this reason: *Any two-person game can be symmetrized* by requiring the competitors to play both sides equal numbers of times. If you and I play the game 20 times, we'll alternate the roles P and Q, so each of us will have the advantage exactly 10 times. Each pair of games constitutes a single symmetric game, which is obviously fair.

Symmetric games look exactly the same to both players. If the payoff matrix is B, then B must be a square matrix with

$$B^T = -B. \tag{16}$$

For instance, suppose $b_{35} = \$7$. That means, if P plays option 3 while Q plays option 5, then P wins \$7 from Q. Therefore, if Q plays 3 while P plays 5, then Q wins \$7 from P, and so $b_{53} = -\$7$.

Let us now prove what must be true: *The value of a zero-sum symmetric game is zero, and an optimal strategy for one player is an optimal strategy for the other.*

Let ω be the value; and let p and q be optimal mixed strategies for the first and second players, respectively. We will prove $\omega = 0$, and we'll prove p and q are optimal for the second and first players, respectively. (We can't hope to prove $q = p$, because optimal strategies are not necessarily unique.)

If $e^T = (1,1,\ldots,1)$, then we assume

$$p^T B \geqslant \omega e^T, \quad Bq \leqslant \omega e. \tag{17}$$

For all x we have $x^T B x \equiv 0$, because $B^T = -B$. Therefore,

$$0 = p^T B p \geqslant \omega e^T p = \omega, \quad 0 = q^T B q \leqslant \omega q^T e = \omega,$$

which proves $\omega = 0$. Now, taking transposes in (17), we get

$$-Bp = B^T p \geqslant 0, \quad -q^T B = q^T B^T \leqslant 0.$$

Multiplying both inequalities by -1, we get

$$Bp \leqslant 0, \quad q^T B \geqslant 0, \tag{18}$$

which proves p and q are optimal for the second and first players, respectively.

In (18) we found a simple characterization of an optimal strategy for a symmetric game: If $B = -B^T$, then the probability vector p is optimal for both players iff $Bp \leqslant 0$.

This gives us a converse of our solution of games by linear programming. We will now prove this: *Every solvable linear program is equivalent to a symmetric zero-sum, two-person game.*

Let's write the program as a standard minimum problem:

$$Ax \geqslant b, \quad x \geqslant 0, \quad c^T x = \min.$$

Here's the dual problem:

$$y^T A \leqslant c^T, \quad y \geqslant 0, \quad y^T b = \max.$$

Feasible solutions x and y and optimal if and only if

$$c^T x \leqslant y^T b,$$

where, in fact, only the "=" may occur.

We can summarize the conditions of feasibility and optimality as follows: For $x \geqslant 0$, $y \geqslant 0$, we have

$$\begin{bmatrix} O, & -A, & b \\ A^T, & O, & -c \\ -b^T, & c^T, & 0 \end{bmatrix} \begin{bmatrix} y \\ x \\ 1 \end{bmatrix} \leqslant 0$$

Here the matrix—call it B—has $m + n + 1$ rows and columns if A has m rows and n columns. The matrix B is antisymmetric: $B = -B^T$. The vector has $m + n + 1$ non-negative components; the last component equals 1. If we divide the vector by the sum of its components, we get a probability vector p. Then $Bp \leqslant 0$ where $B = -B^T$, and so we've found a symmetric game equivalent to the given linear program.

Bluffing. The most interesting thing about games like poker is bluffing. Under what conditions and how often should you bluff? Your answer will depend partly on your reading of the character of the other players, but will also depend on your intuitive grasp of the theory of mixed strategies.

Bluffing occurs in business and in diplomacy. In his book *The Negotiating Game*, Dr. Chester Karrass tells the story of Hitler and Chamberlain at Munich. On pp. 8–10 he has an essay: "The Rape of Czechoslovakia." I'll summarize it for you. Hitler had everything against him; he had every reason to back down. But he bluffed, and Chamberlain failed to call his bluff. Karrass says at the end:

"Chamberlain, businessman turned politician, had lost the greatest negotiation of all time. As a consequence, 25 million people were soon to lose their lives."

Games like diplomacy and poker are too complicated to analyze precisely. But still, game theory gives us, if not knowledge, at least wisdom. Here's an example by S. Vajda:

EXAMPLE 8. You and I will play a simple bluffing game. The first thing we both do is put down a small positive ante a. Then you draw one card from an ordinary deck; after looking at it, you put it face down without showing it to me. We'll say black cards are high, and red cards are low.

Here are the rules. After you draw, you may bet or fold. If you fold, you lose the ante a. If you bet, then I may fold or I may call. If I fold, I lose the ante a, whether you've drawn black or red. If I bet, then you win the amount b if you drew a black card, or I win the amount b if you drew a red card. (The ante a and bet size b are fixed in advance, with $0 < a < b$.)

Your pure strategies. If you draw black, you will certainly bet—there's no question about that; you will bet and win at least the ante a. The only question is this: Will you bet if you draw red? That would be the *bluff* strategy. If you fold when you draw red, that is the *fold* strategy. (Remember, even if you're playing the *fold* strategy, you will bet if you draw black.)

My pure strategies. You've just bet. What should I do? If I know you only bet on black, I will fold; but if I think you may bluff and bet on red, I may decide to call you. I have two pure strategies: the *call* strategy, in which I will call you if you bet; and the *fold* strategy, in which I will fold if you bet.

Can we write down your payoff matrix for this bluffing game? Sure we can. Here it is:

$$\begin{array}{c} \\ \text{bluff} \\ \\ \text{fold} \end{array} \begin{array}{cc} \text{call} & \text{fold} \\ \begin{bmatrix} 0 & a \\ \dfrac{b-a}{2} & 0 \end{bmatrix} \end{array}$$

Let me explain. As usual, let's call the components a_{ij}. For instance, a_{21} is your *average* payoff if you play your *fold* strategy while I play my *call* strategy. I'll explain all four components:

$a_{11} = 0$: If you draw black, you will bet, I will call, and you will win b. If you draw red, you will bet (bluffing), I will call, and you will lose b. Since black and red draws are equally likely, your *average* payoff is $\frac{1}{2}(b - b) = 0$.

$a_{12} = a$: Whatever you draw, you will bet, I will fold, and you will win the ante a.

$a_{21} = (b - a)/2$: If you draw black, you will bet, I will call, and you will win b. If you draw red, you will fold, and you will lose the ante a. Your average payoff is $(b - a)/2$.

$a_{22} = 0$: If you draw black, you will bet, I will fold, and you will win a. If you draw red, you will fold, and you will lose a. Your average payoff is zero.

Optimal mixed strategies. If you always play your *bluff* strategy, I will always play my *call* strategy; if you always play *fold*, I will always play *fold*. So, in pure strategies I can hold your average payoff down to zero.

But you can win with a mixed strategy. Using linear programming, we can easily compute your best mixed strategy p, my best mixed strategy q, and the value ω. Your expected payoff will be ω each time we play; I can't lower it, and you can't raise it.

You can compute these values:

$$p_1 = \frac{b-a}{b+a}, \quad p_2 = \frac{2a}{b+a}; \quad q_1 = \frac{2a}{b+a}, \quad q_2 = \frac{b-a}{b+a}; \tag{19}$$

and $\omega = a(b - a)/(b + a)$. Using the payoff matrix A, please verify the inequalities

$$p^T A \geq (\omega, \omega), \quad Aq \leq \begin{pmatrix} \omega \\ \omega \end{pmatrix}.$$

(Both inequalities will turn out to be equations.)

I promised you wisdom from this example, and now you'll get it. Your optimal bluffing frequency depends on the bet-to-ante ratio $r = b/a$. We assumed $r > 1$. As r goes from 1 to ∞, p_1 goes monotonely from 0 to 1: the bigger r is, the more often you should bluff.

As for me, if I look at q_2 I see this: The bigger r is, the more often I should fold.

The value ω depends on a and r:

$$\omega = a\,\frac{b - a}{b + a} = a \cdot \frac{r - 1}{r + 1}. \tag{20}$$

As a function of r, as r goes from 1 to ∞, ω increases monotonely from 0 to a.

Many-person games. Poker usually has more than two players. How should you play n-person games if n is greater than 2?

Here the theory is very complex. It depends on your assumptions about collusions and side payments. If you want to learn the main ideas simply, it's hard to beat the old book by Luce and Raiffa.

When I was a college freshman, I had two roommates, Fritz and Ted. With regard to all questions (Shall music be played? Shall the lights be on at 2 A.M.?) Fritz and Ted and I played a 3-person game you might call *majority rule*, or *democracy without the Bill of Rights*. Superficially, the game appeared symmetrical, but I soon learned that Fritz-and-Ted together couldn't be beat. It was a lesson in 3-person game theory.

Later, I'll prove the Nash equilibrium theorem for you. This theorem assumes there are no collusions, but it applies to most n-person games, even to nonzero-sum games.

Nonzero-sum games. Zero-sum games are not the most important games. The stock market may be a zero-sum game, but the stock market is not the economy.

If I buy 100 shares of IBM stock, I may think I've made an investment. Ignoring the broker's fees, I play a zero-sum game with the seller. If the price goes up, I'll win and the seller will lose; if the price goes down, I'll lose and the seller will win. One of us is going to profit at the other's expense.

Economists don't call stock purchases *investments* (they call them welfare transfers, or something like that). Stock purchases are no part of the gross national product. To an economist, an *investment* is a purchase made to increase the productivity of a business. If I buy an IBM computer to make my business more productive, *that* is an investment. It's good for IBM *and* good for me. It's even good for you if you're one of my customers. In a wise business transaction everyone comes out ahead. By and large, business is a positive-sum game.

Disarmament: a negative-sum game. But not all is well in the world. For instance, the United States and the Soviet Union divert much of their economic productivity from the civilian sector to the military. Pacifists say this is dangerous; realists say it is necessary. But everyone agrees that it's wasteful.

Poor people in both countries—and rich people, too—would be better off if both countries disarmed.

So why don't they? Let's see if we can understand the paradox of disarmament by making a simple mathematical model.

To begin, we'll assume that the world contains only two countries, the U.S. and the U.S.S.R., so we don't both have to worry about disarming and then getting bombed by China. Second, we'll assume that neither the U.S. nor the U.S.S.R. is totally wicked, stupid, or crazy; we'll assume both countries act in their own interest. Last, we'll make the model symmetric. This is what Bertrand Russell once called a false "love of symmetry" in discussing these two countries, but you'll see that the symmetry won't affect our main conclusion.

Both countries have two pure strategies: *arm* and *disarm*. If we *both arm* (which is what we do in fact), let's say we both get payoffs equal to minus $200 billion, if that is the annual defense budget in each country. If we *both disarm*, both our payoffs rise to zero.

Suppose *we disarm* while *they arm*. Then our payoff could go to minus infinity, or something pretty near. Meanwhile, their payoff could become positive—say $100 billion. Even short of war, they could expect to win a great deal from us by intimidation.

By a false love of symmetry, we'll assume exactly the reverse if *we arm* while *they disarm*. We'll assume our payoff becomes $100 billion while theirs goes to minus infinity.

Since the game isn't zero-sum, we have to write down two payoff matrices—one for us (U.S.) and one for them (U.S.S.R.). We'll do this, in effect, by writing four entries of the form $a \backslash b$, where a is our payoff and b is theirs. So here are the payoffs for the four possible pure-strategy pairs:

		U.S.S.R.	
		arm	disarm
U.S.	arm	$-200 \backslash -200$	$+100 \backslash -\infty$
	disarm	$-\infty \backslash +100$	$0 \backslash 0$

At present, we and the Russians are in the upper left box, since we are both playing *arm*. We're both getting payoff -200. We would both be better off if we both played *disarm*, which would put us in the lower right box.

But whatever they do, we are better off if we arm. If they arm, we must arm; if they disarm, we are still better off if we arm. Similarly, whatever we do, they are better off if they arm. And so we both wind up in the upper left box.

In logic, this is an example of the *fallacy of composition*: what's best for the parts is not always best for the whole. This is the underlying paradox of morality. We would all be better off if we were all good, but then it would pay each one of us to cheat a little.

The bad news from game theory is this: The upper left box is a stable Nash equilibrium. I hope I've roused your interest.

References

1. John von Neumann, Zur Theorie der Gesellschaftsspiele, *Math. Ann.*, Vol. 100 (1928) pp. 295–320.
2. John von Neumann and Oskar Morgenstern, *Theory of Games and Economic Behavior*, Princeton University Press, 1944.
3. George Dantzig, "A Proof of the Equivalence of the Programming Problem and the Game Problem," in Koopmans (ed.) *Activity Analysis of Production and Allocation*, pp. 330–335, Wiley, 1951.
4. Jacob Bronowski, *The Ascent of Man*, p. 432, Little Brown and Company, 1973.
5. Chester Karrass, *The Negotiating Game*, The World Publishing Co., 1970.
6. R. Duncan Luce and Howard Raiffa, *Games and Decisions*, Wiley, 1957.
7. Lloyd Shapley and Martin Shubik, *Game Theory in Economics*, Rand Corporation Reports No. R-904/1, 2, 3, 4, 6 (1971–1974).
8. Bertrand Russell, "What Is Freedom?" in *Fact and Fiction*, p. 56, Simon and Schuster, 1962.
9. S. Vajda, *Theory of Games and Linear Programming*, Wiley, 1956.

PROBLEMS

1. Let $0 \leqslant x \leqslant 1$ and $0 \leqslant y \leqslant 1$. Let $\psi(x,y) = (x - y)^2$. Show:

$$\min_{y} \psi(x,y) = 0 \qquad \text{for all } x,$$

$$\max_{x} \psi(x,y) \geqslant \tfrac{1}{4} \qquad \text{for all } y.$$

Deduce the strict inequality

$$\min_{y}\left[\max_{x} \psi(x,y) \right] > \max_{x}\left[\min_{y} \psi(x,y) \right].$$

2. In general, let X and Y be closed, bounded subsets of R^m and R^n; and let $\psi(x,y)$ be continuous and real-valued for $x \in X$, $y \in Y$. Prove the inequality

$$\min_{y}\left[\max_{x} \psi(x,y) \right] \geqslant \max_{x}\left[\min_{y} \psi(x,y) \right].$$

3. *The minimax property of a matrix game*: Let X be the probability vectors in R^M ($x_I \geqslant 0, \Sigma x_I = 1$); let Y be the probability vectors in R^N. Let A be an $m \times n$ matrix, and define the continuous function $\psi(x,y) = x^T A y$. Let p, q, ω be optimal strategies and the value satisfying (5) and (6). For $x \in X$ and $y \in Y$, show

$$\min_{y}\left[\max_{x} x^T A y \right] \leqslant \max_{x} x^T A q \leqslant \omega,$$

$$\max_{x}\left[\min_{y} x^T A y \right] \geqslant \min_{y} x^T A y \geqslant \omega.$$

Show that all these inequalities are *equalities* by using the result of Problem 2.

4. In *The Ascent of Man*, J. Bronowski presents a version of the game called *Morra*. Each player *shows* one or two fingers, and each player *guesses* the number of fingers the other player will show. Thus, each player has four pure strategies:

(show, guess) = (1,1), (1,2), (2,1), (2,2). The object is to guess how many fingers your opponent will show. The payoff is zero if both players guess right or if both guess wrong. But if only one player guesses right, the payoff to him, from his opponent, equals the sum of the numbers shown by both players. This is a zero-sum, symmetric two-person game; find the payoff matrix. Answer:

$$A = \begin{bmatrix} 0 & 2 & -3 & 0 \\ -2 & 0 & 0 & 3 \\ 3 & 0 & 0 & -4 \\ 0 & -3 & 4 & 0 \end{bmatrix}.$$

5. (Continuation.) Bronowski says that a best mixed strategy for Morra has relative frequencies $0, \frac{7}{12}, \frac{5}{12}, 0$. Prove Bronowski is right: verify $Aq \leqslant 0$, $p^T A \geqslant 0$ if $p = q =$ Bronowski's strategy.

6. (Continuation.) Show that Bronowski's strategy isn't the only optimal strategy: show that p is optimal iff $p_1 = p_4 = 0$ and $\frac{4}{3} \leqslant p_2/p_3 \leqslant \frac{3}{2}$.

7. (Continuation.) Suppose you play Bronowski's optimal strategy while I play the mixed strategy $(0.1, 0.4, 0.3, 0.2)$. On the average, how much do you expect to win per game?

8. Use linear programming to solve the game with payoff matrix

$$A = \begin{bmatrix} 5 & -7 \\ -9 & 4 \end{bmatrix}.$$

("Solve the game" means: find the value ω and optimal mixed strategies p, q.)

9. Use linear programming to solve the game with payoff matrix

$$A = \begin{bmatrix} -2, & 3, -1 \\ 1, -1, & 2 \end{bmatrix}.$$

10. Let a symmetric game have payoff matrix $A = -A^T$. Use the Farkas theorem to prove there exists a vector q satisfying

$$Aq \leqslant 0, \quad \Sigma q_J = 1, \quad q \geqslant 0.$$

(Since every matrix game can be symmetrized, this gives another proof of von Neumann's theorem.)

11. The game *hide and seek* (von Neumann): Given is an $m \times n$ matrix B with components $b_{ij} > 0$. Player P picks a row *or* a column, while player Q picks a single component. Suppose Q picks b_{rs}; then Q must pay P the amount b_{rs} if P picks row r or column s, but the payoff is zero if P picks a row or a column not containing b_{rs}. (Q hides, P seeks.) Player P has $m + n$ pure strategies, while player Q has $m \cdot n$ pure strategies. Suppose P picks row i with probability p_i, column j with probability $p'_j (\Sigma p_i + \Sigma p'_j = 1)$; suppose Q picks component b_{ij} with probability q_{ij}. What is the expected payoff to P from Q? Write the 5×6 payoff matrix A if B is the matrix

$$B = \begin{bmatrix} 1 & 2 & 3 \\ 4 & 5 & 6 \end{bmatrix}.$$

12. (Continuation.) For *hide and seek* take the matrix

$$B = \begin{bmatrix} 1 & 2 \\ 3 & 4 \end{bmatrix}.$$

Find the 4×4 payoff matrix A, and solve the game. [Answer: $\omega = 0.8$; $p^T = (0.4,0.1,0.4,0.1)$; $q^T = (0.8,0,0,0.2).$]

13. A multistage game: Each player is dealt three cards numbered 1, 2, 3. Three tricks will be played. Each player plays one of his cards for the first trick; after observing the first trick, each player plays one of his remaining two cards; then the last play is forced. The payoff is some function of the cards played. Show that each player has 24 pure strategies. (Hint: $24 = 3 \cdot 2^3.$)

*14. Generalize the last problem: let each player hold cards numbered $1, 2, \ldots, n$. Write a formula for the number of pure strategies for each player.

15. For *hide and seek* (Problem 11) show that player Q's optimal mixed strategy has the components $q_{ij} = \omega v_{ij}$, where v solves

$$\sum_{j=1}^{n} b_{ij} v_{ij} \leq 1 \qquad (i = 1, \ldots, m)$$

$$\sum_{i=1}^{m} b_{ij} v_{ij} \leq 1 \qquad (j = 1, \ldots, n)$$

$$v_{ij} \geq 0, \quad \sum_i \sum_j v_{ij} = \max = 1/\omega.$$

(If we set $x_{ij} = b_{ij} v_{ij}$, this linear program becomes what we shall later call an *optimal assignment* problem.)

16. Use linear programming to solve the game with payoff matrix

$$A = \begin{bmatrix} 0 & a \\ c & 0 \end{bmatrix},$$

where a and c are positive. Set $c = \frac{1}{2}(b - a)$, and apply your solution to obtain formula (19) for Vajda's example of bluffing.

17. Find the 6×6 payoff matrix B for a symmetric game equivalent to the linear program

$$\begin{bmatrix} 3 & 2 & 1 \\ 1 & 1 & 5 \end{bmatrix} x \geq \begin{bmatrix} 7 \\ 3 \end{bmatrix}, \quad x \geq 0, \quad [7,5,9]x = \min.$$

Show that the optimal solution of the program is $x^0 = (1,2,0)^T$ by solving the equilibrium equations. Now write the optimal mixed strategy $p = q$ for the game; verify $Bq \leq 0$.

18. For the nonzero-sum game *disarmament*, what are the expected values to the two players if they use *mixed* strategies p and q? If the first player plays p, what strategy is optimal for the second player?

15 Integer Linear Programming: Gomory's Method

In canonical form, a linear programming problem looks like this:

$$Ax = b, \quad x \geqslant 0, \quad c^T x = \min. \tag{1}$$

If the unknowns x_j are required to be integers, we have a problem in integer linear programming.

The canonical program (1) is a minimum problem. On any minimum problem the effect of a new requirement is this: The new problem may have no solution; or if a solution does exist, the new minimum will be greater than or equal to the old minimum.

EXAMPLE 1. The canonical program

$$2x_1 + 4x_2 = 5, \quad x \geqslant 0, \quad x_1 + x_2 = \min.$$

has the solution $x_1 = 0$, $x_2 = \frac{5}{4}$. If we require x_1 and x_2 to be integers, the problem has no solution. In the theory of numbers, equations in integers are called *diophantine equations*; the existence of solutions depends on divisibility relationships.

EXAMPLE 2. The canonical program

$$2x_1 + 4x_2 = 6, \quad x \geqslant 0, \quad x_1 + x_2 = \min.$$

has the optimal real solution $x_1 = 0$, $x_2 = \frac{3}{2}$; the minimum equals $\frac{3}{2}$. The integer program has the solution $x_1 = 1$, $x_2 = 1$; the new minimum equals 2.

EXAMPLE 3. Here is the *knapsack problem*. Given positive values v_j and weights w_j for $j = 1, \ldots, n$, we want to find integers x_j satisfying

$$w_1 x_1 + \cdots + w_n x_n \leqslant \beta, \quad x_j \geqslant 0,$$
$$v_1 x_1 + \cdots + v_n x_n = \max. \tag{2}$$

Here x_j will be the number of objects of type j, each of which has value v_j and weight w_j. The number β is a given positive bound on the total weight. The total value $\Sigma v_j x_j$ is to be maximized.

The knapsack problem is difficult only because of the integer requirement. If we drop the integer requirement, the solution is this: Take as much as possible of an object that maximizes the value-to-weight ratio v_m/w_m. Then the optimal solution has the components

$$x_m = \beta/w_m, \quad \text{where } v_m/w_m = \max(v_j/w_j)$$
$$x_j = 0 \quad \text{if} \quad j \neq m. \tag{3}$$

(If several indices m maximize v_m/w_m, pick any one of them.)

In real numbers the knapsack problem (2) is a trivial standard maximum problem. If we call this the primal problem, then formula (3) gives the optimal primal solution, and

$$y_1 = v_m/w_m \qquad (4)$$

gives the optimal dual solution, satisfying

$$y_1 w_j \geqslant v_j \qquad (j = 1, \ldots, n), \quad y_1 \geqslant 0, \quad \beta y_1 = \min.$$

The optimal value for primal and dual is $\beta v_m/w_m$.

For instance, look at this problem:

$$51x_1 + 50x_2 + 50x_3 \leqslant 100, \quad x_j \geqslant 0$$
$$150x_1 + 100x_2 + 99x_3 = \max. \qquad (5)$$

Here $m = 1$ gives the maximum value-to-weight ratio $150/51$, and the optimal real solution is

$$x_1 = 100/51, \quad x_2 = 0, \quad x_3 = 0; \qquad (6)$$

the total value is $15,000/51 = 294.12$.

In integers the solution is entirely different; it is

$$x_1 = 0, \quad x_2 = 2, \quad x_3 = 0. \qquad (7)$$

The total value goes down to 200. Remember this example when you're tempted to solve an integer program by first solving in reals and then rounding off. If you round off the real solution (6), what you get is nothing like the integer solution (7); and if you round off the real maximum 294.12, the result is far from the integer maximum 200.

The next example will introduce the cutting-plane method. The idea is to convert the integer requirement to new equation constraints. The successive extended linear programs are solved for *real* solutions. When finally an optimal real solution happens to have all components integers, this solution must be optimal for the original integer program.

EXAMPLE 4. Consider this problem in integers:

$$2x_1 - x_2 = 5, \quad x \geqslant 0, \quad x_1 + x_2 = \min. \qquad (8)$$

In real numbers the optimal basic solution is $x_1 = \frac{5}{2}, x_2 = 0$. Of course, you can guess the solution in integers, but pretend you can't, or you'll ruin my example.

In real numbers, the optimal basic variable is x_1. The basis matrix has only the component 2; the inverse has only the component $\frac{1}{2}$. Multiplying the constraint equation by the inverse of the basis, we get

$$x_1 - \tfrac{1}{2}x_2 = \tfrac{5}{2}. \qquad (9)$$

The fractional parts of the non-basic coefficients are

$$\{-\tfrac{1}{2}\} = \tfrac{1}{2}, \quad \{\tfrac{5}{2}\} = \tfrac{1}{2}.$$

(Every real number λ equals an integer $[\lambda]$ plus a fractional part $\{\lambda\}$ with $0 \leqslant \{\lambda\} < 1$.) If x_1 and x_2 are integers, equation (9) implies the congruence

$$\tfrac{1}{2}x_2 \equiv \tfrac{1}{2}, \tag{10}$$

where the congruence sign "$\equiv$" means "differs by an integer from." (For example, $2.718 \equiv 0.718 \equiv -39.282$.) Thus, the congruence (10) is equivalent to an equation

$$\tfrac{1}{2}x_2 = \tfrac{1}{2} + z_1 \qquad (z_1 = \text{integer}). \tag{11}$$

But we have required $x_1 \geqslant 0, x_2 \geqslant 0$. Therefore, the left-hand side must be $\geqslant 0$. *Therefore, the integer z_1 must be $\geqslant 0$.* This is the point. The constraint (11) is new: the old optimal real solution ($x_1 = \tfrac{5}{2}, x_2 = 0$) doesn't solve the new constraint, but an optimal *integer* solution must solve it.

So now we have an extended problem, with a new equation and a new unknown:

$$\begin{aligned} 2x_1 - x_2 &= 5 \\ -z_1 \qquad + \tfrac{1}{2}x_2 &= \tfrac{1}{2} \\ x_1 + x_2 &= \min \end{aligned} \qquad (z_1 \geqslant 0, x_1 \geqslant 0, x_2 \geqslant 0) \tag{12}$$

An optimal integer solution of the original problem (8) must be an optimal integer solution of (12).

For the extended problem (12) we compute the optimal *real* solution, obtaining

$$z_1 = 0, \quad x_1 = 3, \quad x_2 = 1. \tag{13}$$

(The optimal dual solution is $y_1 = \tfrac{1}{2}, y_2 = 3$, and the primal-dual optimum is $c^T x = y^T b = 4$.) The optimal real solution (13) happens to have integer components. Therefore, it is an optimal integer solution of the extended problem (12); and therefore, it is an optimal *integer* solution of the original problem (8).

Gomory's cutting plane. In general, consider the canonical program (1) in integers. Suppose all the given components a_{ij}, b_i, c_j are integers; suppose the set of real feasible solutions is bounded; and suppose an integer feasible solution exists.

Without loss of generality, suppose $x_1, \ldots, x_m$ are the basic variables in an optimal basic *real* solution x^0 (with $x_j^0 = 0$ for $m < j \leqslant n$). If all the x_i^0 are integers, we're done; for then x^0 is a vector with integer components that is optimal over the larger class of reals. (If the best tennis player in the U.S. lives in Nevada, he must be the best tennis player in Nevada.)

But suppose the optimal basic real vector x^0 has some component that is not an integer, say $x_1^0 \neq$ integer. Then we will construct a new equation that x^0 does not satisfy but that an optimal integer solution must satisfy.

First, we multiply the system $Ax = b$ by the inverse of the basis matrix. If the basic variables are $x_1, \ldots, x_m$, the result has the form

$$x_i + \sum_{j > m} t_{ij} x_j = t_{i0} \qquad (i = 1, \ldots, m). \tag{14}$$

The numbers t_{ij} are components of the simplex tableau. If we set $x_j = 0$ for $j > m$, we get the basic components of the optimal real solution x^0:

$$x_i^0 = t_{i0} \geq 0 \qquad (i = 1, \ldots, m).$$

We assume that $t_{10} \neq$ integer.

Look at the single equation

$$x_1 + \sum_{j > m} t_{1j} x_j = t_{10}.$$

If this equation is satisfied by *integers* $x_1, x_{m+1}, \ldots, x_n$, then we have the congruence

$$\sum_{j > m} \{t_{1j}\} x_j \equiv \{t_{10}\}, \tag{15}$$

as in the example (10). The right-hand side satisfies $0 < \{t_{10}\} < 1$; all terms on the left are ≥ 0 because the problem (1) requires $x \geq 0$. (All the fractional parts $\{t_{ij}\}$ are ≥ 0 by definition.) Therefore, either the two sides of the congruence are equal or the left is bigger than the right by an integer. This gives the new constraint

$$\boxed{\sum_{j > m} \{t_{1j}\} x_j = \{t_{10}\} + z_1 \qquad (z_1 \geq 0)} \tag{16}$$

as in the example (11); the new unknown, z_1, is an integer.

Please note this: The old optimal real solution x^0 fails to solve this constraint but an optimal integer solution must solve it.

If we append the equation (16) to the original system of equations, we obtain an extended system of equations, with one more equation and one more unknown, as in the example (12). To continue, we compute an optimal real solution x^1 for the extended system. If all components of x^1 are integers, then x^1 provides an optimal integer solution for the original problem. If not, we get a new inequality exactly as we got the inequality (16). This gives a second extension. And so on.

Ralph Gomory proved that this process succeeds in a finite number of steps. Finally one gets an extended problem with an optimal real solution x^p whose components are all integers. Then x^p must be an optimal integer solution of the original problem.

The proof of Gomory's theorem is difficult. If I could simplify it, I would present it to you. Instead, I'll give you references to some of Gomory's papers and to some texts on integer programming.

As you saw, the general problem of integer programming is difficult because even if all the data are integers, the optimal real solution generally isn't a solution in integers. But there is an important class of integer programs for which an optimal real solution *is* a solution in integers. These problems are called *network flows*; I'll tell you about them next.

References

1. R. E. Gomory, "An Algorithm for Integer Solutions to Linear Programs," in *Recent Advances in Mathematical Programming* (eds.: Graves and Wolfe), McGraw-Hill, 1963.
2. R. E. Gomory, "All Integer Programming Algorithm," in *Industrial Scheduling* (eds.: Muth and Thompson), Prentice Hall, 1963.
3. T. C. Hu, *Integer Programming and Network Flows*, Addison-Wesley, 1969.
4. H. M. Salkin, *Integer Programming*, Addison-Wesley, 1975.

PROBLEMS

1. Consider the knapsack problem (5) with the added constraints $x_j \leqslant 1$ ($j = 1, 2, 3$). Find the optimal *real* solution x^0, and find the optimal *integer* solution x^1.

*2. Consider the general knapsack problem (2) with the added constraints $x_j \leqslant 1$ ($j = 1, \ldots, n$). Find the optimal *real* solution x^0. Write the dual program, and find the optimal dual solution y^0; verify the equality of the primal and dual optimal values. Would you expect equality of the primal and dual optimal values for *integer* programming?

3. Suppose x_1, x_2, x_3 are integers $\geqslant 0$ satisfying

$$21.7x_1 - 18.2x_2 - 19.4x_3 = 5.3$$

Then show

$$7x_1 + 8x_2 + 6x_3 = 3 + 10z_1$$

where all four unknowns are integers $\geqslant 0$.

4. Consider the problem

$$21.7x_1 - 18.2x_2 - 19.4x_3 = 2.3$$
$$x \geqslant 0, \quad x_1 + x_2 + x_3 = \min.$$

Find the optimal *integer* solution.

5. Consider the linear program

$$\begin{bmatrix} 1 & 2 & 3 \\ 3 & 5 & 6 \end{bmatrix} x = \begin{bmatrix} 4 \\ 11 \end{bmatrix}, \quad x \geqslant 0, \quad x_2 = \min.$$

Show that the optimal *real* solution is $x^0 = (3, 0, \frac{1}{3})^T$. Multiply by the inverse basis matrix to obtain

$$x_1 \quad + \; x_2 = 3$$
$$x_3 + \tfrac{1}{3}x_2 = \tfrac{1}{3}$$

Show that the last equation for *integers* $\geqslant 0$ implies $x_2 = 1 + 3z_1$ where x_2 and z_1 are integers $\geqslant 0$.

6. (Continuation.) Consider the linear program

$$\begin{bmatrix} 1 & 2 & 3 & 0 \\ 3 & 5 & 6 & 0 \\ 0 & 1 & 0 & -3 \end{bmatrix} \bar{x} = \begin{bmatrix} 4 \\ 11 \\ 1 \end{bmatrix}, \quad \bar{x} \geqslant 0, \quad \bar{x}_2 = \min.$$

Show that an optimal real solution $\bar{x}$ has the components $2, 1, 0, 0$. Now find an optimal *integer* solution x for Problem 5.

7. The knapsack problem in formula (5) is a standard maximum problem. Restate the problem as a canonical minimum problem, and find the optimal integer solution by Gomory's method.

16 Network Flows

Network flows are integer linear programs with an extraordinary property: some optimal *real* solution is an optimal *integer* solution.

The original theory was discovered by L. R. Ford and D. R. Fulkerson. It has its own theorems and its own algorithms—you don't have to use the simplex method. It has applications ranging from industrial scheduling to combinatorial analysis. But mainly, it's fun.

The basic mathematical model is a *capacitated network* (N,k). The network N is just a finite set of points

$$N = \{s,a,b,\dots,s'\}.$$

Two of the points are special: the *source*, s, and the *sink*, s'. The points in N are sometimes called *nodes*. If x and y are distinct nodes, we'll call (x,y) an edge. The edge (y,x) is different from the edge (x,y). For each edge, we define a *capacity* $k(x,y) \geqslant 0$. We suppose k takes integer values; we don't require $k(y,x) = k(x,y)$.

EXAMPLE 1. In Figure 1 you see a capacitated network.

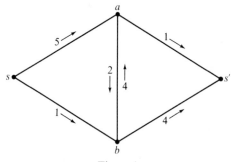

Figure 1

This network has four nodes: s, a, b, s'. Therefore, the number of directed edge must be $4 \cdot 3 = 12$, and for each edge we must have a capacity k. In Figure 1 you see only 6 capacities; those you don't see are assumed to be zero. For instance, you see $k(s,a) = 5$; you don't see $k(a,s)$, so it's zero.

Flows. Suppose (N,k) is a capacitated network with at least one node besides the source and the sink. A flow $f(x,y)$ is an integer-valued function on the edges (x, y); it must have these properties:

   (i) $f(x, y) = -f(y,x)$
   (ii) $f(x, y) \leqslant k(x, y)$
   (iii) $\sum_{y \in N} f(x, y) = 0$ if $x \neq s$ or s'.
   (iv) $f(s,x) \geqslant 0$; $f(x,s') \geqslant 0$.

   Property (i) says that a positive flow from x to y is considered a negative flow from y to x. Property (ii) says that the flow from x to y shouldn't exceed the capacity of that edge. Property (iii) is a conservation law for the interior nodes x: the *net* flow out of x should be zero. Property (iv) says the flow *from* the source may be positive, but not negative; and the flow *into* the sink may be positive, but not negative.

   As you see, $f \equiv 0$ is always an admissible flow. The value of this flow is zero.

   The value of a flow f is defined as

$$v(f) = \sum_x f(s,x). \tag{1}$$

This is the total flow out of the source. As you'll soon see, it's also the total flow into the sink.

EXAMPLE 2. Figure 2.1 and 2.2 give admissible flows for the capacitated network in Figure 1. The first flow has value 1; the second flow has value 4.

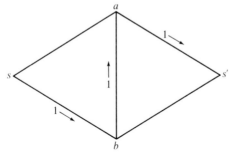

Figure 2.1

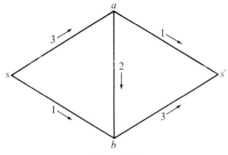

Figure 2.2

The second flow is a *maximal flow*: its value is as big as possible. If you don't believe it, look at Figure 1 and see if you can do better.

Draw a curve around the nodes s and a, as in Figure 2.3; call this subset C. If you look at the capacitated network in Figure 1, you'll see that the total capacity *out* of C is

$$k(s,b) + k(a,b) + k(a,s') = 1 + 2 + 1 = 4. \tag{2}$$

This must be an upper bound for the value of any admissible flow. Since the flow in Figure 2.2 achieves this value, it must be maximal.

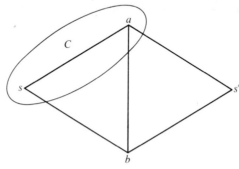

Figure 2.3

Notation. If A and B are subsets of nodes, we define

$$k(A,B) = \sum_{x \in A} \sum_{y \in B} k(x,y), \tag{3}$$

and we define $f(A,B)$ the same way. In this notation property (iii) becomes

$$f(x,N) = 0 \quad \text{if} \quad x \neq s \quad \text{or} \quad s',$$

and the value of the flow is $v(f) = f(s,N)$. We always assume $k(x,x) = f(x,x) = 0$. If $B = A$, we must have $f(A,A) = 0$; that follows from the anti-symmetry property (i).

Cuts. Let C be a subset of the nodes that includes the source but not the sink. Let C' be the complement $N - C$. Thus, C' includes the sink but not the source. The complementary pair C, C' is called a *cut* in the network N.

The capacity of the cut is $k(C,C')$. If f is a flow in the capacitated network (N,k), then $f(C,C')$ is the flow from C to C', and it must satisfy the inequality

$$f(C,C') \leq k(C,C'). \tag{4}$$

That is because we require $f(x,y) \leq k(x,y)$ for every edge.

Different flows have different values; different cuts have different capacities. We called a flow with maximum value a *maximal flow*; we'll call a cut with minimum capacity a *minimal cut*. Later, we will prove the max-flow, min-cut theorem:

Theorem. *Let (N,k) be a capacitated network. Then f_0 is a maximal flow and C_0, C_0' is a minimal cut if and only if*

$$f_0(C_0,C_0') = k(C_0,C_0'). \tag{5}$$

First, let me give you an example of different cuts and different flows in a single capacitated network.

EXAMPLE 3. From Figure 1 let us tabulate all the cuts C, C' and all their capacities, $k(C,C')$.

C	C'	$k(C,C')$
s	a, b, s'	$5 + 1 = 6$
s, a	b, s'	$1 + 2 + 1 = 4$
s, b	a, s'	$5 + 4 + 4 = 13$
s, a, b	s'	$1 + 4 = 5$

Evidently, the second cut is minimal; its capacity equals 4.

In Figure 2.1 and 2.2 you see two different flows in this network. The first flow has value 1; the second has value 4. The second flow is maximal, as we showed after equation (2). As you see, the value of the maximal flow equals the capacity of the minimal cut.

In Figure 2.3 the subset C and its complement are the minimal cut. For the optimal flow, in Figure 2.2, you see that the flow across this cut equals 4, which is the capacity of this cut.

As our example shows, different cuts have different capacities, and different flows have different values. But for *each* flow f the number $f(C,C')$ is the same for *all* cuts C, C':

Lemma. *If f is a flow in (N,k), then the value of the flow satisfies*

$$v(f) = f(C,C')$$

for all cuts C, C'.

PROOF. Because $f(x,y) = -f(y,x)$, we have $f(C,C) = 0$. Therefore,

$$f(C,C') = f(C,C') + f(C,C)$$
$$= f(C,N).$$

But

$$f(C,N) = \sum_{x \in C} f(x,N) = f(s,N),$$

since we require $f(x,N) = 0$ unless $x = s$ or s'. By definition, $f(s,N) = v(f)$.

Thus, the value of a flow equals the flow $f(C,C')$ across *every* cut. Please verify this for the flows in Figures 2.1 and 2.2. Now we can prove the theorem.

PROOF OF THE THEOREM. By assumption, the function $f(x,y)$ is integer-valued. The value $v(f)$ is bounded above by the capacity of any cut. Therefore a maximal flow f_0 exists.

Given the maximal flow f_0, we choose a subset C_0 as follows. We call an edge (x, y) *unsaturated* if

$$f_0(x, y) < k(x, y). \tag{6}$$

We call the *path* $x_0, x_1, x_2, \ldots, x_k$ unsaturated if all of the k edges (x_{i-1}, x_i) are unsaturated. Now we let C_0 consist of the source s and all nodes x that can be reached from s by unsaturated paths. (For example, for the network in Figure 1 and the optimal flow in Figure 2.2 the set C_0 consists of s and a.)

We assert that C_0 cannot contain the sink s'. If C_0 contained s', there would be an unsaturated path going from s to s'. Along this path, in every edge, we could increase f_0 by $+1$ to obtain a new flow f_1. For every interior node x on the path, the flow *into* x would increase by 1 and the flow *out of* x would increase by 1, leaving the net flow $f_1(x, N) = 0$. For the source, the outward flow would increase by 1: $f_1(s, N) = 1 + f_0(s, N)$. So the value of the flow would increase by $+1$, contradicting the maximality of f_0.

Since C_0 contains s but not s', the complementary sets C_0, C_0' form a cut. We now assert

$$f_0(x, x') = k(x, x') \quad \text{if} \quad x \in C_0 \quad \text{and} \quad x' \in C_0'. \tag{7}$$

Proof: Otherwise the edge (x, x') would be unsaturated; then we could reach x' by an unsaturated path going first from s to x and then from x to x'. Then x' would lie not in C_0' but in C_0, since we could reach it by an unsaturated path.

Summing the equations (7), we get $f_0(C_0, C_0') = k(C_0, C_0')$, which is the required equation (5).

Conversely, this equation implies that the flow is maximal and the cut is minimal. For if f is any competing flow, we must have

$$f(C_0, C_0') \leqslant k(C_0, C_0') = f_0(C_0, C_0'),$$

so $v(f) \leqslant v(f_0)$; and if C, C' is any competing cut, we must have

$$k(C, C') \geqslant f_0(C, C') = f_0(C_0, C_0') = k(C_0, C_0'),$$

so $k(C, C') \geqslant k(C_0, C_0')$.   □

EXAMPLE 4. Figure 4.1 shows an optimal flow f_0 for the capacitated network in Figure 4.2. Please look at the subset C_0; check that $f_0(C_0, C_0') = k(C_0, C_0')$.

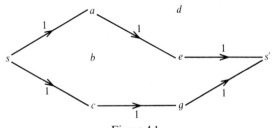

Figure 4.1

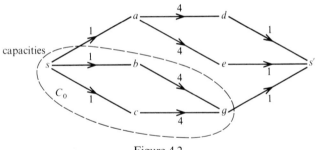

Figure 4.2

The node b can be reached by the unsaturated path s, b. The node g can be reached by the unsaturated path s, b, g.

But what about the node c? Why did I put this node in C_0? Isn't the path s, c saturated?

Yes, it is. But I can reach c by another path, which you might not think of:

$$s, b, g, c.$$

This path has three edges. The figures show that the first two edges are unsaturated. But so is the last one:

$$f_0(g,c) = -f_0(c,g) = -1 < 0 = k(g,c).$$

The point is this: A positive flow in an edge always induces a negative flow in the reverse direction, and so it produces an unsaturated reverse edge, since all capacities are $\geqslant 0$. You have to remember this point when you use the following algorithm.

The unsaturated-path algorithm. The preceding proof suggests a way to construct an optimal flow. Given the capacitated network (N,k), start with any feasible flow, say $f_1(x, y) \equiv 0$. Now let C_1 be the set consisting of s and of all nodes that can be reached from s by unsaturated paths; you can locate these nodes recursively, starting from s. The set C_1 depends on the given (N,k), but also depends on the current feasible flow. If s' lies outside C_1, then f_1 is optimal, as the preceding proof shows; for then $f_1(C_1,C_1') = k(C_1,C_1')$.

If s' lies inside C_1, you can get a better flow. Let $s, a, b, \ldots, s'$ be an unsaturated path from s to s'. Then $f(x, y) < k(x, y)$ on every edge of the path. Since you're dealing with integers, there is a largest positive integer $\varDelta$ such that

$$f_1(x, y) + \varDelta \leqslant k(x, y)$$

for all edges on the path. Now let

$$f_2(x, y) = f_1(x, y) + \varDelta \text{ on the path.}$$

For f_2 to be feasible, let $f_2(y,x) = -f_2(x, y)$ in the reversed edges; and let $f_2(u,v) = f_1(u,v)$ in all the remaining edges of the network.

The new flow is feasible for this reason: If y is any interior node of the path, you've increased the flow into y by Δ, but you've also increased the flow out of y by Δ, keeping the net flow zero.

The new flow is better because the flow out of s has increased by $\Delta \geqslant 1$. Now proceed as before. Form the set C_2 consisting of s and all nodes that can be reached from s by unsaturated paths. If s' lies outside C_2, you're done; if not, you can get a better flow f_3. And so on.

The process must yield an optimal flow f_p in a finite number of steps because

$$k(s,N) \geqslant f_{n+1}(s,N) = f_n(s,N) + \Delta_n(n = 1, 2, \ldots)$$

with $\Delta_n \geqslant 1$.

EXAMPLE 5. Let's use this algorithm on the network (N,k) in Figure 1. We'll start with $f_1 \equiv 0$. Then C_1 is all of N. Let π_1 be the path s, a, s'. Then $\Delta_1 = 1$, and we get the flow f_2 in Figure 5.

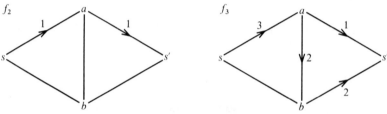

Figure 5

Now the unsaturated path s, a, b, s' has excess capacity $\Delta_2 = 2$. By adding 2 to f_2 along the path, we get the new flow f_3. For f_3 there is only one unsaturated path to s', namely, s, b, s'. By increasing f_3 by the excess capacity $\Delta_3 = 1$ along the path, we get the optimal flow f_4, which appears in Figure 2.2.

Network flows as linear programming. You can state any network-flow problem as a linear program. Given (N,k), let's number the nodes $1, 2, \ldots, n$, with $s = 1$ and $s' = n$. Let k_{ij} be the capacity of the edge (i,j) and let f_{ij} be the flow. Then we require

$$f_{ij} \leqslant k_{ij} \qquad (i,j = 1, \ldots, n)$$
$$f_{ij} + f_{ji} = 0$$

$$\sum_{j=1}^{n} f_{ij} = 0 \qquad (i = 2, \ldots, n-1) \tag{8}$$

$$\sum_{j=2}^{n} f_{1j} = \text{max.}$$

That's one way to state the max-flow problem.

Another way is this. Think of the flow f_{1j} as x_{ij} if the flow is ≥ 0; otherwise, let $x_{ij} = 0$. Using the unknowns $x_{ij} \geq 0$ for $i \neq j$, we get this problem:

$$x_{ij} \leq k_{ij} \qquad (i,j = 1, \ldots, n; i \neq j)$$

$$\sum_{j=2}^{n} x_{ij} - \sum_{k=1}^{n-1} x_{ki} = 0 \qquad (i = 2, \ldots, n-1) \tag{9}$$

$$\sum_{j=2}^{n} x_{1j} = \max$$

This formulation is more in the spirit of linear programming, since we abandon the algebraic flows f_{ij} and use the nonnegative unknowns x_{ij}. Note that the formulation (9) uses fewer constraints than (8) does.

Integer versus real programming. Given the integer capacities $k(x,y) \geq 0$, we have stated the maximum-flow problem for the best *integer* flow $f(x,y)$. As you've just seen, we can restate this problem as an integer linear program (9). Suppose we broaden the domain of competing flows by allowing real non-integer flows. Then we might expect to get a bigger maximum value $f(s,N)$. But that is false; *for this special class of linear programs the maximum over integers equals the maximum over reals.*

PROOF. Let f_r be any admissible *real* flow. Then for all cuts C, C' we must have

$$v(f_r) = f_r(C,C') \leq k(C,C').$$

In particular, this must be true for the cut C_0, C_0' that appears in the proof of the max-flow, min-cut theorem. That particular cut satisfied

$$k(C_0,C_0') = f_0(C_0,C_0') = v(f_0),$$

where f_0 was a maximal *integer* flow. Therefore, we must have

$$v(f_r) \leq k(C_0,C_0') = v(f_0),$$

and so we cannot increase $\max v(f)$ by using non-integer flows.

EXAMPLE 6. For the network (N,k) in Figure 6 there *are* non-integer maximal flows; but for all of them $v(f) = 1$, as for the two maximal integer flows.

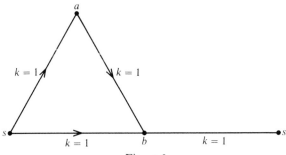

Figure 6

For instance, we could let $f(s,a) = f(a,b) = f(s,b) = \frac{1}{2}$, $f(b,s') = 1$, giving $v(f) = 1$.

I'll give you some applications of network flows in the next section.

References

1. L. R. Ford, Jr., and D. R. Fulkerson, Maximal Flow Through a Network, *Can. J. Math.*, Vol. 8, pp. 399–404, 1956.
2. L. R. Ford, Jr., and D. R. Fulkerson, A Simple Algorithm for Finding Maximal Network Flows and an Application to the Hitchcock Problem, *Can. J. Math.*, Vol. 9, pp. 210–218, 1957.

PROBLEMS

1. Let $N = \{s,a,b,s'\}$. Let the nonzero capacities be

$$k(s,a) = 5, \quad k(a,s') = 2, \quad k(a,b) = 1.$$
$$k(s,b) = 7, \quad k(b,a) = 6, \quad k(b,s') = 9.$$

Draw a picture of the capacitated network (N,k). Make a table of all cuts and capacities (see Example 3). Identify the minimal cut and its capacity $k(C_0,C_0')$.

2. For the network in Problem 1 find the maximal flow f_0 by inspection. Verify formula (7) for this example, and verify that $v(f_0) = k(C_0,C_0')$.

3. Start with $f \equiv 0$, and find the optimal flow f_0 in Problem 2 systematically by the unsaturated-path algorithm.

*4. For the capacited network (N,k), suppose some capacities *into* the source are positive: $k(x,s) > 0$. Show that all these capacities may be replaced by zero without affecting the maximum flow value $v(f)$. (Method: Call the new capacity function k^*, and show that $k(C,C') = k^*(C,C')$ for all cuts.) Similarly, show that positive capacities out of the sink may be replaced by zero.

5. If the network N has m interior nodes, show that the number of cuts equals 2^m.

6. If the network N has m interior nodes, show that the number of unsaturated paths from s to s' has the upper bound $m + m(m-1) + \cdots + m!$

7. Using formula (9), write a linear program equivalent to Example 1.

8. Find a maximal flow and a minimal cut for this symmetric capacitated network:

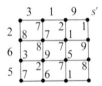

*9. Show that you never have to use flows around loops: Let f be a flow in (N,k). Suppose the flow is positive in every edge in the directed loop $a, b, c, \ldots, a$. If $\varDelta$ is the least of those edge flows, show that $\varDelta$ may be subtracted from every edge flow in the loop to produce a new admissible flow with the same value. Let $\sigma(f)$ be the sum of all the *positive* edge flows $f(x, y)$ in the network. Let f_0 be a maximal flow in (N,k), and let f_0 minimize $\sigma(f)$ over the maximal flows. Deduce that f_0 has no positive flow around any loop.

10. Suppose we generalize network-flow theory by allowing more than one source and more than one sink. Show how to handle this generalization by using only one source and one sink.

17 Assignment and Shortest-Route Problems

In the last section, we proved the max-flow, min-cut theorem, and we discussed the unsaturated-path algorithm for computing a maximal flow. As a first application, I want to show you the *simple-assignment problem*.

This problem is usually stated in terms of *individuals* and *jobs*, but this usage is only figurative. The simple-assignment problem is not a serious problem of personnel management, but it is an interesting problem of combinatorial analysis. In that context it was first solved by P. Hall in 1935.

Suppose we have individuals $i = 1, \ldots, m$ and jobs $j = 1, \ldots, n$. If individual i qualifies for job j, we'll set $q_{ij} = 1$; if not, we'll set $q_{ij} = 0$. The matrix $Q = (q_{ij})$ is called the *qualification matrix*; it has m rows and n columns; all of its components are ones and zeros.

Rules. Each individual may take at most one job; each job may be taken by at most one individual. Individual i may take job j only if $q_{ij} = 1$.

Objective. Assign jobs to as many individuals as possible.

Statement as integer linear programming. Let $x_{ij} = 1$ if individual i takes job j; otherwise let $x_{ij} = 0$. Then the rules say this:

$$\sum_j x_{ij} \leqslant 1$$
$$\sum_i x_{ij} \leqslant 1. \qquad (x_{ij} \geqslant 0, x_{ij} \text{ integer}) \qquad (1)$$
$$x_{ij} \leqslant q_{ij}$$

The objective is to maximize the number of assignments:

$$\sum_i \sum_j x_{ij} = \max. \qquad (2)$$

Statement as network flow. We define the network

$$N: s, a_1, \ldots, a_m, b_1, \ldots, b_n, s', \qquad (3)$$

which contains a source, the m individuals, the n jobs, and a sink. We define the capacities

$$k(s,a_i) = 1 \ (i = 1, \ldots, m); \quad k(b_j,s') = 1 \ (j = 1, \ldots, n)$$
$$k(a_i,b_j) = Mq_{ij},$$

$$(4)$$

where M is a positive integer.

Thus, if individual i qualifies for job j, the capacity $k(a_i,b_j)$ is a positive integer M; otherwise this capacity equals zero. Later we will set $M = m + 1$ in order to prove a theorem. But right now, suppose M is any positive integer.

Suppose x_{ij} gives an assignment that satisfies the rules (1). Then define the flow f as follows:

$$f(a_i,b_j) = x_{ij}$$
$$f(s,a_i) = \sum_j x_{ij}$$
$$f(b_j,s') = \sum_i x_{ij}.$$

$$(5)$$

For the reverse edges use the opposite (negative) flows; for all other edges set $f(x,y) = 0$.

The flow f is admissible for the capacitated network (N,k) because

$$f(s,a_i) = \sum_j x_{ij} \leqslant 1 = k(s,a_i)$$
$$f(a_i,b_j) = x_{ij} \leqslant q_{ij} \leqslant Mq_{ij} = k(a_i,b_j)$$
$$f(b_j,s') = \sum_i x_{ij} \leqslant 1 = k(b_j,s').$$

$$(6)$$

The value of the flow is

$$v(f) = f(s,N) = \sum_i f(s,a_i) = \sum_i \sum_j x_{ij}.$$

$$(7)$$

This is the number of assignments, which we want to maximize.

Conversely, if f is an admissible flow, then $x_{ij} = f(a_i,b_j)$ defines a feasible assignment, satisfying (1). You see, (4) and (5) imply

$$\sum_{j=1}^n x_{ij} = f(s,a_i) \leqslant 1$$
$$\sum_{i=1}^m x_{ij} = f(b_j,s') \leqslant 1$$
$$(x_{ij} = \text{integer} \geqslant 0)$$

$$(8)$$

$$x_{ij} \leqslant Mq_{ij} \quad (i = 1, \ldots, m; j = 1, \ldots, n).$$

These three conditions are the same three conditions that occur in (1) with one exception: the inequality $x_{ij} \leqslant q_{ij}$ in (1) is replaced by $x_{ij} \leqslant Mq_{ij}$ in (8), where M may be any positive integer. This exception makes no difference, for the first two conditions imply $x_{ij} \leqslant 1$, and so $x_{ij} \leqslant Mq_{ij}$ implies $x_{ij} \leqslant q_{ij}$.

Therefore, $x_{ij} = f(a_i, b_j)$ is feasible for (1). By the way, $f(a_i, b_j)$ can't be negative, because we require

$$-f(a_i, b_j) = f(b_j, a_i) \leqslant k(b_j, a_i) = 0.$$

Thus, f is an admissible flow in (N, k) if and only if $x_{ij} = f(a_i, b_j)$ is a feasible assignment, satisfying (1). The value of the flow equals the number of job assignments (7). *The number of assignments is maximized by a maximal flow.*

EXAMPLE 1. Look at the capacitated network in Figure 1. Here we have 3 persons and 3 jobs. The first person qualifies for the first two jobs; the other two persons qualify only for the third job.

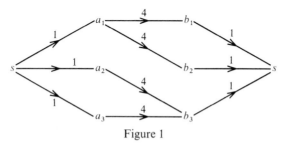

Figure 1

At most two assignments are possible. The first person takes either job 1 or job 2; the second or the third person takes job 3. Correspondingly, there are four maximal flows f; please draw all of them. All four maximal flows have value $v(f) = 2$, which is the biggest possible number of assignments.

Algorithm. Suppose you're given a qualification matrix (q_{ij}), and you want to compute the maximum number of assignments. All you have to do is set up the flow model and apply the unsaturated-path algorithm described in the preceding section.

Complete assignment. Suppose we want to assign *all* m individuals to jobs. An obvious necessary condition is $m \leqslant n$: there must be as many jobs as individuals. But more than that is necessary. Look at Figure 1. There are three individuals and three jobs. Good. But a complete assignment is obviously impossible, because two of the individuals qualify for only one job; there is no admissible assignment for both these individuals (a_2 and a_3).

In general, let I be any subset of individuals. Let $J(I)$ be the subset of jobs for which at least one member of I qualifies. Then the number $|I|$ must be $\leqslant$ the number $|J(I)|$:

$$|I| \leqslant |J(I)|. \tag{9}$$

This must be true for all of the 2^m subsets I.

In Figure 1 we saw this condition violated. For the subset $I = \{a_2, a_3\}$ we found $J(I) = \{b_3\}$, and so $|I| = 2 > |J(I)| = 1$. (There are seven other subsets I, all of which do satisfy (9).)

So (9) is a necessary condition for a complete assignment. Is it also sufficient? Yes. P. Hall proved it in 1935. We will prove it now by using the max-flow, min-cut theorem.

Theorem. *A complete assignment is possible if and only if* $|I| \leqslant |J(I)|$ *for every subset* $I \subset \{a_1, \ldots, a_m\}$.

PROOF. As we've noted, a complete assignment implies the inequality (9) for every subset I. Conversely, let's suppose (9) holds and construct a complete assignment.

Given the qualification matrix (q_{ij}), we use equations (3) and (4) to define the capacitated network (N,k); in (4) we will define M as some integer $>m$, say $M = m + 1$.

Let f_0 be a maximal flow in (N,k). Then (5) implies

$$v(f_0) = f(s,N) = \sum_i f(s,a_i) = \sum_i \sum_j x_{ij}, \tag{10}$$

so the value of a maximal flow equals the maximum possible number of assignments. Thus, we have

$$0 \leqslant v(f_0) \leqslant m, \tag{11}$$

and we want to prove $v(f_0) = m$ if we assume all $|I| \leqslant |J(I)|$.

Let C_0, C_0' be a minimal cut. According to the max-flow, min-cut theorem, we have

$$v(f_0) = k(C_0, C_0'). \tag{12}$$

Let's take a close look at the complementary sets C_0, C_0'.

The set C_0 contains the source, some individuals, and some jobs:

$$C_0 = \{s, I_0, J_0\}.$$

The complement C_0' contains the other individuals, the other jobs, and the sink:

$$C_0' = \{I_0', J_0', s'\}.$$

The capacity of the cut equals

$$k(C_0, C_0') = k(s, I_0') + k(I_0, J_0') + k(J_0, s') \tag{13}$$

because the other three possible terms all equal zero:

$$k(s, J_0') = k(s, s') = k(I_0, s') = 0.$$

Formulas (12) and (13) imply

$$v(f_0) = k(s, I_0') + k(I_0, J_0') + k(J_0, s'). \tag{14}$$

Now you'll see the purpose of using $M > m$. According to (4), all capacities between individuals a_i and jobs b_j equal 0 or M. Therefore, in (14) the term $k(I_0, J_0')$ equals one of the integers $0, M, 2M, 3M, \ldots$. But the sum

$v(f_0)$ must be $\leqslant m$; therefore $k(I_0, J_0') = 0$, and so (14) becomes

$$v(f_0) = k(s, I_0') + k(J_0, s'),$$

or

$$v(f_0) = |I_0'| + |J_0|. \tag{15}$$

We're almost done. Using $M > m$, we proved $k(I_0, J_0') = 0$. That says no individual in I_0 is qualified for any job in J_0'. Therefore,

$$J(I_0) \subset J_0. \tag{16}$$

This says that the individuals in I_0 can qualify only for jobs in J_0. Now, at last, we'll use the inequality (9): $|I_0| \leqslant |J(I_0)|$. Now (16) implies

$$|I_0| \leqslant |J(I_0)| \leqslant |J_0|. \tag{17}$$

Therefore,

$$|I_0'| = m - |I_0| \geqslant m - |J_0|,$$

and (15) yields

$$v(f_0) = |I_0'| + |J_0| \geqslant m.$$

By (11), we have $v(f_0) = m$, and so the maximal flow f_0 gives a complete assignment. ☐

Optimal assignment. We can use the preceding result to solve a somewhat different problem. Again we have m individuals and n jobs, but now we'll assume every individual qualifies for every job. We'll assume that individual i has aptitude $a_{ij} \geqslant 0$ for job j. We want to assign individuals to jobs so as to maximize the sum $\sum a_{ij}$ over all the assignments $i \to j$. Again we assume the exclusion rules: at most one job per individual; at most one individual per job.

Again we'll use the unknowns x_{ij}. We'll say $x_{ij} = 1$ if we assign i to j; otherwise $x_{ij} = 0$. Now the exclusion rules say

$$\sum_{j=1}^{n} x_{ij} \leqslant 1 \qquad (i = 1, \ldots, m)$$

$$\sum_{i=1}^{m} x_{ij} \leqslant 1 \qquad (j = 1, \ldots, n) \tag{18}$$

$$x_{ij} = \text{integer} \geqslant 0.$$

The objective is to maximize the sum of the aptitudes in the assignment:

$$\sum_{i=1}^{m} \sum_{j=1}^{n} a_{ij} x_{ij} = \max \tag{19}$$

And so we have a problem in integer linear programming. I'll show you how to solve this problem by network flows.

With no loss of generality, we may assume $m = n$. If $m < n$, introduce dummy individuals $i = m + 1, \ldots, n$ with a $a_{ij} = 0$ for all j; if $m > n$, introduce dummy jobs $j = m + 1, \ldots, n$ with $a_{ij} = 0$ for all i. Now we can assign all individuals and fill all jobs, and the problem becomes this:

$$\sum_{j=1}^{n} x_{ij} = 1 \qquad (i = 1, \ldots, n)$$

$$\sum_{i=1}^{n} x_{ij} = 1 \qquad (j = 1, \ldots, n) \tag{20}$$

$$x_{ij} = \text{integer} \geqslant 0$$

$$\sum_{i=1}^{n} \sum_{j=1}^{n} a_{ij} x_{ij} = \max$$

(The unknowns x_{ij} constitute a permutation matrix X of 1's and 0's. Each column will contain exactly one 1, and each row will contain exactly one 1.)

If we ignore the integer constraint, the problem (20) is a canonical linear program for n^2 unknowns $x_{ij} \geqslant 0$. We shall get an optimal solution for all *real* x_{ij}. This solution will happen to consist of integers, and so it will solve the integer program (20).

The *dual* of (20) is this problem:

$$u_i + v_j \geqslant a_{ij} \qquad (i, j = 1, \ldots, n) \tag{21}$$

$$\sum u_i + \sum v_j = \min.$$

For example, if $n = 2$ the primal problem is this:

$$\begin{bmatrix} 1 & 1 & 0 & 0 \\ 0 & 0 & 1 & 1 \\ 1 & 0 & 1 & 0 \\ 0 & 1 & 0 & 1 \end{bmatrix} \begin{bmatrix} x_{11} \\ x_{12} \\ x_{21} \\ x_{22} \end{bmatrix} = \begin{bmatrix} 1 \\ 1 \\ 1 \\ 1 \end{bmatrix}, \quad x \geqslant 0 \tag{22}$$

$$\begin{bmatrix} a_{11} & a_{12} & a_{21} & a_{22} \end{bmatrix} x = \max.$$

Corresponding to the upper and lower halves of the matrix, the dual vector has two parts:

$$y^T = [u_1, u_2, v_1, v_2]. \tag{23}$$

Then this is the dual problem:

$$u_1 + v_1 \geqslant a_{11}, \quad u_1 + v_2 \geqslant a_{12}, \quad u_2 + v_1 \geqslant a_{21}, \quad u_2 + v_2 \geqslant a_{22} \tag{24}$$

$$u_1 + u_2 + v_1 + v_2 = \min.$$

For the primal-dual pair (20), (21), the equilibrium theorem gives a necessary and sufficient condition for optimality. Let x be feasible for the primal, and let u, v be feasible for the dual. Then we require this condition:

$$x_{ij} > 0 \qquad \text{only if } u_i + v_j = a_{ij}. \tag{25}$$

In other words, we require

$$x_{ij} = 0 \quad \text{if} \quad u_i + v_j > a_{ij}.$$

In terms of assignments, the equilibrium theorem says this: If (u,v) is optimal for the dual, then individual i may be assigned to job j only if $u_i + v_j = a_{ij}$. An optimal assignment is a *complete* assignment that satisfies the *equilibrium condition* (25).

Algorithm for optimal assignment. We are given the integers $a_{ij} \geqslant 0$. We pick some integers u_i, v_j satisfying the dual feasibility conditions:

$$u_i + v_j \geqslant a_{ij} \qquad (i,j = 1, \ldots, n). \tag{26}$$

Now we'll say i *qualifies for* j $(q_{ij} = 1)$ if $u_i + v_j = a_{ij}$. This gives us a first *qualification matrix* (q_{ij}). Using this qualification matrix, we use the network-flow model for simple assignment to assign the maximum number of individuals to jobs for which they qualify. As usual, we'll use the assignment variables x_{ij}.

If all individuals have been assigned, we're done. For $i, j = 1, \ldots, n$ we have

$$\sum_{j=1}^{n} x_{ij} = 1, \quad \sum_{i=1}^{n} x_{ij} = 1, \quad x_{ij} = 0 \text{ or } 1,$$

and we also have the equilibrium condition (25). Therefore, x is optimal for the primal (20) and (u,v) is optimal for the dual (21).

But suppose some individuals have not been assigned by the maximal flow. Then x_{ij} isn't feasible for the primal (20), and we still have work to do. We will use the maximal flow to get an improved dual solution. Let f_0 be the maximal flow that we've found for the simple-assignment problem defined by the present qualification matrix (q_{ij}) $(i, j = 1, \ldots, n)$. The value $v(f_0)$ is the maximum number of people that can be assigned, and now we are assuming $v(f_0) < n$ (the assignment is incomplete).

Let C_0, C_0' be a minimal cut. Then its capacity satisfies

$$k(C_0, C_0') = v(f_0) < n. \tag{27}$$

As before, let

$$C_0 = \{s, I_0, J_0\}, \quad C_0' = \{I_0', J_0', s'\}, \tag{28}$$

where I_0, J_0 are subsets of individuals and jobs, and I_0', J_0' are their complements. Then

$$k(C_0, C_0') = k(s, I_0') + k(I_0, J_0') + k(J_0, s'). \tag{29}$$

As before, if $M > n$ we conclude $k(I_0, J_0') = 0$ and

$$\begin{aligned} k(C_0, C_0') &= k(s, I_0') + k(J_0, s') \\ &= |I_0'| + |J_0| = n - |I_0| + |J_0|, \end{aligned} \tag{30}$$

and now (27) implies $n - |I_0| + |J_0| < n$, or

$$|J_0| < |I_0|. \tag{31}$$

As in (16), we have $J(I_0) \subset J_0$ because $k(I_0, J_0') = 0$.

The inequality $|J_0| < |I_0|$ is just what we need to get a better dual solution u, v. By "better" I mean we can decrease the dual object function $\sum u_i + \sum v_j$.

We will let

$$\text{new } u_i = \text{old } u_i - \Delta \qquad (i \in I_0)$$
$$\text{new } v_j = \text{old } v_j + \Delta \qquad (j \in J_0), \tag{32}$$

leaving u_i unchanges for i in I_0', and v_j unchanged for j in J_0'. Then

$$\text{new}\left(\sum u_i + \sum v_j\right) = \text{old}\left(\sum u_i + \sum v_j\right) - (|I_0| - |J_0|)\Delta. \tag{33}$$

Since $|I_0| - |J_0|$ is >0, we will choose Δ as big as we can.

How big can we choose Δ without violating the dual feasibility conditions? We require

$$\text{new } u_i - \text{new } v_j \geqslant a_{ij} \qquad (i,j = 1, \ldots, n). \tag{34}$$

Here i may lie in I_0 or in I_0', while j may lie in J_0 or in J_0'. By (32), $u_i + v_j$ is unchanged if $i \in I_0$ and $j \in J_0$. If $\Delta \geqslant 0$, $u_i + v_j$ can only increase if $i \in I_0'$, since v_j either increases or stays the same. So $u_i + v_j$ can decrease only if $i \in I_0$ and $j \in J_0'$:

$$\text{new}(u_i + v_j) = \text{old}(u_i + v_j) - \Delta \qquad (i \in I_0, j \in J_0'). \tag{35}$$

But we have $k(I_0, J_0') = 0$: no i in I_0 qualifies for any j in J_0' in the minimal cut for simple assignment. In the present context that means

$$\text{old}(u_i + v_j) > a_{ij} \qquad (i \in I_0, j \in J_0'). \tag{36}$$

Remember, we defined "i qualifies for j" to mean that $u_i + v_j$ *equals* a_{ij}. Thus, we shall have

$$\text{old}(u_i + v_j) - \Delta \geqslant a_{ij} \qquad (i,j = 1, \ldots, n) \tag{37}$$

if we choose

$$\Delta = \min\{\text{old}(u_i + v_j) - a_{ij}: i \in I_0, j \in J_0'\}. \tag{38}$$

This is the biggest permissible value for Δ; it is some positive integer, since it equals the minimum discrepancy in the strict integer inequalities (36).

Now we use the new dual solution u, v to define a new qualification matrix (q_{ij}). As before, we say i qualifies for j ($q_{ij} = 1$) if $u_i + v_j = a_{ij}$. This gives a new simple-assignment problem. If the new simple assignment is *complete*, that is, if all n individuals get jobs, then we're done: the x_{ij} solve the original *optimal*-assignment problem (20). But if the assignment is incomplete, then we can improve the dual solution again. And so on.

This process must succeed in a finite number of steps. Why? Because every time we improve the feasible dual solution, we decrease the objective $\sum u_i + \sum v_j$ by at least 1. That can happen only a finite number of times, because the dual objective function has a finite lower bound. Indeed, every feasible primal solution x_{ij} gives a lower bound. For instance, $x_{ii} = 1$, $x_{ij} = 0$ ($i \neq j$) gives the lower bound

$$\sum u_i + \sum v_j \geqslant \sum_i \sum_j a_{ij} x_{ij} = \sum_i a_{ii}. \tag{39}$$

So we must get the optimal assignment in a finite number of steps.

EXAMPLE 2. Let this be the aptitude matrix:

$$(a_{ij}) = \begin{bmatrix} 7 & 2 & 6 \\ 3 & 9 & 1 \\ 8 & 4 & 5 \end{bmatrix}$$

One easy way to get a dual feasible solution is to set

$$u_i = \max_j a_{ij}, \quad v_j = 0.$$

Here this says $u_1 = 7$, $u_2 = 9$, $u_3 = 8$, $v_j = 0$. In Figure 2. the aptitude matrix is inside the square; the u_i are at the left; the v_j are on top.

	0	0	0
7	⑦	2	6
9	3	⑨	1
8	⑧	4	5

Figure 2

I've drawn circles around those a_{ij} for which $u_i + v_j = a_{ij}$. These equations define the first qualification matrix:

$$(q_{ij}) = \begin{bmatrix} 1 & 0 & 0 \\ 0 & 1 & 0 \\ 1 & 0 & 0 \end{bmatrix}$$

Here we see that both $i = 1$ and $i = 3$ qualify only for the single $j = 1$. Therefore, complete assignment is impossible.

We will improve the dual by decreasing u_i for $i = 1$ and $i = 3$ and by increasing v_j for $j = 1$:

$$\begin{aligned} \text{new } u_i &= \text{old } u_i - \Delta \qquad (i = 1, 3) \\ \text{new } v_j &= \text{old } v_j + \Delta \qquad (j = 2). \end{aligned}$$

This gives Figure 3.

	Δ	0	0
$7 - \Delta$	7	2	6
9	3	9	1
$8 - \Delta$	8	4	5

Figure 3

The biggest permissible value for Δ is $\Delta = 1$. All bigger values violate the inequality $u_1 + v_3 \geqslant a_{13} = 6$. Choosing $\Delta = 1$, we get Figure 4.

$$
\begin{array}{c}
\quad\ 1\ \ 0\ \ 0 \\
\begin{array}{c|ccc}
6 & ⑦ & 2 & ⑥ \\
9 & 3 & ⑨ & 1 \\
7 & ⑧ & 4 & 5 \\
\end{array}
\end{array}
$$

Figure 4

Now $i = 1$ qualifies for $j = 1$ *and* for the new $j = 3$ (note the new circle around 6).

Now the circles around 8, 9, and 6 show that a complete assignment is possible:

$$x_{31} = 1, \quad x_{22} = 1, \quad x_{13} = 1; \quad \text{all other } x_{ij} = 0.$$

Therefore, this is an optimal assignment.

As a check, we can compute the primal and dual objective functions. First, we find

$$\sum\sum a_{ij}x_{ij} = a_{31} + a_{22} + a_{13} = 23.$$

Next, we find

$$\sum u_i + \sum v_j = (6 + 9 + 7) + 1 = 23.$$

The objective values are equal, and so the check is passed.

Transportation problem. The optimal-assignment problem can be regarded as a special case of the transportation problem, which looks like this:

$$
\sum_{j=1}^{n} x_{ij} = s_i \qquad (i = 1, \ldots, m)
$$

$$
\sum_{i=1}^{m} x_{ij} = d_j \qquad (j = 1, \ldots, n) \tag{40}
$$

$$
x_{ij} \geqslant 0, \quad \sum_{i=1}^{m}\sum_{j=1}^{n} c_{ij}x_{ij} = \min.
$$

Here we are given the costs c_{ij} and the supplies s_i and demands d_j satisfying the consistency condition $\sum s_i = \sum d_j$. The optimal-assignment problem (20) becomes a transportation problem if we set, in (40),

$$m = n, \quad s_i = d_j = 1, \quad c_{ij} = \alpha - a_{ij}, \tag{41}$$

where we may set $\alpha = \max a_{ij}$ if we want to keep the costs c_{ij} nonnegative. Note that (40) and (41) imply

$$\sum\sum c_{ij}x_{ij} = n\alpha - \sum\sum a_{ij}x_{ij}. \tag{42}$$

Since $n\alpha$ is a constant, we shall have

$$\sum\sum c_{ij}x_{ij} = \min. \quad \text{iff} \quad \sum\sum a_{ij}x_{ij} = \max. \tag{43}$$

If the data are integers, the transportation problem can be solved as a network flow. This is done in the beautiful book *Theory of Linear Economic Models* by David Gale. He first solves the *transshipment problem*—a generalization of the simple-assignment problem. Then he uses the transshipment algorithm as a subroutine to solve the transportation problem, just as we used the simple-assignment algorithm as a subroutine to solve the optimal-assignment problem. (See Problems 10–14.)

Later, we will take a different approach. We will solve the transportation problem by using a special, efficient form of the simplex method.

Shortest-route problem. You've been working hard, and you deserve a little recreation. Now I give you something just for fun. It isn't a network flow—but who cares?

We are given a list of cities: $a, b, \ldots, z$. The cities are joined by a network of roads. We want to drive from a to z in the least possible time; we'll call our route a *shortest route*.

We're given a list of direct-travel times τ between every pair of cities. For instance, $\tau(c,q)$ is the time on a direct route from c to q; it is some positive integer number of minutes—infinity if there is no direct route. We don't require $\tau(c,q) = \tau(q,c)$. We assume $\tau(R) < \infty$ for some route R from a to z.

EXAMPLE 3. In Figure 5 the unique shortest route is a, c, b, z.

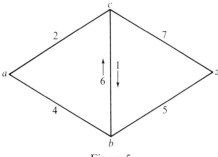

Figure 5

If we call the shortest route R_0, the total time is $\tau(R_0) = 2 + 1 + 5 = 8$. For all other routes R from a to z we have $\tau(R) > 8$.

Algorithm for shortest route. If the number of cities is finite, we can find the shortest route by enumeration, in theory. In practice, if the network is complex, there would be too many routes to look at, and we want a better algorithm.

Start with any route R. Now pick any node function φ that satisfies

$$\tau(c_1,c_2) \geq \varphi(c_2) - \varphi(c_1) \tag{44}$$

for every pair of nodes (cities) c_1 and c_2. A function φ is a sort of *potential*, and we will require $\varphi(a) = 0$ at the start. Thus, we may pick $\varphi \equiv 0$ as a first potential. We'll assume that the functions φ are integer-valued, like τ.

Every potential φ gives a lower bound for the least travel time. If R is the route

$$R: a, x_1, x_2, \ldots, x_k, z,$$

then the total time on this route is

$$\begin{aligned}\tau(R) &= \tau(a,x_1) + \tau(x_1,x_2) + \cdots + \tau(x_k,z) \\ &\geqslant [\varphi(x_1) - \varphi(a)] + [\varphi(x_2) - \varphi(x_1)] + \cdots + [\varphi(z) - \varphi(x_k)].\end{aligned}$$

Since $\varphi(a) = 0$, all the terms cancel except $\varphi(z)$, and so we get the lower bound

$$\tau(R) \geqslant \varphi(z) \text{ for all } R, \text{ for all } \varphi. \tag{45}$$

This says that the travel time is $\geqslant$ the potential at the final node.

If equality holds in (45), then R must be a shortest path. For if R' is any competing path, then we have

$$\tau(R') \geqslant \varphi(z) = \tau(R),$$

which means $\tau(R') \geqslant \tau(R)$ for all R'.

But suppose $\tau(R) > \varphi(z)$. Then we can construct a new potential φ_1 with $\varphi_1(z) > \varphi(z)$. Here's how:

If x^* is any node, we'll say that the path $a, x_1, x_2, \ldots, x_i, x^*$ is *efficient* if

$$\tau(a,x_1) + \tau(x_1,x_2) + \cdots + \tau(x_i,x^*) = \varphi(x^*). \tag{46}$$

For the present potential φ we have assumed there is no efficient path from a to z. (If there were, then this path would be a complete route R satisfying $\tau(R) = \varphi(z)$.)

Let E be the subset of nodes x^* that can be reached by efficient paths. The subset E depends on the potential φ. At least a lies in E; we have assumed that z does not. The final node z lies in the complementary set E'.

We may define a new potential as follows:

$$\varphi_1 = \varphi \text{ in } E, \quad \varphi_1 = \Delta + \varphi \text{ in } E', \tag{47}$$

where Δ is a positive integer constant. In particular, $\varphi_1(a) = 0$ and $\varphi_1(z) = \Delta + \varphi(z)$. The new potential satisfies the requirement

$$\tau(c_1,c_2) \geqslant \varphi_1(c_2) - \varphi_1(c_1). \tag{48}$$

This is obvious unless c_2 lies in E' and c_1 lies in E, in which case

$$\varphi_1(c_2) = \Delta + \varphi(c_2), \quad \varphi_1(c_1) = \varphi(c_1). \tag{49}$$

But we must have

$$\tau(c_1,c_2) > \varphi(c_2) - \varphi(c_1) \quad \text{for} \quad c_2 \in E', c_1 \in E. \tag{50}$$

Otherwise we could reach c_2 by an efficient path going first to c_1 and then directly to c_2. That is impossible if c_2 lies in E', and so the inequality (50) must hold. Therefore, the integers τ and φ must satisfy

$$\tau(c_1,c_2) \geqslant \Delta + \varphi(c_2) - \varphi(c_1) = \varphi_1(c_2) - \varphi_1(c_1)$$

for $c_1 \in E$, $c_2 \in E'$, where Δ is the positive integer

$$\Delta = \min\{\tau(c_1,c_2) - [\varphi(c_2) - \varphi(c_1)]: c_1 \in E, c_2 \in E'\}.$$

This is the biggest permissible value for Δ in (47).

Now we repeat the process. Starting with the new potential, we locate the new subset E of nodes that can be reached by efficient paths. If z lies in E, we're done; otherwise, we construct another new potential. And so on.

This process must yield a shortest route in a finite number of steps. That is because we increase the final potential $\varphi_i(z)$ by a positive integer Δ_i at each step. This process must stop, because all the $\varphi_i(z)$ must be $\leqslant$ the minimum travel time $\tau(R)$. At the end, a shortest route R appears as an efficient path from a to z.

EXAMPLE 4. Let's use this algorithm on the network in Figure 6. Start with the potential $\varphi_0 \equiv 0$. Then E_0 contains only a. For Δ_0 we find

$$\Delta_0 = \tau(a,c) - [\varphi_0(c) - \varphi_0(a)] = 2.$$

This gives the potential

$$\varphi_1(a) = 0, \quad \varphi_1(b) = \varphi_1(c) = \varphi_1(z) = 2.$$

Referring to Figure 6., we see $E_1 = \{a,c\}$. Then we find

$$\Delta_1 = \tau(c,b) - [\varphi_1(b) - \varphi_1(c)] = 1.$$

This gives the potential

$$\varphi_2(a) = 0, \quad \varphi_2(c) = 2, \quad \varphi_2(b) = 3, \quad \varphi_2(z) = 3.$$

Now $E_2 = \{a,c,b\}$ and $\Delta_2 = 5$, giving at last

$$\varphi_3(a) = 0, \quad \varphi_3(c) = 2, \quad \varphi_3(b) = 3, \quad \varphi_3(z) = 8.$$

For the last potential an efficient path from a to z is the required shortest route a, c, b, z.

References

1. David Gale, *Theory of Linear Economic Models*, McGraw-Hill, 1960.
2. L. R. Ford, Jr., "Network Flow Theory", RAND paper p-923, 1956.
3. P. Hall, "On representatives of subsets," *J. London Math. Soc.*, vol. 10 (1935) pp. 26–30.
4. P. R. Halmos and H. E. Vaughan, "The Marriage Problem," *American J. Math*, vol. 72 (1950) pp. 214–215.
5. Marshall Hall, Jr., *Combinatorial Theory*, Ginn Blaisdell, 1967.
6. Richard Bellman, *Dynamic Programming*, Princeton Univ. Press, 1957.

PROBLEMS

1. For the simple-assignment problem, use the qualification matrix

$$\begin{bmatrix} 1 & 0 & 1 & 1 \\ 0 & 0 & 1 & 0 \\ 0 & 1 & 1 & 0 \\ 0 & 1 & 0 & 0 \end{bmatrix}.$$

Set up the flow model. Find an optimal flow f_0 assigning as many persons as possible. Find the minimal cut C_0, C_0'. Find a subset I_0 for which $|J(I_0)| < |I_0|$.

2. Set up the flow model for the simple-assignment problem with qualification matrix

$$\begin{bmatrix} 0 & 0 & 1 & 1 \\ 1 & 1 & 0 & 0 \\ 0 & 1 & 0 & 1 \\ 0 & 1 & 0 & 0 \end{bmatrix}.$$

Solve by inspection. Then, for practice, solve systematically by the flow algorithm.

3. *A combinatoric problem*: Given is an $n \times n$ matrix with n^2 positive-integer components a_{ij}. Call a subset of components OK if no two components lie in the same row or column. The problem is to pick an OK subset of components with maximum sum. State this problem as an optimal-assignment problem.

4. For Problem 3 use the matrix

$$A = \begin{bmatrix} 3 & 3 & 2 \\ 1 & 3 & 5 \\ 2 & 1 & 3 \end{bmatrix}.$$

First solve by inspection. Then use the flow algorithm to see how it works.

5. Use the flow algorithm to solve the optimal-assignment problem with the aptitude matrix

$$A = \begin{bmatrix} 1 & 3 & 3 & 3 & 2 \\ 2 & 1 & 2 & 3 & 5 \\ 3 & 2 & 1 & 1 & 3 \end{bmatrix}.$$

6. In Problem 3 suppose you want an OK subset of n components with *minimum* sum. State this too as an optimal-assignment problem.

7. Use the shortest-route algorithm for this road network, where τ is symmetric:

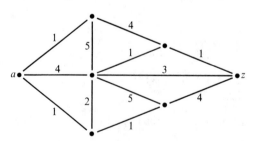

*8. In the calculus of variations one looks for a curve $y(x)$ $(0 \leqslant x \leqslant 1)$ that minimizes an integral

$$\int_0^1 F(x, y(x), y'(x)) \, dx,$$

where $y(0)$ and $y(1)$ are given, and where $F(x,u,v)$ is a prescribed function. Show how a discretized version of this problem might be solved by the shortest-route algorithm. Method: For small positive Δx and small $|\Delta y|$, define the direct time τ between the points (x, y) and $(x + \Delta x, y + \Delta y)$ as

$$\tau = F\left(x, y, \frac{\Delta y}{\Delta x}\right) \Delta x.$$

(You may assume $F > 0$; otherwise, replace F by F plus some large constant.)

9. For the shortest-route problem define the function $\phi(\omega)$ as the shortest total travel time from a to $\omega = b, c, \ldots, z$. Show that ϕ is an admissible potential, satisfying (44). Show that ϕ satisfies this functional equation of *dynamic programming*:

$$\phi(\omega) = \min_{\lambda \neq \omega} \left[\phi(\lambda) + \tau(\lambda, \omega) \right] \quad \text{if} \quad \omega \neq a,$$

where we define $\phi(a) = 0$.

*10. *Transshipment problem.* Let $P_1, \ldots, P_m$ be plants with supplies $\sigma_1, \ldots, \sigma_m$. Let $M_1, \ldots, M_n$ be markets with demands $d_1, \ldots, d_n$. Assume $\Sigma \sigma_i \geqslant \Sigma d_j$. Let $k(P_i, M_j) \geqslant 0$ be the shipping capacity from P_i to M_j; define $k(s, P_i) = \sigma_i$, $k(M_j, s') = d_j$. Prove that all demands can be met unless there is a subset M' of markets for which

$$d(M') > \sigma(P') + k(P, M')$$

where P and P' are complementary subsets of plants. Method: Let C_0, C_0' be a minimal cut in the network $\{s, P_1, \ldots, P_m, M_1, \ldots, M_n, s'\}$. If $C_0 = \{s, P, M\}$, then the minimal cut has capacity $\sigma(P') + k(P, M') + d(M)$. Now what if a maximal flow has value $< d(M) + d(M')$?

11. Show that the dual of the transportation problem (40) is

$$u_i + v_j \leqslant c_{ij} \quad (i = 1, \ldots, m; j = 1, \ldots, n)$$
$$\sum s_i u_i + \sum d_j v_j = \max.$$

*12. Let c_{ij}, s_i, d_j be integers $\geqslant 0$, with $\Sigma s_i = \Sigma d_j$. Define the *transportation problem* (40) and its dual (Problem 11). Suppose $\mathbf{u}, \mathbf{v}$ are feasible for the dual. Let β be some integer bigger than Σd_j, and define the transshipment problem (Problem 10) with supplies s_i, demands d_j, and shipping capacities

$$k(P_i, M_j) = \begin{cases} \beta & \text{if} \quad u_i + v_j = c_{ij} \\ 0 & \text{if} \quad u_i + v_j < c_{ij} \end{cases}.$$

Suppose the transshipment problem is solvable. Let x_{ij} be the amount shipped from P_i to M_j. Show that the x_{ij} give an optimal solution of the transportation problem.

*13. (Continuation.) In Problem 12 suppose the transshipment problem is *not* solvable. For the subsets defined in Problem 10, conclude that $k(P, M') = 0$ because

$k(P,M') \leqslant \sum d_j < \beta$. Hence Problem 10 implies

$$\sum_{M'} d_j > \sum_{P'} s_i.$$

Now show that v_j can be increased on M' and u_i can be decreased on P' to obtain a new feasible dual solution with increased value $\sum s_i u_i + \sum d_j v_j$.

*14. *A network-flow algorithm for the transportation problem*:
   (i) Start with any feasible **u**, **v** (for instance, **0**, **0**).
   (ii) Try to solve the transshipment problem in Problem 12. Stop if there is a solution **x**.
   (iii) Otherwise, improve the feasible **u**, **v** as in Problem 13. Return to step (ii).
   Why must this algorithm solve the transportation problem (40) in a finite number of steps?

18 The Transportation Problem

Suppose a certain commodity, say oil, is produced at *plants* $i = 1, \ldots, m$. And suppose the oil must be shipped to *markets* $j = 1, \ldots, n$. Call x_{ij} the unknown number of barrels of oil to be shipped from plant i to market j. Let c_{ij} be the shipping cost per barrel. Then the shipping cost from i to j will be the product $c_{ij}x_{ij}$, and the total shipping cost from all plants to all markets will be

$$\sum_{i=1}^{m} \sum_{j=1}^{n} c_{ij}x_{ij}. \tag{1}$$

Suppose the supply at plant i is s_i, and suppose the demand at market j is d_j. Let the total supply be $\geqslant$ the total demand:

$$s_1 + \cdots + s_m \geqslant d_1 + \cdots + d_n. \tag{2}$$

Then all demands can be met with the existing supplies; the problem is to meet them with minimum cost.
   We require

$$\sum_{i=1}^{n} x_{ij} \leqslant s_i \qquad (i = 1, \ldots, m), \tag{3}$$

which says that the total shipped out of plant i is $\leqslant s_i$. And we require

$$\sum_{i=1}^{m} x_{ij} \geqslant d_j \qquad (j = 1, \ldots, n), \tag{4}$$

which says that the total shipped into market j must be $\geqslant d_j$. Then no supply will be exceeded, and every demand will be met. By the way, note that these constraints imply (2):

$$\sum_i s_i \geqslant \sum_i \sum_j x_{ij} \geqslant \sum_j d_j. \tag{5}$$

This is the transportation problem: *Find $x_{ij} \geqslant 0$ to meet the constraints* (3), (4) *and minimize the cost* (1).

Figure 1 illustrates the problem for two plants and three markets. The figure suggests that the problem could be regarded as a network flow, and that *has* been done. But we shall here solve the problem by the simplex method. We will not use the simplex tableau, which would fail to use the special features of our problem; but we will use the basic idea.

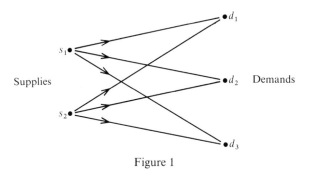

Figure 1

The result will be an exceedingly efficient numerical algorithm. This algorithm is so good that we can use it to solve medium-sized problems by hand, or to solve huge industrial problems by computer. In pure mathematics, certain problems of combinatorial analysis have the mathematical structure of transportation problems; these problems, too, can be solved by the algorithm we're about to discuss.

As it often happens in our subject, the algorithm is easy but the theory is hard. So please bear with it; the reward of understanding will be worth your trouble.

In our approach by the simplex method, we first restate the inequalities as equations. Indeed, if the total supply *equals* the total demand, then the inequalities (3) and (4) must *already* be equations; for only as equations can these inequalities yield equalities on both sides of (5). For instance, if

$$\sum_j x_{6j} < s_6,$$

then (3) implies

$$\sum_i \sum_j x_{ij} < \sum s_i,$$

and now (4) implies $\sum s_i > \sum d_j$ (total supply $>$ total demand). Thus, if $\sum s_i = \sum d_j$, then the "$\leqslant$" in (3) and the "$\geqslant$" in (4) may both be replaced by "$=$".

Suppose instead that total supply exceeds total demand:

$$\sum_{i=1}^{m} s_i > \sum_{j=1}^{n} d_j. \tag{6}$$

We can reduce this case to the former by a trick. Define the excess

$$d_0 \equiv \sum_{i=1}^{m} s_i - \sum_{j=1}^{n} d_j > 0. \tag{7}$$

Now introduce a *dump*, a fictitious market $j = 0$ with demand d_0, and say that there is no shipping cost to the dump:

$$c_{i0} = 0 \qquad (i = 1, \dots, m). \tag{8}$$

If we include the dump, $j = 0$, we now have

$$\sum_{i=1}^{m} s_i = \sum_{j=0}^{n} d_j, \tag{9}$$

and we can proceed as before. The constraints become the *equations*

$$\sum_{j=0}^{n} x_{ij} = s_i \qquad (i = 1, \dots, m)$$
$$\sum_{i=1}^{m} x_{ij} = d_j \qquad (j = 0, \dots, n), \tag{10}$$

and we seek $x_{ij} \geqslant 0$ to

$$\text{minimize } \sum_{i=1}^{m} \sum_{j=0}^{n} c_{ij} x_{ij}. \tag{11}$$

To solve the original problem, we solve the new problem for the unknowns x_{ij}. At the end, we ignore the final slack variables x_{i0}.

Thus, replacing $j = 0$ by $j = 1$, we may always use the *canonical form* of the transportation problem:

$$\sum_{j=1}^{n} x_{ij} = s_i \qquad (i = 1, \dots, m)$$
$$\sum_{i=1}^{m} x_{ij} = d_j \qquad (j = 1, \dots, n) \tag{12}$$

$$x_{ij} \geqslant 0$$

$$\sum_{i=1}^{m} \sum_{j=1}^{n} c_{ij} x_{ij} = \text{minimum}.$$

The $m + n$ equations are redundant, and we must assume that the given supplies and demands satisfy the *consistency condition*

$$\sum_{i=1}^{m} s_i = \sum_{j=1}^{n} d_j. \tag{13}$$

We can think of the unknowns x_{ij} as components of an m-by-n matrix X. We are given the row sums s_i and the column sums d_j. For example, if $m = 2$ and $n = 3$, we have this picture:

$$
\begin{array}{ccc|l}
x_{11} & x_{12} & x_{13} & s_1 \\
x_{21} & x_{22} & x_{23} & s_2 \\
\hline
d_1 & d_2 & d_3 &
\end{array}
\tag{14}
$$

But to understand the theory, we may regard the unknowns x_{ij} as components of a vector $\mathbf{x}$. Then the equations (12) take the form

$$A\mathbf{x} = \mathbf{b}, \tag{15}$$

where A has $m + n$ rows and mn columns. For example, if again $m = 2$ and $n = 3$, then (15) becomes

$$
\begin{bmatrix}
1 & 1 & 1 & 0 & 0 & 0 \\
0 & 0 & 0 & 1 & 1 & 1 \\
1 & 0 & 0 & 1 & 0 & 0 \\
0 & 1 & 0 & 0 & 1 & 0 \\
0 & 0 & 1 & 0 & 0 & 1
\end{bmatrix}
\begin{pmatrix}
x_{11} \\ x_{12} \\ x_{13} \\ x_{21} \\ x_{22} \\ x_{23}
\end{pmatrix}
=
\begin{pmatrix}
s_1 \\ s_2 \\ d_1 \\ d_2 \\ d_3
\end{pmatrix}.
\tag{16}
$$

This formula and formula (14) say the same thing in different ways.

If we use the vector unknown $\mathbf{x}$, then the transportation problem (12) becomes

$$
\begin{aligned}
A\mathbf{x} &= \mathbf{b} \\
\mathbf{x} &\geq 0 \\
\mathbf{c} \cdot \mathbf{x} &= \text{minimum.}
\end{aligned}
\tag{17}
$$

Here $\mathbf{x}$ has the mn components $x_{11}, x_{12}, \ldots, x_{mn}$; $\mathbf{b}$ has the $m + n$ components $s_1, \ldots, s_m, d_1, \ldots, d_n$; and $\mathbf{c}$ has the mn components $c_{11}, c_{12}, \ldots, c_{mn}$. The matrix A is the obvious generalization of the matrix in (16). The redundancy of the equations (12) shows up in A: the sum of the first m rows equals the sume of the last n rows (both sums equal a row vector of all 1's).

The *dual* of (17) is the maximum problem

$$
\begin{aligned}
\mathbf{y} \cdot A &\leq \mathbf{c} \\
\mathbf{y} \cdot \mathbf{b} &= \text{maximum}
\end{aligned}
\tag{18}
$$

Since the first m rows of A are formed differently from the last n rows, we will partition the dual vector as follows:

$$\mathbf{y} = (u_1, \ldots, u_m, v_1, \ldots, v_n). \tag{19}$$

For example, if the primal problem is (16), the dual vector is

$$\mathbf{y} = (u_1, u_2, v_1 v_2, v_3),$$

and the dual problem (18) becomes

$$u_1 + v_1 \leqslant c_{11}$$
$$u_1 + v_2 \leqslant c_{12}$$
$$u_1 + v_3 \leqslant c_{13}$$
$$u_2 + v_1 \leqslant c_{21}$$
$$u_2 + v_2 \leqslant c_{22}$$
$$u_2 + v_3 \leqslant c_{23}$$
$$u_1 s_1 + u_2 s_2 + v_1 d_1 + v_2 d_2 + v_3 d_3 = \text{maximum.}$$

(20)

In general, this is the dual problem (18):

$$u_i + v_j \leqslant c_{ij} \qquad (i = 1, \ldots, m; j = 1, \ldots, n)$$
$$\sum u_i s_i + \sum v_j d_j = \text{maximum.}$$

(21)

A first feasible solution. We know that the consistency condition (13) is *necessary* for the redundant equations (12) to have a solution; now we'll show it is *sufficient*. Given consistent supplies and demands, we will construct a solution x_{ij}. If the given s_i and d_j are $\geqslant 0$, our solution x_{ij} will be $\geqslant 0$. And our solution will have at most $m + n - 1$ non-zero components.

First suppose $m = 1$. Then we just set

$$x_{11} = d_1, x_{12} = d_2, \ldots, x_{1n} = d_n$$

(22)

Here the matrix X has just one row; the single row sum equals s_1, by (13). Similarly, if $n = 1$ we just set $x_{i1} = s_i$ $(i = 1, \ldots, m)$.

Now suppose $m > 1$ and $n > 1$. We will eliminate one row equation or one column equation to get a smaller system of the same type. Set

$$x_{11} = s_1 \quad \text{if} \quad s_1 \leqslant d_1$$

(23.1)

$$x_{11} = d_1 \quad \text{if} \quad d_1 < s_1.$$

(23.2)

In the first case, let the first *row* of X equal

$$s_1 \quad 0 \quad 0 \quad \cdots \quad 0.$$

(24)

Now define a reduced demand

$$d_1' = d_1 - s_1 \geqslant 0$$

(25)

We thus get the reduced system

$$\sum_{j=1}^{n} x_{ij} = s_i \qquad (i = 2, \ldots, m)$$

$$\sum_{i=2}^{m} x_{ij} = d_j' \qquad (j = 1, \ldots, n)$$

(26)

where the demands are now

$$d_1 - s_1, d_2, d_3, \ldots, d_n. \tag{27}$$

The sum of these demands equals the sum of the remaining supplies $s_2, \ldots, s_m$. The new system has $m - 1$ row equations and n column equations. By induction, we can solve the reduced system with at most $[(m - 1) + n] - 1$ non-zero x_{ij}. Since we previously found the first row (24), we now have solved the original system with at most $m + n - 1$ non-zero x_{ij}.

In the case (23.2), we instead eliminate the first *column* equation. We now let the first *column* of X equal

$$\begin{matrix} d_1 \\ 0 \\ \vdots \\ 0 \end{matrix} \tag{28}$$

and we define a reduced supply

$$s_1' = s_1 - d_1 > 0. \tag{29}$$

Now the reduced system has one less unknown; it has one less equation; it has the supplies

$$s_1 - d_1, s_2, \ldots, s_m$$

and the demands

$$d_2, \ldots, d_n.$$

The sum of the new supplies equals the sum of the new demands. As before, we argue by induction and conclude that we can solve the original $m + n$ equations (12). Our solution will have at most $m + n - 1$ non-zero x_{ij}; and if all s_i and d_j are $\geqslant 0$, then all x_{ij} will be $\geqslant 0$. □

EXAMPLE 1. Let's get a feasible solution for this problem

$$\begin{array}{|cccc|c} x_{11} & x_{12} & x_{13} & x_{14} & 3 \\ x_{21} & x_{22} & x_{23} & x_{24} & 5 \\ x_{31} & x_{32} & x_{33} & x_{34} & 9 \\ \hline 7 & 3 & 1 & 6 \end{array} \tag{30}$$

The supplies are at the right; the demands are at the bottom; both totals equal 17.

Since $s_1 = 3$ and $d_1 = 7$, we set $x_{11} = 3$ and eliminate the first row. This give the reduced system

$$\begin{array}{|cccc|c} x_{21} & x_{22} & x_{23} & x_{24} & 5 \\ x_{31} & x_{32} & x_{33} & x_{34} & 9 \\ \hline 4 & 3 & 1 & 6 \end{array}$$

Now the first demand is $<$ the first supply, so we eliminate the first column. We set $x_{21} = 4$ and get the smaller system

$$
\begin{array}{|ccc|c}
x_{22} & x_{23} & x_{24} & 1 \\
x_{32} & x_{33} & x_{34} & 9 \\
\hline
3 & 1 & 6 &
\end{array}
$$

Setting $x_{22} = 1$ and eliminating the first row, we get

$$
\begin{array}{|ccc|c}
x_{32} & x_{33} & x_{34} & 9 \\
\hline
2 & 1 & 6 &
\end{array}
$$

The last three x_{ij} must equal $2, 1, 6$.

In summary, we have found this feasible solution:

$$
\begin{array}{|c|c|c|c|c}
3 & & & & 3 \\
\hline
4 & 1 & & & 5 \\
\hline
 & 2 & 1 & 6 & 9 \\
\hline
7 & 3 & 1 & 6 &
\end{array}
\tag{31}
$$

(The blank squares belong to the x_{ij} that equal zero.) Here $m = 3$, $n = 4$, and $m + n - 1 = 6$, which is just the number of nonzero x_{ij}. If we wrote this example in the form $A\mathbf{x} = \mathbf{b}$, we would find for A a matrix with 7 rows and 12 columns, with rank $A = 6$.

Basic solutions and nondegeneracy. We have proved that we can solve the $m + n$ equations (12) if and only if $\sum s_i = \sum d_j$. In other words, if we write the equations (12) in the form $A\mathbf{x} = \mathbf{b}$, the range of the matrix A is the linear subspace of all vectors $\mathbf{b}$ with $m + n$ components that satisfy the equation

$$
b_1 + \cdots + b_m - b_{m+1} - \cdots - b_{m+n} = 0.
\tag{32}
$$

Thus, the range of A has dimension $m + n - 1$, and so

$$
\text{rank } A = m + n - 1.
\tag{33}
$$

In the general theory of linear programming, we talked about *basic solutions* $\mathbf{x}$ for equations $A\mathbf{x} = \mathbf{b}$. We called the subset of columns $\mathbf{a}^p, \mathbf{a}^q, \ldots, \mathbf{a}^s$ a *basis* if it was a basis for the range of A. Equivalently, if rank $A = r$, a *basis* was any subset of r independent columns of A. We defined a basic solution $\mathbf{x}$ as a solution whose only non-zero components x_j multiplied columns $\mathbf{a}^j$ in a basis:

$$
A\mathbf{x} = x_p\mathbf{a}^p + x_q\mathbf{a}^q + \cdots + x_s\mathbf{a}^s = \mathbf{b}.
\tag{34}
$$

Thus, if rank $A = r$, a basic solution has at most r non-zero components. If $\mathbf{a}^p, \ldots, \mathbf{a}^s$ is a basis, then the components $x_p, \ldots, x_s$ in the equation (34) are called *basic variables* or *variables in the basis*. And sometimes the term *basis* is used for the set of *indices* $p, \ldots, s$ if $x_p, \ldots, x_q$ are basic variables.

Theorems on basic solutions. First, if $A\mathbf{x} = \mathbf{b}$ has any feasible solution $\mathbf{x} \geqslant 0$, then it has a *basic feasible solution*. Second, if the linear program

$$A\mathbf{x} = \mathbf{b}, \quad \mathbf{x} \geqslant 0, \quad \mathbf{c} \cdot \mathbf{x} = \text{minimum} \tag{35}$$

has any optimal solution, then it has a *basic optimal solution*. We proved those two theorems for linear programming in general.

In the transportation problem, the general theorems apply. Only now we have to take care because the unknowns x_{ij} have *two* subscripts. For instance, in the example (16) the unknowns x_{ij} have the subscripts $i = 1, 2$ and $j = 1, 2, 3$. In principle, this cannot matter; for if we wished, we could re-name the six unknowns $x_1, x_2, \ldots, x_6$. Then we'd have conventional, single-indexed unknowns x_j. But in practice, we'll find the original double-indexed unknowns x_{ij} convenient.

EXAMPLE 2. If $m = 2$ and $n = 3$, the equation $A\mathbf{x} = \mathbf{b}$ takes the equivalent forms (14) and (16). Here rank $A = 4$; the first four columns of A are linearly independent, and so they constitute a basis. For this basis the basic variables are

$$x_{11}, x_{12}, x_{13}, x_{21}. \tag{36}$$

Equivalently, we say that this basis is the set of double indices

$$B = \{(1,1), (1,2), (1,3), (2,1)\}. \tag{37}$$

Thus, B *is the set of all double indices* (i,j) *for which* x_{ij} *is a basic variable.* The set B has r members if there are r basic variables. In this example $r = 4$, and so we write

$$|B| = 4, \tag{38}$$

which means the set B has four members.

If instead of (16) we use the picture (14), we can designate the basis B by marking the squares (i,j) that belong to B. For the basis (37) we get this picture:

$$\tag{39}$$

Using any basis, we get a basic solution by solving all the row and column equations with only the basic unknowns (the non-basic unknowns are set equal to zero). For instance, suppose the supplies and demands are

$$s_i = 7, 4; \quad d_j = 5, 0, 6. \tag{40}$$

If (39) gives the basis, then we solve

$$\begin{array}{|c|c|c|c}\hline \bullet & \bullet & \bullet & 7 \\\hline \bullet & & & 4 \\\hline 5 & 0 & 6 \end{array} \qquad (41)$$

for the marked basic unknowns.

Since the second row has only the one mark in square $(2,1)$, we first find $x_{21} = 4$. Then we're left with this picture for the first row

$$\begin{array}{|c|c|c|c}\hline \bullet & \bullet & \bullet & 7 \\\hline 1 & 0 & 6 \end{array} \qquad (42)$$

(the 1 is the residual demand $5-4$). This yields the remaining basic unknowns:

$$x_{11} = 1, \quad x_{12} = 0, \quad x_{13} = 6. \qquad (43)$$

Degeneracy. In linear programming in general, if A has rank r, and if the equation $A\mathbf{x} = \mathbf{b}$ has a solution $\mathbf{x}$ with *fewer* than r non-zero x_j, the problem is called *degenerate*. For instance, the transportation problem with supplies and demands (40) is degenerate. Why? Because the rank equals 4, but we just found a basic solution with only 3 non-zero components (remember, we found $x_{12} = 0$).

In linear programming, degeneracy is more of a worry in principle than in practice. Almost all small perturbations of degenerate programs produce non-degenerate programs. Such perturbations can be made deliberately or inadvertently, for instance, by round-off error. Since the solution depends continuously on the data, no great harm is done. For example, in the data (40) any small perturbation that makes d_2 positive produces a non-degenerate problem, and a small perturbation of the data produces only a small perturbation in the solution.

(Of course, we assume that the perturbed data are consistent; and if they are not, our algorithm will, in effect, make them so. We know that the $m + n$ supply and demand equations are redundant, and that they require the consistency condition $\sum s_i = \sum d_j$. This need never worry us, for we can avoid the redundancy and the consistency condition simply by ignoring any one of the $m + n$ equations.)

So, from now on we will make an *assumption of non-degeneracy*. We will assume that our data have these properties:

(i) *consistency*: $s_1 + \cdots + s_m = d_1 + \cdots + d_n$.

(ii) *fullness*: every solution of the $m + n$ supply and demand equations has *at least* $m + n - 1$ non-zero components.

The fullness property implies this: Suppose a solution $\mathbf{x}$ has *exactly* $m + n - 1$ non-zero components; then $\mathbf{x}$ is a basic solution. For otherwise the non-zero components of $\mathbf{x}$ would belong as coefficients to a *dependent* set of the columns of A, and now some subset of those columns would yield a solution $\mathbf{x}'$ with fewer non-zero components. Then the solution $\mathbf{x}'$ would violate the fullness property.

Equilibrium. Let $\mathbf{x}$ be a basic feasible solution, with $m + n - 1$ positive components x_{ij} for the double indices (i,j) in the basis B. The *equilibrium equations* are the $m + n - 1$ equations

$$u_i + v_j = c_{ij} \qquad \text{for } (i,j) \text{ in } B. \qquad (44)$$

These equations come from the dual problem (21) by writing a *dual equation* for every positive *primal unknown*. We now distinguish two cases:

$$(\alpha) \quad u_p + v_q \leqslant c_{pq} \qquad \text{for } all \ (p,q) \text{ not in } B.$$

In this case we're through: the feasible solution $\mathbf{x}$ is optimal. This follows from the general equilibrium theorem of linear programming. In this case $\mathbf{u}$ and $\mathbf{v}$ are feasible for the dual (21), and they yield

$$\sum_{i=1}^{m} u_i s_i + \sum_{j=1}^{n} v_j d_j = \sum_{i=1}^{m} \sum_{j=1}^{n} (u_i + v_j) x_{ij}$$

$$= \sum_{B} (u_i + v_j) x_{ij}$$

$$= \sum_{B} c_{ij} x_{ij}. \qquad (45)$$

Thus, both our dual and primal solutions are optimal.

Now take the other case:

$$(\beta) \quad u_p + v_q > c_{pq} \qquad \text{for } some \ (p,q) \text{ not in } B.$$

In this case we still have work to do. The inequality (β) implies $\mathbf{u}, \mathbf{v}$ are not feasible for the dual; and we can lower the primal cost by introducing x_{pq} into the basis.

Changing the basis. How can we introduce the small positive amount $x_{pq} = \lambda > 0$? We call the current basis B, and by non-degeneracy (ii) we assume *all* $x_{ij} > 0$ for $(i,j) \in B$.

We may write the current supply equations in this notation, in which an asterisk denotes a sum over *basic* variables:

$$\sum_{j}^{*} x_{ij} = s_i \qquad (i = 1, \dots, m) \qquad (46)$$

Here we sum over the indices j for which (i,j) lies in B.

Similarly, we may write the current demand equations in this notation:

$$\sum_{i}^{*} x_{ij} = d_j \qquad (j = 1, \dots, n) \qquad (47)$$

Here we sum over the indices i for which (i,j) lies in B. The non-basic variable x_{pq} appears in none of the sums (46), (47).

The new shipment $x_{pq} = \lambda > 0$ will use the amount λ from the supply s_p and contribute the amount λ to the demand d_q; this shipment has no effect on the other supplies and demands. Thus, if δ_{ij} is the Kronecker delta, the new shipment uses the amount $\lambda\delta_{ip}$ from the supply s_i and contributes $\lambda\delta_{jq}$ toward the demand d_j.

So the new supply and demand equations take these forms:

$$\lambda\delta_{ip} + \sum_j{}^* (x_{ij} - \lambda t_{ij}) = s_i \qquad (i = 1, \ldots, m) \tag{48}$$

$$\lambda\delta_{jq} + \sum_i{}^* (x_{ij} - \lambda t_{ij}) = d_j \qquad (j = 1, \ldots, n) \tag{49}$$

where the sums $\sum^*$ include only terms with indices (i,j) in the current basis, B. Please compare these formulas with the preceding two formulas, and note the new terms λt_{ij}.

The terms λt_{ij} are defined for $(i,j) \in B$; they are needed to compensate for the new non-basic terms $\lambda\delta_{ip}$ and $\lambda\delta_{jq}$. For $(i,j) \in B$ the t_{ij} are the unique numbers that satisfy the equations

$$\sum_j{}^* t_{ij} = \delta_{ip} \qquad (i = 1, \ldots, m) \tag{50}$$

$$\sum_i{}^* t_{ij} = \delta_{jq} \qquad (j = 1, \ldots, n). \tag{51}$$

These two formulas give $m + n$ consistent equations for $m + n - 1$ basic unknowns t_{ij}. If the original basic equations (46) and (47) hold, then the new equations (48) and (49) hold iff the equations (50) and (51) hold.

The best choice of λ. Since $x_{ij} > 0$ for all $(i,j) \in B$, the new variables, $x_{pq} = \lambda > 0$ and

$$\text{new } x_{ij} = x_{ij} - \lambda t_{ij} \qquad \text{for } (i,j) \text{ in } B, \tag{52}$$

will give a new feasible solution if λ is small enough.

The new cost is

$$\lambda c_{pq} + \sum_B (x_{ij} - \lambda t_{ij}) c_{ij}. \tag{53}$$

Now the equilibrium equations (44) imply

$$\sum_B t_{ij} c_{ij} = \sum_B t_{ij}(u_i + v_j).$$

But (50) implies

$$\sum_B t_{ij} u_i = \sum_{i=1}^m u_i \left(\sum_j{}^* t_{ij} \right) \tag{54}$$

$$= \sum_{i=1}^m u_i \delta_{ip} = u_p,$$

and similarly, (51) implies

$$\sum_B t_{ij} v_j = \sum_{j=1}^n v_j \left(\sum_i{}^* t_{ij} \right)$$

$$= \sum_{j=1}^n v_j \delta_{jq} = v_q. \tag{55}$$

So (53) says the new cost equals

$$\sum_B x_{ij}c_{ij} - \lambda(u_p + v_q - c_{pq}).\tag{56}$$

The sum over B equals the old cost. Therefore,

$$\text{cost decrease} = \lambda(u_p + v_q - c_{pq}),\tag{57}$$

which is positive, by the inequality (β). The bigger we can make λ, the better. If we could make $\lambda \to +\infty$, we could make the cost $\to -\infty$. Obviously, that is impossible if all c_{ij} are ≥ 0.

Just how big may we take λ? From (48) and (49) you see we must require

$$x_{ij} - \lambda t_{ij} \geq 0 \qquad \text{for all } (i,j) \text{ in } B.\tag{58}$$

Otherwise we'd no longer have a feasible solution. If $t_{ij} \leq 0$, we get no trouble, but we could get trouble from any t_{ij} that is >0.

Therefore, this is the biggest and *the best value* for λ:

$$\text{Best } \lambda = \min\{x_{ij}/t_{ij}: t_{ij} > 0, (i,j) \in B\}.\tag{59}$$

That says, we take λ equal to the minimum quotient for which the denominator t_{ij} is positive; any bigger λ would make one of the differences (58) negative. (Later, in formula (63), we will find a better form for Best λ.)

Throughout this discussion, I hope you understand that all we are doing is applying the simplex method to a special problem. Right now, the application may seem complicated, but you will soon find great simplifications. For example, you'll find that the mysterious positive denominator in (59) can take only one value: $t_{ij} = 1$. This helps make the computing easy, and it has an important theoretical consequence: *if the data s_i and d_j are all integers, then the answers x_{ij} will also be integers.* The first basic solution consists of integers, and all later basic solutions will consist of integers.

You will also find this: *All the linear systems we have to solve can be solved recursively, step by step.* This has to be seen to be believed, and I'll give you a numerical example before I prove it for you.

But we're getting ahead of our story. Let's finish our discussion of *changing the basis.*

When we pick the best λ, the minimum in (59) is achieved for *some $t_{\mu v} > 0$* with (μ,v) in B. Then

$$x_{ij} - \lambda t_{ij} = 0 \quad \text{for} \quad (i,j) = (\mu,v).\tag{60}$$

Thus, as x_{pq} enters the basis with the value $\lambda > 0$, $x_{\mu v}$ leaves the basis and becomes zero. In a non-degenerate problem this implies that (μ,v) is unique; for otherwise at least two of the old basic variables would become zero, and we'd be left with a new basic solution with fewer than $m + n - 1$ positive x_{ij}. By the *fullness* property (ii), that's impossible.

Thus we change the basis: (μ,v) leaves; (p,q) enters.

Summary. We will solve non-degenerate transportation problems by the simplex method. (If a problem is degenerate, we perturb it a little and almost surely make it non-degenerate.) These are the steps in the simplex method:

1. Compute the first basic feasible solution x_{ij}.
2. Solve the equilibrium equations for u_i and v_j. Now see which case you're in:

Case (α). The current $\mathbf{x}$ is optimal; STOP.

Case (β). You can lower the cost by introducing $x_{pq} > 0$.

3. In case (β), solve the equations for t_{ij}. Get a new basic solution by bringing (p,q) into the basis and removing (μ, v). Return to step 2.

With each change of basis, the cost decreases. Since the number of possible bases is finite, the process must finally stop with an optimal basic solution.

A COMPLETE NUMERICAL EXAMPLE. Let the costs, supplies, and demands be

$$c_{ij} = \begin{bmatrix} 9 & 7 & 1 \\ 5 & 4 & 0 \end{bmatrix} \quad \begin{array}{l} s_i = 8, 3 \\ d_j = 4, 2, 5 \end{array}$$

Since $\sum s_i = \sum d_j = 1$, the data are consistent. We hope, and assume, that the problem is non-degenerate.

Step 1. We will get a first basic feasible solution by the method discussed before Example 1 (this method is sometimes called the *northwest-corner* method). We set up a 2-by-3 rectangle for the unknowns x_{ij}; we put the supplies at the right, the demands at the bottom

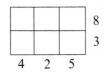

First, we get $x_{11} = 4$, eliminating the first column and leaving the residual supply $s_1' = 8 - 4 = 4$. Continuing, we find the basic $x_{ij} = 4, 2, 2, 3$ in this picture:

$$\begin{array}{|c|c|c|c}
\hline
4 & 2 & 2 & 8 \\
\hline
 & & 3 & 3 \\
\hline
4 & 2 & 5 &
\end{array}$$

We have found *four* basic $x_{ij} > 0$, which is correct here because $m + n - 1 = 4$.

Step 2. We'll solve $u_i + v_j = c_{ij}$ in B. We start with this picture:

$$\begin{array}{|c|c|c|c}
\hline
9 & 7 & 1 & u_1 \\
\hline
 & & 0 & u_2 \\
\hline
v_1 & v_2 & v_3 &
\end{array}$$

The letters are unknowns; the numbers give c_{ij} where $(i,j) \in B$. The picture requires

$$u_1 + v_1 = 9, \quad u_1 + v_2 = 7, \quad u_1 + v_3 = 1, \quad u_2 + v_3 = 0.$$

We have four equations in five unknowns. We arbitrarily make $v_3 = 0$. (We might as well have made $v_3 = 57$ or anything else.)

Now the picture imples $u_2 = 0$ and $u_1 = 1$, for only these values permit $v_3 = 0$. This yields the picture

9	7	1	1
		0	0

$$v_1 \quad v_2 \quad 0$$

Now the 1 at the right forces $v_1 = 8$ and $v_2 = 6$, giving

9	7	1	1
		0	0

$$8 \quad\; 6 \quad\; 0$$

Now all the equilibrium equations are solved. Notice that once we set $v_n = 0$, the other unknowns were forced, one by one.

Finally in step 2, we have to compute $u_i + v_j$ for i,j *not* in B. These are the two primed valued in this picture:

·	·	·	1
8′	6′	·	0

$$8 \quad\; 6 \quad\; 0$$

(The dots occur for $(i,j) \in B$. If we compare the primed numbers with the corresponding costs, we find that we are in case (β):

$$u_2 + v_1 = 8 > 5 = c_{21}$$
$$u_2 + v_2 = 6 > 4 = c_{22}.$$

These two inequalities tell us we could lower the cost by bringing either $(2,1)$ or (2.2). Since the first discrepancy is greater, let's bring in $(p,q) = (2,1)$.

Step 3. We'll solve this picture for the t_{ij}:

·	·	·	0
in		·	1

$$1 \quad\; 0 \quad\; 0$$

The 1's at right and at bottom occur in row p and column q; here $p = 2, q = 1$. We must solve for a t_{ij} wherever there is a dot, that is, where (i,j) is in B. The row sums occur at right; the column sums occur at bottom.

This system is also recursive. Since only one dot occurs in row 2, we find $t_{12} = 1$:

.	.	.	0
		1.	1
1	0	0	

Now only one unknown remains in each of the three columns, and we get the remaining t_{ij}:

1.	0.	$-1.$	0
		1.	1
1	0	0	

Note that *all the t_{ij} equal 1 or 0 or -1*; that will always be true.

Since $t_{ij} > 0$ iff $t_{ij} = 1$, (59) gives

$$\text{Best } \lambda = \min\{x_{ij}: t_{ij} = 1\}$$
$$= \min(x_{11}, x_{23}) \tag{61}$$
$$= \min(4,3) = 3 = x_{23}.$$

Therefore, x_{23} will leave the basis as x_{21} enters with the value $\lambda = 3$. Here $(\mu,v) = (2,3)$, and $(p,q) = (2,1)$. For $(i,j) \in B$, x_{ij} goes to $x_{ij} - \lambda t_{ij}$, and we get the new basic feasible solution

1	2	5	8
3			3
4	2	5	

Note that the supply and demand equations are again satisfied.

How did the cost change? Since we brought in $x_{21} = \lambda = 3$, where $u_2 + v_1 - c_{21} = 3$, the cost must have decreased by the product $3 \times 3 = 9$. In fact, you can compute the first cost

$$\text{old } \sum c_{ij} x_{ij} = 52$$

and you can compute the new cost

$$\text{new } \sum c_{ij} x_{ij} = 43.$$

Return to step 2. We set up the equilibrium equations for the *new* basis B. This is the picture:

9	7	1	u_1
5			u_2
v_1	v_2	v_3	

As before, the letters are unknowns; the numbers give c_{ij} where $(i,j) \in B$.

Again we arbitrarily make $v_3 = 0$. And now, one by one, the picture forces the following values:

$$v_3 = 0, \quad u_1 = 1, \quad v_2 = 6, \quad v_1 = 8, \quad u_2 = -3.$$

And so the picture becomes

9	7	1	1
5			-3

$$8 \quad 6 \quad 0$$

Finally in step 2, we have to compute $u_i + v_j$ for (i,j) *not* in B. These are the two primed numbers in this picture:

·	·	·	1
·	$3'$	$-3'$	-3

$$8 \quad 6 \quad 0$$

Now we compare:

$$u_2 + v_2 = 3 < c_{22} = 4$$
$$u_2 + v_3 = -3 < c_{23} = 0$$

The inequalities $u_i + v_j \leqslant c_{ij}$ for (i,j) not in B define the case (α). And so we discover that *the current* $\mathbf{x}$ *is optimal*.

Check: In the case (α), but not in the case (β), the $\mathbf{u}$ and $\mathbf{v}$ are feasible for the dual. Since they solve the equilibrium equations, they must satisfy

$$\sum s_i u_i + \sum v_j d_j = \sum c_{ij} x_{ij}$$

if $\mathbf{x}$ is optimal for the primal. As a check, we compute

$$\sum s_i u_i = 8 \cdot 1 + 3 \cdot (-3) = -1$$
$$\sum d_j v_j = 4 \cdot 8 + 2 \cdot 6 + 5 \cdot 0 = 44.$$

Sure enough, the sum is 43, which equals the last $\sum c_{ij} x_{ij}$.

General discussion. We just finished solving *by hand* a linear-programming problem with 5 equations and 6 unknowns. All the equations were easy: we could solve them recursively. Now you'll see why that will always be true.

The primal basic equations. In the m-by-n rectangle, put a dot in each square (i,j) where (i,j) is in the basis B. Put m supplies at the right and n demands at the bottom. If $\sum s_i = \sum d_j$, there must be one and only one solution x_{ij} belonging to the basis B. We will prove that we can compute the basic x_{ij} recursively. That is to say, at each stage we can find some equation with only one *new* unknown.

Every equation is a row equation or a column equation. Call either a row or a column a *line*. The matrix X has $m + n$ lines. On the intersections of these lines we have placed $m + n - 1$ dots.

Every line must contain *at least* one dot. Otherwise some row or column equation would contain *no* basic unknown, and so this equation would be unsolvable for any given non-zero supply or demand. For instance, the third column must have a dot; otherwise we could never meet $d_3 \neq 0$.

Lemma. *Some line contains exactly one dot.*

PROOF. Otherwise *every* line would have at least 2 dots. Looking at the m rows, we must see at least $2m$ dots; looking instead at the n columns, we must see at least $2n$ dots. But one or both of those numbers must be $> m + n - 1$:

$$2m > m + n - 1 \quad or \quad 2n > m + n - 1.$$

One way or the other, we see more than $m + n - 1$ dots; that contradicts our assumption.   □

So some line contains just one dot. If the line is a row, we can solve for one basic x_{ij} and eliminate one supply equation; this eliminates one supply, s_i, and changes one demand, d_j, to the residual demand $d_j - s_i$. (The residual need not be ≥ 0, because a basic solution $\mathbf{x}$ need not be feasible.) If the line is a column, we eliminate one demand equation, deleting one demand d_j and changing one supply s_i to the residual supply $s_i - d_j$.

The new supplies and demands are consistent. In terms of dots and lines, we have *one less dot* and *one less line*. The remaining $m + n - 2$ dots designate a basis for the remaining $m + n - 1$ consistent supply and demand equations. Each remaining line must contain at least one dot; and so, by the lemma, some remaining line contains *exactly* one dot.

Continuing in this way, we solve for all the basic x_{ij}. At each stage, some equation contains only one new unknown—some remaining line contains only one remaining dot.

The form of a basic solution. Look at this diagram, in which the dots give a basis B.

We solve for the basic x_{ij} one by one:

$$x_{12} = d_2, \quad x_{11} = s_1 - d_2, \quad x_{21} = d_1 + d_2 - s_1,$$
$$x_{23} = s_2 + s_1 - d_1 - d_2. \tag{62}$$

Every x_{ij} has one of these two forms:

$$(\mathrm{r}) \quad x_{ij} = \sum s_i - \sum d_j$$
$$(\mathrm{c}) \quad x_{ij} = \sum d_j - \sum s_i,$$

where the sums are taken over subsets.

In the example (62), we found x_{11} and x_{23} in the form (r); these unknowns came from *row* equations. We found x_{12} and x_{21} in the form (c); these unknowns came from *column* equations.

In general, every basic x_{ij} has one of the forms (r), (c). This is the reason: At each stage, residual supplies have the form (r) while residual demands have the form (c); that is true for the first stage, and it follows by induction for the later stages. But each new x_{ij} is picked up from some residual row or column equation. From a residual row, x_{ij} will get the form (r); from a column, the form (c).

Now you can see why *all the t_{ij} equal 1, 0, or −1*. Remember, the t_{ij} came from solving a set of basic equations with these data:

$$s_p = 1, \quad s_i = 0 \, (i \neq p); \quad d_q = 1, \quad d_j = 0 \, (j \neq q).$$

Every partial sum $\sum s_i$ equals 0 or 1; every partial sum $\sum d_j$ equals 0 or 1. Every difference (r) or (c) can equal *only* 1, 0, or −1. But every t_{ij} must have the form (r) or (c), and so every $t_{ij} = 1$ or 0 or −1.

Knowing this, you can put formula (59) in better form:

$$\text{Best } \lambda = \min\{x_{ij} : t_{ij} = 1\}. \tag{63}$$

The equilibrium equations. In our complete numerical example, we solved two sets of equilibrium equations

$$u_i + v_j = c_{ij} \quad \text{for} \quad (i,j) \in B, \tag{64}$$

with $v_n = 0$. You saw that we could solve these equations *recursively*. Now I'll show you why that will always be true.

Since we arbitrarily set $v_n = 0$, our first step is to look for some equation (64) that contains v_n:

$$u_i + v_n = c_{in} \quad \text{for} \quad (i,n) \in B. \tag{65}$$

Every equation (65) determines one unknown u_i. In this way we solve for one u_i for each basic dot (i,n) in the last column of the m-by-n rectangle. Since every line in the rectangle must contain at least one basic dot, we must find at least one equation (65).

Now we have computed the u_i for which (i,n) is in the basis. The next step is to look for those equations (64) that contain the *known* u_i; every such equation—if there *is* any—determines a new v_j. If there *isn't* any such equation, our engine must stop: we are out of gas and out of luck. The point of this discussion is to prove we never will run out of gas: we'll be able to keep going till we've reached *all* the u_i and v_j.

After we know some u_i, formula (64) determines all the v_j for j associated with i in the basis; conversely, after we know some v_j, we can get all u_i for i associated with j in the basis. Suppose we've gone on this way as far as we can; suppose we have to stop after computing

$$u_i \text{ for } i \text{ in the set } I, \tag{66}$$

$$v_j \text{ for } j \text{ in the set } J. \tag{67}$$

Then this is what we want to prove:

$$I = \{1,2, \ldots ,m\}$$
$$J = \{1,2, \ldots ,n\}. \tag{68}$$

In other words, we have to stop only when we've got *all* the unknown u_i and v_j.

For every dual variable u_i in (66), write down the corresponding primal basic equation:

$$\sum_j{}^* x_{ij} = s_i \qquad \text{for } i \text{ in } I. \tag{66'}$$

These equations contains only x_{ij} for (i,j) in the basis B. If i is in I, *then j must be in J*; for otherwise we could compute some new v_j by solving some new equation

$$u_i + v_j = c_{ij} \qquad i \in I, j \notin J.$$

Likewise, for every dual variable v_j in (67), write down the corresponding primal basic equation:

$$\sum_i{}^* x_{ij} = d_j \qquad \text{for } j \text{ in } J. \tag{67'}$$

As before, if j is in J, and if x_{ij} is a basic variable, then i must be in I; for otherwise we could solve some new equation

$$u_i + v_j = c_{ij} \qquad i \notin I, j \notin J.$$

Suppose (68) is false. If I is incomplete, then (66') omits some of the m supply equations; if J is incomplete, then (67') omits some of the n demand equations. In either case, the data

$$s_i \, (i \in I), \quad d_j \, (j \in J) \tag{69}$$

are incomplete, and so *they may be chosen independently*. The consistency condition is

$$\sum_{i=1}^m s_i = \sum_{j=1}^n d_j, \tag{70}$$

and that condition applies *only* if I and J are complete. But if I or J is incomplete, then the incomplete primal basic equations (66'), (67') are independent: the data consist of $|I| + |J|$ unconstrained numbers. (Here we use the notation $|S|$ to stand for the number of members of a finite set S.)

So, if I or J is incomplete, the $|I| + |J|$ primal basic equations (66'), (67') are independent. How many basic primal unknowns x_{ij} do these equations contain? These equations contain the unknowns

$$\{x_{ij} : i \in I, j \in J, (i,j) \in B\}. \tag{71}$$

If we call this set X', we will prove

$$|X'| = |I| + |J| - 1. \tag{72}$$

If the $|I| + |J|$ equations are independent, then they contain too few unknowns, and for *some* data (69) the equations would have no solution. That is impossible, since every basis B must provide a solution x_{ij} for every consistent set of primal equations. This argument proves that the $|I| + |J|$ equations cannot be independent, and that means

$$|I| = m \quad \text{and} \quad |J| = n. \tag{73}$$

Now we will prove (72). We have to count the set X' in (71). We let the *primal variable* x_{ij} correspond to the *dual equation*

$$u_i + v_j = c_{ij} : i \in I, j \in J, \text{ and } (i,j) \in B. \tag{74}$$

Each member of X' corresponds to exactly one equation (74), and so $|X'|$ is the number of these equations.

But these are precisely the equilibrium equations that we solved to get the u_i and v_j in (66) and (67). Every time we solved a new equation (74), we computed *one* new dual unknown, u_i or v_j. Before we solved any equation (74), we *started* with the *one* dual unknown $v_n = 0$. After we solved *one* equation, we knew *two* dual unknowns. Finally, we must have solved $|I| + |J| - 1$ equations in order to end with $|I| + |J|$ unknowns. Therefore, we solved exactly $|I| + |J| - 1$ equations (74), and that must be the size of the corresponding set X'. That proves (72) and so we finish our discussion of the transportation problem.

When you do the following problems, you'll see how easy the algorithm is to use.

References

1. F. L. Hitchcock, The distribution of a product from several sources to numerous localities. *J. Math. Phys.* Vol. 20 (1941) pp. 224–230.
2. T. C. Koopmans, Optimum utilization of the transportation system, *Econometrica* Vol. 17 (1949) pp. 136–145.
3. Walter Garvin, *Introduction to Linear Programming* (Part II: The Transporation Problem and its Variants), McGraw-Hill, 1960.

PROBLEMS

1. Let the costs, supplies, and demands be

$$(c_{ij}) = \begin{bmatrix} 9 & 7 & 1 \\ 5 & 4 & 0 \end{bmatrix}, \quad \begin{matrix} s_i = 2, 9 \\ d_j = 4, 2, 5 \end{matrix}.$$

As in the complete numerical example, find optimal **u**, **v**, and **x**. Check: $\Sigma s_i u_i + \Sigma d_j v_j = \Sigma\Sigma c_{ij} x_{ij} = 36$.

2. Let the costs, supplies, and demands be

$$(c_{ij}) = \begin{bmatrix} 9 & 1 & 7 \\ 5 & 4 & 0 \end{bmatrix}, \quad \begin{matrix} s_i = 2, 10 \\ d_j = 4, 3, 5 \end{matrix}.$$

Find optimal $\mathbf{u}$, $\mathbf{v}$, and $\mathbf{x}$. Check: Dual and primal values = 26.

3. Let the costs, supplies, and demands be

$$(c_{ij}) = \begin{bmatrix} 7 & 2 & 5 \\ 4 & 1 & 8 \\ 9 & 6 & 3 \end{bmatrix}, \quad \begin{matrix} s_i = 8, 6, 5 \\ d_j = 3, 9, 7 \end{matrix}.$$

Find optimal $\mathbf{u}$, $\mathbf{v}$, and $\mathbf{x}$. Check: Dual and primal values = 52.

4. Make up a non-trivial transportation problem with 3 supplies and 4 demands. Solve it, and check the equality of dual and primal values.

*5. Solve Problem 3 with the network-flow algorithm described in the last problem in the preceding section. Compare that algorithm with the one in this section. Which algorithm do you prefer? Why? Which one handles degeneracy better? Which one do you think would be better for computer solution of very large problems?

Nonlinear Programming

2

1 Wolfe's Method for Quadratic Programming

Look at the following problem:

$$A\mathbf{x} = \mathbf{b}, \quad \mathbf{x} \geqslant \mathbf{0}$$
$$\mathbf{p} \cdot \mathbf{x} + \tfrac{1}{2}\mathbf{x} \cdot C\mathbf{x} = \text{minimum.} \tag{1}$$

Here A is an $m \times n$ matrix; $\mathbf{b} \in R^m$, $\mathbf{p} \in R^n$; and C is an $n \times n$ *symmetric* matrix. If $C = O$, we have the canonical minimum problem of linear programming; but if $C \neq O$, the problem is nonlinear.

We will obtain necessary and sufficient conditions for $\mathbf{x}^0$ to solve (1). Then we'll discuss Wolfe's method for solving (1) with a computer.

Wolfe's method is easy to program, since his algorithm is a variant of the simplex method of *linear* programming. As we will show, Wolfe's method works if C is positive definite; it also works if $\mathbf{p} = \mathbf{0}$ and C is only positive semi-definite. For these quadratic-programming problems, Wolfe's method gives an elegant and practical solution.

Necessary conditions. It would be easy to deduce necessary and sufficient conditions from the general Kuhn-Tucker theorems, which we will discuss later. But I'll give you an independent derivation that uses only the Farkas theorem.

As in linear programming, we'll say $\mathbf{x}^0$ is *feasible* for (1) if it satisfies the constraints:

$$A\mathbf{x} = \mathbf{b}, \quad \mathbf{x} \geqslant \mathbf{0}. \tag{2}$$

If $\mathbf{x}^0$ is feasible, then all $\mathbf{x} = \mathbf{x}^0 + \varepsilon \mathbf{y}$ are feasible for which

$$A\mathbf{y} = \mathbf{0} \tag{3}$$

and

$$y_j \geqslant 0 \quad \text{if} \quad x_j^0 = 0,$$

where $0 \leqslant \varepsilon \ll 1$. If $\mathbf{x}^0$ is *optimal* for (1), and if we define

$$q(\mathbf{x}) \equiv \mathbf{p} \cdot \mathbf{x} + \tfrac{1}{2}\mathbf{x} \cdot C\mathbf{x}, \tag{4}$$

then the conditions (3) should imply

$$q(\mathbf{x}^0) \leqslant q(\mathbf{x}^0 + \varepsilon \mathbf{y}) \qquad (0 \leqslant \varepsilon \ll 1). \tag{5}$$

Expanding the quadratic, we find

$$q(\mathbf{x}^0 + \varepsilon \mathbf{y}) = q(\mathbf{x}^0) + \varepsilon(\mathbf{p} + C\mathbf{x}^0) \cdot \mathbf{y} + \tfrac{1}{2}\varepsilon^2 \mathbf{y} \cdot C\mathbf{y}. \tag{6}$$

For small $\varepsilon > 0$ the coefficient of ε must be $\geqslant 0$ if (5) holds. Therefore, (3) should imply

$$(\mathbf{p} + C\mathbf{x}^0) \cdot \mathbf{y} \geqslant 0. \tag{7}$$

To use the Farkas theorem, we must put (3) in a familiar form. Let $\mathbf{a}_1, \ldots, \mathbf{a}_m$ be the *rows* of the given matrix A; let $\mathbf{e}^1, \ldots, \mathbf{e}^n$ be the natural basic unit vectors in R^n. Then (3) says

$$\begin{aligned}
\mathbf{a}_i \cdot \mathbf{y} &\geqslant 0 & (i = 1, \ldots, m) \\
-\mathbf{a}_i \cdot \mathbf{y} &\geqslant 0 & (i = 1, \ldots, m) \\
\mathbf{e}^j \cdot \mathbf{y} &\geqslant 0 & \text{if } x_j^0 = 0.
\end{aligned} \tag{8}$$

Since (8) implies (7), the Farkas theorem says

$$\mathbf{p} + C\mathbf{x}^0 = \sum_{i=1}^{m} \rho_i \mathbf{a}_i + \sum_{i=1}^{m} \sigma_i(-\mathbf{a}_i) + \sum{}^0 \tau_j \mathbf{e}^j \tag{9}$$

where the coefficients are all $\geqslant 0$; the sum $\sum^0$ is taken only for j such that $x_j^0 = 0$.

We will now restate (9). If we set $u_i = \sigma_i - \rho_i$, we get a vector $\mathbf{u} \in R^m$. Then

$$\sum_{i=1}^{m} (\sigma_i - \rho_i)\mathbf{a}_i = \mathbf{u}A = A^T\mathbf{u},$$

and (9) says

$$\mathbf{p} + C\mathbf{x}^0 + A^T\mathbf{u} = \mathbf{v}, \tag{10}$$

where

$$0 \leqslant \mathbf{v} = \sum{}^0 \tau_j \mathbf{e}^j \tag{11}$$

Note that

$$\mathbf{x}^0 \cdot \mathbf{v} = \sum{}^0 \tau_j x_j^0 = 0. \tag{12}$$

We have thus proved the following result:

Theorem 1. *Suppose* $\mathbf{x}^0$ *solves the quadratic-programming problem* (1). *Then there exist vectors* $\mathbf{u}^0$ *in* R^m, $\mathbf{v}^0$ *in* R^n *such that* $\mathbf{x}^0, \mathbf{u}^0, \mathbf{v}^0$ *solve*

$$\begin{aligned}
A\mathbf{x} &= \mathbf{b} \\
C\mathbf{x} + A^T\mathbf{u} - \mathbf{v} &= -\mathbf{p} \\
\mathbf{x} \geqslant 0, \quad \mathbf{v} \geqslant 0, \quad \mathbf{x} \cdot \mathbf{v} &= 0.
\end{aligned} \tag{13}$$

(We do *not* require $\mathbf{u} \geqslant 0$; $\mathbf{u}$ is unrestricted in R^m.)

This is a *necessary* condition for x^0 to be optimal. It is remarkable for the following reason: All the equations are *linear*—except the one equation $x \cdot v = 0$. That equation amounts to an *exclusion rule: the components x_j and v_j must not both be positive.* (If one is positive, the other must be zero, since we require $x \geqslant 0$ and $v \geqslant 0$.)

EXAMPLE 1. Consider the problem

$$3x_1 + 4x_2 = 6, \quad x \geqslant 0$$
$$x_1^2 - 5x_1 + 7x_2 = \text{minimum}. \tag{14}$$

Here we identify

$$A = (3,4), \qquad b = (6)$$

$$C = \begin{pmatrix} 2 & 0 \\ 0 & 0 \end{pmatrix}, \quad p = \begin{pmatrix} -5 \\ 7 \end{pmatrix} \tag{15}$$

Now (13) becomes

$$3x_1 + 4x_2 = 6$$

$$\begin{pmatrix} 2x_1 \\ 0 \end{pmatrix} + \begin{pmatrix} 3 \\ 4 \end{pmatrix} u_1 - \begin{pmatrix} v_1 \\ v_2 \end{pmatrix} = \begin{pmatrix} 5 \\ -7 \end{pmatrix}. \tag{16}$$

$$x \geqslant 0, \quad v \geqslant 0, \quad x \cdot v = 0.$$

For $x_1 \leqslant 2$ and $x_2 \geqslant 0$ the quadratic in (14) is minimized iff $x_1 = 2$ and $x_2 = 0$. Therefore, our problem has the unique solution

$$x^0 = \begin{pmatrix} 2 \\ 0 \end{pmatrix}. \tag{17}$$

If we set

$$u^0 = (\tfrac{1}{3}), \quad v^0 = \begin{pmatrix} 0 \\ \frac{25}{3} \end{pmatrix}, \tag{18}$$

we solve (16).

EXAMPLE 2. Consider the problem

$$x_1 + x_2 = 2, \quad x \geqslant 0$$
$$-x_1^2 - x_2^2 = \text{minimum}. \tag{19}$$

This problem has two solutions:

$$x^0 = \begin{pmatrix} 2 \\ 0 \end{pmatrix} \quad \text{and} \quad x^0 = \begin{pmatrix} 0 \\ 2 \end{pmatrix}. \tag{20}$$

Here the system (13) becomes

$$x_1 + x_2 = 2$$

$$-2 \begin{pmatrix} x_1 \\ x_2 \end{pmatrix} + \begin{pmatrix} 1 \\ 1 \end{pmatrix} u_1 - \begin{pmatrix} v_1 \\ v_2 \end{pmatrix} = \begin{pmatrix} 0 \\ 0 \end{pmatrix} \tag{21}$$

$$x \geqslant 0, \quad v \geqslant 0, \quad x \cdot v = 0.$$

One solution is

$$\mathbf{x}^0 = \begin{pmatrix} 2 \\ 0 \end{pmatrix}, \quad \mathbf{u}^0 = (4), \quad \mathbf{v}^0 = \begin{pmatrix} 0 \\ 4 \end{pmatrix}.$$

Another solution is

$$\mathbf{x}^0 = \begin{pmatrix} 0 \\ 2 \end{pmatrix}, \quad \mathbf{u}^0 = (4), \quad \mathbf{v}^0 = \begin{pmatrix} 4 \\ 0 \end{pmatrix}.$$

But look: There is a third solution, namely,

$$\mathbf{x}^0 = \begin{pmatrix} 1 \\ 1 \end{pmatrix}, \quad \mathbf{u}^0 = (2), \quad \mathbf{v}^0 = \begin{pmatrix} 0 \\ 0 \end{pmatrix}. \tag{22}$$

This $\mathbf{x}^0$ does *not* solve (19). Therefore, the necessary condition (13) *is not sufficient for* $\mathbf{x}^0$ *to solve the quadratic program* (1).

Sufficient conditions. We will show that (13) is sufficient, as well as necessary, for $\mathbf{x}^0$ to solve (1) if C is positive semi-definite ($\mathbf{w} \cdot C\mathbf{w} \geqslant 0$ for all $\mathbf{w}$). Note that $C = (-2)$ in Example 2; that accounts for the false solution (22).

Theorem 2. *Suppose* C *is positive semi-definite. Suppose* $\mathbf{x}^0, \mathbf{u}^0, \mathbf{v}^0$ *solve* (13). *Then* $\mathbf{x}^0$ *solves the quadratic program* (1). *If* C *is positive definite, then the solution of* (1) *is unique.*

PROOF. If we expand the quadratic (4), we get

$$q(\mathbf{x}^0 + \mathbf{y}) = q(\mathbf{x}^0) + (\mathbf{p} + C\mathbf{x}^0) \cdot \mathbf{y} + \tfrac{1}{2}\mathbf{y} \cdot C\mathbf{y}. \tag{23}$$

If $\mathbf{x}$ is feasible for (1), let $\mathbf{y} = \mathbf{x} - \mathbf{x}^0$. Then $\mathbf{y}$ must satisfy

$$A\mathbf{y} = \mathbf{0}, \quad y_j \geqslant 0 \quad \text{if} \quad x_j^0 = 0. \tag{24}$$

Since $\mathbf{x}^0, \mathbf{u}^0, \mathbf{v}^0$ satisfy (13), we have

$$\mathbf{p} + C\mathbf{x}^0 = \mathbf{v}^0 - \mathbf{u}^0 A,$$

and so

$$(\mathbf{p} + C\mathbf{x}^0) \cdot \mathbf{y} = \mathbf{v}^0 \cdot \mathbf{y}. \tag{25}$$

But $\mathbf{v}^0 \geqslant \mathbf{0}$; and $v_j^0 > 0$ implies $x_j^0 = 0$, which implies $y_j \geqslant 0$. Therefore, $\mathbf{v}^0 \cdot \mathbf{y} \geqslant 0$; and now (25) and (23) give

$$q(\mathbf{x}^0 + \mathbf{y}) \geqslant q(\mathbf{x}^0) + \tfrac{1}{2}\mathbf{y} \cdot C\mathbf{y} \geqslant q(\mathbf{x}^0). \tag{26}$$

This proves that $\mathbf{x}^0$ minimizes $q(\mathbf{x})$. If C is positive *definite*, then we can say more: If $\mathbf{x}^0 + \mathbf{y}$ is feasible, then (26) implies

$$q(\mathbf{x}^0 + \mathbf{y}) > q(\mathbf{x}^0) \quad \text{unless} \quad \mathbf{y} = \mathbf{0}, \tag{27}$$

and so $\mathbf{x}^0$ is the *unique* solution of (1).

Existence. Does the quadratic program (1) have a solution? If C is positive definite, that question is easy to answer: *A solution exists if there is any* $\mathbf{x}^1$ *that satisfies the constraints.*

Here is the proof. For some $\alpha > 0$ we have

$$\mathbf{x} \cdot C\mathbf{x} \geqslant \alpha |\mathbf{x}|^2 \qquad \text{for all } \mathbf{x},$$

and so the quadratic $q(\mathbf{x})$ equals

$$\mathbf{p} \cdot \mathbf{x} + \tfrac{1}{2}\mathbf{x} \cdot C\mathbf{x} \geqslant -|\mathbf{p}|\,|\mathbf{x}| + \tfrac{1}{2}\alpha|\mathbf{x}|^2$$
$$> q(\mathbf{x}^1) \quad \text{if} \quad |\mathbf{x}| \geqslant R$$

if R is big enough. Therefore, we may restrict the competition to the sphere $|\mathbf{x}| \leqslant R$. Now the set

$$\{\mathbf{x}: A\mathbf{x} = \mathbf{b}, \mathbf{x} \geqslant 0, |\mathbf{x}| \leqslant R\}$$

is closed and bounded, and so some $\mathbf{x}^0$ in this set minimizes $q(\mathbf{x})$.   □

If C is *not* positive definite, the question of existence is harder. In practice, as you know, we usually have some reason for thinking a solution exists, and what we want is a good algorithm for computing it.

Wolfe's algorithm. If C is positive definite, or if $\mathbf{p} = \mathbf{0}$ and C is positive semidefinite, we can use a *simplex method* to solve the system (13). Our two theorems tell us that the system (13) is equivalent to the quadratic program (1).

You object, I'm sure. The system (13) is nonlinear because of the equation $\mathbf{x} \cdot \mathbf{v} = 0$. We can't use the simplex method for a nonlinear problem.

Yes, we can. Let's write the system (13) without the offending nonlinear equation:

$$A\mathbf{x} = \mathbf{b}$$
$$C\mathbf{x} + A^T\mathbf{u} - \mathbf{v} = -\mathbf{p} \tag{28}$$
$$\mathbf{x} \geqslant \mathbf{0}, \quad \mathbf{u} \text{ free}, \quad \mathbf{v} \geqslant \mathbf{0}.$$

This is a problem in *linear* programming. We could compute a solution $\mathbf{x}, \mathbf{v}, \mathbf{u}$ by the simplex method. But probably we would find $\mathbf{x} \cdot \mathbf{v} > 0$, and we must exclude that.

Here is the trick: We will use the equation $\mathbf{x} \cdot \mathbf{v} = 0$ as an *exclusion rule*: x_j and v_j *must not both be positive for any* $j = 1, \ldots, n$. We will use the familiar simplex method with this one modification: At any stage, if x_j is in the old basis ($x_j > 0$), we must not bring v_j into the basis; if v_j is in the old basis ($v_j > 0$), we must not bring x_j into the basis.

We begin by using the simplex method, in the usual way, to obtain a basic feasible solution $\mathbf{x} = \mathbf{x}^1$ for the linear program

$$A\mathbf{x} = \mathbf{b}, \quad \mathbf{x} \geqslant \mathbf{0}. \tag{29}$$

(Here, and in what follows, we assume that the linear programming problems we meet are non-degenerate, so that the simplex method works.) Next we set $\mathbf{u}^1 = \mathbf{0}$ and $\mathbf{v}^1 = \mathbf{0}$. Note that we begin with $\mathbf{x}^1 \cdot \mathbf{v}^1 = 0$.

If, by some miracle, our initial $\mathbf{x}^1$ solves $C\mathbf{x}^1 = -\mathbf{p}$, we are done; for then Theorem 2 tells us that $\mathbf{x}^1$ solves the quadratic program. But if $C\mathbf{x}^1 \neq -\mathbf{p}$, we will introduce slack variables $z_1 \geqslant 0, \ldots, z_n \geqslant 0$ and later drive them to zero. We let

$$\sum_{j=1}^{n} c_{ij}x'_j + d_i z_i^1 = -p_i \qquad (i = 1, \ldots, n) \tag{30}$$

where we fix $d_i = \pm 1$ so that we may take $z_i^1 \geq 0$. This fixes the diagonal matrix

$$D = \begin{pmatrix} d_1 & \cdots & 0 \\ \vdots & \cdots & \vdots \\ 0 & \cdots & d_n \end{pmatrix} = \begin{pmatrix} \pm 1 & \cdots & 0 \\ \vdots & \cdots & \vdots \\ 0 & \cdots & \pm 1 \end{pmatrix}. \tag{31}$$

The slack vector $\mathbf{z} \geq \mathbf{0}$ will later vary (and eventually equal $\mathbf{0}$), but D will always have its initial definition.

We now restate (28) as a minimum problem:

$$\begin{aligned} A\mathbf{x} &= \mathbf{b} \\ C\mathbf{x} + A^T\mathbf{u} - \mathbf{v} + D\mathbf{z} &= -\mathbf{p} \\ \mathbf{x} \geq \mathbf{0}, \quad \mathbf{u} \text{ free}, \quad \mathbf{v} \geq \mathbf{0}, \quad \mathbf{z} &\geq \mathbf{0} \\ \mu \equiv z_1 + \cdots + z_n &= \text{minimum}. \end{aligned} \tag{32}$$

If for the free variable $\mathbf{u}$ we introduce

$$\mathbf{u} = \mathbf{u}' - \mathbf{u}'' \quad \text{with} \quad \mathbf{u}' \geq \mathbf{0} \quad \text{and} \quad \mathbf{u}'' \geq \mathbf{0}, \tag{33}$$

then (32) becomes a canonical minimum problem of linear programming. We start with the initial feasible solution

$$\mathbf{x} = \mathbf{x}^1, \quad \mathbf{u} = \mathbf{0}, \quad \mathbf{v} = \mathbf{0}, \quad \mathbf{z} = \mathbf{z}^1. \tag{34}$$

To the linear-programming problem (32) we now apply the usual simplex method—with just one variance: *at each change of basis we apply the exclusion rule.* If $x_j > 0$, we must not bring in $v_j > 0$; if $v_j > 0$, we must not bring in $x_j > 0$. After a finite number of changes of basis, the computation must stop. Indeed, that would be true even if we did *not* use the exclusion rule.

When the computation stops, μ has some value ≥ 0. Wolfe proved this: If C is *positive definite, the final value of μ is zero.*

Look what that says about the system (32). It says that $\mathbf{z}$ has the final value $\mathbf{0}$. What's more, since we've used the *exclusion rule* at every stage, we have kept $\mathbf{x} \cdot \mathbf{v} = 0$. Under these conditions the system (32) is identical to the *nonlinear* system (13); and that, we know, is necessary and sufficient for the final value $\mathbf{x} = \mathbf{x}^0$ to solve the quadratic program (1).

Now let's prove Wolfe's result: μ takes the final value zero.

When the computation stops, let

$$\begin{aligned} J_1 &= \{j : x_j > 0\} \\ J_2 &= \{j : v_j > 0\} \\ J_0 &= \{j : x_j = v_j = 0\}. \end{aligned} \tag{35}$$

By the exclusion rule, $\mathbf{x} \cdot \mathbf{v} = 0$, and so the index sets J_1 and J_2 are disjoint. And, of course, both J_1 and J_2 are disjoint from J_0. And the union is

$$J_1 \cup J_2 \cup J_0 = \{1, 2, \ldots, n\}. \tag{36}$$

All that says is this: For each j, either $x_j > 0$ or $v_j > 0$ or $x_j = v_j = 0$.

At each stage, this is what the exclusion rule requires: We may bring x_j into the basis only if $j \in J_1 \cup J_0$, since the set J_2 is excluded; we may bring v_j into the basis only if $j \in J_2 \cup J_0$, since the set J_1, is excluded. At the final stage the simplex method tells us this: *No permitted change of basis can lower the cost μ.*

We now write down a linear-programming problem that mentions only the final *permitted* index sets in (32). Let

$$\begin{aligned} \mathbf{a}^1, \ldots, \mathbf{a}^n \text{ be the columns of } A \\ \mathbf{a}_1, \ldots, \mathbf{a}_m \text{ be the columns of } A^T, \end{aligned} \tag{37}$$

and let $\mathbf{c}^j$, $\mathbf{e}^j$, and $\mathbf{d}^j$ be the columns of the matrices C, I, and D. Then the system (32), with only the permitted indices, takes this form:

$$\sum_{J_1 \cup J_0} x_j \mathbf{a}^j = \mathbf{b}$$

$$\sum_{J_1 \cup J_0} x_j \mathbf{c}^j + \sum_{i=1}^{m} u_i \mathbf{a}_i - \sum_{J_2 \cup J_0} v_j \mathbf{e}^j + \sum_{j=1}^{n} z_j \mathbf{d}^j = -\mathbf{p} \tag{38}$$

$$\text{minimize} \sum z_j \equiv \mu$$

$$x_j \geqslant 0, \quad u_i \text{ free}, \quad v_j \geqslant 0, \quad z_j \geqslant 0.$$

When the algorithm stops, the numbers x_j, u_i, v_j, z_j solve the linear program (38). Now we will prove minimum $\mu = 0$ in (38).

We will use the equilibrium theorem of linear programming. The constraints in (38) comprise $m + n$ linear equations. Therefore, the dual vector has $m + n$ components, say

$$r_1, \ldots, r_m, \quad s_1, \ldots, s_n. \tag{39}$$

The dual vector is naturally partitioned into twp parts, $\mathbf{r}$ and $\mathbf{s}$. According to the equilibrium theorem, the optimal dual vector satisfies the following conditions:

$$\begin{array}{llll} (\alpha) & \mathbf{r} \cdot \mathbf{a}^j + \mathbf{s} \cdot \mathbf{c}^j = 0 & \text{if } j \in J_1 \\ (\beta) & \mathbf{r} \cdot \mathbf{a}^j + \mathbf{s} \cdot \mathbf{c}^j \leqslant 0 & \text{if } j \in J_0 \\ (\gamma) & \mathbf{s} \cdot \mathbf{a}_i = 0 & (i = 1, \ldots, m) \\ (\delta) & -\mathbf{s} \cdot \mathbf{e}^j = 0 & \text{if } j \in J_2 \\ (\varepsilon) & -\mathbf{s} \cdot \mathbf{e}^j \leqslant 0 & \text{if } j \in J_0 \\ (\zeta) & \mathbf{s} \cdot \mathbf{d}^j \leqslant 1 & (j = 1, \ldots, n) \\ (\eta) & \mathbf{r} \cdot \mathbf{b} - \mathbf{s} \cdot \mathbf{p} = \mu \end{array}$$

Equality occurs in (α) because $x_j > 0$ in J_1; equality occurs in (γ) because u_i is free; equality occurs in (δ) because $v_j > 0$ in J_2; equality occurs in (η) because the final value of μ is optimal in (38).

Assuming C is positive definite, we will now prove $\mu = 0$.

First we will show $s = 0$. To do so, we only need to show $s \cdot Cs \leqslant 0$. We now assert:

$$(\mathbf{r} \cdot \mathbf{a}^j + \mathbf{s} \cdot \mathbf{c}^j)s_j \begin{cases} \leqslant 0 \text{ in } J_0 \\ = 0 \text{ in } J_1. \\ = 0 \text{ in } J_2 \end{cases} \tag{40}$$

The equality in J_0 follows from the inequality (β) and the inequality (ε), which says $s_j \geqslant 0$ in J_0; the equality in J_1 follows from the equality (α); the equality in J_2 follows from the equality (δ), which says $s_j = 0$ in J_2. Summing over the three subsets, and using

$$\sum_{j=1}^n \mathbf{a}^j s_j = A\mathbf{s}, \quad \sum_{j=1}^n \mathbf{c}^j s_j = C\mathbf{s},$$

we deduce

$$\mathbf{r} \cdot A\mathbf{s} + \mathbf{s} \cdot C\mathbf{s} \leqslant 0, \tag{41}$$

But the vector $A\mathbf{s}$ has the components $\mathbf{a}_i \cdot \mathbf{s}$, and (γ) says all those inner products are zero. Therefore, $A\mathbf{s} = 0$ and

$$\mathbf{s} \cdot C\mathbf{s} \leqslant 0, \tag{42}$$

which proves $\mathbf{s} = 0$. Now (η) says

$$\mu = \mathbf{r} \cdot \mathbf{b} - \mathbf{s} \cdot \mathbf{p} = \mathbf{r} \cdot \mathbf{b}, \tag{43}$$

and we will show this equals zero. We have $\mathbf{b} = A\mathbf{x}$ in Wolfe's linear program (32). Therefore,

$$\mathbf{r} \cdot \mathbf{b} = \mathbf{r} \cdot A\mathbf{x}$$

$$= \sum_{j=1}^n \mathbf{r} \cdot \mathbf{a}^j x_j. \tag{44}$$

Now (α) gives

$$\mathbf{r} \cdot \mathbf{a}^j = -\mathbf{s} \cdot \mathbf{c}^j = 0 \quad \text{in} \quad J_1. \tag{45}$$

But $x_j \neq 0$ iff $j \in J_1$ (that was the definition of the subset J_1). Therefore,

$$\mu = \mathbf{r} \cdot A\mathbf{x} = \sum_{J_1} \mathbf{r} \cdot \mathbf{a}^j x_j = 0, \tag{46}$$

which is the required result.

A *different assumption.* We just proved $\mu = 0$ by assuming C positive definite. Now, instead, let's assume

$$C \text{ positive } semi\text{definite, and } \mathbf{p} = 0. \tag{47}$$

This assumption is neither weaker nor stronger than the former.

Assuming (47) we will again prove $\mu = 0$ when Wolfe's algorithm stops. Since $\mu = \sum z_j$ in (32), and since $\mathbf{x} \cdot \mathbf{v} = 0$, that will again prove that Wolfe's final $\mathbf{x}$ solves the quadratic program (1).

Now we can't show $\mathbf{s} = \mathbf{0}$, but we *can* show $C\mathbf{s} = \mathbf{0}$. To do so, we only need to show $\mathbf{s} \cdot C\mathbf{s} \leqslant 0$. For then the semidefiniteness gives

$$(\mathbf{s} + \varepsilon\mathbf{y}) \cdot C(\mathbf{s} + \varepsilon\mathbf{y}) \geqslant 0 \qquad \text{for all } \mathbf{y},$$

and so

$$\mathbf{s} \cdot C\mathbf{s} + 2\varepsilon\mathbf{y} \cdot C\mathbf{s} + \varepsilon^2\mathbf{y} \cdot C\mathbf{y} \geqslant 0.$$

Now $\mathbf{s} \cdot C\mathbf{s} \leqslant 0$ implies

$$2\varepsilon\mathbf{y} \cdot C\mathbf{s} + O(\varepsilon^2) \geqslant 0 \qquad \text{for all } \mathbf{y}.$$

Letting $\varepsilon \to \pm 0$, we find $\mathbf{y} \cdot C\mathbf{s} = 0$ for all $\mathbf{y}$, and so $C\mathbf{s} = \mathbf{0}$.

Again we make the assertion (40), and the proof is just what it was; and again we deduce (41) and (42). Now (42) implies not $\mathbf{s} = \mathbf{0}$ but only $C\mathbf{s} = \mathbf{0}$.

Again we have $\mathbf{s} \cdot \mathbf{p} = 0$, but now it's true for a different reason: we've assumed $\mathbf{p} = \mathbf{0}$. Therefore, we again have $\mu = \mathbf{r} \cdot \mathbf{b}$. And again ($\alpha$) implies

$$\mathbf{r} \cdot \mathbf{a}^j = -\mathbf{s} \cdot \mathbf{c}^j \quad \text{in} \quad J_1,$$

and now this equals zero because $\mathbf{s} \cdot \mathbf{c}^j$ equals the jth component of the vector

$$\mathbf{s} \cdot C = C^T\mathbf{s} = C\mathbf{s} = \mathbf{0}.$$

Now, as before, (46) yields the result $\mu = 0$.

A NUMERICAL EXAMPLE. Although Wolfe's theoretical arguments are subtle and complex, his computing method is easy. I hope this example will convince you.

We will solve the quadratic program

$$\begin{aligned} x_1 + x_2 &= 1, \quad \mathbf{x} \geqslant \mathbf{0} \\ x_1^2 + x_1 x_2 + x_2^2 - 5x_2 &= \text{minimum}. \end{aligned} \tag{48}$$

You can solve this by inspection if you set $x_1 = 1 - x_2$ in the quadratic. The unique solution is the boundary point where $x_2 = 1$. This problem is a good test for Wolfe's method, since the minimum occurs on the boundary.

The problem (48) has the form

$$\begin{aligned} A\mathbf{x} &= \mathbf{b}, \quad \mathbf{x} \geqslant \mathbf{0} \\ \tfrac{1}{2}\mathbf{x} \cdot C\mathbf{x} + \mathbf{p} \cdot \mathbf{x} &= \text{minimum}, \end{aligned} \tag{49}$$

where

$$A = (1,1), \qquad \mathbf{b} = (1)$$

$$C = \begin{pmatrix} 2 & 1 \\ 1 & 2 \end{pmatrix} \qquad \mathbf{p} = \begin{pmatrix} 0 \\ -5 \end{pmatrix} \tag{50}$$

Since C is positive definite, Wolfe's algorithm must work.

We first get a basic solution to $A\mathbf{x} = \mathbf{b}, \mathbf{x} \geqslant \mathbf{0}$. Let's say our computer gives us

$$\mathbf{x} = \begin{pmatrix} 1 \\ 0 \end{pmatrix}. \tag{51}$$

(This is bad luck; the other basic solution solves the quadratic program.) We now compute

$$C\mathbf{x} = \begin{pmatrix} 2 \\ 1 \end{pmatrix}. \tag{52}$$

If this equaled $-\mathbf{p}$, we would be through; since it does not, we must introduce slack variables $z_i \geqslant 0$. We write

$$C\mathbf{x} + D\mathbf{z} = -\mathbf{p}, \tag{53}$$

which becomes

$$\begin{pmatrix} 2 & 1 \\ 1 & 2 \end{pmatrix}\begin{pmatrix} 1 \\ 0 \end{pmatrix} + \begin{pmatrix} -1 & 0 \\ 0 & 1 \end{pmatrix}\begin{pmatrix} 2 \\ 4 \end{pmatrix} = \begin{pmatrix} 0 \\ +5 \end{pmatrix}. \tag{54}$$

This fixes $d_1 = -1, d_2 = 1$, and it gives the initial slack vector the components $2, 4$. Note that we had to take $d_1 = -1$, not $d_1 = +1$, in order to get $z_1 \geqslant 0$.

We now write down Wolfe's linear program (32):

$$
\begin{aligned}
x_1 + x_2 && = 1 \\
2x_1 + x_2 + u_1 - v_1 && - z_1 && = 0 \\
x_1 + 2x_2 + u_1 && - v_2 && + z_2 = 5
\end{aligned}
\tag{55}
$$
$$x_j \geqslant 0, \quad u_1 \text{ free}, \quad v_j \geqslant 0, \quad z_j \geqslant 0$$
$$\text{Minimize } z_1 + z_2 \equiv \mu$$

All we have to do is solve this problem by the simplex method with just one variance: *the exclusion rule* $\mathbf{x} \cdot \mathbf{v} = 0$.

We start with the basic feasible solution to (55) that we have already computed:

$$x_1 = 1, \quad z_1 = 2, \quad z_2 = 4. \tag{56}$$

All the other unknowns intially equal zero. The initial cost is $\mu \equiv z_1 + z_2 = 6$.

I won't confuse you by writing down the simplex tableau. It's enough to tell you what happens with each change of basis.

First change of basis: x_2 comes in, x_1 goes out. Result: the new basic solution

$$x_2 = 1, \quad z_1 = 1, \quad z_2 = 3, \tag{57}$$

with the reduced cost $\mu = 4$. Please verify that the values (57) do satisfy the three equations in (55).

Next change of basis: v_1 comes in, z_1 goes out. The entrance of v_1 is permitted by the exclusion rule, since $x_1 = 0$ at this stage. Result: the new basic solution

$$x_2 = 1, \quad v_1 = 1, \quad z_2 = 3, \tag{58}$$

with the reduced cost $\mu = 3$. Again, please verify.

Last change of basis: u_1 comes in, z_2 goes out. Result: the basic solution

$$x_2 = 1, \quad u_1 = 3, \quad v_1 = 4, \tag{59}$$

with the cost $\mu = 0$. STOP.

As you see, the computer stops with the right answer: $x_2 = 1$. That's how Wolfe's method does quadratic programming.

Next, I'll tell you about the general theory of nonlinear programming.

References

Philip Wolfe, *The Simplex Method for Quadratic Programming*, Econometrica, vol. 27 (1959) pp. 382–398.

J. J. Sylvester, "A Question in the Geometry of Situation," Quarterly J. Pure and Appl. Math, vol. 1 (1857) p. 79.

PROBLEMS

1. For $C = 0$ show that the optimality condition (13) is the *equilibrium* condition of linear programming.

2. Classical Lagrange multipliers: Suppose x^0 solves the quadratic program (1), and suppose x^0 is an *interior* point: $x^0 > 0$. Then what does the optimality condition (13) become? (The components of u^0 are *Lagrange multipliers*.)

3. Consider the problem

$$2x_1 + 3x_2 \leqslant 6, \quad x \geqslant 0$$
$$(x_1 - 1)^2 + (x_2 - 5)^2 = \min.$$

   Draw a picture and guess the solution. Introduce a slack $x_3 \geqslant 0$, and rewrite the problem in the form (1); identify A, b, C, p. Now use Theorem 2 to prove your guess is optimal: find x^0, u^0, v^0 satisfying (13).

4. Do as in Problem 3 for the problem

$$x_1 + 7x_2 \leqslant 7, \quad x \geqslant 0,$$
$$(x_1 - 1)^2 + (x_2 - 5)^2 = \min.$$

5. Sylvester's problem (1857): "It is required to find the least circle which shall contain a given set of points in the plane." Show that Sylvester's problem for finite point sets in R^n is equivalent to the following quadratic program: *If the points* $a_1, \ldots, a_m$ *are given, find a point* x *and a number* λ *solving*

$$a_i \cdot x + \lambda \geqslant \tfrac{1}{2}|a_i|^2 \qquad (i = 1, \ldots, m),$$
$$\tfrac{1}{2}x \cdot x + \lambda = \min.$$

   Then the required least sphere has center x and has radius $r = \sqrt{(x \cdot x + 2\lambda)}$.

6. In general, suppose $\mathbf{x}^0$ solves

$$Ax \geqslant \mathbf{b}, \quad \mathbf{x} \in R^N,$$
$$\tfrac{1}{2}\mathbf{x} \cdot C\mathbf{x} + \mathbf{p} \cdot \mathbf{x} = \min.$$

where A is an $m \times N$ matrix and C is an $N \times N$ matrix. Show that the following condition is necessary for optimality: *If* $\mathbf{a}_1, \ldots, \mathbf{a}_m$ *are the rows of* A, *suppose*

$$\mathbf{a}_i \cdot \mathbf{x}^0 \quad \begin{cases} = b_i & \text{for } i \text{ in } I \\ > b_i & \text{for } i \text{ not in } I. \end{cases}$$

Then there must be numbers $w_i \geqslant 0$ *for* i *in* I *such that*

$$C\mathbf{x}^0 + \mathbf{p} = \sum_I w_i \mathbf{a}_i.$$

Method: For $0 < \varepsilon \ll 1$ set $\mathbf{x} = \mathbf{x}^0 + \varepsilon \mathbf{y}$. Show that if $\mathbf{y}$ satisfies

$$\mathbf{a}_i \cdot \mathbf{y} \geqslant 0 \qquad \text{for } i \text{ in } I,$$

then $\mathbf{y}$ must satisfy $(C\mathbf{x}^0 + \mathbf{p}) \cdot \mathbf{y} \geqslant 0$. Now use the Farkas theorem.

7. (Continuation.) If C is positive semidefinite in Problem 6, show that the necessary condition is also sufficient.

8. (Continuation.) For Problem 7 show that the optimality condition may be expressed as follows: $\mathbf{x}^0$ is optimal iff there exist vectors $\mathbf{z}$ and $\mathbf{w}$ such that

$$A\mathbf{x}^0 - \mathbf{z} = \mathbf{b}$$
$$C\mathbf{x}^0 + \mathbf{p} = A^T\mathbf{w}$$
$$\mathbf{z} \geqslant 0, \quad \mathbf{w} \geqslant 0, \quad \mathbf{z} \cdot \mathbf{w} = 0.$$

9. (*Continuation.*) For Sylvester's problem in R^n, what is the optimality condition? (Set $N = n + 1$, $x_N = \lambda$.)

*10. (Continuation.) For Sylvester's problem in R^n, show that the optimal sphere has center $\mathbf{x}$ and radius r such that (1) all the given points $\mathbf{a}_1, \ldots, \mathbf{a}_m$ lie in the ball of radius r with center $\mathbf{x}$, and (2) the center $\mathbf{x}$ lies in the convex hull of the points $\mathbf{a}_i$ lying *on* the boundary:

$$\mathbf{x} = \sum_I w_i \mathbf{a}_i, \quad w_i \geqslant 0, \quad \sum_I w_i = 1$$

where $|\mathbf{a}_i - \mathbf{x}| = r$ for $i \in I$. (The optimal sphere is unique because, if two optimal spheres had radius r but had different centers, the intersection of the two balls would lie in a ball of radius $<r$, and this smaller ball would contain the given points.)

11. Consider the quadratic program

$$6x_1 + 3x_2 + 2x_3 = 6, \quad \mathbf{x} \geqslant 0$$
$$x_1^2 + (x_2 - 2)^2 + (x_3 - 3)^2 = \min.$$

Using condition (13), find the optimal solution. (Hint: $x_1 = 0$.)

12. For Problem 11 what is Wolfe's linear program with exclusion rule?

13. Consider the quadratic program

$$Ax \geqslant b, \quad x \geqslant 0.$$
$$\tfrac{1}{2}x \cdot Cx + p \cdot x = \min.$$

Introduce a slack vector and then get an optimality condition from (13).

14. Consider the quadratic program

$$\begin{bmatrix} 1 & 2 & 3 \\ 4 & 5 & 6 \end{bmatrix} x = \begin{bmatrix} 1 \\ 3 \end{bmatrix}, \quad x \geqslant 0$$
$$x_1^2 + x_1 x_2 + x_2^2 + 3x_3^2 - 7x_2 = \min.$$

What is Wolfe's linear program with exclusion rule? If you start with the feasible solution $x = (\tfrac{1}{2}, 0, \tfrac{1}{6})$, what is the diagonal matrix D for Wolfe's method? What is the starting slack vector z?

15. Classical least squares: Let M be an $m \times n$ matrix, and let g be given in R^m. Suppose no x solves $Mx = g$. Consider the problem of minimizing the length of the residual:

$$|Mx - g|^2 = \min. \quad \text{for } x \text{ in } R^n.$$

Show that a necessary and sufficient condition for optimality is

$$M^T M x = M^T g.$$

Show that the optimal x is unique iff the columns of M are linearly independent.

16. Consider least squares with sign constraints:

$$|Mx - g|^2 = \min., \quad x \geqslant 0.$$

Find a necessary and sufficient condition for optimality. Write Wolfe's linear program with exclusion rule.

17. Investment strategy: Let p_1 and p_2 be today's prices per share for two stocks. We wish to buy x_1 and x_2 shares of the two stocks so that

$$p_1 x_1 + p_2 x_2 \leqslant \$100{,}000. \tag{i}$$

We guess that next year the prices per share will be $p_1 + \mu_1$ and $p_2 + \mu_2$, and we want at least $\$10{,}000$ expected profit:

$$\mu_1 x_1 + \mu_2 x_2 \geqslant \$10{,}000. \tag{ii}$$

Let the statistical variance (volatility) of our portfolio be the positive definite quadratic form

$$\sigma_{11} x_1^2 + 2\sigma_{12} x_1 x_2 + \sigma_{22} x_2^2. \tag{iii}$$

The problem is to meet the constraints (i) and (ii) with minimum volatility (iii). From condition (13) find a necessary and sufficient condition for the optimal portfolio x_1, x_2. Draw a picture that illustrates the quadratic program.

18. Generalize the last problem for an optimal portfolio of n stocks.

2 Kuhn-Tucker Theory

When you first studied calculus, you learned how to solve maximum problems. Given a function $g(x)$, if you wanted its maximum value, you solved the equation $g'(x) = 0$.

All we're going to do now is generalize that basic method of calculus. We'll pay special attention to what happens in n dimensions if the maximum occurs on the boundary. We'll discuss a *constrained maximum problem*, and we'll talk about a *saddle-value problem* that generalizes the idea of Lagrange multipliers. We'll follow the classic presentation given by Kuhn and Tucker in 1950.

In a charming, scholarly article published in 1976, Kuhn points out that the famous Kuhn-Tucker conditions were anticipated by William Karush in his Master's Thesis, which he wrote in 1939. Also, there was a paper by Fritz John in 1948.

But still we speak of the *Kuhn-Tucker* conditions. Just so, we speak of *Fourier* series—though Euler used them before Fourier did. We do so with reason: it was Fourier, not Euler, who first presented the full significance of the discovery that continues to bear his name. We do not depreciate the priority of Euler when we continue to value the major contribution of Fourier.

Enough philosophy. Let's get back to calculus.

You remember that little maximum problem? Let's take a close look at it. We are given a function $g(x)$, and we want its maximum for $0 \leqslant x \leqslant a$. Let

$$g(x) = x \sin x \qquad (0 \leqslant x \leqslant a). \tag{1}$$

We take the derivative and set it equal to zero;

$$g'(x) = \sin x + x \cos x = 0. \tag{2}$$

This equation has the roots $x = 0, x_1, x_2, \ldots$ where

$$x_n = -\tan x_n, \quad (n - \tfrac{1}{2})\pi < x_n < n\pi. \tag{3}$$

Now we see some complications. The easy root, $x = 0$, cannot maximize $g(x)$, since $g(x) > 0$ for small $x > 0$. If $a < x_1$, then the maximum occurs on the boundary, at $x = a$. If $a \geqslant x_1$, then the maximum may occur at one of the roots $x_1, x_3, x_5, \ldots$; or it may occur at $x = a$. The maximum cannot occur at any of the roots $x_2, x_4, x_6, \ldots$, since these points provide local minima.

I gave you this example to remind you that when you use calculus for a maximum problem, you have to take a close look at the boundary. And so we proceed with caution to a general *maximum problem of nonlinear programming*:

MAX. Let $g(\mathbf{x})$, $f_1(\mathbf{x}), \ldots, f_m(\mathbf{x})$ be *differentiable for* $\mathbf{x} \geqslant \mathbf{0}$ *in* R^n. *Find* $\mathbf{x}^0$ *to make*

$$g(\mathbf{x}) = \text{maximum} \qquad \text{for } \mathbf{f}(\mathbf{x}) \geqslant \mathbf{0} \text{ and } \mathbf{x} \geqslant \mathbf{0}. \tag{4}$$

In our example (1), we have $n = 1$, $m = 1$,

$$g(x_1) = x_1 \sin x_1, \quad f_1(x_1) = a - x_1. \tag{5}$$

In general, the constraints $\mathbf{x} \geqslant \mathbf{0}$, $\mathbf{f}(\mathbf{x}) \geqslant \mathbf{0}$ define the domain of feasible $\mathbf{x}$. In (1) the feasible x_1 satisfy $0 \leqslant x_1 \leqslant a$.

The problem MAX is more general than it looks. It is like the *standard* form of linear programming: it may be used to express the *general* form. If we want to remove some constraints $x_i \geqslant 0$, we set those $x_i = s_i - t_i$ and then require $s_i \geqslant 0$ and $t_i \geqslant 0$. If we want to require $f_j = 0$, we write the two inequalities $f_j \geqslant 0$ and $-f_j \geqslant 0$.

We will look for necessary conditions for $\mathbf{x}^0$ to solve MAX. If $\mathbf{x}^0 > \mathbf{0}$ and $\mathbf{f}(\mathbf{x}^0) > \mathbf{0}$, we shall obtain the familiar necessary condition of calculus:

$$\nabla g(\mathbf{x}^0) = \mathbf{0} \quad \text{(all } \partial g / \partial x_i = 0 \text{ at } \mathbf{x}^0). \tag{6}$$

Complications occur only if some components $x_i^0 = 0$ or some components $f_j(\mathbf{x}^0) = 0$.

We will obtain conditions for a *local* maximum. We compare $\mathbf{x}^0$ with points $\mathbf{x}$ on a very small arc starting from $\mathbf{x}^0$:

$$\mathbf{x} = \mathbf{x}(t) \quad (0 \leqslant t < t_1). \tag{7}$$

We assume $\mathbf{x}(0) = \mathbf{x}^0$, and we assume that all points on the arc are *feasible*:

$$x_i(t) \geqslant 0 \, (i = 1, \ldots, n); \quad f_j(\mathbf{x}(t)) \geqslant 0 \, (j = 1, \ldots, m). \tag{8}$$

We assume that the arc $\mathbf{x}(t)$ is differentiable at $t = 0$:

$$\mathbf{x}(t) = \mathbf{x}^0 + t\mathbf{v} + \cdots (0 \leqslant t < t_1), \text{ where } \mathbf{v} = \mathbf{x}'(0). \tag{9}$$

If $x_i^0 > 0$, then $x_i(t)$ must remain positive for small t; and if $f_j(\mathbf{x}^0) > 0$, then $f_j(\mathbf{x}(t))$ must remain positive for small t. But we have to be careful about those i or j for which $x_i^0 = 0$ or $f_j(\mathbf{x}^0) = 0$. We now define just those sets of indices:

$$I = I(\mathbf{x}^0) = \{i : x_i^0 = 0\}$$
$$J = J(\mathbf{x}^0) = \{j : f_j(\mathbf{x}^0) = 0\}. \tag{10}$$

To keep $x_i \geqslant 0$ and $f_j \geqslant 0$, we require that the initial velocity $\mathbf{v}$ satisfy

$$\mathbf{v} \cdot \mathbf{e}^i = v_i \geqslant 0 \quad \text{for } i \in I$$
$$\mathbf{v} \cdot \nabla f_j(\mathbf{x}^0) \geqslant 0 \quad \text{for } j \in J. \tag{11}$$

Conversely, if some feasible $\mathbf{x}^0$ is given, let I and J be defined by (10). We then say $\mathbf{x}^0$ satisfies *the constraint qualification* CQ if the following is true: *For all* $\mathbf{v}$ *in* R^n *that satisfy* (11) *there is a small arc of feasible points*

$$\mathbf{x}(t) = \mathbf{x}^0 + t\mathbf{v} + \mathbf{o}(t) \quad (0 \leqslant t < t_1).$$

If the functions f_j are linear, then CQ holds for all feasible $\mathbf{x}^0$; for then we may use the *linear* arc $\mathbf{x} = \mathbf{x}^0 + t\mathbf{v}$. If the f_j are nonlinear, then CQ may fail as we will later show by an example. Typically, the assumption CQ holds, but some care is needed to define the arc $\mathbf{x}(t)$.

The typical case is illustrated in Figure 1.

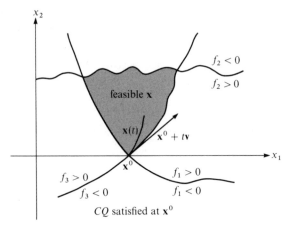

CQ satisfied at $\mathbf{x}^0$

Figure 1

The shaded region gives the feasible points $\mathbf{x}$; they satisfy

$$x_1 \geqslant 0, \quad x_2 \geqslant 0; \quad f_1 \geqslant 0, \quad f_2 \geqslant 0, \quad f_3 \geqslant 0. \tag{12}$$

For the illustrated feasible point $\mathbf{x}^0$, we have

$$x_1^0 > 0, \quad x_2^0 = 0; \quad f_1 = 0, \quad f_2 > 0, \quad f_3 = 0, \tag{13}$$

which means

$$I(\mathbf{x}^0) = \{2\}, \quad J(\mathbf{x}^0) = \{1,3\}. \tag{14}$$

As you see, the sets I and J depend on $\mathbf{x}^0$; if $\mathbf{x}^0$ had been chosen in the interior of the feasible set, then both I and J would be empty, and CQ would be satisfied vacuously.

Look at the linear arc $\mathbf{x}^0 + t\mathbf{v}$ in Figure 1. Here we see

$$v_2 > 0, \quad \mathbf{v} \cdot \nabla f_1 > 0, \quad \mathbf{v} \cdot \nabla f_3 = 0.$$

Though $\mathbf{v}$ satisfies the requirements (11), the *linear* arc is infeasible. Nevertheless, there is a feasible curvilinear arc $\mathbf{x} = \mathbf{x}^0 + t\mathbf{v} + \cdots$.

What about the other feasible points $\mathbf{x}^0$ in Figure 1? As you can see, they all satisfy CQ. For every feasible $\mathbf{x}^0$, if the velocity $\mathbf{v}$ points into or tangent to the feasible set, then there is a small feasible arc $\mathbf{x}(t)$ that starts from $\mathbf{x}^0$ with the *initial* velocity $\mathbf{v}$.

Theorem 1. *Let $\mathbf{x}^0 \geqslant \mathbf{0}$ and $\mathbf{f}(\mathbf{x}^0) \geqslant \mathbf{0}$, and suppose $\mathbf{x}^0$ satisfies the constraint qualification CQ. Define the Lagrange function*

$$\phi(\mathbf{x},\mathbf{u}) = g(\mathbf{x}) + \mathbf{u} \cdot \mathbf{f}(\mathbf{x}) \qquad (\mathbf{x} \geqslant \mathbf{0}, \mathbf{u} \geqslant \mathbf{0}). \tag{15}$$

Suppose $\mathbf{x}^0$ *satisfies the maximum problem* MAX. *Then for some* $\mathbf{u}^0 \geqslant \mathbf{0}$, $\mathbf{x}^0$
and $\mathbf{u}^0$ *satisfy*

$$\nabla_x \phi \leqslant \mathbf{0}, \quad \mathbf{x} \cdot \nabla_x \phi = 0, \quad \mathbf{x} \geqslant \mathbf{0}, \tag{16}$$

$$\nabla_u \phi \geqslant \mathbf{0}, \quad \mathbf{u} \cdot \nabla_u \phi = 0, \quad \mathbf{u} \geqslant \mathbf{0}. \tag{17}$$

PROOF. This theorem is a straightforward application of the Farkas alternative.

If $\mathbf{x}^0$ solves MAX, define the index sets I and J by formula (10). Let $\mathbf{v}$ be any initial velocity satisfying (11). Then there is a feasible arc (9), and so we must have

$$g(\mathbf{x}^0) \geqslant g(\mathbf{x}^0 + t\mathbf{v} + \cdots) \qquad (0 \leqslant t < t_1), \tag{18}$$

which implies

$$\mathbf{v} \cdot \nabla g(\mathbf{x}^0) \leqslant 0. \tag{19}$$

CQ says, in effect, that the inequalities (11) imply the inequality (19).

The Farkas theorem says that if the inequalities $\mathbf{v} \cdot \mathbf{a}^k \geqslant 0$ imply $\mathbf{v} \cdot \mathbf{b} \geqslant 0$, then $\mathbf{b} = \sum \lambda_k \mathbf{a}^k$ with $\lambda_k \geqslant 0$. If we let

$$\mathbf{b} = -\nabla g, \quad \{\mathbf{a}^k\} = \{\mathbf{e}^i : i \in I\} \cup \{\nabla f_j : j \in J\} \tag{20}$$

we get

$$\boxed{-\nabla g(\mathbf{x}^0) = \sum_I \rho_i \mathbf{e}^i + \sum_J \sigma_j \nabla f_j(\mathbf{x}^0)} \tag{21}$$

with $\rho_i \geqslant 0$ and $\sigma_j \geqslant 0$. You may not know it, but we now have all we need; the rest is just a matter of form.

The definition (15) for $\phi(\mathbf{x},\mathbf{u})$ implies

$$\nabla_x \phi = \nabla g(\mathbf{x}) + \sum_{j=1}^{m} u_j \nabla f_j(\mathbf{x}), \tag{22}$$

$$\nabla_u \phi = \mathbf{f}(\mathbf{x}). \tag{23}$$

We now define the vector $\mathbf{u}^0$:

$$u_j^0 = \begin{cases} \sigma_j & (j \in J) \\ 0 & (j \notin J) \end{cases} \tag{24}$$

Then (21) says

$$-\sum_I \rho_i \mathbf{e}^i = \nabla g(\mathbf{x}^0) + \sum_J \sigma_j \nabla f_j(\mathbf{x}^0)$$
$$= \nabla_x \phi(\mathbf{x}^0, \mathbf{u}^0) \tag{25}$$

This vector is $\leqslant \mathbf{0}$; its only nonzero components are the numbers $-\rho_i$ where $i \in I$. Now remember: $i \in I$ means $x_i^0 = 0$. Therefore, at $\mathbf{x}^0, \mathbf{u}^0$ the vector $\nabla_x \phi$ is $\leqslant \mathbf{0}$ and is orthogonal to $\mathbf{x}^0$; but that's just what (16) asserts.

What about the assertion (17)? At $\mathbf{x}^0, \mathbf{u}^0$ we have

$$\nabla_u \phi = \mathbf{f}(\mathbf{x}^0) \geqslant \mathbf{0}, \tag{26}$$

since $\mathbf{x}^0$ is feasible for MAX. And we have

$$\mathbf{u}^0 \cdot \nabla_u \phi(\mathbf{x}^0, \mathbf{u}^0) = \mathbf{u}^0 \cdot \mathbf{f}(\mathbf{x}^0)$$
$$= \sum_J \sigma_j f_j(\mathbf{x}^0). \tag{27}$$

But $j \in J$ means $f_j(\mathbf{x}^0) = 0$, and so the inner product (27) equals zero.

That complets the proof of Theorem 1. As you saw, the key formula was (21), which comes right from the Farkas theorem.

CQ may fail. I promised you an example. Kuhn and Tucker gave this example in their 1950 paper:

MAX. Maximize x_1 for

$$x_1 \geqslant 0, \quad x_2 \geqslant 0, \quad (1 - x_1)^3 - x_2 \geqslant 0. \tag{28}$$

Solution. Here we have $n = 2$, $m = 1$,

$$g = x_1, \quad f_1 = (1 - x_1)^3 - x_2. \tag{29}$$

The feasible set (28) appears shaded in Figure 2.

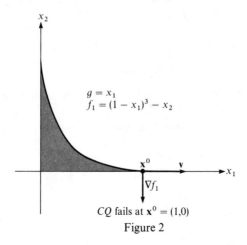

$$g = x_1$$
$$f_1 = (1 - x_1)^3 - x_2$$

CQ fails at $\mathbf{x}^0 = (1,0)$
Figure 2

Right away we see that $g(\mathbf{x})$ is maximized by $\mathbf{x}^0 = (1,0)$; this is the unique solution to MAX.

What about CQ? At $\mathbf{x}^0$ we have

$$x_2 = 0 \quad \text{and} \quad f_1 = 0. \tag{30}$$

Then CQ asks us to consider all $\mathbf{v}$ for which

$$v_2 \geqslant 0 \quad \text{and} \quad \mathbf{v} \cdot \nabla f_1(\mathbf{x}^0) \geqslant 0. \tag{31}$$

Since $\nabla f_1(\mathbf{x}^0) = (0, -1)$, the last formula says $v_2 \geqslant 0$ and $-v_2 \geqslant 0$; that is, $v_2 = 0$. One such $\mathbf{v}$ appears in Figure 2; it is $\mathbf{v} = (1,0)$. But *no* feasible arc $\mathbf{x}(t)$ starts from $\mathbf{x}^0$ with initial velocity $\mathbf{v} = (1,0)$. Therefore, CQ fails.

Now what happens to Theorem 1? Did we really need CQ to deduce (16) and (17)? Here we have

$$\phi(\mathbf{x},\mathbf{u}) = x_1 + u_1[(1 - x_1)^3 - x_2].$$

Formula (16) asserts that or some $u_1 = u_1^0$

$$\nabla_x \phi(\mathbf{x},\mathbf{u}) \leqslant 0 \quad \text{for} \quad \mathbf{x} = (1,0).$$

But this is false, since the first component of $\nabla_x \phi$ equals 1. *So we did need to assume* CQ *in Theorem 1.* A pretty example.

Sufficient conditions. Theorem 1 gives necessary conditions for $\mathbf{x}^0$ to solve MAX. What else may we require of $\mathbf{x}^0$ to obtain *sufficient* conditions?

First consider the unconstrained problem. In elementary calculus, one learns the necessary condition $g'(x_0) = 0$ and the condition $g''(x_0) < 0$, which is sufficient for x_0 to give a local maximum. This conditions works because *it keeps the graph of $g(x)$ below the tangent to the graph at x_0.* Analytically, we may express this as follows:

$$g(x) \leqslant g(x_0) + (x - x_0)g'(x_0). \tag{32}$$

This formula has much to recommend it: it does not use the second derivative g''; if $g'(x_0) = 0$, it guarantees a *global* maximum if it holds for all x; and it is a property of all *concave* functions, as we will now show.

Lemma. *Let $\psi(\mathbf{x})$ be any concave differentiable function in R^n. Then*

$$\psi(\mathbf{x}) \leqslant \psi(\mathbf{x}^0) + (\mathbf{x} - \mathbf{x}^0) \cdot \nabla\psi(\mathbf{x}^0). \tag{33}$$

PROOF. By the definition of concavity, for $0 < \varepsilon < 1$ we have

$$(1 - \varepsilon)\psi(\mathbf{x}^0) + \varepsilon\psi(\mathbf{x}) \leqslant \psi((1 - \varepsilon)\mathbf{x}^0 + \varepsilon\mathbf{x}),$$
$$\psi(\mathbf{x}) \leqslant \psi(\mathbf{x}^0) + \varepsilon^{-1}[\psi(\mathbf{x}^0 + \varepsilon(\mathbf{x} - \mathbf{x}^0)) - \psi(\mathbf{x}^0)]. \tag{34}$$

If we let $\varepsilon \to 0$, we get the result (33).

Local concavity. It's important to notice that the inequality (33) may be used as a *local* condition on $\mathbf{x}^0$: we may require it for all $\mathbf{x}$ *for just one* $\mathbf{x}^0$. Then $\psi(\mathbf{x})$ need not be concave, but still we shall know that $\mathbf{x}^0$ gives a global maximum.

For example, look at Figure 3. Here $g(x)$ is given for $0 \leqslant x \leqslant 1$. We assume $g'(0) \leqslant 0$, which is ncessary, but not sufficient, for $x_0 = 0$ to maximize $g(x)$. Now we require the additional condition of *local concavity*: For $x_0 = 0$

$$g(x) \leqslant g(x_0) + (x - x_0)g'(x_0) \quad \text{for} \quad 0 \leqslant x \leqslant 1.$$

Now Figure 3 shows that x_0 maximizes $g(x)$ though $g(x)$ is only *locally* concave.

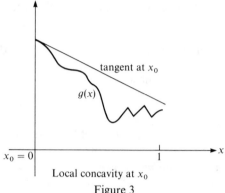

Figure 3

Now we're ready to state general sufficient conditions for $\mathbf{x}^0$ to solve MAX:

Theorem 2. *Let* $g(\mathbf{x}), f_1(\mathbf{x}), \ldots, f_m(\mathbf{x})$ *be differentiable for* $\mathbf{x} \geqslant \mathbf{0}$ *in* R^n. *Define the Lagrange function* (15). *Assume that* $\mathbf{x}^0$ *and* $\mathbf{u}^0$ *satisfy the conditions* (16), (17). *Now assume that the function*

$$\psi(\mathbf{x}) = \phi(\mathbf{x}, \mathbf{u}^0) \qquad (\mathbf{x} \geqslant \mathbf{0}) \tag{35}$$

is locally concave (33) *at* $\mathbf{x}^0$. *Then* $\mathbf{x}^0$ *solves* MAX.

Remark 1. Since $\mathbf{u}^0 \geqslant \mathbf{0}$ in R^m, the function

$$\psi(\mathbf{x}) = g(\mathbf{x}) + \mathbf{u}^0 \cdot \mathbf{f}(\mathbf{x}) \qquad (\mathbf{x} \geqslant \mathbf{0}) \tag{36}$$

will be locally concave at $\mathbf{x}^0$ if all the functions $g(\mathbf{x}), f_1(\mathbf{x}), \ldots, f_m(\mathbf{x})$ are locally concave.

Remark 2. Perhaps with some pain, you remember the constraint qualification CQ. We had to assume CQ to get Theorem 1, but *we shall not have to assume* CQ *to get Theorem* 2.

PROOF OF THE THEOREM. Suppose $\mathbf{x} \geqslant \mathbf{0}$ and $\mathbf{f}(\mathbf{x}) \geqslant \mathbf{0}$. Then, since $\mathbf{u}^0 \geqslant \mathbf{0}$,

$$g(\mathbf{x}) \leqslant g(\mathbf{x}) + \mathbf{u}^0 \cdot \mathbf{f}(\mathbf{x}) = \psi(\mathbf{x}). \tag{37}$$

But we have assumed $\psi(\mathbf{x})$ is locally concave at $\mathbf{x}^0$, and so

$$g(\mathbf{x}) \leqslant \psi(\mathbf{x}^0) + (\mathbf{x} - \mathbf{x}^0) \cdot \nabla\psi(\mathbf{x}^0) \qquad \text{for all } \mathbf{x} \geqslant \mathbf{0}. \tag{38}$$

But that just says

$$g(\mathbf{x}) \leqslant g(\mathbf{x}^0) + \mathbf{u}^0 \cdot \mathbf{f}(\mathbf{x}^0) + (\mathbf{x} - \mathbf{x}^0) \cdot \nabla_x\phi(\mathbf{x}^0, \mathbf{u}^0). \tag{39}$$

But (16) says (at $\mathbf{x}^0, \mathbf{u}^0$)

$$\nabla_x\phi(\mathbf{x}^0, \mathbf{u}^0) \leqslant \mathbf{0}, \quad \mathbf{x}^0 \cdot \nabla_x\phi(\mathbf{x}^0, \mathbf{u}^0) = 0, \tag{40}$$

so (39) gives

$$g(\mathbf{x}) \leqslant g(\mathbf{x}^0) + \mathbf{u}^0 \cdot \mathbf{f}(\mathbf{x}^0). \tag{41}$$

Now (17) says

$$\mathbf{u}^0 \cdot \mathbf{f}(\mathbf{x}^0) = \mathbf{u}^0 \cdot \nabla_u \phi(\mathbf{x}^0, \mathbf{u}^0) = 0, \tag{42}$$

and so (41) gives the result: $g(\mathbf{x}) \leqslant g(\mathbf{x}^0)$.

The case of linear programming. Whenever you learn something new, you can test its strength by applying it to something you knew before. Let's see what our two theorems say about the standard maximum problem of linear programming:

$$A\mathbf{x} \leqslant \mathbf{c}, \quad \mathbf{x} \geqslant \mathbf{0}, \quad \mathbf{b} \cdot \mathbf{x} = \max. \tag{43}$$

This is a special case of MAX if we set

$$g(\mathbf{x}) = \mathbf{b} \cdot \mathbf{x}, \quad \mathbf{f}(\mathbf{x}) = \mathbf{c} - A\mathbf{x}. \tag{44}$$

Then this is the Lagrange functional:

$$\phi(\mathbf{x}, \mathbf{u}) = \mathbf{b} \cdot \mathbf{x} + \mathbf{u} \cdot (\mathbf{c} - A\mathbf{x}).$$

Its gradients with respect to $\mathbf{x}$ and $\mathbf{u}$ are

$$\nabla_x \phi = \mathbf{b} - \mathbf{u}A, \quad \nabla_u \phi = \mathbf{c} - A\mathbf{x}. \tag{45}$$

Theorem 1 gives necessary conditions for $\mathbf{x}^0$ to solve MAX; Theorem 2 gives sufficient conditions. The constraint qualification CQ is satisfied for all feasible $\mathbf{x}$ because $\mathbf{f}(\mathbf{x})$ is linear (this is proved in the first paragraph after the definition of CQ). The function $\phi(\mathbf{x}, \mathbf{u}^0)$ is concave in $\mathbf{x}$ because it is linear. Therefore, the two theorems say this about *linear programming*: $\mathbf{x}^0$ *solves* MAX *if and only if it and some* $\mathbf{u}^0$ *satisfy* (16) *and* (17).

If we insert the gradients (45) into formulas (16) and (17), we get

$$\mathbf{b} - \mathbf{u}A \leqslant \mathbf{0}, \quad (\mathbf{b} - \mathbf{u}A) \cdot \mathbf{x} = 0, \quad \mathbf{x} \geqslant \mathbf{0}, \tag{16'}$$

$$\mathbf{c} - A\mathbf{x} \geqslant \mathbf{0}, \quad \mathbf{u} \cdot (\mathbf{c} - A\mathbf{x}) = 0, \quad \mathbf{u} \geqslant \mathbf{0}. \tag{17'}$$

These formulas require: $\mathbf{x}$ is feasible for the primal; $\mathbf{u}$ is feasible for the dual; and the *equilibrium conditions* hold.

Indeed, we knew before that these conditions were necessary and sufficient for optimality in linear programming; they are equivalent to the duality theorem. I hope you are pleased that our two theorems pass this test of strength. But you shouldn't be surprised; for we did use the Farkas theorem to prove Theorem 1, and we know that the Farkas theorem implies the duality theorem.

A saddle-value problem. In the linear case, which we just discussed, we maximized with respect to $\mathbf{x}$, and we minimized with respect to $\mathbf{u}$. That suggests the following general problem:

SV. *Let* $\phi(\mathbf{x}, \mathbf{u})$ *be differentiable for* $\mathbf{x} \geqslant \mathbf{0}$ *in* R^n *and* $\mathbf{u} \geqslant \mathbf{0}$ *in* R^m. *Find* $\mathbf{x}^0 \geqslant \mathbf{0}$ *and* $\mathbf{u}^0 \geqslant \mathbf{0}$ *to solve*

$$\phi(\mathbf{x}, \mathbf{u}^0) \leqslant \phi(\mathbf{x}^0, \mathbf{u}^0) \leqslant \phi(\mathbf{x}^0, \mathbf{u}) \tag{46}$$

for all $\mathbf{x} \geqslant \mathbf{0}$ *and* $\mathbf{u} \geqslant \mathbf{0}$.

This just says: At $\mathbf{x}^0, \mathbf{u}^0$ the function $\phi(\mathbf{x},\mathbf{u})$ is maximized with respect to $\mathbf{x}$ if $\mathbf{u}$ stays fixed, and ϕ is minimized with respect to $\mathbf{u}$ if $\mathbf{x}$ stays fixed. We know that the saddle-value property is important in game theory, and so we will consider the general problem SV; we will not restrict the definition of ϕ to formula (15), though that is the most important case.

This is what we want to know in general: *what relationship exists between the saddle-value property* (46) *and the two formulas*

$$\nabla_x\phi(\mathbf{x}^0,\mathbf{u}^0) \leqslant \mathbf{0}, \quad \mathbf{x}^0 \cdot \nabla_x\phi(\mathbf{x}^0,\mathbf{u}^0) = 0, \quad \mathbf{x}^0 \geqslant \mathbf{0} \tag{i}$$

$$\nabla_u\phi(\mathbf{x}^0,\mathbf{u}^0) \geqslant \mathbf{0}, \quad \mathbf{u}^0 \cdot \nabla_u\phi(\mathbf{x}^0,\mathbf{u}^0) = 0, \quad \mathbf{u}^0 \geqslant \mathbf{0}. \tag{ii}$$

In the context of nonlinear programming, these were formulas (16) and (17). The following theorem gives a relationship.

Theorem 3. *Suppose* $\mathbf{x}^0, \mathbf{u}^0$ *solve the saddle-value problem* SV. *Then they satisfy formulas* (i) *and* (ii). *Conversely, suppose* $\mathbf{x}^0, \mathbf{u}^0$ *satisfy* (i) *and* (ii); *suppose also that they satisfy*

$$\phi(\mathbf{x},\mathbf{u}^0) \leqslant \phi(\mathbf{x}^0,\mathbf{u}^0) + (\mathbf{x} - \mathbf{x}^0) \cdot \nabla_x\phi(\mathbf{x}^0,\mathbf{u}^0) \quad \text{for} \quad \mathbf{x} \geqslant \mathbf{0} \tag{iii}$$

and

$$\phi(\mathbf{x}^0,\mathbf{u}) \geqslant \phi(\mathbf{x}^0,\mathbf{u}^0) + (\mathbf{u} - \mathbf{u}^0) \cdot \nabla_u\phi(\mathbf{x}^0,\mathbf{u}^0) \quad \text{for} \quad \mathbf{u} \geqslant 0. \tag{iv}$$

Then $\mathbf{x}^0, \mathbf{u}^0$ *solve* SV.

Before the proof, here are a few remarks:

1. The supplementary conditions (iii) and (iv) require that ϕ be locally concave in $\mathbf{x}$ and locally convex in $\mathbf{u}$. That's what you'd expect if ϕ is maximized with respect to $\mathbf{x}$ and minimized with respect to $\mathbf{u}$.

2. Without some supplementary conditions, (i) and (ii) do not imply SV. For example, if $m = n = 1$, let

$$\phi(x,u) = (x - 7)^2 - (u - 9)^2 \qquad (x \geqslant 0, u \geqslant 0)$$

Here (i) and (ii) are both satisfied at $x_0 = 7$, $u_0 = 9$. But SV fails, since

$$\phi(x,9) > \phi(7,9) > \phi(7,u) \quad \text{if} \quad x \neq 7 \text{ and } u \neq 9,$$

which is the opposite of the SV inequality (46).

3. In the most important case, ϕ is a Lagrange function:

$$\phi(\mathbf{x},\mathbf{u}) = g(\mathbf{x}) + \mathbf{u} \cdot \mathbf{f}(\mathbf{x}). \tag{47}$$

Then the inequality (iv) is automatically satisfied as an equality, since ϕ is linear in $\mathbf{u}$. And the inequality (iii) is just the condition of local concavity (35), which we used as a supplementary condition in Theorem 2. After proving Theorem 3, we'll relate the SV problem to the MAX problem.

PROOF OF THE THEOREM. Suppose $\mathbf{x}^0, \mathbf{u}^0$ solve SV. Since ϕ is maximized with respect to its first argument, we have

$$\phi((1 - \varepsilon)\mathbf{x}^0 + \varepsilon\mathbf{x}, \mathbf{u}^0) - \phi(\mathbf{x}^0,\mathbf{u}^0) \leqslant 0 \tag{48}$$

for all $\mathbf{x} \geqslant \mathbf{0}$ if $0 < \varepsilon < 1$. If we divide by ε and let $\varepsilon \to 0$, we get

$$(\mathbf{x} - \mathbf{x}^0) \cdot \nabla_x \phi(\mathbf{x}^0, \mathbf{u}^0) \leqslant 0 \qquad \text{for all } \mathbf{x} \geqslant \mathbf{0}. \tag{49}$$

Since $\mathbf{x} - \mathbf{x}^0$ may equal any $\mathbf{v} \geqslant \mathbf{0}$, (49) implies

$$\nabla_x \phi(\mathbf{x}^0, \mathbf{u}^0) \leqslant \mathbf{0}. \tag{50}$$

And since $\mathbf{x}$ may equal $\mathbf{0}$, (49) implies

$$-\mathbf{x}^0 \cdot \nabla_x \phi(\mathbf{x}^0, \mathbf{u}^0) \leqslant 0. \tag{51}$$

But since $\mathbf{x}^0 \geqslant \mathbf{0}$, only equality can occur in (51). This proves (i). Exactly the same argument proves (ii), since SV says that *minus* ϕ is maximized with respect to its *second* argument.

Conversely, suppose $\mathbf{x}^0, \mathbf{u}^0$ satisfy all four conditions (i), ..., (iv). Then for all $\mathbf{x} \geqslant \mathbf{0}$

$$\begin{aligned}
\phi(\mathbf{x}, \mathbf{u}^0) &\leqslant \phi(\mathbf{x}^0, \mathbf{u}^0) + (\mathbf{x} - \mathbf{x}^0) \cdot \nabla_x \phi(\mathbf{x}^0, \mathbf{u}^0) \\
&= \phi(\mathbf{x}^0, \mathbf{u}^0) + \mathbf{x} \cdot \nabla_x \phi(\mathbf{x}^0, \mathbf{u}^0) \\
&\leqslant \phi(\mathbf{x}^0, \mathbf{u}^0).
\end{aligned}$$

And for all $\mathbf{u} \geqslant \mathbf{0}$

$$\begin{aligned}
\phi(\mathbf{x}^0, \mathbf{u}) &\geqslant \phi(\mathbf{x}^0, \mathbf{u}^0) + (\mathbf{u} - \mathbf{u}^0) \cdot \nabla_u \phi(\mathbf{x}^0, \mathbf{u}^0) \\
&= \phi(\mathbf{x}^0, \mathbf{u}^0) + \mathbf{u} \cdot \nabla_u \phi(\mathbf{x}^0, \mathbf{u}^0) \\
&\geqslant \phi(\mathbf{x}^0, \mathbf{u}^0).
\end{aligned}$$

That proves SV and completes the proof of the theorem.

For *concave* functions the problems SV and MAX are almost equivalent:

Theorem 4. *Let* $g(\mathbf{x}), f_1(\mathbf{x}), \ldots, f_m(\mathbf{x})$ *be differentiable and concave for* $\mathbf{x} \geqslant \mathbf{0}$ *in* R^n. *Let* $\phi(\mathbf{x}, \mathbf{u})$ *be the Lagrange function* (47). *Suppose* $\mathbf{x}^0$ *and some* $\mathbf{u}^0$ *solve* SV. *Then* x^0 *solves* MAX. *Conversely, suppose* $\mathbf{x}^0$ *solves* MAX *and* CQ; *or suppose directly that* $\mathbf{x}^0$ *and some* $\mathbf{u}^0$ *solve* (i) *and* (ii). *Then* $\mathbf{x}^0$ *and some* $\mathbf{u}^0$ *solve* SV.

PROOF. Since $\phi(\mathbf{x}, \mathbf{u})$ is concave in $\mathbf{x}$, condition (iii) holds for *every* $\mathbf{x}^0$ and $\mathbf{u}^0$. Since ϕ is linear in $\mathbf{u}$, condition (iv) holds (as an equality). Thus, for concave functions we may take (iii) and (iv) for granted.

If $\mathbf{x}^0$ and $\mathbf{u}^0$ solve SV, then Theorem 3 says they solve (i) and (ii). Now Theorem 2 says that $\mathbf{x}^0$ solves MAX.

Conversely, if $\mathbf{x}^0$ solves MAX and CQ, then Theorem 1 says $\mathbf{x}^0$ and some $\mathbf{u}^0$ solve (i) and (ii). Now Theorem 3 says that $\mathbf{x}^0$ and $\mathbf{u}^0$ solve SV.

Slater's theorem. The last theorem relates the SV and MAX problems for concave functions that are *differentiable*. But a concave function need not be differentiable. (For example, in one dimension, $1 - |x|$ is not differentiable.) And yet one may state saddle-value and maximum problems for non-differentiable functions. How are these problems related for general concave functions?

In the following discussion we will assume that, for all $\mathbf{x} \geqslant \mathbf{0}$ in R^n, the given functions $g(\mathbf{x}), f_1(\mathbf{x}), \ldots, f_m(\mathbf{x})$ are not necessarily differentiable. We define two problems:

MAX. Find $\mathbf{x}^0 \geqslant \mathbf{0}$ to solve

$$g(\mathbf{x}) = \text{maximum} \qquad \text{for } \mathbf{x} \geqslant \mathbf{0} \text{ and } \mathbf{f}(\mathbf{x}) \geqslant \mathbf{0}.$$

SV. Find $\mathbf{x}^0 \geqslant \mathbf{0}$, $\mathbf{u}^0 \geqslant \mathbf{0}$ to solve

$$g(\mathbf{x}) + \mathbf{u}^0 \cdot \mathbf{f}(\mathbf{x}) \leqslant g(\mathbf{x}^0) + \mathbf{u}^0 \cdot \mathbf{f}(\mathbf{x}^0) \leqslant g(\mathbf{x}^0) + \mathbf{u} \cdot \mathbf{f}(\mathbf{x}^0)$$

for all $\mathbf{x} \geqslant \mathbf{0}$ in R^n and all $\mathbf{u} \geqslant \mathbf{0}$ in R^m.

First we have an easy result:

Theorem 5. *Suppose* $\mathbf{x}^0, \mathbf{u}^0$ *solve* SV. *Then* $\mathbf{x}^0$ *solves* MAX. (*And this true for all real-valued functions* $g, f_1, \ldots, f_m$—*concave or not*). *Moreover,* $\mathbf{u}^0 \cdot \mathbf{f}(\mathbf{x}^0) = 0$.

PROOF. In SV the second inequality implies

$$(\mathbf{u} - \mathbf{u}^0) \cdot \mathbf{f}(\mathbf{x}^0) \geqslant 0 \qquad \text{for all } \mathbf{u} \geqslant \mathbf{0}.$$

If we let all $u_j \to +\infty$, we deduce $\mathbf{f}(\mathbf{x}^0) \geqslant \mathbf{0}$; if instead we set $\mathbf{u} = \mathbf{0}$, we find $-\mathbf{u}^0 \cdot \mathbf{f}(\mathbf{x}^0) \geqslant 0$, and now $\mathbf{u}^0 \geqslant \mathbf{0}$ implies $\mathbf{u}^0 \cdot \mathbf{f}(\mathbf{x}^0) = 0$.

The first inequality SV now states

$$g(\mathbf{x}) + \mathbf{u}^0 \cdot \mathbf{f}(\mathbf{x}) \leqslant g(\mathbf{x}^0) \qquad \text{for all } \mathbf{x} \geqslant \mathbf{0}.$$

Since SV assumes $\mathbf{u}^0 \geqslant \mathbf{0}$, we find $g(\mathbf{x}) \leqslant g(\mathbf{x}^0)$ if $\mathbf{f}(\mathbf{x}) \geqslant \mathbf{0}$. And so $\mathbf{x}^0$ solves MAX.

I repeat: This theorem is a platitude; it holds for *all* real-valued functions. But the next theorem—proved by M. Slater in 1950—is no platitude. It proves a converse of Theorem 5 for concave functions.

Slater's Theorem. *Suppose* $g(\mathbf{x}), f_1(\mathbf{x}), \ldots, f_m(\mathbf{x})$ *are concave for all* $\mathbf{x} \geqslant \mathbf{0}$; *suppose* $\mathbf{f}(\mathbf{a}) > \mathbf{0}$ *for some* $\mathbf{a} \geqslant \mathbf{0}$; *and suppose* $\mathbf{x}^0$ *solves* MAX. *Then* $\mathbf{x}^0$ *and some* $\mathbf{u}^0$ *solve* SV.

First, here are some remarks on the assumptions:

1. If we drop the assumption of concavity, the theorem becomes false. For example, let $m = n = 1$ and set

$$g(x) = x^2, \quad f(x) = 2 - x.$$

Then $f(a) > 0$ if $a = 1$; and $x_0 = 2$ solves MAX. But SV requires for all $x \geqslant 0$:

$$g(x) + u_0 f(x) \leqslant g(x_0) + u_0 f(x_0),$$

and so

$$x^2 + u_0(2 - x) \leqslant \text{constant}.$$

This is impossible, since the term x^2 dominates as $x \to \infty$.

2. More surprising is that we need the assumption $f(\mathbf{a}) > 0$ for some $\mathbf{a} \geq 0$. If we drop this assumption, we have this counter-example:
Let $m = 1$, $n = 2$, and set

$$g(\mathbf{x}) = x_1, \quad f(\mathbf{x}) = -x_2 - (x_1 - 1)^2.$$

Both functions are concave. If $\mathbf{x} \geq 0$, only one point $\mathbf{x}^0$ is feasible for MAX:

$$\mathbf{x}^0 \geq 0 \quad \text{and} \quad f(\mathbf{x}^0) \geq 0 \quad \text{iff } \mathbf{x}^0 = (1,0).$$

Therefore, this point solves MAX. Please note this: No point $\mathbf{a} \geq 0$ makes $f(\mathbf{a}) > 0$.

Now suppose $\mathbf{x}^0$ and some u_0 solve SV. Then, for all $\mathbf{x} \geq 0$,

$$g(\mathbf{x}) + u_0 f(\mathbf{x}) \leq g(\mathbf{x}^0) + u_0 f(\mathbf{x}^0),$$

which says

$$x_1 + u_0(-x_2 - (x_1 - 1)^2) \leq 1 \quad (x_1 \geq 0, x_2 \geq 0).$$

If we set $x_2 = 0$, $x_1 = 1 + \varepsilon$, this says

$$1 + \varepsilon + u_0(-\varepsilon^2) \leq 1$$

which is false for small $\varepsilon > 0$. Therefore, there is no u_0 for which $\mathbf{x}^0$ and u_0 solve SV.

PROOF OF SLATER'S THEOREM. We will use the separating-plane theorem for convex sets: *Suppose Y and Z are disjoint convex sets in R^M; then there is a fixed vector $\mathbf{w} \neq 0$ for which*

$$\mathbf{w} \cdot \mathbf{y} \leq \mathbf{w} \cdot \mathbf{z} \tag{52}$$

for all $\mathbf{y}$ in Y and all z in Z.

Let $\mathbf{x}^0$ solve MAX. We now define sets Y and Z in R^{m+1}. Let Y be the set of all points

$$\mathbf{y} = (y_0, y_1, \ldots, y_m)$$

such that, for *some* $\mathbf{x} \geq 0$ in R^n,

$$y_0 \leq g(\mathbf{x}), \text{ and } y_j \leq f_j(\mathbf{x}) \quad (j = 1, \ldots, m). \tag{53}$$

Let Z be set of all points

$$z = (z_0, z_1 \ldots, z_m)$$

such that

$$z_0 > g(\mathbf{x}^0), \text{ and } z_j > 0 \quad (j = 1, \ldots, m). \tag{54}$$

We will show that Y and Z are *disjoint* and *convex*. They are disjoint because if $\mathbf{y} = \mathbf{z}$, then for some $\mathbf{x} \geq 0$

$$g(\mathbf{x}) \geq y_0 = z_0 > g(\mathbf{x}^0),$$

and

$$f_j(\mathbf{x}) \geq y_j = z_j > 0 \quad (j = 1, \ldots, m),$$

and $\mathbf{x}^0$ would not solve MAX. The set Z is convex because it is an open half-space. The set Y is convex because the functions g, f_j are concave: if

$$\mathbf{y} \leqslant \mathbf{f(x)} \quad \text{and} \quad \mathbf{y'} \leqslant \mathbf{f(x')},$$

where $f_0 \equiv g$, then

$$(1 - \theta)\mathbf{y} + \theta\mathbf{y'} \leqslant (1 - \theta)\mathbf{f(x)} + \theta\mathbf{f(x')}$$
$$\leqslant \mathbf{f}((1 - \theta)\mathbf{x} + \theta\mathbf{x'}) \qquad (0 \leqslant \theta \leqslant 1),$$

and so Y contains $(1 - \theta)\mathbf{y} + \theta\mathbf{y'}$ if it contains $\mathbf{y}$ and $\mathbf{y'}$.

Now the separating-plane theorem says there is a vector $\mathbf{w} \neq \mathbf{0}$ that satisfies (52) for all $\mathbf{y}$ in Y and all $\mathbf{z}$ in Z:

$$w_0 y_0 + w_1 y_1 + \cdots + w_m y_m \leqslant w_0 z_0 + w_1 z_1 + \cdots + w_m z_m. \tag{55}$$

Since we may let all $z_j \to +\infty$ for $z \in Z$, we deduce $w_j \geqslant 0$ ($j = 0, \ldots, m$).

By the definition (53), if $\mathbf{x} \geqslant \mathbf{0}$ in R^n, then we may take

$$y_0 = g(\mathbf{x}), \quad y_j = f_j(\mathbf{x}) \qquad (j = 1, \ldots, m). \tag{56}$$

And by the definition (54), if $\varepsilon > 0$ we may take

$$z_0 = g(\mathbf{x}^0) + \varepsilon, \quad z_j = \varepsilon \qquad (j = 1, \ldots, m). \tag{57}$$

If we insert these values in (55) and let $\varepsilon \to 0$, we get

$$w_0 g(\mathbf{x}) + w_1 f_1(\mathbf{x}) + \cdots + w_m f_m(\mathbf{x}) \leqslant w_0 g(\mathbf{x}^0) \qquad (\mathbf{x} \geqslant \mathbf{0}). \tag{58}$$

The purpose of Slater's assumption $\mathbf{f(a)} > \mathbf{0}$ is to prove $w_0 > 0$. If we set $\mathbf{x} = \mathbf{a}$ in (58), and if $w_0 = 0$, we find

$$w_1 f_1(\mathbf{a}) + \cdots + w_m f_m(\mathbf{a}) \leqslant 0. \tag{59}$$

But that is impossible, because $\mathbf{w} \neq \mathbf{0}$ and $\mathbf{w} \geqslant \mathbf{0}$, and so the sum in (59) is positive. Therefore, $w_0 > 0$.

Now we may divide by w_0 in (58) to obtain

$$g(\mathbf{x}) + u_1^0 f_1(\mathbf{x}) + \cdots + u_m^0 f_m(\mathbf{x}) \leqslant g(\mathbf{x}^0) \qquad (\mathbf{x} \geqslant \mathbf{0}), \tag{60}$$

where $u_j^0 = w_j/w_0$ ($j = 1, \ldots, m$); the point $\mathbf{u}^0$ is $\geqslant \mathbf{0}$ in R^m.

Since $\mathbf{x}^0$ is assumed to solve MAX, it satisfies $\mathbf{f(x^0)} \geqslant \mathbf{0}$, and so

$$g(\mathbf{x}^0) \leqslant g(\mathbf{x}^0) + \mathbf{u} \cdot \mathbf{f(x^0)} \qquad (\mathbf{u} \geqslant \mathbf{0}). \tag{61}$$

If we set $\mathbf{x} = \mathbf{x}^0$ in (60), we get

$$g(\mathbf{x}^0) + \mathbf{u}^0 \cdot \mathbf{f(x^0)} \leqslant g(\mathbf{x}^0). \tag{62}$$

But $\mathbf{u}^0 \cdot \mathbf{f(x^0)} \geqslant 0$, and so (62) implies $\mathbf{u}^0 \cdot \mathbf{f(x^0)} = 0$. Now (60) and (61) yield SV: For all $\mathbf{x} \geqslant \mathbf{0}$ and all $\mathbf{u} \geqslant \mathbf{0}$,

$$g(\mathbf{x}) + \mathbf{u}^0 \cdot \mathbf{f(x)} \leqslant g(\mathbf{x}^0) = g(\mathbf{x}^0) + \mathbf{u}^0 \cdot \mathbf{f(x^0)}$$
$$\leqslant g(\mathbf{x}^0) + \mathbf{u} \cdot \mathbf{f(x^0)}. \tag{63}$$

We will use Slater's theorem in the theory of *geometric programming*.

References

1. H. W. Kuhn and A. W. Tucker, "Nonlinear Programming," in Proceedings of the Second Berkeley Symposium on Mathematical Statistics and Probability (Berkeley, U. of California Press, 1950), 481–492.
2. William Karush, "Minima of Functions of Several Variables with Inequalities as Side Conditions," Master's Thesis, Department of Mathematics, University of Chicago, December, 1939, 26 pp.
3. Fritz John, "Extremum Problems with Inequalities as Subsidiary Conditions," Studies and Essays, Courant Anniversary Volume (New York, Interscience, 1948), 187–204.
4. H. W. Kuhn, "Nonlinear Programming: a Historical View," in R. W. Cottle and C. E. Lemke (ed.) *Nonlinear Programming*, SIAM-AMS Proceedings, Vol. 9 (1976) pp. 1–26.
5. M. Slater, "Lagrange Multipliers Revisited," Cowles Commission Discussion Paper No. 403, November, 1950.

PROBLEMS

1. Define the gradient $\nabla f(\mathbf{x})$ as the vector with components $\partial f/\partial x_i$. If $\mathbf{x}$ is a function of t with derivative $\mathbf{x}'(t) = \mathbf{v}(t)$, show that

$$\mathbf{v} \cdot \nabla f(\mathbf{x}) \geqslant 0 \qquad \text{when } t = 0$$

   if $f(\mathbf{x}(0)) = 0$ and if $f(\mathbf{x}(t)) \geqslant 0$ when $t > 0$.

2. The text says: "If the functions f_j are linear, then CQ holds for all feasible $\mathbf{x}^0$; for then we may use the *linear* arc $\mathbf{x} = \mathbf{x}^0 + t\mathbf{v}$." Why is that so?

3. In Theorem 1 replace the inequality constraint $\mathbf{f}(\mathbf{x}) \geqslant \mathbf{0}$ by the equality constraint $\mathbf{f}(\mathbf{x}) = \mathbf{0}$. Show that the conclusion still holds except that $\mathbf{u}$ need not be $\geqslant \mathbf{0}$ in (17). Method: Write the equality as a pair of inequalities, and apply Theorem 1.

4. If C is a symmetric matrix, show that the function $\mathbf{x} \cdot C\mathbf{x}$ is convex iff C is positive semi-definite.

5. Consider the quadratic program

$$A\mathbf{x} = \mathbf{b}, \quad \mathbf{x} \geqslant \mathbf{0},$$
$$\tfrac{1}{2}\mathbf{x} \cdot C\mathbf{x} + \mathbf{p} \cdot \mathbf{x} = \min.$$

   Find necessary and sufficient conditions for optimality by using Theorems 1 and 4. Check your conditions with the theorems in Section 1.

6. Assume the general constraints:

$$x_i \geqslant 0 \text{ for } i \text{ in } I_1, \quad x_i \text{ real for } i \text{ in } I_0,$$
$$f_j \geqslant 0 \text{ for } j \text{ in } J_1, \quad f_j = 0 \text{ for } j \text{ in } J_0.$$

   Assuming CQ and differentiability, use Theorem 1 to obtain necessary conditions for $g(\mathbf{x}) = \max$.

7. Consider the problem

$$x_1^2 + x_2^2 \leqslant 25, \quad \mathbf{x} \geqslant \mathbf{0}$$
$$(x_1 - 3)^2 + (x_2 - 4)^2 = \max.$$

Guess the solution $\mathbf{x}^0$, and verify the necessary conditions (16), (17). State and verify the constraint qualification CQ; draw a picture.

8. Solve the problem

$$x_1^2 + x_2^2 \leqslant 25$$
$$x_1 + x_2 \geqslant 7, \quad \mathbf{x} \geqslant 0$$
$$(x_1 - 3)^6 + (x_2 - 4)^6 = \max.$$

Verify all the necessary conditions for optimality, including CQ. (Answer: $\mathbf{x}^0 = (4,3)$; $\mathbf{u}^0 = (6,42)$.) Draw a picture.

9. In R^1 a function is convex if, for all x and y,

$$g((1 - \theta)x + \theta y) \leqslant (1 - \theta)g(x) + \theta g(y) \qquad (0 \leqslant \theta \leqslant 1).$$

If g'' exists, show that g is convex if $g'' \geqslant 0$.

10. For $\mathbf{x}$ in R^n, a function $f(\mathbf{x})$ is convex if

$$f((1 - \theta)\mathbf{x} + \theta \mathbf{y}) \leqslant (1 - \theta)f(\mathbf{x}) + \theta f(\mathbf{y}) \qquad (0 \leqslant \theta \leqslant 1).$$

If f is twice continuously differentiable, show that f is convex if the matrix $(\partial^2 f/\partial x_i \partial x_j)$ is positive semi-definite. (Method: For $0 \leqslant \theta \leqslant 1$ define the function $g(\theta) = f((1 - \theta)\mathbf{x} + \theta \mathbf{y})$, and require

$$g(\theta) \leqslant (1 - \theta)g(0) + \theta g(1) \qquad (0 \leqslant \theta \leqslant 1).$$

Now use the result of Problem 9.)

11. Get a variant of Slater's theorem that holds for $\mathbf{x}$ with *no* sign constraints (we will use this variant for *geometric* programming). (Method: Make the change of variable $\mathbf{x} = \mathbf{y} - \mathbf{z}$, and require $\mathbf{y} \geqslant 0, \mathbf{z} \geqslant 0$.)

12. Let the functions $\psi(\mathbf{x}), \varphi_1(\mathbf{x}), \ldots, \varphi_m(\mathbf{x})$ be convex for $\mathbf{x} \geqslant 0$. Suppose $\mathbf{x}^0$ minimizes $\psi(\mathbf{x})$ for all $\mathbf{x} \geqslant 0$ such that

$$\varphi_i(\mathbf{x}) \leqslant b_i \qquad (i = 1, \ldots, m).$$

What does Slater's theorem imply?

13. Let $x_1, \ldots, x_n$ be probabilities $(x_j \geqslant 0, \sum x_j = 1)$. Claude Shannon defined the *entropy of information* as $-\sum x_i \log x_i$. Show that the entropy function is concave. Then find necessary and sufficient conditions for the entropy to be maximized under constraints $f_i(\mathbf{x}) \geqslant 0$ $(i = 1, \ldots, m)$ if the functions f_i are differentiable and concave.

14. (Continuation.) Again suppose $\mathbf{x} \geqslant 0, \sum x_j = 1$. Derive conditions to maximize the Shannon entropy if the constraints are linear equations

$$\sum_{j=1}^{n} a_{ij} x_j = b_i \qquad (i = 1, \ldots, r).$$

(This problem occurs in communication engineering; see D. Slepian, "On Maxentropic Discrete Stationary Processes," Bell System Technical J., vol. 51 (1972) pp. 629–653.)

3 Geometric Programming

Geometric Programming is the title of an important book by R. J. Duffin, E. L. Peterson, and Clarence Zener. The authors give a simple analytical method for solving a class of nonlinear programming problems that arise in engineering design.

Let $t_1, t_2, \ldots, t_n$ be positive unknowns. Consider this problem:

$$q(\mathbf{t}) = \text{minimum} \qquad \text{for } \mathbf{t} > \mathbf{0}, \; p_1(\mathbf{t}) \leqslant 1, \ldots, p_m(\mathbf{t}) \leqslant 1. \tag{1}$$

Here $\mathbf{t}$ stands for $(t_1, \ldots, t_n)$, and $\mathbf{t} > \mathbf{0}$ means all $t_j > 0$. The functions $q, p_1, \ldots, p_m$ are given nonlinear functions of $t_1, \ldots, t_n$.

In engineering design, the given functions can often be satisfactorily represented as sums of finite numbers of terms of the form

$$c t_1^{k_1} t_2^{k_2} \cdots t_n^{k_n} \tag{2}$$

with *positive* coefficients c. The exponents $k_1, k_2, \ldots, k_n$ may be any real numbers—positive, negative, or zero. The authors D, P, and Z call these functions *posynomials*:

$$p(\mathbf{t}) = \sum_{\mathbf{k}} c(\mathbf{k}) t_1^{k_1} \cdots t_n^{k_n}. \tag{3}$$

They are polynomials with *positive* coefficients. Geometric *programming applies to nonlinear programming problems* (1) *in which the given functions are posynomials.*

Here are two examples of posynomials:

$$\begin{aligned}
p(x, y, z) &= \pi + 3x^{-\sqrt{2}} y^{19.6} + x^3 y z^{-45} + \sqrt{7} z^{13} \\
q(\mathbf{t}) &= q(t_1, t_2) = 5 t_1 t_2^{-1} + \sqrt{2} t_2^{-7.2}.
\end{aligned} \tag{4}$$

But the following functions are not posynomials:

$$\begin{aligned}
f(x) &= (1 - x)^{-1} = 1 + x + x^2 + \cdots \qquad (0 < x < 1) \\
g(x) &= 3 - x \\
h(x, y) &= e^{x+y} \\
\varphi(\mathbf{t}) &= (1 + t_1 + t_2 + t_3)^{-1}.
\end{aligned} \tag{5}$$

NOTATION. It will be convenient to represent the cumbersome product in (2) by

$$t_1^{k_1} \cdots t_n^{k_n} \equiv t^{\mathbf{k}}. \tag{6}$$

Now the posynomial (3) takes the form

$$p(\mathbf{t}) = \sum_{\mathbf{k}} c(\mathbf{k}) t^{\mathbf{k}}, \tag{7}$$

where the vector $\mathbf{k}$ ranges over a *finite* set of points in R^n; let's call this set K.

For example, in (4) the posynomial $p(x, y, z)$ depends on three real variables, so we may write $p(x, y, z) = p(\mathbf{t})$ where $\mathbf{t} = (x, y, z)$. Then $\mathbf{t}$ and $\mathbf{k}$ lie in R^3. The variable $\mathbf{t}$ ranges over all points (x, y, z) with positive coordinates. The exponent vector $\mathbf{k}$ ranges over the set K that consists of just these four points:

$$(0,0,0) \quad (-\sqrt{2},19.6,0) \quad (3,1,-45) \quad (0,0,13).$$

The associated coefficients $c(\mathbf{k})$ are the four positive numbers $\pi, 3, 1$ and $\sqrt{7}$; for instance,

$$c(-\sqrt{2},19.6,0) = 3.$$

In this way we can represent the posynomial $p(x,y,z)$ in the general form

$$p(\mathbf{t}) = \sum_K c(\mathbf{k})t^k \tag{8}$$

where we sum over $\mathbf{k}$ in K.

When we deal with a collection of posynomials $p_1(\mathbf{t}), \ldots, p_m(\mathbf{t})$, we have to distinguish the different exponent sets $K_1, \ldots, K_m$ and the different associated coefficients $c_1(\mathbf{k}), \ldots, c_m(\mathbf{k})$. We will denote the ith posynomial by

$$p_i(\mathbf{t}) = \sum_{K_i} c_i(\mathbf{k})t^k \tag{9}$$

where we sum over $\mathbf{k}$ in the set K_i. (It would perhaps be clearer if we wrote $\mathbf{k} \in K_i$ below the $\sum$ instead of just K_i; but later we'll be writing multiple sums and products, and the shorter notation will be easier.)

Posynomials are nasty functions. In general, they are neither convex nor concave. But the authors D, P, and Z observed this: *A simple change of variables makes every posynomial a convex function.* That saves the subject: it reduces geometric programming to a topic in convex programming.

This is the change of variables that does the trick:

$$t_1 = e^{x_1}, t_2 = e^{x_2}, \ldots, t_n = e^{x_n}. \tag{10}$$

Now the posynomial $p(\mathbf{t})$ equals a convex function $f(\mathbf{x})$. We'll prove this in a minute, but first I'd better say something about convex functions.

A function $f(\mathbf{z})$ is called convex if it satisfies

$$f((1-\theta)\mathbf{x} + \theta\mathbf{y}) \leqslant (1-\theta)f(\mathbf{x}) + \theta f(\mathbf{y}) \qquad (0 \leqslant \theta \leqslant 1). \tag{11}$$

As θ goes from 0 to 1, the point $(1-\theta)\mathbf{x} + \theta\mathbf{y}$ moves on the line segment from $\mathbf{x}$ to $\mathbf{y}$. The definition (11) says f lies *below* or on the straight line joining the ordinates at endpoints.

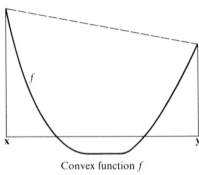

Convex function f

Figure 1

A function f is called *concave* if $-f$ is convex. Then the inequality (11) is reversed.

In (11), if you define $g(\theta)$ by

$$g(\theta) = f((1 - \theta)\mathbf{x} + \theta\mathbf{y}) \qquad (0 \leq 1),$$

then (11) says

$$g(\theta) \leq (1 - \theta)g(0) + \theta g(1) \qquad (0 \leq \theta \leq 1). \tag{12}$$

This inequality holds if $g''(\theta)$ is ≥ 0; this is proved in the Appendix. (Thus, we may take $g(\theta) = \theta^2$ or $e^{-\theta}$; these functions satisfy (12) because their second derivatives are positive.)

Therefore, $f(\mathbf{z})$ will be convex if

$$\left(\frac{d}{d\theta}\right)^2 f((1 - \theta)\mathbf{x} + \theta\mathbf{y}) \geq 0 \qquad (0 \leq \theta \leq 1). \tag{13}$$

If you work this out, it says

$$\sum_{i=1}^{n} \sum_{j=1}^{n} u_i(\partial_{ij} f)u_j \geq 0, \tag{14}$$

where $u_i = y_i - x_i$ and where $\partial_{ij} f$ is the second derivative of $f(\mathbf{z})$ with respect to z_i and z_j. If H is the symmetric matrix with components $\partial_{ij} f$, the inequality (14) says $\mathbf{u} \cdot H\mathbf{u} \geq 0$. Thus, the function f is convex if *the matrix of its second derivatives is positive semidefinite.*

EXAMPLE 1. Let

$$f(\mathbf{x}) = e^{\mathbf{k} \cdot \mathbf{x}} = \exp(k_1 x_1 + k_2 x_2 + \cdots + k_n x_n). \tag{15}$$

Differenting twice, we get

$$\partial_{ij} f(\mathbf{x}) = k_i k_j e^{\mathbf{k} \cdot \mathbf{x}} = k_i k_j f(\mathbf{x})$$

and so

$$\sum_i \sum_j u_i(\partial_{ij} f)u_j = \sum_i u_i k_i \sum_j u_j k_j e^{\mathbf{k} \cdot \mathbf{x}}$$

$$= \left(\sum_s u_s k_s\right)^2 e^{\mathbf{k} \cdot \mathbf{x}} \geq 0. \tag{16}$$

Therefore, $e^{\mathbf{k} \cdot \mathbf{x}}$ is convex.

EXAMPLE 2. As a function of $\mathbf{t}$, consider the one-term posynomial

$$p(\mathbf{t}) = t_1 t_2 \qquad \text{for } \mathbf{t} > \mathbf{0}. \tag{17}$$

Is this function convex? Let's see.

This is the matrix of second derivatives:

$$H = (\partial_{ij} p) = \begin{pmatrix} 0 & 1 \\ 1 & 0 \end{pmatrix}.$$

This is *not* positive semidefinite, for if we let $\mathbf{u} = (1, -1)$, we get

$$\mathbf{u} \cdot H\mathbf{u} = -2 < 0.$$

Finally, let $\mathbf{y} - \mathbf{x} = \mathbf{u}$, where we may take

$$\mathbf{x} = (2,2), \quad \mathbf{y} = (3,1).$$

Then

$$p(\mathbf{x}) = 4, \quad p(\mathbf{y}) = 3.$$

But at the midpoint,

$$p(\tfrac{1}{2}(\mathbf{x} + \mathbf{y})) = p(\tfrac{5}{2},\tfrac{3}{2}) = \tfrac{15}{4} > \tfrac{1}{2}p(\mathbf{x}) + \tfrac{1}{2}p(\mathbf{y}),$$

so $p(\mathbf{t})$ is not convex.

Example 2 proves that posynomials need not be convex. (They don't have to be concave either, as you can see from the example $t_1 t_2$, which equals s^2 on the line $t_1 = t_2 = s > 0$.)

EXAMPLE 3. Look again at the non-convex function $t_1 t_2$. Make the change of variables $t_1 = e^{x_1}, t_2 = e^{x_2}$. Then

$$t_1 t_2 = \exp(x_1 + x_2),$$

which equals $e^{\mathbf{k} \cdot \mathbf{x}}$ if $\mathbf{k} = (1,1)$. Now Example 1 says $p(\mathbf{t})$ is a convex function of the new variable $\mathbf{x}$.

This leads to the general result: *the change of variables* (10) *makes the polynomial $p(\mathbf{t})$ into a convex function $f(\mathbf{x})$*. And now $\mathbf{x}$ is free in R^n: whereas t_j was restricted to $t_j > 0$, now x_j ranges over $-\infty < x_j < \infty$.
    To prove the general result, we first show that each term

$$t_1^{k_1} \cdots t_n^{k_n} = e^{\mathbf{k} \cdot \mathbf{x}} \tag{18}$$

is convex in $\mathbf{x}$. But that's just what we proved in Example 1. Now the linear combination

$$f(\mathbf{x}) = \sum_K c(\mathbf{k}) e^{\mathbf{k} \cdot \mathbf{x}} \tag{19}$$

has *positive* coefficients $c(\mathbf{k})$. As you see from the defining inequality (11), a linear combination of convex functions is convex if the coefficients are positive. Therefore $f(\mathbf{x})$ is convex.   □

We'll use the theory of convex programming later. But first let's discuss the technique of solving problems. This depends on a general inequality, from which "geometric" programming derives its name—*the inequality of arithmetic and geometric means*.
    Assume

$$u_j > 0, \quad \theta_j \geqslant 0, \quad \sum \theta_j = 1 \quad (j = 1, \ldots, n). \tag{20}$$

Then

$$u_1 + \cdots + u_n \geqslant \left(\frac{u_1}{\theta_1}\right)^{\theta_1} \cdots \left(\frac{u_n}{\theta_n}\right)^{\theta_n}, \tag{21}$$

where we define $(u/\theta)^\theta = 1$ if $\theta = 0$. Equality occurs in (21) iff all θ_j are positive and

$$\frac{u_1}{\theta_1} = \cdots = \frac{u_n}{\theta_n}. \tag{22}$$

The inequality (21) is illustrated and proved in the Appendix. As a matter of notation, we will often write (21) in this form:

$$\sum u_j \geqslant \prod (u_j/\theta_j)^{\theta_j}. \tag{23}$$

EXAMPLE 4. We'll use the geometric inequality to solve a simple problem in geometric programming: In R^3 find $\mathbf{t} > \mathbf{0}$ to minimize

$$q(\mathbf{t}) \equiv 4t_1^{-1}t_2^{-1}t_3^{-1} + 4t_2t_3 + 2t_1t_3 + t_1t_2. \tag{24}$$

(Here we assume no constraints $p_i(\mathbf{t}) \leqslant 1$.)

SOLUTION. We'll use the geometric inequality (21) with exponents θ_j that we'll determine later. If we write $q(\mathbf{t})$ as a sum of four terms, we find

$$q(\mathbf{t}) = u_1 + \cdots + u_4 \geqslant u_1^{\theta_1} \cdots u_4^{\theta_4}$$
$$q(t) \geqslant (4t_1^{-1}t_2^{-1}t_3^{-1}/\theta_1)^{\theta_1}(4t_2t_3/\theta_2)^{\theta_2}(2t_1t_3/\theta_3)^{\theta_3}(t_1t_2/\theta_4)^{\theta_4}. \tag{25}$$

This inequality holds for all $\mathbf{t} > \mathbf{0}$; both sides are functions of $\mathbf{t}$.

To find a lower bound for $q(\mathbf{t})$, we'll try to choose the θ's to make the right-hand side of (25) independent of $\mathbf{t}$. If we collect the terms, (25) takes the form

$$q(\mathbf{t}) \geqslant v(\boldsymbol{\theta})t_1^{b_1}t_2^{b_2}t_3^{b_3}, \tag{26}$$

where the constant term is

$$v(\boldsymbol{\theta}) = (4/\theta_1)^{\theta_1}(4/\theta_2)^{\theta_2}(2/\theta_3)^{\theta_3}(1/\theta_4)^{\theta_4} \tag{27}$$

and where the powers b_j are

$$\begin{aligned} b_1 &= -\theta_1 && + \theta_3 + \theta_4 \\ b_2 &= -\theta_1 + \theta_2 && + \theta_4 \\ b_3 &= -\theta_1 + \theta_2 + \theta_3 \end{aligned} \tag{28}$$

As (26) shows, if we can make all the powers b_j equal zero, then we'll get the lower bound

$$q(\mathbf{t}) \geqslant v(\boldsymbol{\theta}) \qquad \text{for all } \mathbf{t} > \mathbf{0}. \tag{29}$$

If then we can choose $\mathbf{t}$ to achieve equality in (29), we'll get the minimum value of $q(\mathbf{t})$.

If we set $b_i = 0$ $(i = 1, 2, 3)$, we get 3 equations in 4 unknowns. A fourth equation comes from the assumption (20):

$$\theta_1 + \theta_2 + \theta_3 + \theta_4 = 1.$$

You can solve the 4 equations by elimination. Here are the answers:

$$\theta_1 = \tfrac{2}{5}, \quad \theta_2 = \theta_3 = \theta_4 = \tfrac{1}{5}. \tag{30}$$

Good news: All the θ's are *positive*. Remember, we need $\theta_j > 0$ to satisfy assumption (20), and we'll need $\theta_j > 0$ to satisfy the condition of equality, (22).

If we insert the values (30) in the inequality (26), we get this lower bound for all $t > 0$:

$$q(t) \geqslant v(\tfrac{2}{5}, \tfrac{1}{5}, \tfrac{1}{5}, \tfrac{1}{5}). \tag{31}$$

Now (27) gives the lower bound $q(t) \geqslant 10$.

Since $q(t) \geqslant 10$ for all $t > 0$, we can minimize $q(t)$ if we can find some t that achieves the equality $q(t) = 10$. Now what does that say? It says we want to achieve *equality* of the arithmetic and geometric means. For this we use the general condition (22).

Here $u_1, \ldots, u_4$ are the 4 terms in the posynomial $q(t)$; $\theta_1, \ldots, \theta_4$ are the exponents we computed in (29). So the condition of equality (22) says

$$4t_1^{-1}t_2^{-1}t_3^{-1}/(\tfrac{2}{5}) = 4t_2t_3/(\tfrac{1}{5}) \tag{32}$$
$$= 2t_1t_3/(\tfrac{1}{5}) = t_1t_2/(\tfrac{1}{5}).$$

This amounts to 3 equations in 3 unknowns. The equations are nonlinear in the t_j, but they are *linear* in $x_j = \log t_j$. You can easily get these answers:

$$t_1 = 2, \quad t_2 = 1, \quad t_3 = \tfrac{1}{2}.$$

These are the unique positive numbers that minimize $q(t)$, giving $q(t) = 10$.

I've given all the details in this simple example because it so well illustrates the general method. But it should raise some questions in your mind:

• Shall we always get the same number of equations and unknowns? (Unfortunately, the answer is no.)

• Shall we always get the equality $q(t) = v(\theta)$ if q is minimum? (The answer is yes, and we will prove it.)

• If we have trouble getting the minimum of $q(t)$ by this technique, can we at least get some good lower bounds? (Yes, we can.)

• In this simple example, which we could have done by ordinary calculus, we didn't have any constraints $p_i(t) \leqslant 1$. Is the technique usable if we have constraints? (Yes, it is; the next example will show you how.)

EXAMPLE 5. Here's a problem with a constraint. For $t > 0$ minimize

$$q(t) \equiv t_1^{-1}t_2^{-1}t_3^{-1} + t_2t_3 \tag{33}$$

under the constraint

$$p(t) \equiv \tfrac{1}{2}t_1t_3 + \tfrac{1}{4}t_1t_2 \leqslant 1. \tag{34}$$

SOLUTION. Here's how you work in the constraint. If α is any number $\geqslant 0$, then of course

$$q(t) \geqslant q(t)[p(t)]^\alpha \tag{35}$$

for all feasible $\mathbf{t}\,(\mathbf{t} > 0,\, p(\mathbf{t}) \leqslant 1)$. Now we're set up for the geometric inequality. For the term $q(\mathbf{t})$ we write

$$q(\mathbf{t}) \geqslant (t_1^{-1} t_2^{-1} t_3^{-1}/\theta_1)^{\theta_1}(t_2 t_3/\theta_2)^{\theta_2},$$

requiring $\theta_j \geqslant 0$, $\sum \theta_j = 1$. For the term $p(\mathbf{t})$ we write

$$p(\mathbf{t}) \geqslant (\tfrac{1}{2} t_1 t_3/\varphi_1)^{\varphi_1}(\tfrac{1}{4} t_1 t_2/\varphi_2)^{\varphi_2},$$

requiring $\varphi_j \geqslant 0$, $\sum \varphi_j = 1$. Now the composite inequality (35) yields

$$q(\mathbf{t}) \geqslant v t_1^{b_1} t_2^{b_2} t_3^{b_3} \tag{36}$$

where v is the constant

$$v = \theta_1^{-\theta_1} \theta_2^{-\theta_2} (2\varphi_1)^{-\alpha\varphi_1}(4\varphi_2)^{-\alpha\varphi_2} \tag{37}$$

and b_1, b_2, b_3 are the powers

$$\begin{aligned}
b_1 &= -\theta_1 && + \alpha\varphi_1 + \alpha\varphi_2 \\
b_2 &= -\theta_1 + \theta_2 && \quad\ \ + \alpha\varphi_2 \\
b_3 &= -\theta_1 + \theta_2 + \alpha\varphi_1 &&
\end{aligned} \tag{38}$$

To get the lower bound $q(\mathbf{t}) \geqslant v$, we need to solve these equations:

$$\begin{aligned}
b_j &= 0 \quad (j = 1, 2, 3) \\
\theta_1 + \theta_2 &= 1 \\
\varphi_1 + \varphi_2 &= 1,
\end{aligned} \tag{39}$$

where we require all five unknowns $\theta_1, \theta_2, \varphi_1, \varphi_2, \alpha$ to be $\geqslant 0$. If we introduce the new unknowns

$$\alpha\varphi_1 = \omega_1, \quad \alpha\varphi_2 = \omega_2, \tag{40}$$

then the system (39) becomes linear:

$$\begin{aligned}
-\theta_1 && + \omega_1 + \omega_2 &= 0 \\
-\theta_1 + \theta_2 && + \omega_2 &= 0 \\
-\theta_1 + \theta_2 + \omega_1 && &= 0 \\
\theta_1 + \theta_2 && &= 1.
\end{aligned} \tag{41}$$

All four unknowns are required $\geqslant 0$. Note that the constraint $\varphi_1 + \varphi_2 = 1$ has disappeared. When we've found ω_1 and ω_2, we'll define α by

$$\alpha = \omega_1 + \omega_2 \geqslant 0. \tag{42}$$

Now (40) gives

$$\varphi_1 = \omega_1/\alpha, \quad \varphi_2 = \omega_2/\alpha \quad \text{if} \quad \alpha > 0. \tag{43}$$

If $\alpha = 0$, we arbitrarily set $\varphi_1 = \varphi_2 = \tfrac{1}{2}$. (If $\alpha = 0$, the choice of the φ_j is irrelevant, because the factor p^α in (35) equals 1.)

This is the unique solution of the linear system (41):

$$\theta_1 = \tfrac{2}{3}, \quad \theta_2 = \tfrac{1}{3}, \quad \omega_1 = \tfrac{1}{3}, \quad \omega_2 = \tfrac{1}{3}. \tag{44}$$

Please check it. Now (42) and (43) give the original unknowns

$$\alpha = \tfrac{2}{3}, \quad \varphi_1 = \tfrac{1}{2}, \quad \varphi_2 = \tfrac{1}{2}. \tag{45}$$

Bear in mind that at this stage, before we've proved any theorems, you must regard it as pure good luck that all the unknowns (44) turned out positive. If any one of them had turned out negative, our discussion of this example would be over: the method would have failed.

If we use the computed values in (37), we get

$$v = (\tfrac{2}{3})^{-2/3}(\tfrac{1}{3})^{-1/3}(1)^{-1/3}(2)^{-1/3} = \tfrac{3}{2}.$$

Therefore, for all feasible $\mathbf{t}$, $q(\mathbf{t}) \geqslant 1.5$.

How do we get equality? As you know, this requires $\mathbf{t}$ to make the terms equal in the two geometric inequalities:

$$t_1^{-1}t_2^{-1}t_3^{-1}/\theta_1 = t_2 t_3/\theta_2$$
$$\tfrac{1}{2}t_1 t_3/\varphi_1 = \tfrac{1}{4}t_1 t_2/\varphi_2. \tag{46}$$

But that isn't all. Since we found α positive ($\alpha = \tfrac{2}{3}$), and since we require $p(\mathbf{t}) \leqslant 1$, the factor p^α in (35) will be <1 unless $p(\mathbf{t}) = 1$. Therefore, we must require $p(\mathbf{t}) = 1$:

$$p(\mathbf{t}) \equiv \tfrac{1}{2}t_1 t_3 + \tfrac{1}{4}t_1 t_2 = 1. \tag{47}$$

(Equivalently, we may require that the second pair of terms in (46) both equal 1.)

If we use the computed values $\theta_1, \theta_2, \varphi_1, \varphi_2$ in (46) and (47), we have three equations for the three unknowns t_j. (Once again, if we wished, we could replace these nonlinear equations by *linear* equations for $x_j = \log t_j$.) The solutions are (please verify)

$$t_1 = 2, \quad t_2 = 1, \quad t_3 = \tfrac{1}{2}. \tag{48}$$

That's the answer. These components make $q(\mathbf{t}) = 1.5$; all other feasible $\mathbf{t}$ make $q(\mathbf{t}) > 1.5$.

EXAMPLE 6. I hope you're not tired of examples, but I have to give you one more before you can use this technique on the harder problems. On the easier problems, like the last two, the number of equations equals the number of unknowns, and you get an exact solution; on the harder problems, like the one I'll show you now, the number of equations is greater than the number of unknowns, and you get only upper and lower bounds. Often these bounds are close, and they may give you all the accuracy you need for an engineering problem.

PROBLEM. For $\mathbf{t} > 0$ minimize

$$q(\mathbf{t}) \equiv t_1^{-1}t_2^{-1}t_3^{-1} + t_2 t_3 + t_3^7 \tag{49}$$

under the constraint

$$p(\mathbf{t}) \equiv \tfrac{1}{2}t_1 t_3 + \tfrac{1}{4}t_1 t_2 \leqslant 1. \tag{50}$$

SOLUTION. This problem is identical to Example 5 except that the new term t_3^7 has been added to $q(t)$. If we proceed as before, for feasible t we get

$$q(t) \geqslant q(t)[p(t)]^\alpha \tag{51}$$

$$\begin{aligned} \geqslant & (t_1^{-1}t_2^{-1}t_3^{-1}/\theta_1)^{\theta_1}(t_2t_3/\theta_2)^{\theta_2}(t_3^7/\theta_3)^{\theta_3} \\ & \cdot [(\tfrac{1}{2}t_1t_3/\varphi_1)^{\varphi_1}(\tfrac{1}{2}t_1t_2/\varphi_2)^{\varphi_2}]^\alpha, \end{aligned} \tag{52}$$

provided $\alpha \geqslant 0,\ \theta_1 \geqslant 0,\ \theta_2 \geqslant 0,\ \varphi_1 \geqslant 0,\ \varphi_2 \geqslant 0$ and

$$\theta_1 + \theta_2 + \theta_3 = 1 \quad \text{and} \quad \varphi_1 + \varphi_2 = 1. \tag{53}$$

Note that now we have a new unknown, θ_3, which has appeared because of the new term t^7.

If, as before, we define

$$\omega_1 = \alpha\varphi_1 \geqslant 0, \quad \omega_2 = \alpha\varphi_2 \geqslant 0,$$

and if we set the powers of the t_j equal to zero, we get these linear equations:

$$-\theta_1 \qquad\qquad\quad + \omega_1 + \omega_2 = 0 \tag{i}$$

$$-\theta_1 + \theta_2 \qquad\qquad + \omega_2 = 0 \tag{ii}$$

$$-\theta_1 + \theta_2 + 7\theta_3 + \omega_1 \qquad = 0; \tag{iii}$$

and the only constraint that remains from (53) is

$$\theta_1 + \theta_2 + \theta_3 = 1. \tag{iv}$$

These *four* equations contain *five* unknowns. This is an under-determined system, for which there are infinitely many solutions. The unknowns are called the *dual* unknowns.

Every nonnegative solution gives a different lower bound

$$q(t) \geqslant v(\theta_1,\theta_2,\theta_3,\omega_1,\omega_2) \tag{54}$$

for all feasible t. From (52), we see that v has the form

$$v = \theta_1^{-\theta_1}\theta_2^{-\theta_2}\theta_3^{-\theta_3}(2\varphi_1)^{-\omega_1}(4\varphi_2)^{-\omega_2} \tag{55}$$

where $\varphi_j = \alpha\omega_j$ and $\varphi_1 + \varphi_2 = 1$.

Ideally, to get the best lower bound v, we would *maximize* the expression (55) for all nonnegative variables satisfying the equations (i)–(iv). Then (54) would give

$$q(t) \geqslant \max v(\theta_1,\theta_2,\theta_3,\omega_1,\omega_2) \tag{56}$$

for all feasible t. Later, we'll prove this remarkable general result of D, P, and Z:

$$\boxed{\min q = \max v} \tag{57}$$

In other words, some feasible t gives equality in (56), and *that* value of t minimizes $q(t)$.

If we can't easily get max v, at least we can get *some* v to use in (54). All we have to do is find any nonnegative numbers $\theta_1, \ldots, \omega_2$ that solve (i)–(iv). These equations are the same as equations (41) except for the new terms in θ_3. So if we set $\theta_3 = 0$ and use the old values (44) for the other unknowns, we get five numbers that solve the new equations; we get

$$\theta_1 = \tfrac{2}{3}, \quad \theta_2 = \tfrac{1}{3}, \quad \theta_3 = 0, \quad \omega_1 = \tfrac{1}{3}, \quad \omega_2 = \tfrac{2}{3}.$$

If we plug these numbers into formula (55), using $0^0 = 1$, we get $v = 1.5$. This is just the value of v that we computed in the preceding example, where there was no θ_3. In the present example, this value of v gives the lower bound

$$q(\mathbf{t}) \geqslant 1.5 \qquad \text{for all feasible } \mathbf{t}.$$

To get an upper bound for min $q(\mathbf{t})$, all we have to do is pick *any* feasible $\mathbf{t}$. For instance, let's pick the $\mathbf{t}$ that was optimal for the preceding example, namely $\mathbf{t} = (2,1,\tfrac{1}{2})$. This $\mathbf{t}$ is feasible for the present example, and it gives q the value

$$q(2,1,\tfrac{1}{2}) = 1.5078.$$

Along with the lower bound $q \geqslant 1.5$, this gives the bracket

$$1.5 \leqslant \min q(\mathbf{t}) \leqslant 1.5078.$$

This much accuracy is good enough for most engineering problems.

The degree of difficulty. In the last problem there were five dual unknowns $\theta_1, \theta_2, \theta_3, \omega_1, \omega_2$ but only four dual equations (i)–(iv). That made the problem more difficult than the preceding two problems, where the number of dual unknowns equaled the number of dual equations. What determines these numbers?

If you look at the last example, you see that the three dual unknowns $\theta_1, \theta_2, \theta_3$ arose from the three terms in the sum for $q(\mathbf{t})$; likewise, the two dual unknowns ω_1, ω_2 arose from the two terms in the sum for $p(\mathbf{t})$. In general, you will see this: *The number of dual unknowns equals the total number of terms summed in all the given posynomials.* Call this number N.

Now let's count the dual equations. In the last example, one dual equation $b_j = 0$ arose for each primal unknown t_j, where b_j was the composite exponent of t_j. This accounted for the three dual equations (i), (ii), (iii). But we had one more dual equation, (iv), which came from normalizing the weights $\theta_1, \theta_2, \theta_3$ in the geometric inequality for $q(\mathbf{t})$. There were no more dual equations. The normalization $\varphi_1 + \varphi_2 = 1$, for the weights belonging to the constraint posynomial $p(\mathbf{t})$, disappeared when we introduced the new variables $\omega_1 = \alpha\varphi_1$, $\omega_2 = \alpha\varphi_2$. This example is typical: one dual equation will arise for each primal unknown t_j ($j = 1, \ldots, n$); one more equation will arise from normalizing the weights θ_i in the inequality for q. In general, *the number of dual equations will equal the number of primal unknowns plus one: $n + 1$.*

Let's check. In Example 4 we had $N = 4$ summands in $q(\mathbf{t})$; there was no $p(\mathbf{t})$; we had $n = 3$ primal unknowns t_j; and we had N dual equations in

$n + 1$ dual unknowns. In Example 5 we had $N = 4$ summands in the posynomials q and p; we had $n = 3$; and again we had N dual equations in $n + 1$ dual unknowns. We've already checked Example 5, where $N = 5$ and $n = 3$.

As a rule, the number of summands will be greater than the number of variables t_j, and so we shall have $N \geqslant n + 1$. If $N = n + 1$, the number of dual equations equals the number of unknowns. If $N > n + 1$, there are more dual equations than dual unknowns; for this case D, P, and Z define

$$\text{the degree of difficulty} \equiv N - (n + 1). \tag{58}$$

This quantity usually, but not always, gives the dimension of the set of solutions of the dual equations.

It is possible, though unusual, for the degree to be negative. Then we have $N \leqslant n$, which usually means that the N summands are independent variables. For instance, if the only given posynomial is

$$q(\mathbf{t}) = u_1 + u_2 = t_1^5 t_2^{-1} + t_1^{-3.7} t_2^{\pi}, \tag{59}$$

then $N = n = 2$; the degree is -1, and the summands u_1 and u_2 are independent. The function $q(\mathbf{t})$ has no minimum for $\mathbf{t} > 0$, though q can be made to approach the lower bound zero. (Set $t_1 = \varepsilon$, $t_2 = \varepsilon^2$; let $\varepsilon \to 0$.)

But look at this strange example:

$$q(\mathbf{t}) = t_1 t_2 t_3 + t_1^{-1} t_2^{-1} t_3^{-1}. \tag{60}$$

Here $N - (n + 1) = 2 - 4 = -2$, but there is a respectable minimum, 2, which is achieved on the whole surface $t_1 t_2 t_3 = 1$ for $\mathbf{t} > 0$. You can easily see how this sort of thing can happen. Though q appears to be a function of three variables, it is really a function of just the one variable $u = t_1 t_2 t_3$. Then $q = u + u^{-1} \geqslant 2$, with equality iff $u = 1$.

General discussion. Let $q(\mathbf{t}), p_1(\mathbf{t}), \ldots, p_m(\mathbf{t})$ be posynomials for $\mathbf{t} > 0$ in R^n. Consider this problem:

$$q(\mathbf{t}) = \text{minimum for } \mathbf{t} > 0 \text{ and } p_i(\mathbf{t}) \leqslant 1 (i = 1, \ldots, m). \tag{61}$$

We'll now discuss a general application of the geometric inequality.

For feasible $\mathbf{t}$, which satisfy the constraints, we have

$$q(\mathbf{t}) \geqslant q(\mathbf{t})[p_1(\mathbf{t})]^{\alpha_1} \cdots [p_m(\mathbf{t})]^{\alpha_m} \tag{62}$$

if $\alpha_i \geqslant 0$ $(i = 1, \ldots, m)$. We now write the posynomial $p_i(\mathbf{t})$ in the notation (9); for convenience, we define $p_0(\mathbf{t}) = q(\mathbf{t})$ and $\alpha_0 = 1$. In this notation, (62) says

$$q(\mathbf{t}) \geqslant \prod_{i=0}^{m} \left[\sum_{K_i} c_i(\mathbf{k}) t^{\mathbf{k}} \right]^{\alpha_i}. \tag{63}$$

For $\mathbf{k}$ in the finite set K_i, let the weights $\theta_i(k)$ satisfy

$$\theta_i(\mathbf{k}) \geqslant 0, \quad \sum_{K_i} \theta_i(\mathbf{k}) = 1.$$

Define $\omega_1(\mathbf{k}) = \alpha_i \theta_i(\mathbf{k})$. Then we have

$$\sum_{K_i} c_i(\mathbf{k}) t^k \geq \prod_{K_i} \{c_i(\mathbf{k}) t^k / \theta_i(\mathbf{k})\}^{\theta_i(\mathbf{k})}, \tag{64}$$

and (63) gives

$$q(\mathbf{t}) \geq \prod_{i=0}^{m} \prod_{K_i} \{c_i(\mathbf{k}) t^k / \theta_i(\mathbf{k})\}^{\omega_i(\mathbf{k})}. \tag{65}$$

To get a lower bound for $q(\mathbf{t})$, we try to make the product on the right independent of $\mathbf{t}$. Using the definition (6) for t^k, we collect the terms in (65) to obtain

$$q(\mathbf{t}) \geq v(\omega) t_1^{b_1} t_2^{b_2} \cdots t_n^{b_n},$$

where $v(\omega)$ is the constant

$$v(\omega) = \prod_{i=0}^{m} \prod_{K_i} \{c_i(\mathbf{k}) / \theta_i(\mathbf{k})\}^{\omega_i(\mathbf{k})} \tag{66}$$

and b_j is the collected power of t_j, namely,

$$b_j \equiv \sum_{i=0}^{m} \sum_{K_i} k_j \omega_i(\mathbf{k}) \qquad (j = 1, \ldots, n). \tag{67}$$

Since $\alpha_0 = 1$, the unknowns $\omega_0(\mathbf{k}) = \theta_0(\mathbf{k})$ are required to satisfy

$$\sum_{K_0} \omega_0(\mathbf{k}) = 1. \tag{68}$$

The other n dual equations are

$$b_j = 0 \qquad (j = 1, \ldots, n). \tag{69}$$

All the dual unknowns $\omega_i(\mathbf{k})$ are required to be ≥ 0. The number of dual unknowns equals $|K_0| + \cdots + |K_m|$, which is the number of summands in all the posynomials $p_0, \ldots, p_m$. If the numbers $\omega_i(\mathbf{k}) \geq 0$ satisfy the $n+1$ dual equations, they are called *feasible for the dual problem*, and they provide the lower bound

$$q(\mathbf{t}) \geq v(\omega) \tag{70}$$

for all $\mathbf{t}$ that are feasible for *primal problem* (61).

This is the *dual problem*:

$$v(\omega) = \text{maximum for feasible } \omega. \tag{71}$$

that is, for $\omega \geq 0$ satisfying equations (68) and (69).

Now we will prove the main theorem of geometric programming.

Theorem. *Assume that some* $\mathbf{t}$ *satisfies the strict primal constraints*

$$\mathbf{t} > 0, \quad p_i(\mathbf{t}) < 1 \qquad (i = 1, \ldots, m). \tag{72}$$

Suppose the primal problem (61) has a solution. Then the dual problem (71) has a solution, and

$$\min q(\mathbf{t}) = \max v(\omega). \tag{73}$$

REMARKS. This is not an elementary theorem, since the proof uses Slater's theorem for convex programming (see Section 2).

The equality $\min q = \max v$ states that for some feasible primal t and dual ω, we can attain equality in the composite geometric inequality (65). For equality to hold we must first have equality in (62), and so we require

$$\alpha_i = 0 \quad \text{if} \quad p_i(\mathbf{t}) < 1 \qquad (i = 1, \ldots, m), \tag{74}$$

where

$$\alpha_i \equiv \sum_{K_i} \omega_i(\mathbf{k}) \qquad (i = 0, 1, \ldots, m).$$

If $\alpha_i = 0$, the weights $\theta_i(\mathbf{k})$ are irrelevant, since $p_i^{\alpha} = p_i^0 = 1$. But if $\alpha_i > 0$, we require equality in the inequality (64) for the posynomial $p_i(\mathbf{t})$. So, if $\alpha_i > 0$, we require

$$c_i(\mathbf{k})t^k/\theta_i(\mathbf{k}) = \text{constant} \qquad \text{for } \mathbf{k} \text{ in } K_i.$$

Since $\theta_i(\mathbf{k}) = \omega_i(\mathbf{k})/\alpha_i$, this says

$$\omega_i(\mathbf{k}) = \lambda_i c_i(\mathbf{k})t^k \qquad \text{for } \mathbf{k} \text{ in } K_i \text{ if } \alpha_i > 0 \tag{75}$$

where λ_i equals some constant for $\mathbf{k}$ in K_i. (Please note that the requirement (75) must apply to the index $i = 0$, since we assume $\alpha_0 = 1$.)

The conditions (74) and (75) are necessary and sufficient for the equality $q(\mathbf{t}) = v(\omega)$ if $\mathbf{t}$ and ω are feasible. For all other feasible $\mathbf{t}$ and ω we get only the strict inequality $q(\mathbf{t}) > v(\omega)$. So the proof of the theorem must boil down to the conditions (74) and (75). If $\mathbf{t}$ solves the primal minimum problem, we have to prove the existence of an ω that is feasible for the dual and that solves the *equilibrium conditions* (74) and (75).

In Section 2 we proved Slater's theorem for concave functions $g(\mathbf{x})$, $f_1(\mathbf{x}), \ldots, f_m(\mathbf{x})$ defined for $\mathbf{x} \geq \mathbf{0}$. For the following proof, we need a version of Slater's theorem that applies for *all* $\mathbf{x}$. To get this version, set $\mathbf{x} = \mathbf{y} - \mathbf{z}$ where $\mathbf{y}$ and $\mathbf{z}$ are $\geq \mathbf{0}$. Then, for instance,

$$g(\mathbf{x}) = g(\mathbf{y} - \mathbf{z}) \qquad (\mathbf{y} \geq \mathbf{0}, \mathbf{z} \geq \mathbf{0}),$$

and if $g(\mathbf{x})$ is concave in $\mathbf{x}$ for all $\mathbf{x}$, then $g(\mathbf{y} - \mathbf{z})$ is concave in $\mathbf{y}$ and $\mathbf{z}$ for all $\mathbf{y} \geq \mathbf{0}$ and $\mathbf{z} \geq \mathbf{0}$.

Define the Lagrangian

$$\begin{aligned}\phi(\mathbf{x},\mathbf{u}) &= g(\mathbf{x}) + \mathbf{u} \cdot \mathbf{f}(\mathbf{x}) \\ &= g(\mathbf{x} - \mathbf{y}) + \mathbf{u} \cdot \mathbf{f}(\mathbf{y} - \mathbf{z})\end{aligned} \tag{76}$$

for $\mathbf{y}$ and $\mathbf{z} \geq \mathbf{0}$ in R^n, $\mathbf{u} \geq \mathbf{0}$ in R^m. Suppose $\mathbf{x}^0$ maximizes $g(\mathbf{x})$ for all $\mathbf{x}$ such that $\mathbf{f}(\mathbf{x}) \geq \mathbf{0}$. Set $\mathbf{x}^0 = \mathbf{y}^0 - \mathbf{z}^0$. Then our first version of Slater's theorem implies, for some $\mathbf{u}^0 \geq \mathbf{0}$ in R^m,

$$\phi(\mathbf{y} - \mathbf{z}, \mathbf{u}^0) \leq \phi(\mathbf{y}^0 - \mathbf{z}^0, \mathbf{u}^0) \leq \phi(\mathbf{y}^0 - \mathbf{z}^0, \mathbf{u})$$

for all $\mathbf{y}$ and $\mathbf{z} \geq \mathbf{0}$ in R^n and for all $\mathbf{u} \geq \mathbf{0}$ in R^m. Setting $\mathbf{x} = \mathbf{y} - \mathbf{z}$, we get, for some $\mathbf{u}^0 \geq \mathbf{0}$ in R^m,

$$\phi(\mathbf{x},\mathbf{u}^0) \leq \phi(\mathbf{x}^0,\mathbf{u}^0) \leq \phi(\mathbf{x}^0,\mathbf{u}) \tag{77}$$

for *all* x in R^n and for all $u \geqslant 0$ in R^m. The conclusion (77) holds under Slater's assumption

$$f(a) > 0 \qquad \text{for some } a \text{ in } R^n. \tag{78}$$

PROOF OF THE THEOREM. If we make the change of variables $t_j = e^{x_j}$, then all the posynomials defined for $t > 0$ become convex functions of x for all x in R^n. (We proved this after Example 3.) To use Slater's theorem, we define the following *concave* functions of x:

$$g(x) = -q(t) \tag{79}$$
$$f_i(x) = 1 - p_i(t) \qquad (i = 1, \ldots, m). \tag{80}$$

Slater's theorem now gives the conclusion (77):

$$g(x) + u^0 \cdot f(x) \leqslant g(x^0) + u^0 \cdot f(x^0) \leqslant g(x^0) + u \cdot f(x^0) \tag{81}$$

for all x in R^n and all $u \geqslant 0$ in R^m.

If we set $u = 0$, the second inequality (81) gives $u^0 \cdot f(x^0) \leqslant 0$. But $u^0 \geqslant 0$ and $f(x^0) \geqslant 0$, and so $u^0 \cdot f(x^0) \geqslant 0$. Therefore, $u^0 \cdot f(x^0) = 0$. Since both vectors are $\geqslant 0$, we deduce

$$u_i^0 = 0 \quad \text{if} \quad f_j(x^0) > 0. \tag{82}$$

Since $u^0 \cdot f(x^0) = 0$, the first inequality (81) says

$$g(x) + u^0 \cdot f(x) \leqslant g(x^0) \tag{83}$$

with equality for $x = x^0$. Now elementary calculus implies for $x = x^0$

$$\frac{\partial}{\partial x_j} [g(x) + u^0 \cdot f(x)] = 0 \qquad (j = 1, \ldots, n). \tag{84}$$

Now everything is done but the bookkeeping. Using $t^k = e^{k \cdot x}$, we find

$$g(x) = -q(t) = -\sum_{K_0} c_0(k) e^{k \cdot x}$$

$$\frac{\partial}{\partial x_j} g(x) = -\sum_{K_0} c_0(k) k_j e^{k \cdot x} \qquad (j = 1, \ldots, n).$$

Similarly, for $i = 1, \ldots, m$, we find

$$\frac{\partial}{\partial x_j} f_i(x) = -\sum_{K_i} c_i(k) k_j e^{k \cdot x} \qquad (j = 1, \ldots, n).$$

Now (84) becomes

$$-\sum_{i=0}^{m} u_i^0 \sum_{K_i} c_i(k) k_j \exp k \cdot x^0 = 0 \qquad (j = 1, \ldots, n), \tag{85}$$

where we've set $u_0^0 \equiv 1$.

Let $q_0 = q(t^0) = -g(x^0)$. If we divide the last formula by $-q_0$, we get

$$\sum_{i=0}^{m} \sum_{K_i} k_j \omega_i(k) = 0 \qquad (j = 1, \ldots, n) \tag{86}$$

where we identify

$$\omega_i(\mathbf{k}) = q_0^{-1} u_i^0 c_i(\mathbf{k}) \exp \mathbf{k} \cdot \mathbf{x}^0 \qquad (i = 0, \ldots, m). \tag{87}$$

We divided by q_0 to make

$$\sum_{K_0} \omega_0(\mathbf{k}) = 1. \tag{88}$$

If you compare the last three formulas to the dual equations defined by (67), (68), (69), you see that the nonnegative numbers $\omega_i(\mathbf{k})$ defined in (87) satisfy the $n + 1$ dual equations.

All we have to do now is verify the equilibrium conditions (74) and (75). First let's compute the sum α_i. Formula (87) gives

$$\alpha_i \equiv \sum_{K_i} \omega_i(\mathbf{k}) \qquad (i = 0, 1, \ldots, m)$$

$$= q_0^{-1} u_i^0 \sum_{K_i} c_i(\mathbf{k}) \exp \mathbf{k} \cdot \mathbf{x}^0,$$

and so

$$\alpha_i = q_0^{-1} u_i^0 f_i(\mathbf{x}^0) \qquad (i = 1, \ldots, m).$$

But we have $f_i = 1 - p_i \geqslant 0$, and so formula (82) implies $\alpha_i = 0$ if $p_i < 1$ $(i = 1, \ldots, m)$. That verifies condition (74).

Finally, we put $\omega_i(\mathbf{k})$ in the required form

$$\omega_i(\mathbf{k}) = \lambda_i c_i(\mathbf{k}) t^k.$$

This comes from (87) if we set $\mathbf{t} = \mathbf{t}^0$ and identify

$$\lambda_i = q_0^{-1} u_i^0, \quad t^k = \exp \mathbf{k} \cdot \mathbf{x}^0.$$

That verifies condition (75) and completes the proof.   □

Reference

R. J. Duffin, E. L. Peterson, and Clarence Zener, *Geometric Programming*, 1967, John Wiley and Sons.

Appendix: The Inequality of Arithmetic and Geometric Means

In the simplest case this inequality states

$$\tfrac{1}{2}(a + b) \geqslant \sqrt{ab} \tag{1}$$

for positive numbers a and b. Equality occurs iff $a = b$. On the left is the arithmetic mean; on the right is the geometric mean.

The geometric mean really does occur in geometry. If a rectangle has sides a and b, the geometric mean equals the side of a square with the same area. The inequality (1) implies that the square has the least perimeter of all rectangles with the same area.

$\quad$ *Generalization.* Let $x_1, \ldots, x_n$ be positive numbers. Let $\theta_1, \ldots, \theta_n$ satisfy

$$\theta_j > 0, \quad \sum \theta_j = 1. \tag{2}$$

Then we assert

$$\theta_1 x_1 + \cdots + \theta_n x_n \geqslant x_1^{\theta_1} \cdots x_n^{\theta_n} \tag{3}$$

with equality iff $x_1 = \cdots = x_n$.

EXAMPLE. If $n = 2$ and if $\theta_1 = \theta_2 = \frac{1}{2}$, we get the inequality (1).

$\quad$ *Equivalent assertion.* In geometric programming one uses this form of the inequality:

$$u_1 + \cdots + u_n \geqslant \left(\frac{u_1}{\theta_1}\right)^{\theta_1} \cdots \left(\frac{u_n}{\theta_n}\right)^{\theta_n} \tag{4}$$

where

$$u_j > 0, \quad \theta_j > 0, \quad \sum \theta_j = 1. \tag{5}$$

Formula (4) comes from (3) by setting $\theta_j x_j = u_j$. Equality occurs in (4) iff

$$\frac{u_1}{\theta_1} = \cdots = \frac{u_n}{\theta_n}. \tag{6}$$

PROOF. Let $f(x) = \log x$ for $x > 0$. Taking logarithms in (3), we get this assertion:

$$f(\theta_1 x_1 + \cdots + \theta_n x_n) \geqslant \theta_1 f(x_1) + \cdots + \theta_n f(x_n) \tag{7}$$

with equality iff $x_1 = \cdots = x_n$. This asserts that $\log x$ is a *strictly concave function.* We will prove (7) by induction after we've proved it for $n = 2$.

$\quad$ If $n = 2$, set $\theta_1 = t$ and $\theta_2 = 1 - t$. For $0 \leqslant t \leqslant 1$ define the function

$$g(t) = \log((1 - t)x_1 + tx_2) - (1 - t) \log x_1 - t \log x_2. \tag{8}$$

If $x_1 \neq x_2$, the function $g(t)$ satisfies

$$\begin{aligned} g(0) &= g(1) = 0, \\ g''(t) &< 0 \quad \text{for} \quad 0 \leqslant t \leqslant 1. \end{aligned} \tag{9}$$

$\quad$ We now assert

$$g(t) > 0 \quad \text{for} \quad 0 < t < 1. \tag{10}$$

If this were false, then $g(t)$ would be $\leqslant 0$ at some *interior* point of the interval $[0,1]$. Then $g(t)$ would achieve its *minimum* value at some interior point t_0, where calculus would require

$$g'(t_0) = 0, \quad g''(t_0) \geqslant 0.$$

But this is impossible, because $g''(t) < 0$. This proves (10), and if we take exponentials, we get the required result (7) if $n = 2$.

If $n > 2$, we use induction. First we define a positive number y by

$$\theta_1 x_1 + \theta_2 x_2 + \cdots + \theta_n x_n = \theta_1 x_1 + (1 - \theta_1)y.$$

The result for $n = 2$ now gives

$$f(\theta_1 x_1 + (1 - \theta_1)y) \geqslant \theta_1 f(x_1) + (1 - \theta_1)f(y). \tag{11}$$

Now induction gives

$$\begin{aligned}
f(y) &= f((1 - \theta_1)^{-1}(\theta_2 x_2 + \cdots + \theta_n x_n)) \\
&\geqslant (1 - \theta_1)^{-1}\theta_2 f(x_2) + \cdots + (1 - \theta_1)^{-1}\theta_n f(x_n)
\end{aligned} \tag{12}$$

If we use this in (11) we get the required inequality (7). Looking at (12) and (13) we see that equality occurs iff

$$x_1 = y = x_2 = \cdots x_n.$$

This completes the proof of the inequality of arithmetic and geometric means.

What happens if some $\theta_j = 0$? We've proved

$$\sum_{j=1}^{n} u_j \geqslant \prod_{j=1}^{n} (u_j/\theta_j)^{\theta_j} \tag{13}$$

assuming

$$\theta_j > 0, \quad u_j > 0, \quad \sum_{j=1}^{n} \theta_j = 1. \tag{14}$$

If some $\theta_j \to +0$, we define the term

$$(u_j/\theta_j)^{\theta_j} \equiv 1 \quad \text{if} \quad \theta_j = 0, \tag{15}$$

which is the limiting value, since u_j is assumed positive. Now we can replace (14) by the broader assumption

$$\theta_j \geqslant 0, \quad u_j > 0, \quad \sum_{j=1}^{n} \theta_j = 1, \tag{16}$$

allowing some $\theta_j = 0$.

If $\theta_j > 0$ for $j \in J$, we find

$$\sum_{j=1}^{n} u_j > \sum_{J} u_j \quad \text{if some } \theta_j = 0. \tag{17}$$

Now the inequality (13) for *positive* θ_j says

$$\sum_{J} u_j \geqslant \prod_{J} (u_j/\theta_j)^{\theta_j}. \tag{18}$$

But the *product* over J may be taken over *all* $j = 1, \ldots, n$, since the extra factors (15) all equal 1. Now the last two formulas imply the *strict* inequality

$$\sum_{j=1}^{n} u_j > \prod_{j=1}^{n} (u_j/\theta_j)^{\theta_j} \quad \text{if some } \theta_j = 0. \tag{19}$$

PROBLEMS

1. Use the geometric inequality (21) to minimize

$$7\sqrt{t} + 9t^{-3} \quad \text{for} \quad t > 0,$$

2. Use the geometric inequality (21) to minimize

$$3t_1^{-1}t_2^{-1} + 4t_1^3 + 15t_1t_2^5 \quad \text{for} \quad t > 0.$$

In the optimum, what are the relative weights $\theta_1, \theta_2, \theta_3$?

3. Find positive x, y minimizing

$$3x^2 + 7y^4 \quad \text{for} \quad xy \geqslant 5.$$

4. Show that linear programming is a special case of geometric programming: Consider the linear program

$$\sum_{i=1}^{m} y_i a_{ij} \leqslant c_j \qquad (j = 1, \ldots, n)$$

$$\sum y_i b_i = \max.$$

Set $t_i = \exp y_i > 0$ and define

$$q(\mathbf{t}) = t_1^{-b_1} \cdots t_m^{-b_m},$$
$$p_j(\mathbf{t}) = e^{-c_j} t_1^{a_{1j}} \cdots t_m^{a_{mj}}.$$

Consider the geometric program to minimize $q(\mathbf{t})$ for $\mathbf{t} > 0$ satisfying $p_j(\mathbf{t}) \leqslant 1$ $(j = 1, \ldots, n)$.

*5. (Continuation.) Show that the fundamental theorem of geometric programming implies the duality principle and the equilibrium theorem of linear programming. (Note: For the geometric program in Problem 4, the exponents α_j satisfy

$$\alpha_j \geqslant 0, \quad \sum_{j=1}^{n} a_{ij}\alpha_j = b_i \qquad (i = 1, \ldots, m),$$

where (74) requires $\alpha_j = 0$ if $p_j(\mathbf{t}) < 1$.)

6. Let A, B, C, D be positive constants. Problem: Find positive x, y, z minimizing

$$q = A(xyz)^{-1} + Byz + Cxz + Dxy.$$

Show that the optimal weights are $\theta_1 = \frac{2}{5}$, $\theta_2 = \theta_3 = \theta_4 = \frac{1}{5}$, as in formula (30). Get formulas for the optimal x, y, z. Verify the primal-dual equality min $q = \max v$.

7. For positive x, y, z minimize

$$q = 5x^{-1}y^{-3}z^{-1} + 7y^3z$$

under the constraint

$$2xz + xy^3 \leqslant 9.$$

Verify the primal-dual equality min $q = \max v$.

8. Consider the problem to minimize

$$q = x^{-1}y^{-1}z^{-1} + yz + x^{-5}y^2z^3$$

for positive x, y, z satisfying

$$\tfrac{1}{2}xz + \tfrac{1}{4}xy \leqslant 1.$$

Find upper and lower bounds for min q. (Look at Examples 5 and 6.)

9. For $\mathbf{t} > \mathbf{0}$ in R^n, what is the minimum value of $\sum t_i$ if $\prod t_i^{-1} \leqslant 1$? For $\theta_i \geqslant 0$ $(i = 1, \ldots, n)$ and $\sum \theta_i = 1$, what is the maximum value of $\prod \theta_i^{-\theta_i}$?

10. Use geometric programming to minimize

$$t_1 + 2t_2 + \cdots + nt_n \quad \text{for} \quad \mathbf{t} > \mathbf{0}$$

if $\sum t_i^{-2} \leqslant 1$.

11. This problem is *not* a geometric program: Find positive x, y minimizing

$$(x^2 + y^4)^{1/2} + x^{-1} + xy + y^{-3}.$$

State the problem as a geometric program to find positive x, y, z minimizing

$$z + x^{-1} + xy + y^{-3}$$

where x, y, z satisfy an appropriate constraint $p(x, y, z) \leqslant 1$.

12. A rectangular box in three dimensions has volume V, surface area A, and edge length L. State the following problem as a geometric program: Maximize V for $A \leqslant 10$ in.^{2} and $L \leqslant 16$ in.

13. Show that the volume, area, and edge length of a box satisfy the inequalities

$$V^{1/3} \leqslant (A/6)^{1/2} \leqslant L/12.$$

Which boxes produce equalities?

3 Fixed-Point Theorems

1 Introduction to Fixed Points; Contraction Mappings

In the theory of zero-sum, two-person games the basic theorem was proved by John von Neumann; he used the Brouwer fixed-point theorem. In the theory of many-person games the basic theorem was proved by J. F. Nash; he also used the Brouwer fixed-point theorem. We will prove Nash's theorem with the Kakutani fixed-point theorem.

What is a fixed-point theorem? It is a theorem that refers to an equation

$$x = f(x). \tag{1}$$

Usually, the theorem gives conditions for the *existence* of a solution. The function f may be thought of as a mapping. Then a solution x is a point that the mapping leaves fixed. There are many varieties of fixed-point theorems. Some give conditions for uniqueness or multiplicity of solutions. The Kakutani theorem refers to a generalization of the equation (1). In the Schauder theorem the fixed "point" lies in a "space" of functions, and this "point" may be a function that solves a nonlinear integral equation or partial differential equation.

Some fixed-point theorems are constructive; most are not. The Brouwer theorem is not. It just tells you a solution exists; it's up to you to find it. You ask: What good is that? What good is a mere existence theorem?

Gauss called mathematics the science of relationships. Perhaps the most basic mathematical relationship is existence, relating a problem to a solution. Gauss was a formidable computer, and when he could compute something important, he did; when he couldn't, he proved it existed. For instance, he proved the fundamental theorem of algebra: For every polynomial equation, a complex root exists. That's not as good as the quadratic formula, but it will have to do—as Galois showed later.

Even the practical computer user can take comfort from an existence theorem. When you're trying to find something, it's a comfort to know it exists.

Look at the fixed-point equation: $x = f(x)$. Have you ever seen it before? Yes, you have—perhaps more often than you know. You see, *every* equation is a fixed-point equation.

The reason is simple. Suppose this equation is given: $g(x) = 0$. Then we can write the fixed-point equation

$$x = x + g(x), \tag{2}$$

or if you prefer,

$$x = x - 79g(x).$$

In general we can write the equation $g(x) = 0$ as the fixed-point equation

$$x = x + \Phi[g(x)] \tag{3}$$

provided that $\Phi[g] = 0$ iff $g = 0$. So when we talk generally about fixed-point equations, we are talking about *all* equations.

The contraction mapping principle is an exception among fixed-point theorems: it is constructive. You can use the method of proof to construct a solution. The method is called the *method of successive approximations*. (When I was a graduate student, I liked this method so much that I wrote my thesis on it.)

In its elementary form, the contraction mapping theorem says this: Let M be a closed set of real numbers, and suppose the function f maps M into itself. (If you like, think of M as the set of all real numbers.) Finally, suppose f is a contraction mapping:

$$|f(a) - f(b)| \leqslant \theta|a - b|, \tag{4}$$

where $0 \leqslant \theta < 1$. Conclusion: The mapping f has a unique fixed point in M.

Uniqueness is easy to prove. If there were two fixed points, a and b, then the contraction property imples

$$|a - b| = |f(a) - f(b)| \leqslant \theta |a - b|. \tag{5}$$

Then $a - b = 0$ because $0 \leqslant \theta < 1$.

To prove the existence of a fixed point, we'll use an iterative scheme. Start with any x_0 in M, and compute the successive approximations

$$x_{n+1} = f(x_n) \qquad (n = 0, 1, 2, \ldots). \tag{6}$$

We'll prove that the sequence x_n converges.

That will suffice. If $x_n \to x$, then the limit x must lie in M because all the x_n lie in M and M is *closed* (M contains all its limit points). Next, (4) implies

$$|f(x_n) - f(x)| \leqslant \theta|x_n - x|, \tag{7}$$

so $x_n \to x$ implies $f(x_n) \to f(x)$. Now (6) yields the fixed-point equation $x = f(x)$.

To prove that x_n converges, we subtract from the equation (6) the same equation with n replaced by $n - 1$:

$$x_{n+1} - x_n = f(x_n) - f(x_{n-1}) \qquad (n = 1, 2, \ldots). \tag{8}$$

The contraction property implies

$$|x_{n+1} - x_n| \leqslant \theta |x_n - x_{n-1}| \qquad (n = 1, 2, \ldots).$$

Then $|x_{n+1} - x_n| \leqslant \theta^2 |x_{n-1} - x_{n-2}|$, etc. At last, we get

$$|x_{n+1} - x_n| \leqslant \theta^n |x_1 - x_0| \qquad (n = 1, 2, \ldots). \tag{9}$$

For all $q > p$ this implies

$$\begin{aligned}
|x_q - x_p| = \left| \sum_{n=p}^{q-1} (x_{n+1} - x_n) \right| &\leqslant \sum_{p}^{q-1} |x_{n+1} - x_n| \\
&\leqslant |x_1 - x_0|(\theta^p + \theta^{p+1} + \cdots + \theta^{q-1}). \\
&< |x_1 - x_0|\theta^p(1 - \theta)^{-1} \to 0 \quad \text{as} \quad p \to \infty.
\end{aligned} \tag{10}$$

Since $x_q - x_p \to 0$ for $q > p \to \infty$, the sequence x_n converges, and so we have constructed a fixed point. $\qquad\square$

EXAMPLE 1. Suppose we want to solve the fixed-point equation

$$x = 1 - x^5. \tag{11}$$

As x goes from 0 to 1, the right-hand side goes from 1 to 0. Evidently, the graphs cross and there is a unique root between 0 and 1.

Let M be the closed interval $0 \leqslant x \leqslant 1$. The function $1 - x^5$ maps M into itself. Start with $x_0 = 0.5$ and compute the successive approximations

$$x_{n+1} = 1 - x_n^5 \qquad (n = 0, 1, 2, \ldots). \tag{12}$$

The limit should be a root of (11), shouldn't it?

Here's what you get for the sequence $x_0, x_1, x_2, \ldots$ with 3-digit accuracy:

$$0.5, 0.969, 0.147, 1, 0, 1, 0, 1, 0, \ldots.$$

Good grief. What's wrong?

What's wrong is this: The root x lies near 1, but the function $1 - x^5$ is not a contraction mapping near 1, since the derivative equals $-5x^4 = -20$ at $x = 1$. But, as you see by dividing by $b - a$ and letting $b \to a$ in (4), a differentiable contraction mapping should satisfy

$$|f'(a)| \leqslant \theta < 1, \tag{13}$$

This simple example is typical of the frustrations of the contraction mapping theorem. The root obviously exists, but we can't get it. Or can we?

EXAMPLE 2. We are determined to solve the equation (11) by successive approximations. We introduce a parameter λ and write the equation in the form

$$x = (1 - \lambda)x + \lambda(1 - x^5) \equiv f(x) \qquad (0 \leqslant x \leqslant 1). \qquad (14)$$

This equation is equivalent to (11) unless $\lambda = 0$. We will choose λ so as to make $|f'(x)| \leqslant \theta < 1$.

If we choose $\lambda = \frac{2}{7}$, then we shall have $|f'| \leqslant \frac{5}{7}$ on the whole interval. Then we get the iterative scheme

$$x_{n+1} = \tfrac{5}{7}x_n + \tfrac{2}{7}(1 - x_n^5) \qquad (n = 0, 1, \ldots).$$

Starting with $x_0 = 0.5$, we compute this sequence:

$$0.5, 0.634, 0.709, 0.741, 0.751, 0.754, 0.755, 0.755, \ldots.$$

At last we get $x = 0.7548776662$. That's more like it.

EXAMPLE 3. What happens if you try to solve $x = 1 - x$ by successive approximations? Try, and see what happens. (This is like the story about mothballs: Do mothballs kill moths? Yes, but only if you make a direct hit.)

EXAMPLE 4. *Newton's method* is an automatic way to convert an equation $g(x) = 0$ into a fixed-point equation $x = f(x)$ in which $f(x)$ is a contraction in the neighborhood of a root. If $g(x)$ is differentiable, we write

$$x = f(x) \equiv x - g'(x)^{-1}g(x). \qquad (15)$$

For simplicity, suppose $g'(x) \neq 0$ and suppose g'' exists near the root. Then $f'(x) = (g')^{-2}g''g = 0$ at the root, and $|f'|$ is very small near the root. So the contraction principle must work if M is a small closed interval containing the root.

With its generalizations to N-dimensional space and to function spaces, the Newton equation (15) gives the most important example of the equation (3). Here $\Phi[g(x)]$ stands for $-g'(x)^{-1}g(x)$. (In N dimensions $g'(x)$ is the Jacobian matrix; in function spaces $g'(x)$ is the Fréchet derivative.)

We proved the contraction-mapping theorem in 1 dimension. You will have many uses for this theorem in N dimensions and in function spaces. Don't let those terms intimidate you. The proof looks almost the same as what you know already. Now I'm going to show you Banach's 1922 version. Please compare the proof line for line with our old formulas (4)–(10); you'll see there's not much new.

Banach talks abstractly about a *complete metric space M*. This is a set on which we have a function $d(a,b)$ measuring a kind of distance between every two points in M. We require these properties:

(i) $d(a,b) = d(b,a) \geqslant 0$, with $d(a,b) = 0$ iff $a = b$.
(ii) $d(a,b) + d(b,c) \geqslant d(a,c)$, (triangle inequality).

(iii) If $d(x_p,x_q) \to 0$ as $p, q \to \infty$, then there exists in M a "limit" x such that $d(x_n,x) \to 0$ (completeness—the Cauchy property).

Theorem. *Let f map a complete metric space M into itself. Assume, for every a and b,*

$$d(f(a),f(b)) \leqslant \theta d(a,b), \tag{4'}$$

where $0 \leqslant \theta < 1$. Then f has a unique fixed point in M.

PROOF. Uniqueness: If there were two fixed points, a and b, then

$$d(a,b) = d(f(a),f(b)) \leqslant \theta d(a,b). \tag{5'}$$

Then $d(a,b) = 0$ because $0 \leqslant \theta < 1$, and so $a = b$.

Existence: Start with any x_0 in M and compute $x_1, x_2, \ldots$ by

$$x_{n+1} = f(x_n) \qquad (n = 0, 1, 2, \ldots). \tag{6'}$$

We will prove that $d(x_p,x_q) \to 0$ as $p, q \to \infty$.

That will suffice. For then completeness implies there is a point x in M such that $d(x_n,x) \to 0$. Next, (4') implies

$$d(f(x_n),f(x)) \leqslant \theta d(x_n,x); \tag{7'}$$

hence, $d(f(x_n),f(x)) \to 0$. By the triangle inequality,

$$d(x,f(x)) \leqslant d(x,x_{n+1}) + d(x_{n+1},f(x)),$$

and now (6') yields $d(x_{n+1},f(x)) = d(f(x_n),f(x)) \to 0$, and so $d(x,f(x)) = 0$ and $x = f(x)$.

To prove $d(x_p,x_q) \to 0$, we write

$$d(x_n,x_{n+1}) = d(f(x_{n-1}),f(x_n)) \leqslant \theta d(x_{n-1},x_n) \qquad (n = 1, 2, \ldots).$$

Repetition gives us

$$d(x_n,x_{n+1}) \leqslant \theta^n d(x_0,x_1) \qquad (n = 1, 2, \ldots). \tag{9'}$$

If $q > p$, the triangle inequality and (9') imply

$$\begin{aligned}
d(x_p,x_q) &\leqslant \sum_{n=p}^{q-1} d(x_n,x_{n+1}) \\
&\leqslant d(x_0,x_1)(\theta^p + \theta^{p+1} + \cdots + \theta^{q-1}) \\
&< d(x_0,x_1)\theta^p(1 - \theta)^{-1} \to 0 \quad \text{as} \quad p \to \infty.
\end{aligned} \tag{10'}$$

This completes the proof of Banach's theorem.

As I said, nothing much is new here. So why did I bother to show it to you? Why did I show you both versions? For two reasons:

1. Abstraction intimidates me. Unless I'm talking about something I can touch, smell, or taste, I don't know what I'm talking about. I can taste

the real numbers, but complete metric spaces make me uneasy. Perhaps you feel the same way.

2. The abstract version has tremendous unexpected consequences. With no trouble, it implies the Cauchy-Lipschitz theorem on the existence and uniqueness of solutions to systems of ordinary nonlinear differential equations. With no trouble, it implies the implicit-function theorem. It is enough to make you believe in pure mathematics. (See Problems 1 and 2.)

Let me give you just one small example—a Hammerstein integral equation.

EXAMPLE 5. Consider the nonlinear integral equation

$$x(t) = \int_0^1 e^{-st} \cos(\lambda x(s)) \, ds \qquad (0 \leqslant t \leqslant 1), \tag{16}$$

with $0 < \lambda < 1$. Using Banach's theorem, we will prove that this equation has a unique continuous real-valued solution $x(t)$.

We'll let M be the space of "points" $\mathbf{x}$ equal to continuous functions $x(t)$ for $0 \leqslant t \leqslant 1$. If $\mathbf{a} = a(t)$ and $\mathbf{b} = b(t)$, we'll define the distance $d(\mathbf{a},\mathbf{b})$ by the maximum norm

$$d(\mathbf{a},\mathbf{b}) = \max|a(t) - b(t)| \qquad (0 \leqslant t \leqslant 1). \tag{17}$$

For instance, if $a(t) = t$ and $b(t) = \sin t$, then $d(\mathbf{a},\mathbf{b}) = 1 - \sin 1 = 0.1585$.

Our space M is a complete metric space. You see at once that $d(\mathbf{a},\mathbf{b})$ has the properties (i) and (ii). It also has property (iii): a uniformly convergent sequence of continuous functions has a continuous limit. (See Problem 5.)

Now then. What is the mapping? If $\mathbf{x}$ lies in M, we define $\mathbf{f}(\mathbf{x}) \equiv \mathbf{y}$, where

$$y(t) = \int_0^1 e^{-st} \cos(\lambda x(s)) \, ds \qquad (0 \leqslant t \leqslant 1). \tag{18}$$

The problem (16) asks for a fixed point: $\mathbf{x} = \mathbf{f}(\mathbf{x})$.

The mapping is a contraction because we've assumped $0 < \lambda < 1$. You see,

$$\cos \lambda a - \cos \lambda b = \lambda(b - a) \sin \theta,$$

where θ lies between λa and λb. Therefore,

$$|\cos \lambda a - \cos \lambda b| \leqslant \lambda|b - a|.$$

For the functions $a(t)$ and $b(t)$, we get

$$|\cos(\lambda a(t)) - \cos(\lambda b(t))| \leqslant |b(t) - a(t)| \leqslant d(\mathbf{a},\mathbf{b}).$$

For the integrals $\mathbf{u} = \mathbf{f}(\mathbf{a})$ and $\mathbf{v} = \mathbf{f}(\mathbf{b})$, we get

$$|u(t) - v(t)| \leqslant \int_0^1 e^{-st}|\cos(\lambda a(s)) - \cos(\lambda b(s))| \, ds$$
$$\leqslant \lambda d(\mathbf{a},\mathbf{b}) \int_0^1 e^{-st} \, ds \leqslant \lambda d(\mathbf{a},\mathbf{b}).$$

Taking the maximum for $0 \leqslant t \leqslant 1$, we get

$$d(\mathbf{f(a)},\mathbf{f(b)}) \leqslant \lambda d(\mathbf{a},\mathbf{b}).$$

Beautiful. That's all there is to it. Banach's theorem says there is one and only one solution $x(t)$ to the nonlinear integral equation (16).

We assumed $0 < \lambda < 1$; you might wonder what happens if $\lambda \geqslant 1$. Then we can't use the contraction-mapping principle.

For $\lambda = 1$ we can get a solution by taking a convergent subsequence of solutions $x(t;\lambda)$ belonging to parameters $\lambda < 1$ with $\lambda \to 1$. It's easy to show that the solutions $x(t;\lambda)$ are uniformly bounded and equicontinuous for $0 \leqslant t \leqslant 1$; a classical theorem gives a convergent subsequence and hence a solution $x(t,1)$ for $\lambda = 1$.

For $\lambda > 1$ we have a different story. Then the Hammerstein equation (16) becomes a hard problem; I have no elementary way to prove a solution exists. For $\lambda > 1$ we shall later get a solution from the Schauder fixed-point theorem, which extends to Banach space the great theorem of Brouwer.

I will give you three proofs of the Brouwer fixed-point theorem. If you wish, you can study any one of them without the other two. The first of the three proofs has never before appeared in print. It was told to me by my colleague Adriano Garsia.

References

1. S. Banach, Sur les operations dans les ensembles abstraits et leur application aux equations integrales. *Fund. Math.* Vol. 3 (1922) pp. 133–181.
2. D. R. Smart, *Fixed Point Theorems*, Cambridge Univ. Press, 1974.

PROBLEMS

1. Cauchy-Lipschitz theorem. Consider the initial-value problem of ordinary differential equations

$$\frac{d}{dt} x(t) = f(x(t),t), \quad x(0) = 0.$$

Assuming f satisfies a *Lipschitz condition*, you can prove a solution $x(t)$ exists and is unique in some interval $0 \leqslant t \leqslant t_1$. Here's how:

Assume the function $f(s,t)$ is continuous for $|s| \leqslant s_0$ and $0 \leqslant t \leqslant t_0$, with

$$|f(s,t) - f(s',t)| \leqslant \lambda|s - s'|$$

for some Lipschitz constant λ. Rewrite the initial-value problem as the integral equation

$$x(t) = \int_0^t f(x(u),u)\, du.$$

If μ is an upper bound of $|f(s,t)|$, let t_1 satisfy

$$0 < t_1 \leqslant t_0, \quad t_1 \lambda < 1, \quad t_1 \mu \leqslant s_0.$$

Define the complete metric space of continuous functions $x(t)$ with $|x(t)| \leqslant s_0$ for $0 \leqslant t \leqslant t_1$. Define the "distance" between two such functions as

$$d(\mathbf{x}_1, \mathbf{x}_2) = \max |x_1(t) - x_2(t)| \quad \text{for} \quad 0 \leqslant t \leqslant t_1.$$

Show that the integral in the integral equation gives a contraction mapping of the metric space into itself. Now get a unique fixed point $\mathbf{x}$ from Banach's theorem. The fixed point $\mathbf{x} = x(t)$ solves the initial-value problem.

2. Implicit-function theorem. Assume $g(x,t)$ is continuously differentiable in some neighborhood of the origin; assume $g(0,0) = 0$. Given t near zero, you want a solution x to the equation $g(x,t) = 0$ (the solution x is an *implicit function* of t). Assume the partial derivative $g_x \neq 0$, and proceed as follows:
   Define the constant $c = g_x(0,0) \neq 0$. Define the function $f(x,t) = x - c^{-1}g(x,t)$. Show $f_x = 0$ for $x,t = 0,0$; deduce that $|f_x| \leqslant \theta < 1$ in some closed rectangle $|x| \leqslant x_1, |t| \leqslant t_1$. Now, given t, consider the fixed-point equation $x = f(x,t)$. Use the contraction-mapping theorem.

*3. Generalize Problem 1: State and prove the Cauchy-Lipschitz theorem for R^n.

*4. Generalize Problem 2: State and prove the implicit-function theorem for an equation $\mathbf{g}(\mathbf{x},\mathbf{t}) = \mathbf{0}$ where $\mathbf{g}$ and $\mathbf{x}$ lie in R^n while $\mathbf{t}$ lies in R^m.

*5. Assume $x_n(t) \to x(t)$ as $n \to \infty$, *uniformly* in t for $0 \leqslant t \leqslant 1$. That means: Given $\varepsilon > 0$, you can find $N = N(\varepsilon)$, *independent* of t, such that

$$|x_n(t) - x(t)| \leqslant \varepsilon \quad \text{if} \quad n \geqslant N(\varepsilon).$$

If the $x_n(t)$ are continuous, prove that $x(t)$ is continuous. Hint:

$$x(s) - x(t) = [x(s) - x_N(s)] + [x_N(s) - x_N(t)] + [x_N(t) - x(t)].$$

6. Newton's method. Let $g(a) = 0$. Assume $g(x)$ is twice continuously differentiable for x near a. Assume $g'(a) \neq 0$. Pick x_0 near a, and define the iteration scheme

$$x_{n+1} = x_n - g'(x_n)^{-1}g(x_n) \quad (n = 0, 1, 2, \ldots).$$

Prove $x_n \to a$ if x_0 is picked close enough to a; this is called *local convergence*.

7. For Problem 6, prove *quadratic convergence*:

$$|x_{n+1} - x_n| \leqslant \text{constant} \cdot |x_n - x_{n-1}|^2.$$

*8. Newton's method if $g'(a) = 0$. Assume

$$g(x) = b(x - a)^p + \cdots,$$
$$g'(x) = bp(x - a)^{p-1} + \cdots,$$

where $b \neq 0$ and $p > 1$ (the dots stand for smaller terms). Again prove local convergence for Newton's method; disprove quadratic convergence.

9. Consider the function $f(x) = x + e^{-x}$ on the half-line $x \geqslant 0$. Observe that $0 \leqslant f'(x) < 1$, and deduce that $|f(a) - f(b)| < |a - b|$. Is $f(x)$ a contraction mapping? Does the

equation $x = f(x)$ have a root? Would it help to restrict $f(x)$ to a closed interval $0 \leqslant x \leqslant A$? Why not?

10. If λ is a positive constant, consider the function $f(x) = \sin \lambda x$ for $-\infty < x < \infty$. For which constants λ does $f(x)$ give a contraction mapping of R^1 into itself? For which λ does the equation $x = f(x)$ have a root? For which λ is the root unique?

11. If M is an interval of real numbers, and if $f(x)$ is differentiable on M, show that $f(x)$ is a contraction if and only if $|f'(x)| \leqslant \theta < 1$, for some constant θ. If M is the union of *disjoint* intervals, show that $f(x)$ need *not* be a contraction if $|f'(x)| \leqslant \theta < 1$: let M be the union of disjoint intervals I_1, I_2; define $f(x)$ mapping M into itself with no fixed point, though $f'(x) \equiv 0$.

*12. Let M be a closed, bounded, convex subset of R^n, and let $\mathbf{f}(\mathbf{x})$ map M into itself. Assume all n components of $\mathbf{f}$ are continuously differentiable, and define the $n \times n$ Jacobian matrix $J = (\partial f_i / \partial x_j)$. Using Euclidian length, show that $\mathbf{f}(\mathbf{x})$ gives a contraction mapping iff the Jacobian matrix has norm $|J| < 1$. (The norm of a matrix A is defined as the maximum of the length quotients $|A\mathbf{z}| \div |\mathbf{z}|$ for vectors $\mathbf{z} \neq \mathbf{0}$.)

*13. Generalize Newton's method (Problem 6) to R^n. With an appropriate assumption, prove local convergence.

2 Garsia's Proof of the Brouwer Fixed-Point Theorem

The Brouwer fixed-point theorem is one of the most important results in modern mathematics. It is easy to state but hard to prove. The statement is easy enough to be understood by anyone, even by someone who can't add or subtract. But its proof has usually been so difficult that it has been taught only in graduate courses on topology.

The Brouwer theorem has many applications in mathematical analysis. For instance, it is an essential tool in the theory of ordinary differential equations. In its extension by Schauder and Leray, the fixed-point theorem is used to establish previously unattainable results in the theory of nonlinear partial differential equations and integral equations. In mathematical economics, it is used to prove the existence of equilibria in many-person games.

This is what the Brouwer theorem says in everyday terms: Sit down with a cup of coffee. Gently and continuously swirl the coffee about in the cup. Put the cup down, and let the motion subside. When the coffee is still, Brouwer says there is at least one point in the coffee that has returned to the exact spot in the cup where it was when you first sat down.

In mathematical terms the Brouwer theorem says: *If a ball (or its topological equivalent) is mapped continuously into itself, then at least one point must be mapped into itself.*

Now that is fascinating. Somehow it should be easy to prove.

When I was a student, like all mathematics students, I knew the statement of the Brouwer theorem. Of course, I wanted to understand it. I knew that sooner or later I would have to understand it if I wanted to call myself a competent professional mathematician. But I never took a course in topology, and so I failed to learn a proof.

As a post-doctoral fellow in New York University, I decided to attend lectures on topology with the purpose of understanding the Brouwer theorem. The professor was the eminent mathematician Emil Artin. His first lectures were all about something called "the free group," which I found vexing. After a while, I felt we would never reach the Brouwer theorem, and I stopped attending; I let the matter slide. I tried to prove the theorem for myself, but always failed. I looked at books on topology, but lacked the patience to study them.

One day ten years later, I was complaining to my colleague Adriano Garsia:

"Why isn't there an easy proof of the Brouwer fixed-point theorem?"

"Didn't you ever take a course in topology?" he asked.

"No," I admitted. Why not be honest?

"Well, what would you consider a simple proof?" he asked.

"One that I can understand," I said.

"Do you know Green's theorem?" he asked.

"You mean Green's theorem in integral calculus? Of course I know Green's theorem; everyone knows Green's theorem," I said huffily.

"Then I can give you an easy proof of the Brouwer theorem," he said.

"I dare you," I said.

He told me his proof, and now I'm going to tell it to you. His proof is beautiful and fairly easy. I would say it is about twice as hard to learn as Stokes's theorem in calculus, but not harder than that. If you can understand ordinary engineering mathematics, then you can understand Garsia's proof of the Brouwer fixed-point theorem.

First, some terminology. Topologists use the word *ball* for the solid $|\mathbf{x}| \leqslant 1$; they use the word *sphere* for the surface $|\mathbf{x}| = 1$. Other mathematicians use *sphere* for either the solid or its surface, and then they have to explain what they mean. I think the topologists are right, and I will use the words *ball* and *sphere* as they do.

Brouwer's fixed-point theorem says:

Let $\mathbf{f}(\mathbf{x})$ be a continuous function defined in the N-dimensional unit ball $|\mathbf{x}| \leqslant 1$. Let $\mathbf{f}(\mathbf{x})$ map the ball into itself: $|\mathbf{f}(\mathbf{x})| \leqslant 1$ for $|\mathbf{x}| \leqslant 1$. Then some point in the ball is mapped into itself: $\mathbf{f}(\mathbf{x}^{\circ}) = \mathbf{x}^{\circ}$.

For $N = 1$ the theorem says this: If $-1 \leqslant f(x) \leqslant 1$ for $-1 \leqslant x \leqslant 1$, then $f(x) = x$ for some x. In other words, the graph $y = f(x)$ must intersect the line $y = x$ for some x. This is illustrated in Figure 1.

For $N = 1$ the theorem is easy to prove. The function $f(x) - x$ is continuous for $-1 \leqslant x \leqslant 1$. It is $\leqslant 0$ at $x = 1$; it is $\geqslant 0$ at $x = -1$. Therefore it equals 0 somewhere in the closed interval $-1 \leqslant x \leqslant 1$.

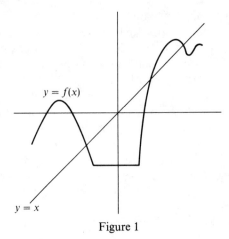

Figure 1

Note that the assumptions on $f(x)$ are all used; if any assumption is dropped, the theorem is false. For instance, if $f(x) = x + 1$, then $f(x) \neq x$ for $-1 \leqslant x \leqslant 1$; here $f(x)$ does not satisfy $|f(x)| \leqslant 1$ for $|x| \leqslant 1$. For another instance, if $f(x) = -x$ for $|x| \leqslant 1$ except for the single point $x = 0$ where $f(x) = \frac{1}{2}$, then $f(x) \neq x$ for $-1 \leqslant x \leqslant 1$; here $f(x)$ is discontinuous.

For $N = 2$ dimensions, the theorem says this: If the disk $|x| \leqslant 1$ is mapped continuously into itself, at least one point is mapped into itself.

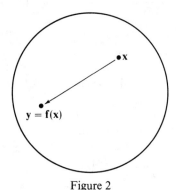

Figure 2

Here again we see that if any of the assumptions on the mapping $\mathbf{f}(\mathbf{x})$ is dropped, the theorem becomes false. Note also this: If the disk is replaced by some other domain, the theorem may become false. For instance, consider the annulus $\frac{1}{2} \leqslant |\mathbf{x}| \leqslant 1$. This domain can be mapped continuously into itself by a rotation through an angle θ. Unless θ is a multiple of 2π, there is no fixed point.

This brings us to the topology of the domain. We say that the ball $|\mathbf{x}| \leqslant 1$ is topologically equivalent to a domain D if there is a continuous mapping

$\mathbf{y} = T\mathbf{x}$ from the ball into D, with a continuous inverse mapping $\mathbf{x} = T^{-1}\mathbf{y}$ from D back to the ball.

For instance, in 2 dimensions the disk $|\mathbf{x}| \leqslant 1$ is topologically equivalent to the square $-1 \leqslant y_1 \leqslant 1$, $-1 \leqslant y_2 \leqslant 1$. (For T^{-1} we may take the mapping

$$x_1 = y_1/\sigma, \quad x_2 = y_2/\sigma \text{ if } \sigma = |\mathbf{y}'|,$$

where $\mathbf{y}'$ is the boundary point on the ray from $\mathbf{0}$ through $\mathbf{y}$.) But we may not let D be the whole plane; and we may not let D be an annulus.

Let D be topologically equivalent to the unit ball. *Suppose the Brouwer theorem is true for the unit ball; then it is true for D.*

Here is the proof. Suppose $\mathbf{f}(\mathbf{y})$ maps D into itself, and suppose $\mathbf{f}$ is continuous; we want to show that $\mathbf{f}$ has a fixed point $\mathbf{y}° = \mathbf{f}(\mathbf{y}°)$. Set up the continuous correspondence

$$\mathbf{y} = T\mathbf{x}, \quad \mathbf{x} = T^{-1}\mathbf{y}$$

for $\mathbf{y}$ in D and $|\mathbf{x}| \leqslant 1$. This is illustrated in Figure 3.

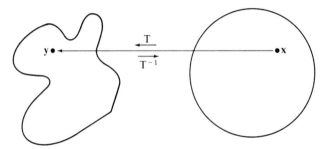

Figure 3

Now define the function

$$\mathbf{g}(\mathbf{x}) = T^{-1}\mathbf{f}(T\mathbf{x})$$

This function maps $|\mathbf{x}| \leqslant 1$ into itself, and $\mathbf{g}$ is continuous because T^{-1}, $\mathbf{f}$, and T are continuous. Now Brouwer's theorem for the ball says: $\mathbf{g}$ has a fixed point $\mathbf{x}° = \mathbf{g}(\mathbf{x}°)$. If $\mathbf{y}° = T\mathbf{x}°$, then

$$T^{-1}\mathbf{y}° = \mathbf{g}(T^{-1}\mathbf{y}°)$$

If we apply T, we get the fixed point

$$\mathbf{y}° = T\mathbf{g}(T^{-1}\mathbf{y}°) = \mathbf{f}(\mathbf{y}°) \quad \text{in} \quad D.$$

Now we will approach the proof of Brouwer's theorem for the ball. Let $\mathbf{f}$ map the unit ball continuously into itself. Define the function

$$\mathbf{h}(\mathbf{x}) = \mathbf{x} - \mathbf{f}(\mathbf{x}).$$

A fixed point of $\mathbf{f}$ is a root of the equation $\mathbf{h}(\mathbf{x}) = \mathbf{0}$. If we suppose $\mathbf{f}(\mathbf{x})$ has no fixed point for $|\mathbf{x}| \leqslant 1$, then $\mathbf{h}(\mathbf{x}) \neq \mathbf{0}$ for $|\mathbf{x}| \leqslant 1$.

The discriminant. If $\mathbf{h}(\mathbf{x})$ is any function in R^N that is continuous and non-zero on the surface $|\mathbf{x}| = 1$, we will define a discriminant $\delta[\mathbf{h}]$. We require δ to be a real-valued functional with three properties:

(i) $\delta[\mathbf{h}(\mathbf{x})] \neq 0$ if $\mathbf{h}(\mathbf{x}) \equiv \mathbf{x}$
(ii) $\delta[\mathbf{h}(\mathbf{x})] = 0$ *if* $\mathbf{h}(\mathbf{x})$ *can be defined as a continuous non-zero function in the whole unit ball* $|\mathbf{x}| \leqslant 1$.
(iii) *If* $\mathbf{h}_1(\mathbf{x})$ *and* $\mathbf{h}_2(\mathbf{x})$ *never point in opposite directions on the surface, then they have equal discriminants*:

$$\delta[\mathbf{h}_1] = \delta[\mathbf{h}_2] \quad \text{if} \quad (1 - \theta)\mathbf{h}_1(\mathbf{x}) + \theta\mathbf{h}_2(\mathbf{x}) \neq 0 \qquad \text{for } 0 \leqslant \theta \leqslant 1 \text{ and } |\mathbf{x}| = 1$$

EXAMPLE. For $N = 1$, we can construct a functional $\delta[h]$ as follows. The function $h(x)$ is given on the boundary of the unit ball $-1 \leqslant x \leqslant 1$; in other words the two numbers $h(-1) \neq 0$ and $h(1) \neq 0$ are given. Let $s =$ the sign of $h(1)$: $s = 1$ if $h(1) > 0$; $s = -1$ if $h(1) < 0$. Let $s' =$ the sign of $h(-1)$. Then define

$$\delta[h] = s - s'.$$

Now verify the three properties:

(i) $\delta[\mathbf{x}] = 1 - (-1) = 2 \neq 0$.
(ii) $s - s' = 0$ if $h(x)$ has any continuous non-zero extension into the whole interval, since $s - s' \neq 0$ implies that $h(1)$ and $h(-1)$ have opposite signs.
(iii) In one dimension "$h_1(x)$ and $h_2(x)$ never point in opposite directions on the surface" means: $h_1(1)$ and $h_2(1)$ have the same sign, and $h_1(-1)$ and $h_2(-1)$ have the same sign. Then the two discriminants are equal.

Use of the discriminant. If we can construct a discriminant $\delta[\mathbf{h}]$ with the three required properties, then we can prove the fixed-point theorem. Here's how:

Given is $\mathbf{f}(\mathbf{x})$ mapping $|\mathbf{x}| \leqslant 1$ continuously into itself. Define $\mathbf{h}(\mathbf{x}) = \mathbf{x} - \mathbf{f}(\mathbf{x})$ for $|\mathbf{x}| = 1$. If $\mathbf{f}$ has no fixed point, then $\mathbf{h}(\mathbf{x}) \neq \mathbf{0}$. We now assert that $\mathbf{x}$ and $\mathbf{h}(\mathbf{x})$ nowhere point in opposite directions if $|\mathbf{x}| = 1$. Indeed,

$$\mathbf{x} \cdot \mathbf{h}(\mathbf{x}) = \mathbf{x} \cdot \{\mathbf{x} - \mathbf{f}(\mathbf{x})\} = 1 - \mathbf{x} \cdot \mathbf{f}(x)$$

while

$$0 < |\mathbf{x} - \mathbf{f}(\mathbf{x})|^2 = 1 - 2\mathbf{x} \cdot \mathbf{f} + |\mathbf{f}|^2 \leqslant 2(1 - \mathbf{x} \cdot \mathbf{f}).$$

Therefore, $\mathbf{x} \cdot \mathbf{h}(\mathbf{x}) > 0$ and

$$(1 - \theta)\mathbf{x} + \theta\mathbf{h}(\mathbf{x}) \neq \mathbf{0} \quad \text{if} \quad 0 \leqslant \theta \leqslant 1,$$

since the equality would imply $1 - \theta + \theta\mathbf{x} \cdot \mathbf{h} = 0$.

Now property (iii) says that $\delta[\mathbf{h}] = \delta[\mathbf{x}]$. But $\delta[\mathbf{x}] \neq 0$, and so $\delta[\mathbf{h}] \neq 0$. Now property (ii) says that any continuous definition of $\mathbf{h}(\mathbf{x})$ in the whole ball must somewhere $= \mathbf{0}$. Then $\mathbf{x} - \mathbf{f}(\mathbf{x}) = \mathbf{0}$, that is, $\mathbf{f}$ has a fixed point.

The operator D. The definition of the discriminant will depend on a certain differential operator D. Here we suppose R^N is the space of vectors with

N real components. The operator D will apply to functions $\mathbf{g}(\mathbf{x})$ with these properties: $\mathbf{g}(\mathbf{x})$ lies in R^N and is twice continuously differentiable as a function of $\mathbf{x}$ in a neighborhood of the surface $|\mathbf{x}| = 1$. For such functions, $D\mathbf{g}(\mathbf{x}) = \mathbf{h}(x)$ will lie in R^N and will be continuously differentiable on the surface $|\mathbf{x}| = \rho = 1$.

Let ∂_j represent $\partial/\partial x_j$. Then $\partial_j\mathbf{g}$ is the vector whose ith component is $\partial_j g_i$. We first define the Jacobian matrix

$$J = [\partial_1\mathbf{g}, \partial_2\mathbf{g}, \ldots, \partial_N\mathbf{g}]$$

with determinant

$$\det J = \Delta = \Delta[\mathbf{g}].$$

Define J_k to be the matrix obtained by replacing the column $\partial_k\mathbf{g}$ by $\mathbf{g}$. Call its determinant

$$\det J_k = \Delta_k[\mathbf{g}].$$

Now define $\mathbf{h} = D\mathbf{g}$ to be the vector whose kth component is

$$h_k = \Delta_k[\mathbf{g}].$$

We will illustrate these definitions for $N = 1, 2,$ and 3.

$N = 1$. Here we have

$$J = [\partial_1 g_1], \quad \Delta = \partial_1 g_1 = g_1'(x_1),$$
$$J_1 = [g_1], \quad h_1 = \Delta_1 = g_1(x_1) = Dg.$$

$N = 2$. Here we have

$$J = [\partial_1\mathbf{g}, \partial_2\mathbf{g}], \quad \Delta = \det J$$
$$J_1 = [\mathbf{g}, \partial_2\mathbf{g}], \quad \Delta_1 = \det J_1,$$
$$J_2 = [\partial_1\mathbf{g}, \mathbf{g}], \quad \Delta_2 = \det J_2,$$

$$D\mathbf{g} = \begin{bmatrix} \Delta_1 \\ \Delta_2 \end{bmatrix}.$$

For example, suppose

$$\mathbf{g} = \begin{bmatrix} x_1^2 + x_2 \\ x_1 \cos x_2 \end{bmatrix}$$

then

$$J = \begin{bmatrix} 2x_1, \ 1 \\ \cos x_2, \ -x_1 \sin x_2 \end{bmatrix}$$

$$J_1 = \begin{bmatrix} x_1^2 + x_2, \ 1 \\ x_1 \cos x_2, \ -x_1 \sin x_2 \end{bmatrix}$$

$$\Delta_1 = (x_1^2 + x_2)(-x_1 \sin x_2) - x_1 \cos x_2$$

$$J_2 = \begin{bmatrix} 2x_1, \ x_1^2 + x_2 \\ \cos x_2, \ x_1 \cos x_2 \end{bmatrix}$$

$$\Delta_2 = 2x_1^2 \cos x_2 - (x_1^2 + x_2) \cos x_2$$

and so

$$D\begin{bmatrix} x_1^2 + x_2 \\ x_1 \cos x_2 \end{bmatrix} = \begin{bmatrix} (x_1^2 + x_2)(-x_1 \sin x_2) - x_1 \cos x_2 \\ 2x_1^2 \cos x_2 - (x_1^2 + x_2) \cos x_2 \end{bmatrix}$$

$N = 3$. Here we have

$$\begin{aligned} J &= [\partial_1 \mathbf{g}, \partial_2 \mathbf{g}, \partial_3 \mathbf{g}], & \Delta &= \det J \\ J_1 &= [\mathbf{g}, \partial_2 \mathbf{g}, \partial_3 \mathbf{g}], & \Delta_1 &= \det J_1 \\ J_2 &= [\partial_1 \mathbf{g}, \mathbf{g}, \partial_3 \mathbf{g}], & \Delta_2 &= \det J_2 \\ J_3 &= [\partial_1 \mathbf{g}, \partial_2 \mathbf{g}, \mathbf{g}], & \Delta_3 &= \det J_3 \end{aligned}$$

$$D\mathbf{g} = \begin{bmatrix} \Delta_1 \\ \Delta_2 \\ \Delta_3 \end{bmatrix}$$

Thus, the operator D is a first-order differential operator mapping vectors into vectors. In this sense it is like the operator *curl* (usually written as $\nabla \times$); it is unlike the divergence (usually written as $\nabla \cdot$), which maps vectors into scalars.

The operator D satisfies an identity that will make it useful to us: the divergence of $D\mathbf{g}$ in N dimensions equals N times the Jacobian determinant.

Lemma. $\nabla \cdot (D\mathbf{g}) = N \det J$.

EXAMPLE. In the example we used for $N = 2$, we find
$$\begin{aligned} \nabla \cdot (D\mathbf{g}) &= \partial_1 [(x_1^2 + x_2)(-x_1 \sin x_2) - x_1 \cos x_2] \\ &\quad + \partial_2 [2x_1^2 \cos x_2 - (x_1^2 + x_2) \cos x_2] \\ &= 2[-x_1^2 \sin x_2 - \cos x_2] = 2 \det J. \end{aligned}$$

EXAMPLE. For $N = 2$ this is the proof of the lemma: The vector $D\mathbf{g}$ has the two components

$$\det[\mathbf{g}, \partial_2 \mathbf{g}] \quad \text{and} \quad \det[\partial_1 \mathbf{g}, \mathbf{g}].$$

The divergence of this vector equals

$$\det[\partial_1 \mathbf{g}, \partial_2 \mathbf{g}] + \det[\mathbf{g}, \partial_1 \partial_2 \mathbf{g}] + \det[\partial_2 \partial_1 \mathbf{g}, \mathbf{g}] + \det[\partial_1 \mathbf{g}, \partial_2 \mathbf{g}].$$

The second and third terms cancel, because they are determinants with two columns interchanged. The remaining two terms each equal $\det J$.

PROOF OF THE LEMMA. For $N \geq 2$ the proof directly generalizes the proof just given for $N = 2$. The vector function $D\mathbf{g}$ has the components $\Delta_1, \Delta_2, \ldots, \Delta_N$, and so the divergence equals

$$\nabla \cdot (D\mathbf{g}) = \partial_1 \Delta_1 + \partial_2 \Delta_2 + \cdots + \partial_N \Delta_N.$$

Each Δ_k is a determinant

$$\Delta_k = \det J_k.$$

The rule for differentiating determinants says

$$\partial_k \Delta_k = \sum_{v=1}^{N} \det J_{kv}$$

where J_{kv} is the matrix obtained by applying the operator ∂_k to the vth column of the matrix J_k.

If $v = k$ this rule gives

$$\det J_{kk} = \det J = \Delta.$$

That is because J_k was formed from J by replacing the kth column, $\partial_k \mathbf{g}$, by $\mathbf{g}$; now if ∂_k is applied to this column, we get back the original column $\partial_k \mathbf{g}$.

If $v \neq k$, the matrix J_{kv} has column v equal to $\partial_k \partial_v \mathbf{g}$; it has column k equal to $\mathbf{g}$; and for column $j \neq v$ or k it has $\partial_j \mathbf{g}$. Thus the matrices J_{kv} and J_{vk} are identical except that columns k and v are interchanged. Therefore,

$$\det J_{kv} = -\det J_{vk} \quad \text{if} \quad v \neq k.$$

Now we find

$$\mathbf{V} \cdot (D\mathbf{g}) = \sum_{k=1}^{N} \partial_k \Delta_k$$

$$= \sum_{k=1}^{N} \sum_{v=1}^{N} \det J_{kv} = N \det J,$$

since the terms with $k = v$ equal $\det J$, and the terms with $k \neq v$ cancel.

Corollary. *If* $\mathbf{u}(\mathbf{x})$ *is twice continuously differentiable and if* $|\mathbf{u}(\mathbf{x})| = 1$, *then* $\mathbf{V} \cdot (D\mathbf{u}) = 0$.

PROOF. We must show that $\det J = 0$, where

$$J = [\partial_1 \mathbf{u}, \partial_2 \mathbf{u}, \ldots, \partial_N \mathbf{u}].$$

It is enough to show that the columns of J are dependent. But that is true, since every column $\partial_j \mathbf{u}$ is orthogonal to the unit vector $\mathbf{u}$:

$$0 = \partial_j |\mathbf{u}|^2 = 2\mathbf{u} \cdot \partial_j \mathbf{u}.$$

Now we are ready to *define the discriminant* $\delta[\mathbf{u}]$ for functions *that are twice continuously differentiable unit vectors in a neighborhood of the unit sphere.* For these functions we define

$$\delta[\mathbf{u}] \equiv \int_{|\mathbf{x}|=1} (D\mathbf{u}) \cdot \mathbf{n} \, dS$$

Note that $\mathbf{x}$ equals $\mathbf{n}$, the outer normal, on the surface $|\mathbf{x}| = 1$. Here we assume $N \geqslant 2$ dimensions. If A_N is the area of the surface $|\mathbf{x}| = 1$, topologists call $A_N^{-1} \delta(\mathbf{u}]$ *the degree of mapping.*

EXAMPLE. What does this mean for $N = 2$? Here $\mathbf{x}$ on the unit circle is the unit normal, and

$$\mathbf{n}\,dS = \begin{bmatrix} dx_2 \\ -dx_1 \end{bmatrix}.$$

Then

$$
\begin{aligned}
(D\mathbf{u}) \cdot \mathbf{n}\,dS &= \det[\mathbf{u},\partial_2\mathbf{u}]\,dx_2 - \det[\partial_1\mathbf{u},\mathbf{u}]\,dx_1 \\
&= \det[\mathbf{u},\partial_2\mathbf{u}\,dx_2] + \det[\mathbf{u},\partial_1\mathbf{u}\,dx_1] \\
&= \det[\mathbf{u},d\mathbf{u}] \\
&= u_1\,du_2 - u_2\,du_1 \\
&= d\arctan\left(\frac{u_2}{u_1}\right) \qquad (\text{since } u_1^2 + u_2^2 = 1) \\
&= d\arg\mathbf{u}.
\end{aligned}
$$

This gives the definition for $N = 2$:

$$\delta[\mathbf{u}] = \oint_{\rho=1} d\arg\mathbf{u}.$$

The discriminant is the net change of argument around the unit circle.

EXAMPLE. For general N we shall need to know $\delta[\mathbf{u}]$ if $\mathbf{u}$ is the unit vector

$$\mathbf{u}(\mathbf{x}) = \rho^{-1}\mathbf{x} \quad \text{where} \quad \rho = |\mathbf{x}| > 0$$

Let $\mathbf{e}^1, \ldots, \mathbf{e}^N$ be the basic unit vectors

$$\mathbf{e}^1 = \begin{pmatrix} 1 \\ \vdots \\ 0 \end{pmatrix}, \ldots, \mathbf{e}^N = \begin{pmatrix} 0 \\ \vdots \\ 1 \end{pmatrix}.$$

Then

$$
\begin{aligned}
\partial_k(\rho^{-1}\mathbf{x}) &= -\rho^{-3}x_k\mathbf{x} + \rho^{-1}\mathbf{e}^k \\
&= -x_k\mathbf{x} + \mathbf{e}^k \quad \text{for} \quad \rho = 1.
\end{aligned}
$$

This is the kth column of the Jacobian matrix J.

To obtain the jth component of the vector $D\mathbf{u}$, we must replace the jth column of J by $\mathbf{u}$ and take the determinant; for $\rho = 1$ this gives

$$\det[-x_1\mathbf{x} + \mathbf{e}^1, \ldots, \mathbf{x}, \ldots, -x_N\mathbf{x} + \mathbf{e}^N]$$

where $\mathbf{x}$ is the jth column. We can eliminate the terms $-x_1\mathbf{x}, \ldots, -x_N\mathbf{x}$ in the other columns by adding multiples of the column $\mathbf{x}$. This gives the determinant

$$\det[\mathbf{e}^1, \ldots, \mathbf{x}, \ldots, \mathbf{e}^N] = x_j.$$

This shows that for $\mathbf{u}(\mathbf{x}) = \mathbf{x}/\rho$

$$D\mathbf{u} = \mathbf{x} \quad \text{for} \quad \rho = 1.$$

Now we find at once

$$\delta[\rho^{-1}\mathbf{x}] = \int_{\rho=1} \mathbf{x} \cdot \mathbf{x} \, dS = \int_{\rho=1} 1 \, dS = A_N > 0,$$

where A_N is the area of the unit sphere ($A_2 = 2\pi$, $A_3 = 4\pi$, etc.).

EXAMPLE. It will also be useful to know $\delta[\mathbf{v}]$ where $\mathbf{v} = -\mathbf{u} = -\rho^{-1}\mathbf{x}$. If we look over the preceding computation, we see that in the determinants every column is multiplied by -1 if $\mathbf{u}$ is replaced by $-\mathbf{u}$; therefore, since there are N columns, the result x_j must be multiplied by $(-1)^N$. This gives

$$D\mathbf{v} = D(-\mathbf{u}) = (-1)^N D\mathbf{u} = (-1)^N \mathbf{x},$$

and we find

$$\delta[-\rho^{-1}\mathbf{x}] = (-1)^N A_N.$$

Now we'll find a few more properties of $\delta[\mathbf{u}]$ for functions $\mathbf{u}(\mathbf{x})$ in the class U^2 (twice continuously differentiable unit vectors in a neighborhood of $|\mathbf{x}| = 1$).

Lemma. *Suppose $\mathbf{u}(\mathbf{x})$ is in U^2. And suppose that $\mathbf{u}(\mathbf{x})$ can be defined as a twice continuously differentiable unit vector in the* **whole** *unit ball $|\mathbf{x}| \leqslant 1$. Then $\delta[\mathbf{u}] = 0$.*

EXAMPLE. We have computed $\delta[\mathbf{u}] = A_N > 0$ if $\mathbf{u}(\mathbf{x}) = \mathbf{x}/\rho$ near $\rho = 1$. Now the lemma implies that there is no way to extend the definition of $\mathbf{u}(\mathbf{x})$ inside the ball $\rho \leqslant 1$ so that $\mathbf{u}(\mathbf{x})$ remains a twice continuously differentiable unit vector.

PROOF OF THE LEMMA. Suppose that $|\mathbf{u}(\mathbf{x})| = 1$ for $\rho \leqslant 1$. Then we have $\nabla \cdot D\mathbf{u} = 0$ for $\rho \leqslant 1$. Now we can use Green's theorem:

$$\delta[\mathbf{u}] \equiv \int_{\rho=1} (D\mathbf{u}) \cdot \mathbf{n} \, dS$$

$$= \int_{\rho \leqslant 1} \nabla \cdot (D\mathbf{u}) \, dV = 0.$$

That's all there is to it.   □

Next we will obtain a remarkable invariance property of the discriminant.

Lemma. *If $\mathbf{u}(\mathbf{x})$ and $\mathbf{v}(\mathbf{x})$ are both in the class U^2, and if $\mathbf{u} + \mathbf{v}$ is nowhere zero on the unit sphere $\rho = 1$, then $\delta[\mathbf{u}] = \delta[\mathbf{v}]$.*

EXAMPLE. In two dimensions this says that if the unit vectors $\mathbf{u}$ and $\mathbf{v}$ are never opposite on the unit circle, then they have the same net change of argument as $\mathbf{x}$ moves around the circle. For instance, suppose $\mathbf{u}(\mathbf{x}) = \mathbf{x}$ for $\rho = 1$, and suppose $\mathbf{v}(\mathbf{x}) \neq -\mathbf{x}$. Then $\arg \mathbf{v}(\mathbf{x})$ changes by 2π as $\mathbf{x}$ moves around the circle.

PROOF OF THE LEMMA. The functions $\mathbf{u(x)}$ and $\mathbf{v(x)}$ are given for $1 - \varepsilon <$ $\rho < 1 + \varepsilon$. Let $\varphi(\rho)$ be defined for $1 - \varepsilon \leqslant \rho \leqslant 1 + \varepsilon$ with these properties:

(i) $0 \leqslant \varphi(\rho) \leqslant 1$ for $1 - \varepsilon \leqslant \rho \leqslant 1 + \varepsilon$
(ii) φ, φ', and φ'' are continuous
(iii) $\varphi(\rho) \equiv 0$ for $1 - \varepsilon \leqslant \rho \leqslant \rho_0$
(iv) $\varphi(\rho) \equiv 1$ for $\rho_1 \leqslant \rho \leqslant 1 + \varepsilon$

where $1 - \varepsilon < \rho_0 < \rho_1 < 1$. In other words: $\varphi(\rho) \equiv 0$ in a small interval; $\varphi(\rho)$ increases smoothly to the value 1; and then $\varphi(\rho) \equiv 1$ in a small interval.

We can use $\varphi(\rho)$ to make a smooth transition between $\mathbf{u(x)}$ and $\mathbf{v(x)}$ in the spherical shell $1 - \varepsilon < \rho \leqslant 1$. We first define the vector

$$\mathbf{q(x)} = (1 - \varphi(\rho))\mathbf{u(x)} + \varphi(\rho)\mathbf{v(x)}$$

Then $\mathbf{q(x)} \neq \mathbf{0}$ because $\mathbf{u}$ and $\mathbf{v}$ are unit vectors that are never opposite if ε is small enough. Now we define the unit vector

$$\mathbf{w(x)} = \mathbf{q(x)}/|\mathbf{q(x)}|.$$

The properties of $\varphi(\rho)$ guarantee that $\mathbf{w(x)}$ lies in U^2 and that

$$\mathbf{w(x)} = \mathbf{u(x)} \quad \text{for} \quad 1 - \varepsilon < \rho \leqslant \rho_0$$
$$\mathbf{w(x)} = \mathbf{v(x)} \quad \text{for} \quad \rho_1 \leqslant \rho \leqslant 1 + \varepsilon.$$

We will now apply Green's theorem in a spherical shell. Let σ lie between $1 - \varepsilon$ and ρ_0; we will integrate for $\sigma \leqslant \rho \leqslant 1$:

$$\int_{\sigma \leqslant \rho \leqslant 1} \nabla \cdot D\mathbf{w(x)} \, dV = \left(\int_{\rho=1} - \int_{\rho=\sigma} \right)(D\mathbf{w}) \cdot \mathbf{n} \, dS$$

(Here $\mathbf{x}\rho^{-1} = \mathbf{n}$, the outward normal.) We note these facts:

$$\nabla \cdot D\mathbf{w(x)} = 0 \quad \text{since } \mathbf{w} \in U^2$$
$$D\mathbf{w} = D\mathbf{u} \quad \text{for } \rho = \sigma$$
$$D\mathbf{w} = D\mathbf{v} \quad \text{for } \rho = 1.$$

The Green's identity now becomes

$$0 = \int_{\rho=1} (D\mathbf{v}) \cdot \mathbf{n} \, dS - \int_{\rho=\sigma} (D\mathbf{u}) \cdot \mathbf{n} \, dS \qquad (*)$$

The first integral equals $\delta[\mathbf{v}]$; we will show that the second integral equals $\delta[\mathbf{u}]$. That follows if we replace $\mathbf{w}$ by $\mathbf{u}$ in the Green's identity. Since $\mathbf{u(x)}$ lies in U^2, we find

$$0 = \left(\int_{\rho=1} - \int_{\rho=\sigma} \right)(D\mathbf{u}) \cdot \mathbf{n} \, dS$$

which says

$$0 = \delta[u] - \int_{\rho=\sigma} (D\mathbf{u}) \cdot \mathbf{n} \, dS$$

Formula $(*)$ now yields the result:

$$0 = \delta[\mathbf{v}] - \delta[\mathbf{u}].$$

The definition of $\delta[\mathbf{h}]$. So far, we have defined the discriminant $\delta[\mathbf{u}]$ only for functions $\mathbf{u}(\mathbf{x})$ in U^2. Using the properties of $\delta[\mathbf{u}]$, we can now define $\delta[\mathbf{h}]$ for all functions $\mathbf{h}(\mathbf{x})$ with these properties: $\mathbf{h}(\mathbf{x})$ lies in R^N if $|\mathbf{x}| = 1$ and $\mathbf{x} \in R^N$; $\mathbf{h}(\mathbf{x})$ is continuous and non-zero if $|\mathbf{x}| = 1$.

First we extend the definition of $\mathbf{h}(\mathbf{x})$ by the formula

$$\mathbf{h}(\mathbf{x}) \equiv \rho\mathbf{h}(\rho^{-1}\mathbf{x}) \quad \text{for} \quad 0 < \rho = |\mathbf{x}| < \infty.$$

This function is continuous for all $\mathbf{x} \in R^N$; it is non-zero; and it approaches $\mathbf{0}$ as $\rho \to 0$.

If $\mathbf{h}(\mathbf{x})$ does not have continuous second derivatives, we can approximate it as well as we like by a function $\mathbf{k}(\mathbf{x})$ with continuous second derivatives for $\mathbf{x}$ in a bounded region, e.g., for $|\mathbf{x}| \leqslant 2$. For instance, we can use the Weierstrass approximation theorem to obtain a function $\mathbf{k}(\mathbf{x})$ whose components $k_i(\mathbf{x})$ are polynomials in the N variables $x_1, \ldots, x_N$. Since $\mathbf{h}(\mathbf{x}) \neq \mathbf{0}$ for $\rho > 0$, we shall have

$$\mathbf{k}(\mathbf{x}) \cdot \mathbf{h}(\mathbf{x}) > 0 \quad \text{if} \quad \tfrac{1}{2} \leqslant \rho \leqslant 2$$

if $\mathbf{k}$ is close enough to $\mathbf{h}$. If the original $\mathbf{h}(\mathbf{x})$ does have continuous second derivatives, we simply define $\mathbf{k}(\mathbf{x}) \equiv \mathbf{h}(\mathbf{x})$ for $\tfrac{1}{2} \leqslant \rho \leqslant 2$.

Now we define the function

$$\mathbf{u}(\mathbf{x}) = \mathbf{k}(\mathbf{x})/|\mathbf{k}(\mathbf{x})| \qquad (\tfrac{1}{2} < \rho < 2)$$

This function lies in U^2, and it has the essential property

$$\mathbf{u}(\mathbf{x}) \cdot \mathbf{h}(\mathbf{x}) > 0 \qquad (\tfrac{1}{2} < \rho < 2)$$

Since $\mathbf{u}(\mathbf{x})$ lies in U^2, we have $\delta[\mathbf{u}]$ defined by the integral

$$\delta[u] = \int_{\rho=1} (D\mathbf{u}) \cdot \mathbf{x} \, dS.$$

Definition. Let $\mathbf{h}(\mathbf{x})$ be continuous and non-zero for $\rho = 1$. Let $\mathbf{u}(\mathbf{x})$ be any function in U^2 such that

$$\mathbf{u}(\mathbf{x}) \cdot \mathbf{h}(\mathbf{x}) > 0 \quad \text{for} \quad \rho = 1.$$

Then we define

$$\boxed{\delta[\mathbf{h}] \equiv \delta[\mathbf{u}]}$$

We must show that this definition makes sense. Suppose that $\mathbf{u}(\mathbf{x})$ and $\mathbf{v}(\mathbf{x})$ are two different functions in U^2 such that

$$\mathbf{u} \cdot \mathbf{h} > 0 \quad \text{and} \quad \mathbf{v} \cdot \mathbf{h} > 0 \quad \text{for} \quad \rho = 1.$$

Then definition says $\delta[\mathbf{h}]$ equals both $\delta[\mathbf{u}]$ and $\delta[\mathbf{v}]$; we must show that these two numbers are equal. It will be enough to show that $\mathbf{u} + \mathbf{v} \neq \mathbf{0}$ for $\rho = 1$, because we have shown that this implies $\delta[\mathbf{u}] = \delta[\mathbf{v}]$. But

$$(\mathbf{u} + \mathbf{v}) \cdot \mathbf{h} = \mathbf{u} \cdot \mathbf{h} + \mathbf{v} \cdot \mathbf{h} > 0$$

Therefore, $\mathbf{u} + \mathbf{v} \neq \mathbf{0}$, and our definition of $\delta[\mathbf{h}]$ makes sense.

Theorem. *The discriminant* $\delta[\mathbf{h}]$ *has the required properties* (i), (ii), *and* (iii).

PROOF. (i) If $\mathbf{h}(\mathbf{x}) = \mathbf{x}$, we define $\mathbf{u}(\mathbf{x}) = \mathbf{x}/\rho$, and we have shown

$$\delta[\mathbf{x}] \equiv \delta[\mathbf{x}/\rho] = A_N > 0.$$

(ii) Suppose $\mathbf{h}(\mathbf{x})$ is continuous and non-zero in the whole unit ball $\rho \leqslant 1$.

If $\mathbf{h}(\mathbf{x})$ is not twice continuously differentiable, we can approximate it by a function $\mathbf{k}(\mathbf{x}) \in C^2$. If $|\mathbf{k}(\mathbf{x}) - \mathbf{h}(\mathbf{x})| < \varepsilon$, then for very small $\varepsilon > 0$

$$|\mathbf{k}| = |\mathbf{k} - \mathbf{h} + \mathbf{h}| \geqslant |\mathbf{h}| - |\mathbf{k} - \mathbf{h}| > |\mathbf{h}| - \varepsilon > 0$$
$$2\mathbf{k} \cdot \mathbf{h} = |\mathbf{h}|^2 + |\mathbf{k}|^2 - |\mathbf{h} - \mathbf{k}|^2 > |\mathbf{h}|^2 + (|\mathbf{h}| - \varepsilon)^2 - \varepsilon^2 > 0$$

Now we define $\mathbf{u}(\mathbf{x}) = \mathbf{k}(\mathbf{x})/|\mathbf{k}(\mathbf{x})|$ for $\rho \leqslant 1$. Then

$$\mathbf{u} \cdot \mathbf{h} > 0, \quad \delta[\mathbf{h}] = \delta[\mathbf{u}] = 0.$$

(iii) Suppose $\mathbf{h}_1(\mathbf{x})$ and $\mathbf{h}_2(\mathbf{x})$ nowhere have opposite directions on the surface $\rho = 1$. Then we can approximate them by $\mathbf{k}_1(\mathbf{x})$ and $\mathbf{k}_2(\mathbf{x})$ that are never opposite and that lie in C^2 in a neighborhood of $\rho = 1$; we also require $\mathbf{k}_i \cdot \mathbf{h}_i > 0$ for $\rho = 1$.

For ρ near 1, we now define the unit vectors

$$\mathbf{u}_1 = \mathbf{k}_1/|\mathbf{k}_1|, \quad \mathbf{u}_2 = \mathbf{k}_2/|\mathbf{k}_2|$$

Since $\mathbf{k}_1$ and $\mathbf{k}_2$ nowhere have opposite directions, we have $\mathbf{u}_1 + \mathbf{u}_2 \neq \mathbf{0}$. We have proved that this implies

$$\delta[\mathbf{u}_1] = \delta[\mathbf{u}_2].$$

Finally, we note that

$$\delta[\mathbf{h}_1] = \delta[\mathbf{u}_1] \quad \text{and} \quad \delta[\mathbf{h}_2] = \delta[\mathbf{u}_2]$$

since $\mathbf{k}_i \cdot \mathbf{h}_i > 0$ implies $\mathbf{u}_i \cdot \mathbf{h}_i > 0$ for $\rho = 1$. This completes the proof that $\delta[\mathbf{h}_1] = \delta[\mathbf{h}_2]$.

PROOF OF THE BROUWER FIXED-POINT THEOREM. We have now defined the discriminant $\delta[\mathbf{h}]$, and we've proved it has the required three properties. Now the proof of the Brouwer theorem is very short; it appears in the preceding remark "Use of the discriminant."

We've done what we set out to do: prove the great Brouwer fixed-point theorem. We'll close our discussion with just a few remarks.

Elementary proofs of Brouwer's theorem. Garsia's proof makes Brower's theorem an exercise in determinants and vector calculus—engineering mathematics, you might say. Similar proofs had been published by E. Heinz and by Dunford and Schwartz.

These proofs are not considered "elementary," because they use calculus There is an elementary proof based on an ingenious combinatorial lemma of Sperner. But do not be misled by the word *elementary*: a proof may be elementary but nevertheless difficult. The whole theory of finite groups is elementary. But is it easy? I do not think so.

The number of zeros. Suppose $\mathbf{h}(\mathbf{x}) \neq \mathbf{0}$ for $\rho = 1$. Suppose $\mathbf{h}(\mathbf{x})$ is continuous for $\rho \leqslant 1$. If $\delta[\mathbf{h}] \neq 0$, we know that $\mathbf{h}(\mathbf{x}) = \mathbf{0}$ for some $\mathbf{x}$ with $\rho < 1$. Is it possible that $\delta[\mathbf{h}]$ somehow counts the number of roots?

In one famous case the answer is yes. In two dimensions let $x_1 + ix_2$ be a complex variable, and let $h_1 + ih_2$ be an analytic function. In two dimensions we found that $\delta[\mathbf{h}]$ equals the net change of argument as $\mathbf{x}$ moves around the unit circle. Now the *principle of the argument* for analytic functions says the net change in arg $\mathbf{h}$ equals 2π times the number of zeros of $\mathbf{h}$ inside the unit circle $\rho < 1$. (Here the zeros are counted with their multiplicities; for instance, $x^3(x - \frac{1}{2})$ has four zeros.) So for analytic functions the discriminant $\delta[\mathbf{h}]$ equals 2π times the number of zeros.

But in general the answer is no: $\delta[\mathbf{h}]$ *cannot be expected to yield the number of zeros.* Why not? Because $\delta[\mathbf{h}]$ depends only on the boundary values of $\mathbf{h}$; and we can modify $\mathbf{h}$ to produce a continuous function $\mathbf{k}$ that equals $\mathbf{h}$ on the boundary, but has one more zero inside. Then $\delta[\mathbf{h}] = \delta[\mathbf{k}]$, but $\mathbf{h}$ and $\mathbf{k}$ have different numbers of zeros.

To construct $\mathbf{k}$, suppose the continuous function $\mathbf{h}(\mathbf{x}) \neq \mathbf{0}$ at the point $\mathbf{x} = \mathbf{a}$ inside the unit ball. For each $\mathbf{x} \neq \mathbf{a}$, let $\lambda(\mathbf{x})$ equal the distance from $\mathbf{a}$ to the unit sphere $\rho = 1$ in the direction of the vector $\mathbf{x} - \mathbf{a}$. Then

$$\lambda(\mathbf{x}) = |\mathbf{x} - \mathbf{a}| \quad \text{for} \quad \rho = 1$$
$$0 < 1 - |\mathbf{a}| \leqslant \lambda(\mathbf{x}) \leqslant 1 + |\mathbf{a}| < 2 \qquad \text{for all } \mathbf{x} \neq \mathbf{a}$$

and the function $\lambda(\mathbf{x})$ is continuous except at $\mathbf{x} = \mathbf{a}$. Now construct the function

$$\mathbf{k}(\mathbf{x}) = \lambda^{-1}(\mathbf{x})|\mathbf{x} - \mathbf{a}|\mathbf{h}(\mathbf{x})$$

This function is continuous for all $\rho \leqslant 1$ if we define $\mathbf{k}(\mathbf{a}) = \mathbf{0}$. On the boundary $\rho = 1$ we have $\mathbf{k}(\mathbf{x}) \equiv \mathbf{h}(\mathbf{x})$. But $\mathbf{k}(\mathbf{x})$ has exactly one more zero than $\mathbf{h}(\mathbf{x})$ inside $\rho < 1$, namely, $\mathbf{x} = \mathbf{a}$.

(This construction does not violate the principle of the argument. If $h_1 + ih_2$ is analytic, then $k_1 + ik_2$ is continuous but not analytic.)

Continuous direction fields on spheres. Here's a puzzle for you: On a globe representing the earth, can you draw a continuous family of unit tangents? At any point $\mathbf{x}$ on the globe, a unit tangent $\mathbf{u}(\mathbf{x})$ represents a direction. The question is this: Can the function $\mathbf{u}(\mathbf{x})$ be continuous on the whole spherical surface? Our experience with geography suggests the answer is no: there has to be trouble at the north pole or somewhere.

If the earth were a two-dimensional disk, the surface would be a circle, and the puzzle would be easy. Solution:

$$\mathbf{u}(\mathbf{x}) = \begin{pmatrix} -x_2 \\ x_1 \end{pmatrix} \quad \text{if} \quad \mathbf{x} = \begin{pmatrix} x_1 \\ x_2 \end{pmatrix} \quad \text{and} \quad \rho = 1.$$

If the earth were four-dimensional, we could extend the two-dimensional solution to obtain

$$\mathbf{u}(\mathbf{x}) = \begin{pmatrix} -x_2 \\ x_1 \\ -x_4 \\ x_3 \end{pmatrix} \quad \text{if} \quad \mathbf{x} = \begin{pmatrix} x_1 \\ x_2 \\ x_3 \\ x_4 \end{pmatrix} \quad \text{and} \quad \rho = 1.$$

This trick works for any *even* number of dimensions. If N is even, just define

$$u_1 = -x_2, \quad u_2 = x_1, \ldots, u_{N-1} = -x_N, u_N = x_{N-1}$$

But suppose N is odd. Then we can prove that the puzzle has no solution. This is a beautiful application of the discriminant.

Theorem. *In N dimensions, if N is odd then there is no continuous $\mathbf{u}(\mathbf{x})$ on the surface $\rho = 1$ such that*

$$|\mathbf{u}(\mathbf{x})| \equiv 1 \quad \text{and} \quad \mathbf{u}(\mathbf{x}) \cdot \mathbf{x} \equiv 0.$$

PROOF. You remember we computed

$$\delta[\mathbf{x}] = A_N > 0 \quad \text{and} \quad \delta[-\mathbf{x}] = (-)^N A_N.$$

These numbers are different if N is odd.

Now suppose $\mathbf{u}(\mathbf{x})$ solves the puzzle. Let's compute its discriminant, $\delta[\mathbf{u}]$. We can do this if we can find any continuous $\mathbf{v}(\mathbf{x})$ for $\rho = 1$ such that $|\mathbf{v}| \equiv 1$ and $\mathbf{v} + \mathbf{u} \neq \mathbf{0}$. Then we know $\delta[\mathbf{u}] = \delta[\mathbf{v}]$, by property (iii) of the discriminant.

For $\mathbf{v}(\mathbf{x})$ we may choose $\mathbf{v}(\mathbf{x}) \equiv \mathbf{x}$, since

$$(\mathbf{x} + \mathbf{u}) \cdot \mathbf{x} = \mathbf{x} \cdot \mathbf{x} + 0 = 1,$$

and so

$$\mathbf{x} + \mathbf{u} \neq \mathbf{0}$$

by our assumption that $\mathbf{u} \cdot \mathbf{x} = 0$. Therefore,

$$\delta[\mathbf{u}] = \delta[\mathbf{x}] = A_N > 0$$

But wait a minute. We may also choose $\mathbf{v}(\mathbf{x}) \equiv -\mathbf{x}$, since

$$(-\mathbf{x} + \mathbf{u}) \cdot (-\mathbf{x}) = 1, \text{ and so } -\mathbf{x} + \mathbf{u} \neq \mathbf{0}.$$

Therefore

$$\delta[\mathbf{u}] = \delta[-\mathbf{x}] = (-)^N A_N.$$

This is impossible if N is odd, for then $\delta[\mathbf{u}]$ would be both positive and negative.

References

1. L. E. J. Brouwer, Uber Abbildung und Mannigfaltigkeiten, *Math. Ann.* Vol. 71 (1910) pp. 97–115.
2. E. Heinz, An elementary analytic theory of the degree of mapping in n-dimensional space, *J. Math. Mech.* Vol. 8 (1959) p. 231.
3. N. Dunford and J. T. Schwartz, *Linear Operators*, Vol. 1, 1958, Interscience, New York.

Appendix: Convex bodies. We define a *convex body* to be a closed, bounded, convex set.[1] Suppose a convex body is mapped continuously into itself. Must there be a fixed point? As we've shown, the answer is yes if the body is topologically equivalent to the unit ball.

We will now prove this equivalence. But we must be careful, because a degenerate convex body in R^N may have dimension $M < N$. For instance, in R^3 a line segment has dimension $M = 1$; a triangle has dimension $M = 2$. But still, the segment is a ball in 1 dimension, and a triangle is equivalent to a ball in 2 dimensions. That is enough for our purpose.

Theorem. *Let C be a convex body in R^N. Suppose C contains more than one point. Then, for some $M \leqslant N$, C is topologically equivalent to a closed ball in R^M.*

PROOF. Choose points in C: $\mathbf{x}^0, \mathbf{x}^1, \ldots, \mathbf{x}^M$. Choose as many points as possible so that the M differences

$$\mathbf{x}^1 - \mathbf{x}^0, \mathbf{x}^2 - \mathbf{x}^0, \ldots, \mathbf{x}^M - \mathbf{x}^0$$

are linearly independent in R^N. These M points span an M-dimensional linear subspace L^M.

We now say this: The whole body C lies in the hyperplane $P^M = \mathbf{x}^0 + L^M$. Indeed, if some point $\mathbf{x}^{M+1}$ in C lay outside P^M, then $\mathbf{x}^{M+1} - \mathbf{x}^0$ would be a new independent point in L; and that is impossible.

From now on we will think of the body C only as a subset of the plane P^M. If we say that a point $\mathbf{b}$ *is an interior point of* C, we shall mean that C contains an M-dimensional ball centered at $\mathbf{b}$ and lying in P^M. (If $M = N$, then P^M is the original space R^N.)

We now construct the barycenter

$$\mathbf{b} = (M + 1)^{-1}(\mathbf{x}^0 + \mathbf{x}^1 + \cdots + \mathbf{x}^M).$$

Since C is convex, this is an interior point of C.

---

[1] Definitions: A *closed* set contains its limit points; a *bounded* set lies inside some sphere; a *convex* set contains the segment between every pair of its points.

Let $\mathbf{u}$ be any unit vector in L^M. Then the body C contains a boundary point $\mathbf{b} + \lambda\mathbf{u}$ with $\lambda > 0$. For each $\mathbf{u}$ there is only one such boundary point. Why? Suppose there were two, with $\lambda_1 < \lambda_2$. Remember that C contains some small ball S centered at $\mathbf{b}$. But then the point $\mathbf{b} + \lambda_1\mathbf{u}$ lies *interior* to the convex hull of the ball S and the point $\mathbf{b} + \lambda_2\mathbf{u}$. Then $\mathbf{b} + \lambda_1\mathbf{u}$ is interior to C, which is impossible for a boundary point.

Thus, for each $\mathbf{u}$ in L^M, there is a *unique*

$$\lambda = \lambda(\mathbf{u}) > 0$$

such that $\mathbf{b} + \lambda\mathbf{u}$ lies on the boundary of C. The function $\lambda(\mathbf{u})$ is called *the radial function*.

We assert that *the radial function is continuous* as a function of the unit vector $\mathbf{u} \in L^M$. If $\mathbf{u}^0$ were a point of discontinuity, then the boundary of C would contain points

$$\mathbf{b} + \lambda_k\mathbf{u}^k \qquad (k = 1, 2, 3, \ldots)$$

with $\mathbf{u}^k \to \mathbf{u}^0$ but with positive λ_k *not* converging to $\lambda(\mathbf{u}^0)$. Since $\lambda_1, \lambda_2, \ldots$ is a bounded sequence, there is a subsequence with a limit $\lambda^* \neq \lambda(\mathbf{u}^0)$. But then $\mathbf{b} + \lambda^*\mathbf{u}^0$ must lie on the boundary of C, since a limit of boundary points must be a boundary point. Now we would have *two* boundary points

$$\mathbf{b} + \lambda\mathbf{u}^0 \quad \text{with} \quad \lambda = \lambda^* \quad \text{and} \quad \lambda = \lambda(\mathbf{u}^0),$$

and that is impossible, since the boundary point in the direction $\mathbf{u}^0$ is unique.

Now we have all we need for a bicontinuous mapping of C into the unit ball $|\mathbf{y}| \leqslant 1$ in R^M. Let $\mathbf{u}^1, \mathbf{u}^2, \ldots, \mathbf{u}^M$ be orthogonal unit vectors that constitute a basis for the linear subspace L^M. For all $\mathbf{x}$ in L^M, define $\mathbf{y}$ in R^M by the identity

$$\mathbf{x} = y_1\mathbf{u}^1 + y_2\mathbf{u}^2 + \cdots + y_M\mathbf{u}^M.$$

Then $|\mathbf{x}| \leqslant 1$ corresponds bicontinuously to $|\mathbf{y}| \leqslant 1$.

The convex body C consists of $\mathbf{b}$ and of all the points

$$\mathbf{c} = \mathbf{b} + \rho\lambda(\mathbf{u})\mathbf{u} \quad \text{with} \quad 0 < \rho \leqslant 1, |\mathbf{u}| = 1,$$

$\mathbf{u} \in L^M$. Setting $\mathbf{x} = \rho\mathbf{u}$, we let this point correspond to $\mathbf{y}$ in R^M, where $0 < \rho = |\mathbf{x}| = |\mathbf{y}| \leqslant 1$. We let $\mathbf{b}$ correspond $\mathbf{y} = \mathbf{0}$, and we now have the required bicontinuous mapping of C into the unit ball $|\mathbf{y}| \leqslant 1$.

Explicitly, if U is the $N \times M$ matrix whose columns are the orthogonal unit vectors $\mathbf{u}^j$, then

$$\mathbf{b} + \rho\lambda(\mathbf{u})\mathbf{u} = \mathbf{c}$$

maps the unit ball $|\mathbf{y}| \leqslant 1$ continuously into C, where

$$\rho = |\mathbf{y}| \quad \text{and} \quad \rho\mathbf{u} = \mathbf{y} = \mathbf{x} = U\mathbf{y}.$$

Conversely, the inverse mapping

$$\lambda^{-1}(\mathbf{u})U^T(\mathbf{c} - \mathbf{b}) = \mathbf{y}$$

maps C continuously into $|\mathbf{y}| \leqslant 1$, where

$$\mathbf{u} = (\mathbf{c} - \mathbf{b})/|\mathbf{c} - \mathbf{b}| \quad \text{if} \quad \mathbf{c} \neq \mathbf{b},$$

and where $\mathbf{c} = \mathbf{b}$ maps into $\mathbf{y} = \mathbf{0}$. The inverse mapping is continuous because the radial function $\lambda(\mathbf{u})$ is continuous and positive.

PROBLEMS

1. A famous theorem of Oskar Perron states that an $n \times n$ *positive* matrix must have a positive eigenvalue with a positive eigenvector. (In other words, if all a_{ij} are >0, then $A\mathbf{x} = \lambda\mathbf{x}$ for some $\lambda > 0$, with all $x_j > 0$.) Prove Perron's theorem fast: If A is the matrix, let S be the set of probability vectors $(x_j \geqslant 0, \sum x_j = 1)$. Let $\lambda(\mathbf{x})$ equal the sum of the components of the vector $A\mathbf{x}$. Define the function $\mathbf{f}(\mathbf{x}) = \lambda^{-1}(\mathbf{x})A\mathbf{x}$. Show that $\mathbf{f}(\mathbf{x})$ maps the simplex S continuously into itself. And so ...?

2. Prove the fundamental theorem of algebra: Let $p(z) = z^n + c_1 z^{n-1} + \cdots + c_n$. Assume $p(z) \neq 0$ for all complex z, and get a contradiction as follows. For $\lambda > 0$, define the function $f(z) = \lambda^{-n} p(\lambda z)$. For $|z| = 1$ show that $f(z) \to z^n$ as $\lambda \to +\infty$. Deduce that the discriminant satisfies

$$\delta[f(z)] = \delta[z^n] = 2n\pi \neq 0$$

for all sufficiently large λ. Conclude that $f(z) = 0$ for some z in the unit disk.

3. Differential equations: Consider the nonlinear system $d\mathbf{x}/dt = \mathbf{f}(\mathbf{x})$ in R^n. An *equilibrium* is a constant solution $\mathbf{x}(t) \equiv \mathbf{x}^0$; an equilibrium satisfies $\mathbf{f}(\mathbf{x}^0) = \mathbf{0}$. Let the function $\mathbf{f}(\mathbf{x})$ be continuous. For $\mathbf{x}$ on some sphere $|\mathbf{x}| = R$, assume that $\mathbf{f}(\mathbf{x})$ nowhere points in the direction $\mathbf{x}$ (or instead, assume that $\mathbf{f}(\mathbf{x})$ nowhere points in the direction $-\mathbf{x}$). Then show that the sphere must enclose an equilibrium $\mathbf{x}^0$.

4. Differential equations: Let $\mathbf{f}(\mathbf{x},t)$ be Lipschitz-continuous in $\mathbf{x}$, and let $\mathbf{f}$ be continuous and *periodic* in t: $\mathbf{f}(\mathbf{x}, t + 1) \equiv \mathbf{f}(\mathbf{x},t)$. For the nonlinear system $d\mathbf{x}/dt = \mathbf{f}(\mathbf{x},t)$, consider the mapping $\mathbf{x}(0) \mapsto \mathbf{x}(1)$ for solutions $\mathbf{x}(t)$. Suppose this mapping carries a domain D into itself, where D is topologically equivalent to a ball. Then show there is a *periodic* solution $\mathbf{x}(t) \equiv \mathbf{x}(t + 1)$.

*5. Game theory: Using the Brouwer fixed-point theorem, you can prove von Neumann's theorem on zero-sum two-person games. Let A be an $m \times n$ matrix. Let D be the set of pairs of vectors $\mathbf{x}, \mathbf{y}$, with $\mathbf{x} \in R^m$, $\mathbf{y} \in R^n$, $x_i \geqslant 0$, $\sum x_i = 1$, $y_j \geqslant 0$, $\sum y_j = 1$. You want a pair $\mathbf{x}^0, \mathbf{y}^0$ in D satisfying

$$\mathbf{x} \cdot A\mathbf{y}^0 \leqslant \mathbf{x}^0 \cdot A\mathbf{y}^0 \leqslant \mathbf{x}^0 \cdot A\mathbf{y}$$

for all $\mathbf{x}, \mathbf{y}$ in D. Map D into itself as follows. First define the ramp function $\{\lambda\}^+ = \max(\lambda, 0)$ for real λ. Now define

$$u_i(\mathbf{x},\mathbf{y}) = \left\{ \sum_j a_{ij} y_j - \sum_i \sum_j x_i a_{ij} y_j \right\}^+$$

$$v_j(\mathbf{x},\mathbf{y}) = \left\{ -\sum_i x_i a_{ij} + \sum_i \sum_j x_i a_{ij} y_j \right\}^+$$

Map $\mathbf{x}, \mathbf{y} \mapsto \mathbf{x}', \mathbf{y}'$ as follows:

$$x_i' = (x_i + u_i)/(1 + u_1 + \cdots + u_m)$$
$$y_j' = (y_j + v_j)/(1 + v_1 + \cdots + v_n).$$

Show that this mapping maps D continuously into itself, and show that a fixed point provides the required $\mathbf{x}^0, \mathbf{y}^0$. (J. F. Nash used this method to prove his general equilibrium theorem.)

6. A mapping $\mathbf{x} \mapsto \mathbf{g}(\mathbf{x})$ is called a *retract* if (i) it keeps every point on the *boundary* of the domain fixed, and (ii) it maps the interior into the boundary. Using Brouwer's theorem, prove that the ball $|\mathbf{x}| \leqslant 1$ has no continuous retract. Hint: Define $\mathbf{f}(\mathbf{x}) = \frac{1}{2}(\mathbf{x} - \mathbf{g}(\mathbf{x}))$, and look at a fixed point $\mathbf{x} = \mathbf{f}(\mathbf{x})$.

7. (Converse.) Suppose Brouwer's theorem were false. Then show how to construct a continuous retract of the unit ball. Hint: If $\mathbf{x} \neq \mathbf{f}(\mathbf{x})$, look at the arrow pointing from $\mathbf{f}$ to $\mathbf{x}$; extend the arrow to a boundary point $\mathbf{x}'$; look at the mapping $\mathbf{x} \mapsto \mathbf{x}'$.

8. Let the letter E be mapped continuously into itself. Must there be a fixed point? (For the letter O the answer is no.) What about the letter e?

9. (Rothe's theorem.) For $\mathbf{x}$ in the closed unit ball in R^n, let $\mathbf{f}(\mathbf{x})$ be continuous. Assume $|\mathbf{f}(\mathbf{x})| \leqslant 1$ if $|\mathbf{x}| = 1$, but do not assume $|\mathbf{f}(\mathbf{x})| \leqslant 1$ if $|\mathbf{x}| < 1$. Still, show that $\mathbf{f}(\mathbf{x})$ has a fixed point in the unit ball. Method: First define the function $\mathbf{g}(\mathbf{x}) = \mathbf{x}/|\mathbf{x}|$ for $|\mathbf{x}| \geqslant 1$; define $\mathbf{g}(\mathbf{x}) = \mathbf{x}$ for $|\mathbf{x}| \leqslant 1$. Look at $\mathbf{g}(\mathbf{f}(\mathbf{x}))$.

*10. Extend Rothe's theorem (Problem 9) to general convex bodies in R^n.

11. Theorem on homotopy: Let $\mathbf{u}(\mathbf{x},t)$ be a continuous non-zero vector in R^n for $\mathbf{x}$ on the unit sphere in R^n for $0 \leqslant t \leqslant 1$, so that the discriminant $\delta[\mathbf{u}]$ is a function of t for $0 \leqslant t \leqslant 1$. Show that $\delta[\mathbf{u}]$ is *constant*. Method: From the continuity of $\mathbf{u}$, deduce for small $|\varepsilon|$:

$$\mathbf{u}(\mathbf{x},t) \cdot \mathbf{u}(\mathbf{x}, t + \varepsilon) > 0,$$

and so the discriminant is constant.

12. For $|\mathbf{x}| = r \neq 0$, define this unit vector in R^2:

$$\mathbf{u}(\mathbf{x}) = r^{-2}(x_1^2 - x_2^2, 2x_1 x_2).$$

Form the Garsian $D\mathbf{u}$, and verify that its divergence is zero: $\nabla \cdot D\mathbf{u} = 0$. Evaluate the discriminant $\delta[\mathbf{u}]$. (Answer: $\delta = 4\pi$. Note that in the complex plane $\mathbf{u}$ is just z^2/r^2.)

13. Let S be the set of probability vectors in R^n ($x_i \geqslant 0, \sum x_i = 1$). Construct a bicontinuous function $\mathbf{f}(\mathbf{x})$ that maps S one-one onto the unit ball in R^{n-1}.

14. Let $|\mathbf{x}| \leqslant 1, \mathbf{x} \in R^m$; let $|\mathbf{y}| \leqslant 1, \mathbf{y} \in R^n$. Consider the set D comprising all pairs $\mathbf{x}, \mathbf{y}$. Show that D is topologically equivalent to the unit ball in R^{m+n}.

15. Show that there is no way to define a continuous direction field on the surface of an ellipsoid in R^3.

16. Consider a continuously circulating fluid flow inside a torus. Assume the flow is *steady*, so that the velocity at a point $\mathbf{x}$ depends on $\mathbf{x}$ but not on the time t. Show

that there must be at least one *closed* streamline: there must be some *periodic* solution $\mathbf{x}(t)$ for the position $\mathbf{x}$ of a particle at time t. Poincare proved results like that. The trick is to look at one cross-sectional disk D. Each particle in D leaves and returns to D after one complete circuit around the torus. Thus, the flow maps D continuously onto itself. Look at a fixed point of this mapping.

3 Milnor's Proof of the Brouwer Fixed-Point Theorem

Until recently, all proofs of the Brouwer fixed-point theorem have been difficult; they have used combinatorial arguments, homology theory, differential forms, or geometric topology. Most people who have wanted to use the Brouwer theorem have never understood a proof of it. I should know; I was one of them.

In 1978 John Milnor published a simple proof, which I'm going to present to you now. All you need to know first is calculus.

Brouwer's theorem says this: *Let $\mathbf{f}(\mathbf{x})$ be any continuous function that maps the ball $|\mathbf{x}| \leqslant 1$ into itself. Then there is a fixed point, $\mathbf{c}$, which is mapped into itself*: $\mathbf{c} = \mathbf{f}(\mathbf{c})$.

We will use the term *unit ball* for the n-dimensional solid comprising all points $\mathbf{x}$ whose coordinates satisfy

$$x_1^2 + \cdots + x_n^2 \leqslant 1.$$

(In other words, $|\mathbf{x}|^2 \leqslant 1$, where $\mathbf{x} \cdot \mathbf{x} = |\mathbf{x}|^2 = \sum x_i^2$.) We'll call this ball B^n.

The surface of B^n is the *sphere* S^{n-1} comprising all points $\mathbf{x}$ whose coordinates satisfy

$$x_1^2 + \cdots + x_n^2 = 1.$$

Thus, in three-dimensional space S^2 is the 2-dimensional sphere that bounds the unit ball B^3.

If $n = 1$, the unit ball is the line segment $-1 \leqslant x \leqslant 1$. If $f(x)$ maps B^1 into itself, we get Figure 1. Each point x goes to a point $f(x)$. Draw an arrow from x to $f(x)$; the arrow has length zero if x is a fixed point.

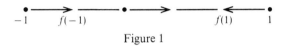

$$\begin{array}{cccc} -1 & f(-1) & & f(1) \quad 1 \end{array}$$

Figure 1

Suppose there were no fixed point. Then the arrow at -1 would point to the right; the arrow at $+1$ would point to the left. Let x move continuously from -1 to $+1$, and watch the arrow from x to $f(x)$. Somewhere between -1 and $+1$ the arrow has to flip from right to left. This is impossible if the arrow is continuous and nowhere zero.

In analytical terms, the arrow is represented by the difference $f(x) - x$. This function is positive at $x = -1$; it is negative at $x = +1$. Since $f(x) - x$ is continuous, it must equal zero at some intermediate point c. Then $f(c) = 0$, and c is the required fixed point.

If $n = 2$, we get Figure 2. Each point $\mathbf{x}$ goes to another point $\mathbf{f}(\mathbf{x})$ in the ball B^2. Draw the arrow from each point $\mathbf{x}$ to its image $\mathbf{f}(\mathbf{x})$. On the boundary S^1 all the arrows point inward. Brouwer's theorem says some arrow in the ball has length zero.

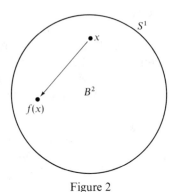

Figure 2

Notice that we need the hypothesis of continuity. Otherwise, we could let $\mathbf{f}(\mathbf{x})$ be, say, a rotation through $90°$; that would leave the center fixed, so we could agree to map the center $\mathbf{x} = \mathbf{0}$ into some other point $\mathbf{f}(\mathbf{0}) \neq \mathbf{0}$. Then $\mathbf{f}(\mathbf{x})$ would be a discontinuous function with no fixed point.

Already for $n = 2$ the Brouwer theorem is somewhat difficult. It could be proved by using the *winding number* of Poincare, but we won't take time for that now.

For $n > 2$, all proofs have been difficult, or they required advanced, specialized preparation. But now we have the astonishing proof by John Milnor, which depends on this fact: *the function* $(1 + t^2)^{n/2}$ *is not a polynomial if n is an odd integer.*

Why should that have anything to do with the Brouwer fixed-point theorem? You will see.

We begin with a puzzle: *In n dimensions, construct a continuous field of unit tangents to the sphere S^{n-1}.*

For $n = 2$ the solution is easy. Look at Figure 3. At each point $\mathbf{u}$ on S^1 we construct the tangent $\mathbf{v}(\mathbf{u}) = (-u_2, u_1)$. Then

$$|\mathbf{v}| = 1 \quad \text{and} \quad \mathbf{v} \cdot \mathbf{u} = 0.$$

For $n = 3$ we have 3-space, as in the real world. Regard the earth as the unit ball. Can you put a continuous direction field on the surface? I'll bet you can't. Think about it; you're bound to have trouble at the north pole or somewhere else.

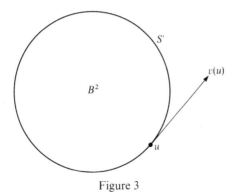

Figure 3

How about $n = 4$? Now you can't visualize the problem, but you can easily solve it. If you use the trick we used for $n = 2$, first on u_1, u_2 and then on u_3, u_4, you get the unit tangents

$$\mathbf{v}(\mathbf{u}) = (-u_2, u_1; -u_4, u_3).$$

Clearly, this trick works for all even n. We get this continuous field of tangents:

$$\mathbf{v}(\mathbf{u}) = (-u_2, u_1; \ldots; -u_n, u_{n-1}). \tag{1}$$

But if n is odd, the *hairy-ball theorem* says there is no solution:

Theorem 1. *If n is odd, then there is no continuous field of non-zero tangents to the unit sphere S^{n-1}.*

PROOF. For $|\mathbf{u}| = 1$, let $\mathbf{v}(\mathbf{u})$ be a field of unit tangents:

$$\mathbf{u} \cdot \mathbf{v}(\mathbf{u}) = 0, \quad |\mathbf{v}(\mathbf{u})| = 1 \text{ for } |\mathbf{u}| = 1.$$

For the moment, assume that $\mathbf{v}(\mathbf{u})$ is continuously differentiable.
    Let A be the spherical shell (or annulus)

$$A: \tfrac{1}{2} \leqslant r \leqslant \tfrac{3}{2}, \tag{2}$$

where $r = |\mathbf{x}|$. The shell A surrounds the unit sphere. We now extend the definition of $\mathbf{v}$ to the shell A. For $|\mathbf{u}| = 1$ define

$$\mathbf{v}(r\mathbf{u}) = r\mathbf{v}(\mathbf{u}) \qquad (\tfrac{1}{2} \leqslant r \leqslant \tfrac{3}{2}). \tag{3}$$

This definition makes $\mathbf{v}(\mathbf{x})$ continuously differentiable in A, with

$$\mathbf{x} \cdot \mathbf{v}(\mathbf{x}) = 0 \quad \text{and} \quad |\mathbf{v}(\mathbf{x})| = |\mathbf{x}| \equiv r.$$

Now let t be a small real constant, and define the mapping

$$\mathbf{x} \mapsto \mathbf{x} + t\mathbf{v}(\mathbf{x}) \qquad (\mathbf{x} \in A). \tag{4}$$

This maps A into some set A_t. (Can you guess what A_t is? Look at Figure 4.)

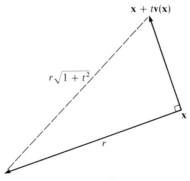

$$\mathbf{x} + t\mathbf{v}(\mathbf{x})$$

$$r\sqrt{1+t^2}$$

$$\mathbf{x}$$

$$r$$

Figure 4

We have to show that the mapping (4) is one-to-one. Since $\mathbf{v}(\mathbf{x})$ is continuously differentiable, there is some constant $\lambda > 0$ for which

$$|\mathbf{v}(\mathbf{x}) - \mathbf{v}(\mathbf{y})| \leqslant \lambda|\mathbf{x} - \mathbf{y}| \tag{5}$$

for every couple of points $\mathbf{x}$ and $\mathbf{y}$ in A. Now suppose $\mathbf{x}$ and $\mathbf{y}$ map into the same point:

$$\mathbf{x} + t\mathbf{v}(\mathbf{x}) = \mathbf{y} + t\mathbf{v}(\mathbf{y})$$

Then

$$|\mathbf{x} - \mathbf{y}| = |t|\,|\mathbf{v}(\mathbf{y}) - \mathbf{v}(\mathbf{x})| \leqslant |t|\lambda|\mathbf{x} - \mathbf{y}|$$

This implies $\mathbf{x} = \mathbf{y}$ if $|t| < 1/\lambda$. Thus, for small $|t|$ the mapping is one-to-one.

Now we'll show that the image A_t is just another annulus. If $|\mathbf{x}| = r$, then the image has length

$$|\mathbf{x} + t\mathbf{v}(\mathbf{x})| = r(1 + t^2)^{1/2}, \tag{6}$$

since $\mathbf{x}$ and $\mathbf{v}(\mathbf{x})$ are orthogonal vectors of length r. This identity shows that the sphere of radius r maps *into* the sphere of radius $r\sqrt{(1 + t^2)}$.

Now we need to show that the first sphere maps *onto* the second, which means that *every* point in the second sphere is the image of some point in the first sphere. In other words, we need to prove that the following equation must have a solution:

$$\mathbf{x} + t\mathbf{v}(\mathbf{x}) = \mathbf{c}, \tag{7}$$

where

$$\tfrac{1}{2} \leqslant |\mathbf{x}| \leqslant \tfrac{3}{2} \quad \text{and} \quad |\mathbf{c}| = (1 + t^2)^{1/2}|\mathbf{x}|.$$

Here $\mathbf{c}$ is given, and we must find $\mathbf{x}$.

First suppose $|\mathbf{c}| = 1$. Write the equation in the form

$$\mathbf{x} = \mathbf{c} - t\mathbf{v}(\mathbf{x}). \tag{8}$$

We will use the contraction-mapping principle. The function on the right maps the shell A into itself if $|t| < \tfrac{1}{3}$, for then

$$|t\mathbf{v}(\mathbf{x})| < \tfrac{1}{3}|\mathbf{v}(\mathbf{x})| = \tfrac{1}{3}r \leqslant \tfrac{1}{2}(\tfrac{1}{2} \leqslant r \leqslant \tfrac{3}{2})$$

and so
$$\tfrac{1}{2} = |\mathbf{c}| - \tfrac{1}{2} \leqslant |\mathbf{c} - t\mathbf{v}(\mathbf{x})| \leqslant |\mathbf{c}| + \tfrac{1}{2} = \tfrac{3}{2}.$$

If also $|t| < 1/\lambda$, then
$$|t\mathbf{v}(\mathbf{x}) - t\mathbf{v}(\mathbf{y})| \leqslant |t| \cdot \lambda \cdot |\mathbf{x} - \mathbf{y}|$$

and so the function $\mathbf{c} - t\mathbf{v}(\mathbf{x})$ is a contracting mapping on A. This mapping has a fixed point, which solves the equation (8) if $|\mathbf{c}| = 1$.

If $|\mathbf{c}| \neq 1$, define the unit vector $\mathbf{c}^1 = \mathbf{c}/|\mathbf{c}|$. Then we can solve this equation for $\mathbf{x}^1$:
$$\mathbf{x}^1 + t\mathbf{v}(\mathbf{x}^1) = \mathbf{c}^1.$$

If we multiply this equation by $|\mathbf{c}|$, we get the required solution $\mathbf{x} = |\mathbf{c}|\mathbf{x}^1$.

Now we have completed a proof that, for small t, the function
$$\mathbf{f}(\mathbf{x}) = \mathbf{x} + t\mathbf{v}(\mathbf{x}) \tag{9}$$

maps the shell A one-to-one onto the shell
$$A_t: \tfrac{1}{2}(1 + t^2)^{1/2} \leqslant r \leqslant \tfrac{3}{2}(1 + t^2)^{1/2}.$$

What is the volume $|A_t|$? In n dimensions, since A_t is geometrically similar to A, we have
$$|A_t| = (1 + t^2)^{n/2}|A|, \tag{10}$$

where the constant $|A|$ is the volume of the n-dimensional shell $\tfrac{1}{2} \leqslant r \leqslant \tfrac{3}{2}$. For instance, if $n = 3$,
$$|A| = \tfrac{4}{3}\pi[(\tfrac{3}{2})^3 - (\tfrac{1}{2})^3].$$

But suppose we use calculus. The function $\mathbf{f}(\mathbf{x})$ maps A one-to-one onto A_t. Therefore,
$$|A_t| = \int \det\left(\frac{\partial f_i}{\partial x_j}\right) dx_1 \cdots dx_n \tag{11}$$

if the Jacobian determinant is positive.

Now the definition (9) gives
$$\left(\frac{\partial f_i}{\partial x_j}\right) = \left(\delta_{ij} + t\frac{\partial v_i}{\partial x_j}\right) \qquad (i, j = 1, \ldots, n) \tag{12}$$

where $\delta_{ij} = \partial x_i/\partial x_j = 1$ or 0. Thus, the Jacobian matrix (12) tends to I as $t \to 0$, and so the determinant tends to 1.

As a function of the parameter t, each component (12) is a linear function. Therefore, the Jacobian determinant is some polynomial
$$\det\left(\frac{\partial f_i}{\partial x_j}\right) = 1 + a_1(\mathbf{x})t + \cdots + a_n(\mathbf{x})t^n.$$

If we integrate over $\mathbf{x}$, we get another *polynomial*:
$$|A_t| = b_0 + b_1 t + b_2 t^2 + \cdots + b_n t^n, \tag{13}$$

where b_k is the integral of $a_k(\mathbf{x})$ over the annulus A.

EXAMPLE. If $n = 2$ let

$$\mathbf{f}(\mathbf{x}) = \begin{pmatrix} x_1 \\ x_2 \end{pmatrix} + t\begin{pmatrix} -x_2 \\ x_1 \end{pmatrix}$$

The Jacobian determinant equals

$$\begin{vmatrix} 1 & -t \\ t & 1 \end{vmatrix} = 1 + t^2.$$

Integrating over $\mathbf{x}$ for $\frac{1}{2} \leqslant \mathbf{x} \leqslant \frac{3}{2}$, we compute

$$|A_t| = |A|(1 + t^2)$$

where $|A| = \pi[(\frac{3}{2})^2 - (\frac{1}{2})^2] = 2\pi$.

In general, formula (13) says $|A_t|$ is a polynomial in t. But formula (10) says $|A_t|$ is a constant times $(1 + t^2)^{n/2}$. These conclusions are inconsistent if n is odd. Thus, we have proved that for odd n the sphere S^{n-1} has no field of unit tangents $\mathbf{v}(\mathbf{x})$ if $\mathbf{v}(\mathbf{x})$ is continuously differentiable.

Finally, we have to remove the assumption of differentiability.

Let $\mathbf{v}(\mathbf{x})$ be any *continuous* field of non-zero tangents to S^{n-1}. Using $\mathbf{v}(\mathbf{x})$, we will construct a differentiable tangent field $\mathbf{w}(\mathbf{x})$. First extend the definition of $\mathbf{v}(\mathbf{x})$ to the whole space by the formula

$$\mathbf{v}(r\mathbf{u}) = r\mathbf{v}(\mathbf{u}) \qquad (0 \leqslant r < \infty, |\mathbf{u}| = 1).$$

Now consider $\mathbf{v}(\mathbf{x})$ in the closed n-dimensional cube

$$C: -1 \leqslant x_i \leqslant 1 \qquad (i = 1, \ldots, n).$$

Using the Weierstrass approximation theorem in the cube C, we can approximate each component $v_i(x_1, \ldots, x_n)$ by some polynomial $p_i(x_1, \ldots, x_n)$, and we can make this approximation as good as we like in the whole cube C. Since the cube C includes the unit sphere, we can make $\mathbf{p}$ so close to $\mathbf{v}$ that

$$\mathbf{p} - (\mathbf{p} \cdot \mathbf{u})\mathbf{u} \neq 0 \quad \text{for} \quad |\mathbf{u}| = 1. \tag{14}$$

(Note that this expression tends to $\mathbf{v}$ as $\mathbf{p} \to \mathbf{v}$. Remember, $\mathbf{v} \neq 0$ for $|\mathbf{u}| = 1$.)

If $\mathbf{p} = \mathbf{p}(\mathbf{u})$, the vectors (14) constitute an infinitely differentiable non-zero tangent field $\mathbf{w}(\mathbf{u})$ on the unit sphere. If you require unit tangents, just form $\mathbf{w}/|\mathbf{w}|$. Now our proof for differentiable tangents gives the full result: *there can be no continuous field of non-zero tangents to S^{n-1} if n is odd.* ☐

That proves the hairy-ball theorem. I hope the details didn't make you lose track of the idea, which was this: The function $\mathbf{x} + t\mathbf{v}(\mathbf{x})$ maps the annulus A onto the annulus

$$A_t = (1 + t^2)^{1/2}A,$$

because $\mathbf{x} \cdot \mathbf{v} = 0$. The volume of A_t in n dimensions is

$$|A_t| = (1 + t^2)^{n/2}|A|.$$

But calculus says $|A_t|$ is a *polynomial* in t. Therefore n is even.

Now we can prove the Brouwer fixed-point theorem.

This is the idea: Suppose the Brouwer theorem is false in n dimensions. Then we will construct a field of non-zero vectors in the ball B^n that are *normal* to sphere S^{n-1}. We will then regard the ball B^n as the equatorial disk inside the higher-dimensional ball B^{n+1}. By stereographic projections from the north and south poles, we construct a continuous field of tangents to the sphere S^n. But we know this is impossible if n is even. But Brouwer's theorem for n dimensions implies Brouwer's theorem for $n-1$ dimensions, as you will see. This proves Brouwer's theorem for all n, even or odd.

Theorem 2. *Let* $f(x)$ *map the unit ball* B^n *continuously into itself. Then there is a fixed point* $x = f(x)$.

PROOF. Suppose $f(x)$ has no fixed point. Let $|x| \leqslant 1$; let $y = f(x)$, and form all the vectors $z = x - y$. Then $z \neq 0$, and on the unit sphere the vectors z point outward:

$$x \cdot z = x \cdot (x - y) = 1 - x \cdot y > 0 \quad \text{if} \quad |x| = 1. \tag{15}$$

Why? Because

$$0 < |x - y|^2 = |x|^2 + |y|^2 - 2x \cdot y \leqslant 2 - 2x \cdot y.$$

We will now construct a field of *vectors* w *that are continuous and non-zero in* B^n, *with* $w(x) = x$ *if* $|x| = 1$. Define

$$w = x - \lambda y \qquad (y = f(x)) \tag{16}$$

where λ is the scalar

$$\lambda = \frac{1 - x \cdot x}{1 - x \cdot y}. \tag{17}$$

The denominator is non-zero, by (15), and so $w(x)$ is a continuous function of x in B^n.

On the sphere $|x| = 1$ we have $\lambda = 0$, and so $w = x$. This says $w(x)$ is the outward unit normal at the surface point x.

It remains to show $w \neq 0$ inside the ball. If $w = 0$, multiply the equation (16) by the denominator of the fraction λ. This gives the equation

$$0 = (1 - x \cdot y)x - (1 - x \cdot x)y. \tag{18}$$

But $w = 0$ says $x = \lambda y$, which gives

$$(x \cdot y)x = \lambda^2(y \cdot y)y = (x \cdot x)y.$$

Now (18) becomes $0 = -x + y$, which we have ruled out. Therefore $w \neq 0$ in the ball B^n.

Now regard B^n as the equatorial disk inside the ball B^{n+1}. Using the vectors w in the disk B^n, we will construct a field of tangents to the sphere S^n, which is the boundary of B^{n+1}.

First we'll work on the southern hemisphere. Look at Figure 5. You're looking at a side view of the ball B^{n+1}. Your eyes are at the level of the equator, so the equatorial disk B^n looks to you like a line segment. From the north pole, $\mathbf{N}$, we project each point $\mathbf{x}$ in the disk onto a point $\mathbf{u}$ in the southern hemisphere. We're going to construct a tangent $\mathbf{v}$ at the point $\mathbf{u}$.

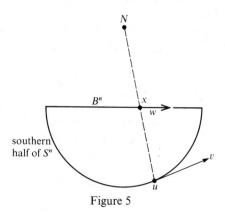

Figure 5

In case you are uncomfortable with all this n-dimensional visualizing, you can use formulas:

If $\mathbf{x}$ has the coordinates $x_1, \ldots, x_n$ in n dimensions, then
$$\mathbf{x} = (x_1, \ldots, x_n, 0) \tag{19}$$
in $n + 1$ dimensions. The north pole is
$$\mathbf{N} = (0, \ldots, 0, 1) \tag{20}$$

The point $\mathbf{x}$ lies on the line segment between $\mathbf{N}$ and the stereographic projection $\mathbf{u}$ in the southern hemisphere. Therefore, for some $\theta = \theta(\mathbf{x})$ between 0 and 1, we have
$$\mathbf{x} = (1 - \theta)\mathbf{N} + \theta\mathbf{u}. \tag{21}$$

The coordinates satisfy these equations:
$$\begin{aligned} x_i &= \theta u_i \qquad (i = 1, \ldots, n) \\ 0 &= (1 - \theta) + \theta u_{n+1}. \end{aligned} \tag{22}$$

Given the x_i, we can solve for the u_i and θ. First, we write
$$u_i = x_i/\theta \qquad (i = 1, \ldots, n); \quad u_{n+1} = (\theta - 1)/\theta. \tag{23}$$

Since $|\mathbf{u}| = 1$ on the sphere S^n, we require
$$1 = \sum_{i=1}^{n+1} u_i^2 = (x_1/\theta)^2 + \cdots + (x_n/\theta)^2 + (\theta - 1)^2/\theta^2.$$

Multiplying by θ^2, we find $\theta^2 = |\mathbf{x}|^2 + (\theta - 1)^2$, and so

$$\theta = \tfrac{1}{2}(|\mathbf{x}|^2 + 1). \tag{24}$$

Note that θ is $\geqslant \tfrac{1}{2}$. In equation (21), this says $\mathbf{x}$ is closer to $\mathbf{u}$ than to $\mathbf{N}$. But that is clear from Figure 5.

Now we are going to construct a tangent $\mathbf{v}$ at the point $\mathbf{u}$. We have projected a point $\mathbf{x}$ in the equatorial disk B^n onto the point $\mathbf{u}$ in the southern half of S^n. We will now use the vector $\mathbf{w}(\mathbf{x})$ defined in (16), satisfying

$$\mathbf{w} \in B^n, \quad \mathbf{w} \neq \mathbf{0}, \quad \mathbf{w} = \mathbf{x} \text{ if } |\mathbf{x}| = 1. \tag{25}$$

If $|\mathbf{x}| < 1$, we can construct a small line segment

$$\mathbf{x}(t) = \mathbf{x} + t\mathbf{w}(\mathbf{x}) \qquad (0 \leqslant t \ll 1). \tag{26}$$

If we project this segment stereographically from $\mathbf{N}$, we get a small arc

$$\mathbf{u}(t) = \mathbf{u}(\mathbf{x} + t\mathbf{w}(\mathbf{x})) \qquad (0 \leqslant t \ll 1) \tag{27}$$

If you regard t as time, the point $\mathbf{x}(t)$ has velocity $\mathbf{w}(\mathbf{x})$ in the disk B^n. The projection $\mathbf{u}(t)$ then has the velocity

$$\mathbf{v} = \frac{d}{dt}\mathbf{u}(t) \quad \text{for } t = 0. \tag{28}$$

The vector $\mathbf{v}$ is tangent to S^n at the point $\mathbf{u}$. That follows by differentiating the identity $\mathbf{u}(t) \cdot \mathbf{u}(t) \equiv 1$.

To show $\mathbf{v} \neq \mathbf{0}$, we write the projection identity (21) as a function of time:

$$\mathbf{x}(t) = (1 - \theta(t))\mathbf{N} + \theta(t)\mathbf{u}(t) \qquad (0 \leqslant t \ll 1). \tag{29}$$

If we take derivatives at $t = 0$, we get

$$\mathbf{w} = -\theta'\mathbf{N} + \theta'\mathbf{u} + \theta\mathbf{v}.$$

Then

$$\mathbf{v} = \theta^{-1}[\mathbf{w} + \theta'(\mathbf{N} - \mathbf{u})]. \tag{30}$$

If $\theta' = 0$, then $\mathbf{v} \neq \mathbf{0}$ because $\mathbf{w} \neq \mathbf{0}$; if $\theta' \neq 0$, then $\mathbf{v} \neq \mathbf{0}$ because

$$v_{n+1} = \theta^{-1}[0 + \theta'(1 - u_{n+1})] \neq 0, \tag{31}$$

since $w_{n+1} = 0$ and $u_{n+1} < 0$.

We have shown $\mathbf{v} \neq \mathbf{0}$ and $\mathbf{v} \cdot \mathbf{u} = 0$ if $u_{n+1} < 0$. Now let $\mathbf{u}$ approach the equator $u_{n+1} = 0$. According to the projection identity (21), this happens if

$$\theta \to 1, \quad |\mathbf{x}| \to 1, \quad \mathbf{x} - \mathbf{u} \to \mathbf{0}.$$

Then formula (30) gives, in the limit,

$$\mathbf{v} = [\mathbf{w} + \theta'(\mathbf{N} - \mathbf{x})] \tag{32}$$

as $\mathbf{u}$ approaches a point $\mathbf{x}$ on the equator. But then $\mathbf{w} = \mathbf{x}$, by (25); and

$$\theta' = \frac{d}{dt} \tfrac{1}{2}(1 + \mathbf{x} \cdot \mathbf{x}) = \mathbf{w} \cdot \mathbf{x} = 1,$$

by (24) and (25). Therefore,

$$\mathbf{v} = [\mathbf{x} + \mathbf{N} - \mathbf{x}] = \mathbf{N} \quad \text{if} \quad u_{n+1} = 0. \tag{33}$$

This completes the definition of $\mathbf{v}$ as a non-zero field of tangents to the *closed* southern hemisphere in S^n. At the equator the tangents $\mathbf{v}$ are unit vectors pointing straight up.

As a function of $\mathbf{u}$, the vector $\mathbf{v}$ is continuous. Why? All the functions $\theta, \theta', \mathbf{w}$, and $\mathbf{u}$ are continuous functions of $\mathbf{x}$, as we've seen. Then (30) says $\mathbf{v}$ is a continuous function of $\mathbf{x}$, since θ is $\geq \tfrac{1}{2}$. But (22) gives $\mathbf{x}$ as a continuous function of $\mathbf{u}$. And so $\mathbf{v}$ is a continuous function of $\mathbf{u}$.

What have we done so far? First, we assumed the Brouwer theorem false for the ball B^n. We then regarded B^n as the equatorial disk in B^{n+1}. By stereographic projection from the *north* pole, we constructed a continuous field of non-zero tangents to the *lower* half of S^n. For $\mathbf{u}$ on the equator the tangent $\mathbf{v}(\mathbf{u})$ equals a unit vector pointing straight *up* ($\mathbf{v} = \mathbf{N}$).

We used the *north* pole and projected *down*. Suppose we had used the *south* pole and projected *up*. What would we have got? By symmetry, we would have got a continuous field of non-zero tangents to the *upper* half of S^n; call these tangents $\mathbf{v}^+(\mathbf{u})$. By symmetry, for $\mathbf{u}$ on the equator the tangent $\mathbf{v}^+(\mathbf{u})$ equals a unit vector pointing straight *down* ($\mathbf{v} = \mathbf{S}$). Look at Figure 6 and compare it to Figure 5.

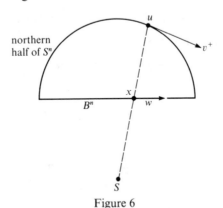

Figure 6

As you can see, $\mathbf{v}^+$ makes a perfect mismatch with $\mathbf{v}$ on the equator:

$$\mathbf{v}^+(\mathbf{u}) = -\mathbf{v}(\mathbf{u}) \quad \text{for} \quad u_{n+1} = 0 \, (|\mathbf{u}| = 1). \tag{34}$$

That's awful—just what we don't want. What we want is a continuous field of tangents on the whole sphere S^n: the limits from above and below have to match on the equator.

But we can get that. We have defined $\mathbf{v}(\mathbf{u})$ in the *lower* hemisphere. We can define $\mathbf{v}(\mathbf{u})$ in the *upper* hemisphere as follows:

$$\mathbf{v}(\mathbf{u}) \equiv -\mathbf{v}^+(\mathbf{u}) \quad \text{for} \quad u_{n+1} \geqq 0.$$

This turns the mismatch (34) into a match, and now we have a *continuous* field of non-zero tangents on the whole sphere S^n.

But the hairy-ball theorem says that is impossible if $n = 2, 4, 6, \ldots$. Therefore, the Brouwer fixed-point theorem must be true for the ball B^n if $n = 2, 4, 6, \ldots$.

What about $n = 1, 3, 5, \ldots$? Then the hairy-ball theorem is no help. On the contrary, if $n = 1, 3, 5, \ldots$, then S^n does have a continuous field of tangents. Could it be that the Brouwer theorem is false for odd n?

No, the Brouwer theorem is true for all n. Here's why:

Let $n = 1, 3, 5, \ldots$. Let $\mathbf{f}(\mathbf{x})$ map B^n continuously into itself; we want a fixed point $\mathbf{x} = \mathbf{f}(\mathbf{x})$. For $\mathbf{y}$ in B^{n+1} define the function

$$\mathbf{g}(\mathbf{y}) = (f_1(\mathbf{x}), \ldots, f_n(\mathbf{x}), 0)$$

where we set $y_j \equiv x_j$ for $j = 1, \ldots, n$. The function $\mathbf{g}(\mathbf{y})$ first vertically projects $\mathbf{y}$ onto the point $\mathbf{x}$ in the equatorial disk $y_{n+1} = 0$, then applies the mapping $\mathbf{f}$ from the disk into itself.

The function $\mathbf{g}(\mathbf{y})$ maps B^{n+1} continuously into itself. By what we have proved, $\mathbf{g}(\mathbf{y})$ must have a fixed point if $n + 1 = 2, 4, 6, \ldots$. The fixed point satisfies $\mathbf{y} = \mathbf{g}(\mathbf{y})$, which says

$$y_j = x_j = f_j(\mathbf{x}) \, (j = 1, \ldots, n); \quad y_{n+1} = 0.$$

Thus, the Brouwer theorem for B^{n+1} implies the Brouwer theorem for B^n, and so the proof is done.

Think it over; it's an amazing proof. Milnor makes the hairy-ball theorem depend on the fact that $(1 + t^2)^{n/2}$ isn't a polynomial if n is odd. Then a little projecting gives the Brouwer theorem for even dimensions, and a little more projecting gives it for odd dimensions.

Milnor's original article is only four pages long. I've written everything out in great detail—stereographic projections and all. I hope it's helped you.

References

1. J. Milnor, Analytic proofs of the "hairy ball theorem" and the Brouwer fixed point theorem, American Math. Monthly, Vol. 85 No. 7 (1978), pp. 521–524.
2. D. Asimov, Average Gaussian curvature of leaves of foliations, preprint, 1976. Bull. Amer. Math. Soc. 84, (1978) pp. 131–133.
3. W. M. Boothby, On two classical theorems of algebraic topology, Amer. Math. Monthly, Vol. 78 (1971) pp. 237–249.
4. P. Hilton and S. Wylie, Homology Theory, Cambridge University Press, New York, 1960, pp. 218–219.

5. M. Hirsch, Differential Topology, Springer-Verlag, New York, 1976, pp. 73, 134.
6. S. Lang, Analysis II, Addison-Wesley, Reading, Mass., 1969, pp. 50, 121.
7. J. Milnor, Topology from the Differentiable Viewpoint, Univ. Press of Va., Charlottesville, 1965, pp. 14, 30.
8. E. Spanier, Algebraic Topology, McGraw-Hill, New York, 1966, pp. 151, 194.

Problems. If you haven't done any of the problems in the last section, you might want to do some of them now. After studying this section, you can do any of the sixteen problems in the last section except Problems 2, 3, 11, and 12, which need the idea of *degree of mapping.*

4 Barycentric Coordinates, Sperner's Lemma, and an Elementary Proof of the Brouwer Fixed-Point Theorem

Garsia's proof of the Brouwer fixed-point theorem is fairly easy; but it is not *elementary*, since it uses calculus. So does Milnor's proof. Now we'll discuss an elementary proof. In my opinion, it is more difficult than Garsia's or Milnor's, but perhaps you will find it easier. Anyway, the elementary proof is worth learning because it introduces some techniques that we can use for other purposes.

Barycentric coordinates. In 2 dimensions a *simplex* is a triangle; in 1 dimension a simplex is a line segment; in N dimensions a simplex is the set of all points

$$\mathbf{x} = x_0\mathbf{v}^0 + x_1\mathbf{v}^1 + \cdots + x_N\mathbf{v}^N \tag{1}$$

such that

$$x_0 \geqslant 0, \ldots, x_N \geqslant 0, \text{ and } x_0 + \cdots + x_N = 1. \tag{2}$$

Here $\mathbf{v}^0, \ldots, \mathbf{v}^N$ are the vertices of the simplex. The numbers $x_0, \ldots, x_N$ are the *barycentric coordinates* of the point $\mathbf{x}$.

Do not confuse the $N + 1$ barycentric coordinates of $\mathbf{x}$ with the N cartesian coordinates. In this discussion we will always mean by x_i the ith barycentric coordinate of a point $\mathbf{x}$ inside the fixed simplex with vertices $\mathbf{v}^0, \ldots, \mathbf{v}^N$. Our whole world will be that one simplex; we will have no interest in any point outside our simplex.

Of course, there are easy identities relating barycentric and cartesian coordinates. If the vertex $\mathbf{v}^k$ has the cartesian coordinates $c_1^{(k)}, \ldots, c_N^{(k)}$, then $\mathbf{x}$ has the N cartesian coordinates $c_1, \ldots, c_N$ where (1) gives

$$c_j = x_0 c_j^{(0)} + \cdots + x_N c_j^{(N)} \qquad (j = 1, \ldots, N). \tag{3}$$

Conversely, *if the simplex is nondegenerate*, that is, if the N vectors

$$\mathbf{v}^1 - \mathbf{v}^0, \mathbf{v}^2 - \mathbf{v}^0, \ldots, \mathbf{v}^N - \mathbf{v}^0 \text{ are independent,} \tag{4}$$

then the cartesian coordinates of $\mathbf{x}$ *uniquely* determine its barycentric coordinates. For then the equation

$$\mathbf{x} - \mathbf{v}^0 = a_1(\mathbf{v}^1 - \mathbf{v}^0) + a_2(\mathbf{v}^2 - \mathbf{v}^0) + \cdots + a_N(\mathbf{v}^N - \mathbf{v}^0) \tag{5}$$

has a unique solution $a_1, \ldots, a_N$. If we now define

$$x_1 = a_1, x_2 = a_2, \ldots, x_N = a_N, \text{ and}$$
$$x_0 = 1 - a_1 - \cdots - a_N, \tag{6}$$

then (5) gives

$$\mathbf{x} = x_0\mathbf{v}^0 + x_1\mathbf{v}^1 + \cdots + x_N\mathbf{v}^N. \tag{7}$$

By the definition of the simplex, all the numbers x_k in (6) are ≥ 0 if $\mathbf{x}$ lies in the simplex; and (6) implies $x_0 + \cdots + x_N = 1$.

By the way, why are those coordinates called *barycentric*? Because the barycenter $\mathbf{b}$ is the center of gravity, namely,

$$\mathbf{b} = \frac{1}{N+1}(\mathbf{v}^0 + \mathbf{v}^1 + \cdots + \mathbf{v}^N),$$

and this point has the simple barycentric coordinates

$$b_0 = b_1 = \cdots = b_N = 1/(N+1).$$

Brouwer's fixed-point theorem for the simplex. A triangle is topologically equivalent to the disk $|\mathbf{x}| \leq 1$ in 2 dimensions; and tetrahedron is equivalent to the ball $|\mathbf{x}| \leq 1$ in 3 dimensions; and a nondegenerate simplex of points (1) is equivalent to the ball $|\mathbf{x}| \leq 1$ in N dimensions. Therefore, it suffices to state Brouwer's theorem for the simplex.

Theorem. *If* $\mathbf{f}(\mathbf{x})$ *maps a nondegenerate simplex continuously into itself, then there is a fixed point* $\mathbf{x}^* = \mathbf{f}(\mathbf{x}^*)$.

In barycentric coordinates, a fixed point satisfies the equations

$$x_k^* = f_k(\mathbf{x}^*) \qquad (k = 0, \ldots, N). \tag{8}$$

In the proof that follows, we shall find it easier to prove *inequalities*:

$$x_k^* \geq f_k(\mathbf{x}^*) \qquad (k = 0, \ldots, N). \tag{9}$$

But for *barycentric* coordinates *the equations* (8) *and the inequalities* (9) *imply each other*: trivially, (8) implies (9); but also (9) implies (8), because

$$\sum_k x_k^* = 1 = \sum_k f_k.$$

On the boundary faces of the simplex certain inequalities $x_k > f_k(\mathbf{x})$ cannot occur. In 2 dimensions you can see this if you look at Figure 1.

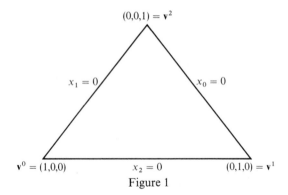

Figure 1

The vertex $\mathbf{v}^k$ has kth coordinate equal to 1 and all other coordinates equal to zero. The boundary face opposite $\mathbf{v}^k$ consists of all $\mathbf{x}$ with $x_k = 0$.

Let $\mathbf{y} \equiv \mathbf{f(x)}$. If $\mathbf{y} \neq \mathbf{x}$, then some coordinate $y_j \neq x_k$. Therefore, since $\sum y_j = \sum x_j$, we must have *both*

$$\text{some } x_k > y_k \text{ and some } x_i < y_i. \tag{10}$$

Focus on the first inequality, $x_k > y_k$; clearly this cannot occur where $x_k = 0$. In other words, $x_k > y_k$ *cannot occur on the segment opposite* $\mathbf{v}^k$.

In three dimensions the boundary of the simplex is more complicated. The simplex is determined by 4 vertices. Any 3 vertices determine a boundary face; any 2 vertices determine a boundary segment. Let us call all the faces, segments, and vertices *boundary elements*. Each element has dimension 2, 1, or 0.

In N dimensions each boundary element has dimension $N-1, N-2, \ldots$, or 0. A boundary element of dimension $d < N$ is determined by a set of $d + 1$ vertices, say

$$\mathbf{v}^p, \mathbf{v}^q, \ldots, \mathbf{v}^s. \tag{11}$$

On *this* boundary element the points $\mathbf{x}$ have coordinates

$$x_p \geqslant 0, x_q \geqslant 0, \ldots, x_s \geqslant 0. \tag{12}$$

All other coordinates $x_k = 0$, and so the inequality $x_k > y_k \geqslant 0$ cannot occur on this boundary element. In other words:

$$\text{If } x_j > y_j \text{ for } \mathbf{x} \text{ in } \langle \mathbf{v}^p, \mathbf{v}^q, \ldots, \mathbf{v}^s \rangle \text{ then } j = p \text{ or } q \text{ or } \cdots \text{ or } s. \tag{13}$$

(Here the notation $\langle \mathbf{v}^p, \ldots, \mathbf{v}^s \rangle$ stands for the boundary element determined by $\mathbf{v}^p, \ldots, \mathbf{v}^s$.)

Now we can define the scheme of indexing that will play the crucial role in our use of Sperner's lemma. For all $\mathbf{x}$ in the N-dimensional simplex, let $\mathbf{y}$ be any function of $\mathbf{x}$ such that $\mathbf{y}$ lies in the simplex but $\mathbf{y} \neq \mathbf{x}$. Then, as we've seen, for each $\mathbf{x}$ we have some $x_j > y_j$. Now define the index $m(\mathbf{x})$ as the *smallest* such j:

$$m(\mathbf{x}) \equiv \min\{j : x_j > y_j\}. \tag{14}$$

(We choose the *smallest* j only as one definite way to pick some index satisfying $x_j > y_j$; we might as well have chosen the largest such j, but we didn't.)

The function $m(\mathbf{x})$ takes one of the values $0, 1, \ldots, N$ for each $\mathbf{x}$ the simplex. But on the boundary, we know that the function $m(\mathbf{x})$ is restricted. Formula (13) implies this:

$$\textit{For } \mathbf{x} \textit{ in } \langle \mathbf{v}^p, \mathbf{v}^q, \ldots, \mathbf{v}^s \rangle \textit{ the function } m(\mathbf{x}) = p \textit{ or } q \textit{ or } \cdots \textit{ or } s. \qquad (15)$$

For $N = 2$ this result is illustrated in Figure 2.

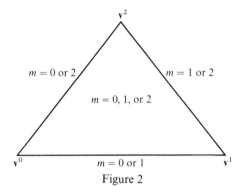

Figure 2

Do you remember why we are doing all this? We are looking for a fixed point of $\mathbf{f}(\mathbf{x})$. That is a point $\mathbf{x}$ whose barycentric coordinates satisfy all the inequalities

$$x_0 \geqslant y_0, x_1 \geqslant y_1, \ldots, x_N \geqslant y_N, \qquad (16)$$

where $\mathbf{y} \equiv \mathbf{f}(\mathbf{x})$. Here's how we will do it:

For $n = 2, 3, \ldots$ we form the *nth barycentric subdivision* of our simplex. In two dimensions we show the fifth subdivision in Figure 3.

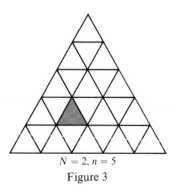

$N = 2, n = 5$

Figure 3

In Figure 3 the vertices in the subdivision are the points

$$\mathbf{x} = \tfrac{1}{5}(k_0, k_1, k_2) \qquad (17)$$

where the k_i are integers with

$$\text{all } k_i \geqslant 0 \quad \text{and} \quad \sum k_i = 5, \tag{18}$$

In general, for the nth subdivision in N dimensions, the vertices are the points

$$\mathbf{x} = \frac{1}{n}(k_0, k_1, \ldots, k_N), \tag{19}$$

where the k_i are integers satisfying

$$\text{all } k_i \geqslant 0 \quad \text{and} \quad \sum k_i = n.$$

Look again at Figure 3. We will call the little shaded triangle a *cell*. The original simplex is the whole *body*; the subsimplexes are its *cells*. In Figure 3 we see 25 cells. Each cell is small; the diameter of each cell is $\frac{1}{5}$ of the diameter of the body.

In general, in the nth subdivision of a simplex in N dimensions, the number of cells tends to infinity as $n \to \infty$; but the diameter of each cell tends to zero. If $\varDelta$ is the diameter of the body, then the diameter of each cell is $\varDelta/n$.

We are given a continuous function $\mathbf{y} = \mathbf{f}(\mathbf{x})$ that maps the body into itself. We *assume* that $\mathbf{f}(\mathbf{x})$ has no fixed point, and we will now deduce the opposite: $\mathbf{f}(\mathbf{x})$ *must* have a fixed point. That will prove Brouwer's theorem.

Since we assume $\mathbf{y} \neq \mathbf{x}$, we may use formula (14) to label each point $\mathbf{x}$ with an index $m(\mathbf{x})$. The index takes one of the values $0, \ldots, N$ at each point in the body, and on the boundary of the body the index satisfies the restriction (15), which we have illustrated in Figure 2.

Now look at Figure 3. We count 21 vertices. Label each vertex $\mathbf{x}$ with an index $m(\mathbf{x}) = 0, 1,$ or 2. On the boundary you must obey the rule (15), which is pictured in Figure 2. That means you must use $m = 0$ or 1 on the bottom side, $m = 0$ or 2 on the left, and $m = 1$ or 2 on the right. In Figure 3, that leaves 6 interior vertices, each to be labeled 0, 1, or 2.

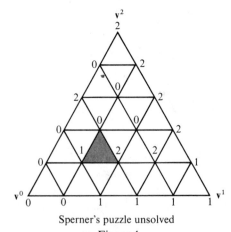

Sperner's puzzle unsolved

Figure 4

Now's here a puzzle. Follow the rules we've just given, and label all 21 vertices in Figure 3, so that none of the 25 cells has *all* the labels 0, 1, 2. (See Figure 4, for one attempt.)

Sperner's lemma, which we will prove, says the puzzle is impossible. *At least one of the cells must have a complete set of labels.* (Sperner's lemma applies to all regular simplicial subdivisions, but for our purposes we will only state and prove it for what we've called the *n*th barycentric subdivision.)

Sperner's Lemma *Form the nth barycentric subdivision of a nondegenerate simplex in N dimensions. Label each vertex with an index $m(\mathbf{x}) = 0, \ldots, N$ that satisfies the restriction (15) on the boundary. Then some cell in the subdivision must have vertices with the complete set of labels: $0, 1, \ldots,$ and N.*

Before we prove Sperner's lemma, *let's show how it proves the Brouwer fixed-point theorem:*

Let $\mathbf{y} = \mathbf{f}(\mathbf{x})$ map the simplex continuously into itself. If we assume $\mathbf{y} \neq \mathbf{x}$, we can use (14) to define an index $m(\mathbf{x})$ that satisfies (15).

Form the *n*th barycentric subdivision. Now Sperner's lemma guarantees that some cell has vertices with the complete set of labels; say

$$
\begin{array}{ll}
m = 0 & \text{at the vertex } \mathbf{x}^0(n) \\
m = 1 & \text{at the vertex } \mathbf{x}^1(n) \\
\multicolumn{2}{c}{\ldots\ldots} \\
m = N & \text{at the vertex } \mathbf{x}^N(n).
\end{array}
\tag{20}
$$

What does this say about the function $\mathbf{y} = \mathbf{f}(\mathbf{x})$? If $m = j$ at the point $\mathbf{x}$, then the definition (14) says something about the *j*th barycentric coordinate, namely, $x_j > y_j$. Therefore, (20) says this:

$$
\begin{array}{ll}
x_0 > y_0 & \text{at the vertex } \mathbf{x}^0(n) \\
x_1 > y_1 & \text{at the vertex } \mathbf{x}^1(n) \\
\multicolumn{2}{c}{\ldots\ldots} \\
x_N > y_N & \text{at the vertex } \mathbf{x}^N(n).
\end{array}
\tag{21}
$$

But all the vertices of the cell are close to each other if *n* is large, since the diameter of the cell is the diameter of the body divided by *n*:

$$
\max_{0 \leq p < q \leq N} \left| \mathbf{x}^p(n) - \mathbf{x}^q(n) \right| = \Delta/n \to 0 \quad \text{as} \quad n \to \infty.
\tag{22}
$$

As $n \to \infty$, let's watch the single vertex $\mathbf{x}^0(n)$. This vertex wanders through the body in some bounded infinite sequence. The sequence may or may not have a limit, but this we do know: Some *subsequence* has a limit[1]; say

$$
\mathbf{x}^0(n_s) \to \mathbf{x}^* \quad \text{as} \quad s \to \infty.
\tag{23}
$$

---

[1] The limit is guaranteed by the Bolzano-Weierstrass theorem.

But now the closeness of the vertices (22) implies that they *all* tend to $\mathbf{x}^*$ as $n_s \to \infty$:

$$x^p(n_s) \to x^* \quad \text{as} \quad s \to \infty \; (p = 0, 1, \ldots, N). \tag{24}$$

Now the continuity of $\mathbf{f}(\mathbf{x})$ implies

$$\mathbf{f}(\mathbf{x}^p(n_s)) \to \mathbf{f}(\mathbf{x}^*) \equiv \mathbf{y}^* \quad \text{as} \quad s \to \infty \; (p = 0, 1, \ldots, N). \tag{25}$$

But the barycentric coordinates of a point $\mathbf{x}$ depend continuously on $\mathbf{x}$. Therefore, if we let $n = n_s \to \infty$ in (21), we obtain the limiting inequalities

$$
\begin{aligned}
x_0 &\geqslant y_0 && \text{at the limit } \mathbf{x}^* \\
x_1 &\geqslant y_1 && \text{at the limit } \mathbf{x}^* \\
&\cdots\cdots \\
x_N &\geqslant y_N && \text{at the limit } \mathbf{x}^*.
\end{aligned}
\tag{26}
$$

In other words,

$$x_j^* \geqslant y_j^* \quad (j = 0, 1, \ldots, N), \tag{27}$$

and for barycentric coordinates this says $\mathbf{x}^* = \mathbf{y}^*$. *This is an elementary proof of the Brouwer fixed-point theorem.*

Wonderful. Now all we have to do is *prove Sperner's lemma*. This we will do by using induction on the dimension N. As it often happens in inductive proofs, we will find it easier to prove more than the original assertion. We will prove this:

Assertion. In Sperner's lemma the number of fully labeled cells must be **odd**.

In other words, the number of cells with the complete set of labels must be 1 or 3 or 5 or . . . . As it happens in Figure 4, the number is 1; by changing a label, you can make the number 3; but in no way can you make the number 0 or 2 or 4 or . . . or 24.

NOTATION. In N dimensions, if the vertices of a cell have the labels $m_0, m_1, \ldots, m_N$, we say the cell has type $(m_0, m_1, \ldots, m_N)$. Here permutations don't matter, but multiplicities do matter. For instance,

$$(0,1,2,0) = (2,0,0,1) = (2,1,0,0) \neq (2,1,1,0).$$

A cell in N dimensions has *boundary elements* of dimensions $0, 1, \ldots,$ $N - 1$. Those of dimension 0 we will call *vertices*; those of dimension $N - 1$ we will call *faces*. We will call the *whole* cell an element of dimension N.

The counting function. We are given a barycentric subdivision labeled by the rules of Sperner's lemma. *By $F(a,b, \ldots, q)$ we shall mean the number of elements in the body of type* $(a,b, \ldots, q)$.

For example, in Figure 4 we count:

$$
\begin{aligned}
&F(0) = 8 \qquad\quad F(1) = 6 \qquad\quad F(2) = 7 \\
&F(0,0) = 9, \qquad F(0,1) = 5, \\
&F(0,1,0) = 3, \quad F(0,1,1) = 1, \quad F(0,1,2) = 1
\end{aligned}
\tag{28}
$$

This is just a sampling; for instance, we omitted $F(1,2)$ and $F(1,1,2)$.

In terms of the counting function, this is our assertion: *In N dimensions*

$$F(0,1,\ldots,N) \text{ is odd.} \tag{29}$$

That is true in (28), where $F(0,1,2) = 1$.

The case N = 1. We must show that $F(0,1)$ is odd if we number the segment

$$0 \cdot\!\!-\!\!\!-\!\!\!-\!\!\cdot\!\!-\!\!\!-\!\!\!-\!\!\cdot\!\!-\!\!\!-\!\!\!-\!\!\cdot\!\!-\!\!\!-\!\!\cdot1$$

by our rules.

Let's look at the faces labeled 0 (if $N = 1$, a face is a single point). *Two* labels 0 occur in each cell of type $(0,0)$; *one* label 0 occurs in each cell of type $(0,1)$.

Now look at the sum

$$2F(0,0) + F(0,1).$$

This sum counts every *interior* 0 twice, since every interior 0 is the face that is shared by two cells; but the sum counts the single 0 on the boundary of the segment only once. Therefore,

$$2F(0,0) + F(0,1) = 2F_i(0) + 1, \tag{30}$$

where $F_i(0)$ stands for the number of interior 0's. This proves $F(0,1)$ is odd.

For example, look at the bottom edge in Figure 4. This edge is numbered

$$\underset{\bullet}{0}\underset{\bullet}{\quad\quad}\underset{\bullet}{0}\underset{\bullet}{\quad\quad}\underset{\bullet}{1}\underset{\bullet}{\quad\quad}\underset{\bullet}{1}\underset{\bullet}{\quad\quad}\underset{\bullet}{1}\underset{\bullet}{\quad\quad}1 \tag{31}$$

This body has

$$F(0,0) = 1, \quad F(0,1) = 1, \quad F_i(0) = 1, \tag{32}$$

and these numbers satisfy (30).

We could now go right to the general case, but it will be easier for you if you first understand this:

The case N = 2. Let's look at the faces labeled $(0,1)$. *Two* faces $(0,1)$ occur in each cell of type

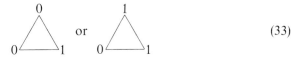

$$\text{(33)}$$

One face $(0,1)$ occurs in each cell of type

$$\text{(34)}$$

Now look at the sum

$$2[F(0,1,0) + F(0,1,1)] + F(0,1,2). \tag{35}$$

This sum counts every *interior* face $(0,1)$ twice, since every interior face is shared by two cells; but the sum counts every face $(0,1)$ on the *boundary* of the body only once, because each face on the boundary belongs to only one cell. Therefore, our sum (35) satisfies

$$2[F(0,1,0) + F(0,1,1)] + F(0,1,2) = 2F_i(0,1) + F_b(0,1), \qquad (36)$$

where F_i and F_b stand for the numbers of faces (0,1) in the interior and on the boundary.

We now say this: $F_b(0,1)$ *is odd.* Why? Because this is the number of segments (0,1) on the boundary. These segments can lie only on the element between the vertices $\mathbf{v}^0$ and $\mathbf{v}^1$. On this element Sperner's lemma applies with dimension $N - 1 = 1$, and so $F_b(0,1)$ is odd *by induction.*

Now formula (36) takes the form

$$2[\ldots] + F(0,1,2) = 2(\ldots) + (\text{odd}). \qquad (37)$$

This proves $F(0,1,2)$ is odd.

For example, look at Figure 4. In (28), we counted

$$F(0,1,0) = 3, \quad F(0,1,1) = 1, \quad \text{and} \quad F(0,1,2) = 1. \qquad (38)$$

We now count the interior and boundary faces (0,1):

$$F_i(0,1) = 4 \quad \text{and} \quad F_b(0,1) = 1. \qquad (39)$$

These numbers satisfy formula (36): $2[3 + 1] + 1 = 2(4) + 1$.

Note that the count $F_b(0,1)$ uses only the element between $\mathbf{v}^0$ and $\mathbf{v}^1$; we looked at this element before in formula (31), and our present $F_b(0,1)$ appeared before as $F(0,1)$ in (32).

Now I'm sure you get the idea, and you'll easily understand what follows.

The general case $N > 1$. Let's look at the faces labeled $(0, 1, \ldots, N - 1)$. *Two* such faces occur in each cell of type

$$(0, 1, \ldots, N - 1, m) \quad \text{if} \quad m \leqslant N - 1.$$

One face $(0, 1, \ldots, N - 1)$ occurs in each cell of type

$$(0, 1, \ldots, N - 1, N).$$

Now look at the sum

$$S \equiv 2 \sum_{m=0}^{n-1} F(0, 1, \ldots, N - 1, m) + F(0, 1, \ldots, N - 1, N). \qquad (40)$$

This sum counts every *interior* face $(0, \ldots, N - 1)$ twice, since every interior face is shared by two cells; but the sum counts every face $(0, \ldots, N - 1)$ on the *boundary* of the body only once, because each face on the boundary belongs to only one cell. Therefore, our sum satisfies

$$S = 2F_i(0, \ldots, N - 1) + F_b(0, \ldots, N - 1). \qquad (41)$$

We now say this: $F_b(0, \ldots, N - 1)$ *is odd.* Why? *Because, in $N - 1$ dimensions,* this is the number of *cells* of type $(0, \ldots, N - 1)$ in a Sperner subdivision of the $(N - 1)$-dimensional simplex $\langle \mathbf{v}^0, \ldots, \mathbf{v}^{N-1} \rangle$. Now Sperner's lemma applies with dimension $N - 1$, and so $F_b(0, \ldots, N - 1)$ is odd by induction.

Now formulas (40) and (41) take the forms

$$S = 2 \sum + F(0, 1, \ldots, N - 1, N)$$

and

$$S = 2F_i + F_b = \text{even} + \text{odd} = \text{odd}.$$

This proves Sperner's lemma; and as we saw, Sperner's lemma proves the Brouwer fixed-point theorem. We shall later use the technique of barycentric subdivision to prove the fixed-point theorem of Kakutani.

But first we will extend Brouwer's theorem to infinite dimensions. We will prove the Schauder fixed-point theorem, which is one of the most powerful tools in mathematical analysis.

PROBLEMS

1. In the plane, let the vertices v^0, v^1, v^2 have the cartesian coordinates $(3, -2)$, $(1,5)$, $(-7,1)$. Let x have cartesian coordinates (c_1, c_2), and let x have barycentric coordinates (x_0, x_1, x_2) in the simplex $\langle v^0, v^1, v^2 \rangle$. Write the cartesian coordinates of x as functions of its barycentric coordinates; also write the barycentric coordinates as functions of the cartesian coordinates.

2. For Problem 1 show that the simplex is nondegenerate.

3. For Problem 1 draw the simplex, and draw the five lines

$$x_1 = 0, \quad x_1 = \tfrac{1}{5}, \quad x_1 = \tfrac{2}{5}, \quad x_1 = \tfrac{3}{5}, \quad x_1 = \tfrac{4}{5}.$$

4. For Problem 1 draw the sixth barycentric subdivision. Locate the point with barycentric coordinates $\tfrac{1}{6}(3,1,2)$. Also locate the barycenter, and write its barycentric coordinates.

5. For the simplex in Problem 1 define the mapping $y = f(x)$ by

$$y_1 = x_2, \quad y_2 = x_3, \quad y_3 = x_1$$

unless x is the barycenter b; for $x = b$ define $y_1 = 1$, $y_2 = 0$, $y_3 = 0$. Show that this mapping is discontinuous, and show that it has no fixed point.

6. For Problem 5 define the index function $m(x)$ according to formula (14). Draw the third barycentric subdivision. For each of the ten vertices in the subdivision write the barycentric coordinates of x and of $y = f(x)$; then find the ten numbers $m(x)$. In a separate picture, attach the labels $m(x)$ to the ten subdivision vertices. What does formula (15) say for this example? How many of the nine cells have vertices labeled $0, 1, 2$?

7. In Figure 4 evaluate $F(2,1)$ and $F(1,2,1)$.

8. Draw a triangle, and mark a point a in the interior. Label the three vertices v^0, v^1, v^2. Now draw the subset of points y in the simplex with $y_0 \geqslant a_0$. Draw the subset with $y_1 \geqslant a_1$, and draw the subset with $y_2 \geqslant a_2$. Draw the intersection of two of these subsets. Draw the intersection of all three.

9. The text says that the barycentric coordinates of a point in a nondegenerate simplex are continuous functions of the point. What does that mean and why is it true? Is it true for a degenerate simplex?

10. The diameter of a closed, bounded set is the maximum distance between two points. If a simplex has diameter Δ, why does *every* cell in the nth barycentric subdivision have diameter Δ/n? (Hint: First show that the diameter of a simplex is the greatest distance between two of its *vertices*.)

11. If a simplex in N dimensions has diameter Δ, and if $\mathbf{b}$ is the barycenter, show that

$$|\mathbf{x} - \mathbf{b}| \leqslant \frac{N}{N+1} \Delta \qquad \text{for all } \mathbf{x} \text{ in the simplex.}$$

12. Let $\mathbf{x}$ and $\mathbf{y}$ be two points in an N-dimensional simplex. Suppose their barycentric coordinates satisfy

$$x_i \geqslant y_i - \varepsilon \qquad (i = 0, 1, \ldots, N),$$

where $\varepsilon \geqslant 0$. Then prove

$$x_i \leqslant y_i + N\varepsilon \qquad (i = 0, \ldots, N).$$

*13. Approximate fixed points: Suppose $\mathbf{f}(\mathbf{x})$ maps a nondegenerate N-dimensional simplex continuously into itself. Suppose $\mathbf{f}$ satisfies $|\mathbf{f}(\mathbf{x}) - \mathbf{f}(\mathbf{x}')| \leqslant \lambda|\mathbf{x} - \mathbf{x}'|$. Let the simplex have diameter Δ. Form the nth barycentric subdivision. Let $\mathbf{b}^*$ be the barycenter of a cell with a complete set of Sperner labels as in formula (20). Now derive an upper bound for the Euclidian distance $|\mathbf{b}^* - \mathbf{f}(\mathbf{b}^*)|$. (Your upper bound should be $O(1/n)$ as $n \to \infty$.)

*14. Consider the nth barycentric subdivision of an N-dimensional simplex. Easy: Show that the number of cells is n^N. Hard: Show that the number of vertices is the binomial coefficient

$$\binom{n+N}{N} = \frac{(n+1)(n+2)\cdots(n+N)}{1 \cdot 2 \cdots N}$$

5 The Schauder Fixed-Point Theorem

In his popular book *How to Solve It*, the distinguished mathematician George Pólya said: "A great discovery solves a great problem. . . ."

Professor Pólya was one of my teachers. He always filled his lectures with examples. He believed that the more abstract a subject was, the more it called for vivid examples.

So let's begin with a great problem and with an example. The problem is to prove the existence of solutions to nonlinear integral equations. The example is this equation:

$$x(t) = \int_0^1 e^{-st} \cos(7x(s))\, ds \qquad (0 \leqslant t \leqslant 1). \tag{1}$$

If a real-valued, integrable solution $x(s)$ exists, it makes the integral a continuous function of t, and so $x(t)$ must be continuous. And if $x(t)$ exists, it must satisfy

$$|x(t)| \leqslant 1 \qquad (0 \leqslant t \leqslant 1), \tag{2}$$

since

$$|x(t)| = \left| \int_0^1 e^{-st} \cos(\cdots) \, ds \right| \leqslant \int_0^1 e^{-st} \, ds \leqslant 1.$$

Let's define the set of all real-valued functions $x(t)$ that are continuous for $0 \leqslant t \leqslant 1$. This set is called a *Banach space*, and we will denote it by $\mathbb{B}$. A "point" $\mathbf{x}$ in the "space" $\mathbb{B}$ is a real-valued, continuous function $x(t)$. If we think of $\mathbf{x}$ as a vector, we may think of $x(t)$ as its components for $0 \leqslant t \leqslant 1$. The vector $\mathbf{x}$ has infinitely many components, and $\mathbb{B}$ has dimension infinity.

The integral in (1) transforms every continuous function $x(s)$ into a continuous function

$$y(t) \equiv \int_0^1 e^{-st} \cos(7x(s)) \, ds \qquad (0 \leqslant t \leqslant 1). \tag{3}$$

In the Banach space $\mathbb{B}$, let us write this identity in the form

$$\mathbf{y} = \mathbf{f}(\mathbf{x}). \tag{4}$$

Here $\mathbf{f}(\mathbf{x})$ is given by the integral in (3). Since a continuous $x(s)$ produces a continuous $y(t)$, we may say that the function $\mathbf{f}(\mathbf{x}) = \mathbf{y}$ maps the Banach space $\mathbb{B}$ into itself.

And we can say more. Let us define the "unit ball" in $\mathbb{B}$. This will consist of the points $\mathbf{x}$ that satisfy the inequality $\max|x(t)| \leqslant 1$. As we saw, the function $\mathbf{f}$ maps every point $\mathbf{x}$ into the unit ball $|\mathbf{y}| \leqslant 1$; here we use the norm

$$|\mathbf{y}| \equiv \max_{0 \leqslant t \leqslant 1} |y(t)|. \tag{5}$$

In particular, *the function $\mathbf{f}$ maps the unit ball into itself.*

It's beginning to sound familiar, isn't it? It sounds like the language of the Brouwer fixed-point theorem. In this language, what does the original equation (1) ask for? It asks for a *fixed point*:

$$\mathbf{x} = \mathbf{f}(\mathbf{x}). \tag{6}$$

By analogy with the Brouwer theorem, we shall want to know that the function $\mathbf{f}$ is continuous. But what does *continuity* mean in a Banach space? It means this: If $\mathbf{x}_n \to \mathbf{x}^*$, then $\mathbf{f}(\mathbf{x}_n) \to \mathbf{f}(\mathbf{x}^*)$. And by this we mean that

$$\text{if } |\mathbf{x}_n - \mathbf{x}^*| \to 0, \text{ then } |\mathbf{f}(\mathbf{x}_n) - \mathbf{f}(\mathbf{x}^*)| \to 0. \tag{7}$$

In our space $\mathbb{B}$, the convergence $|\mathbf{x}_n - \mathbf{x}^*| \to 0$ means

$$\max_{0 \leqslant t \leqslant 1} |x_n(t) - x^*(t)| \to 0 \quad \text{as} \quad n \to \infty. \tag{8}$$

This is what we ordinarily call *uniform convergence* of the sequence $x_n(t)$ on the interval $0 \leqslant t \leqslant 1$. If $\mathbf{y} \equiv \mathbf{f}(\mathbf{x})$, the function $\mathbf{f}$ is continuous if the uniform convergence $x_n(s) \to x^*(s)$ implies the uniform convergence $y_n(t) \to y^*(t)$. If formula (3) defines $\mathbf{y} \equiv \mathbf{f}(\mathbf{x})$, then the function $\mathbf{f}$ is indeed continuous. In the Banach space $\mathbb{B}$, our function $\mathbf{f}$ maps the unit ball continuously into itself.

Therefore, the integral equation (1) has a solution if the following generalization of Brouwer's theorem is correct:

Theorem 0. *In a Banach space $\mathbb{B}$, let $\mathbf{f}(\mathbf{x})$ map the unit ball continuously into itself. Then the mapping has a fixed point $\mathbf{x} = \mathbf{f}(\mathbf{x})$.*

Alas, this theorem is false, as an example will show. We shall need to require something more than continuity; then we shall have the Schauder fixed point theorem. The Schauder theorem proves the existence of solutions for an enormous class of nonlinear functional equations—including our little integral equation (1).

Now let's get down to business. In general, *what is a Banach space $\mathbb{B}$?* It is a linear vector space of points $\mathbf{x}$ defined over a field of scalars, which we shall take to be the field of real constants c. There is a zero vector, $\mathbf{0}$, for which

$$\mathbf{x} + \mathbf{0} = \mathbf{x} \qquad \text{for all } \mathbf{x} \text{ in } \mathbb{B}. \tag{9}$$

There is a norm $|\mathbf{x}|$ that satisfies

$$|\mathbf{x}| \geqslant 0, \text{ with } |\mathbf{x}| = 0 \text{ iff } \mathbf{x} = \mathbf{0}, \tag{10}$$

$$|c\mathbf{x}| = |c|\,|\mathbf{x}|, \tag{11}$$

$$|\mathbf{x} + \mathbf{y}| \leqslant |\mathbf{x}| + |\mathbf{y}|. \tag{12}$$

Finally, the space must satisfy the Cauchy property: If the sequence $\mathbf{x}_1, \mathbf{x}_2, \ldots$ satisfies

$$|\mathbf{x}_n - \mathbf{x}_m| \to 0 \quad \text{as} \quad n, m \to \infty, \tag{13}$$

then there is a limit $\mathbf{x}^*$, for which

$$|\mathbf{x}_n - \mathbf{x}^*| \to 0 \quad \text{as} \quad n \to \infty. \tag{14}$$

We do not need to assume that, conversely, (14) implies (13), since that is implied by the triangle inequality (12).

EXAMPLE 1. Let $\mathbb{B}$ be the space of real-valued continuous functions $x(t)$ for $0 \leqslant t \leqslant 1$. One easily verifies the properties (9)–(12). The point $\mathbf{x} = \mathbf{0}$ in $\mathbb{B}$ is the continuous function $x(t) \equiv 0$ for $0 \leqslant t \leqslant 1$. The norm is

$$|\mathbf{x}| = \max_{0 \leqslant t \leqslant 1} |x(t)|. \tag{15}$$

The Cauchy property states a basic theorem about continuous functions: If a sequence of continuous functions $x_1(t), x_2(t), \ldots$ satisfies (13), then the sequence converges uniformly to a continuous function $x^*(t)$. I'm assuming that you know this theorem.

EXAMPLE 2. Consider the space of points

$$\mathbf{x} = (x_1, x_2, x_3, \ldots \ ) \tag{16}$$

with infinitely many real components x_i. This is the obvious extension of the N-dimensional vector space R^N as $N \to \infty$. We define the norm as

$$|\mathbf{x}| = (x_1^2 + x_2^2 + \cdots \ )^{1/2}, \tag{17}$$

and we define H to be the set of $\mathbf{x}$ with $|\mathbf{x}| < \infty$.

The space H is a Banach space. The properties (9)–(12) are easy to verify if you know the Schwarz inequality. The Cauchy property, (13) $\Rightarrow$ (14), requires some care to prove. Here is a sketch of the proof: You first show that if $\mathbf{x}_n$ has the components x_{nj}, then (13) implies that there exist limits

$$x_j^* = \lim_{m \to \infty} x_{mj}. \tag{18}$$

You then show, for finite N,

$$\sum_{j=1}^{N} (x_{nk} - x_j^*)^2 \leqslant \limsup_{m \to \infty} |\mathbf{x}_n - \mathbf{x}_m|^2. \tag{19}$$

If you first let $N \to \infty$ and then let $n \to \infty$, you get the Cauchy limit (14).

The space H is called a Hilbert space because it has an inner product

$$\mathbf{x} \cdot \mathbf{y} = \sum x_j y_j \tag{20}$$

that satisfies $\mathbf{x} \cdot \mathbf{x} = |\mathbf{x}|^2$. And the inner product has other familiar properties.

Every Hilbert space is a Banach space, but the converse is false. In a Hilbert space the norm satisfies the parallelogram law:

$$|\mathbf{x} + \mathbf{y}|^2 + |\mathbf{x} - \mathbf{y}|^2 = 2(|\mathbf{x}|^2 + |\mathbf{y}|^2). \tag{21}$$

You can show that the Banach space $\mathbb{B}$ in Example 1 fails the parallelogram law; therefore $\mathbb{B}$ is no Hilbert space.

Theorem 0 is false. The Hilbert space H provides a pretty counterexample to our naive extension of the Brouwer fixed-point theorem. For all $\mathbf{x}$ in the unit ball $|\mathbf{x}| \leqslant 1$, define

$$y_1 = (1 - |\mathbf{x}|^2)^{1/2}; \quad y_2 = x_1, \quad y_3 = x_2, \quad y_4 = x_3, \ldots. \tag{22}$$

Then $\mathbf{y}$ is a continuous function of $\mathbf{x}$: if $\mathbf{x} \to \mathbf{x}^*$, then $\mathbf{y} \to \mathbf{y}^*$, where $y_1^* = (1 - |\mathbf{x}^*|)^{1/2}$ and $y_{i+1}^* = x_i^*$.

If $|\mathbf{x}| \leqslant 1$, then $|\mathbf{y}| \leqslant 1$; indeed, $|\mathbf{y}| = 1$.

But can there be a fixed point $\mathbf{x} = \mathbf{y}$? If so, then all its components are equal. Only one $\mathbf{x}$ in H has equal components: $\mathbf{x} = \mathbf{0}$. But then (22) says $y_1 = 1$, and so $\mathbf{y} \neq \mathbf{x}$. (This example is due to S. Kakutani.)

What goes wrong in spaces of infinite dimension? I'll tell you the secret: The finite-dimensional ball is *compact*; the infinite-dimensional ball is not.

Compactness. A set is compact if every infinite sequence in the set has a limit point in the set. In the N-dimensional vector space R^N every closed, bounded set is compact; that is the Bolzano-Weierstrass theorem. For example, in R^N the unit ball $|\mathbf{x}| \leqslant 1$ is compact.

But look at the unit ball in the Hilbert space H. The ball is bounded; and it is closed, because

$$|\mathbf{x}_n| \leqslant 1 \quad \text{and} \quad \mathbf{x}_n \to \mathbf{x}^* \quad \text{imply} \quad |\mathbf{x}^*| \leqslant 1.$$

But the ball cannot be compact, since it contains an infinite sequence of orthogonal unit vectors:

$$\mathbf{x}_1 = (1,0,0,\ldots), \quad \mathbf{x}_2 = (0,1,0,\ldots), \quad \mathbf{x}_3 = (0,0,1,\ldots),\ldots.$$

No subsequence can converge, since

$$|\mathbf{x}_m - \mathbf{x}_n| = \sqrt{2} \qquad \text{for all } m \neq n.$$

Look also at the Banach space $\mathbb{B}$ of continuous functions $x(t)$ $(0 \leqslant t \leqslant 1)$. Here also, the unit ball $|\mathbf{x}| \leqslant 1$ is closed and bounded; but it cannot be compact, since no subsequence of the continuous functions $x_n(t) = t^n$ converges uniformly for $0 \leqslant t \leqslant 1$. The convergence could not be uniform, because the pointwise limit has a discontinuity at $t = 1$.

The sequence $x_n(t) = \sin nt$ gives a more dramatic example. Here each subsequence diverges for infinitely many t in every subinterval; so uniform convergence on the whole interval $[0,1]$ is out of the question.

In the false Theorem 0 the function $\mathbf{f}(\mathbf{x})$ maps the ball continuously into itself. We know this is not enough to guarantee a fixed point. But Schauder showed that *a fixed point is guaranteed if* $\mathbf{f}(\mathbf{x})$ *has one more property: it maps the unit ball into a* **compact** *set*. This requirement adds no new restriction in finite dimensions, since in R^N the unit ball is compact.

How severe is this new requirement? We can infer from an example that Schauder's requirement if often met.

You remember our integral equation (1). Here the identity (3) defines, in the Banach space $\mathbb{B}$, a function $\mathbf{y} \equiv \mathbf{f}(\mathbf{x})$ that maps the unit ball continuously *into* itself. *Into* but, as we will show, *not onto*. Let Y be the range of $\mathbf{f}$:

$$Y = \{\mathbf{y}: \mathbf{y} = \mathbf{f}(\mathbf{x}), |\mathbf{x}| \leqslant 1\}. \tag{23}$$

We will show that *Y is compact*.

We shall rely on the classical *selection principle*, which is proved in Appendix 1: For $0 \leqslant t \leqslant 1$ let the sequence $y_n(t)$ $(n = 1, 2, \ldots)$ *be uniformly bounded and equicontinuous. Then the sequence has a uniformly convergent subsequence.*

To show that Y is compact, let $\mathbf{x}_n$ be a sequence in the unit ball in $\mathbb{B}$; then show that the resulting sequence $\mathbf{y}_n$ has a convergent subsequence. That is, show that the sequence of continuous functions

$$y_n(t) = \int_0^1 e^{-st} \cos(7x_n(s))\,ds \qquad (0 \leqslant t \leqslant 1) \tag{24}$$

has a uniformly convergent subsequence.

The sequence is uniformly bounded: $|y_n(t)| \leqslant 1$. To show that it is equicontinuous, we estimate:

$$|y_n(t) - y_n(\tau)| \leqslant \int_0^1 |e^{-st} - e^{-s\tau}| \cdot 1 \, ds.$$

By the mean-value theorem of calculus,

$$|e^{-st} - e^{-st}| \leqslant s|t - \tau|,$$

and so

$$|y_n(t) - y_n(\tau)| \leqslant \tfrac{1}{2}|t - \tau|.$$

The bound on the right tends to zero as $\tau \to t$, and *the bound is independent of n*; that is the definition of equicontinuity. The classical selection principle now guarantees a uniformly convergent subsequence $y_{n_i}(t)$. Therefore, the range Y is compact.

Now our nonlinear integral equation (1) is guaranteed a solution by *the Schauder fixed-point theorem*:

Theorem 1. *Let X be a non-empty convex set in a Banach space; let Y be a compact subset of X. Suppose* $\mathbf{y} = \mathbf{f}(\mathbf{x})$ *maps X continuously into Y. Then there is a fixed point* $\mathbf{x}^* = \mathbf{f}(\mathbf{x}^*)$.

PROOF. Choose any $\varepsilon > 0$. Successively, pick $\mathbf{y}_1, \mathbf{y}_2, \mathbf{y}_3, \ldots$ in Y so that

$$|\mathbf{y}_i - \mathbf{y}_j| \geqslant \varepsilon \quad \text{for} \quad 1 \leqslant i < j \leqslant n. \tag{25}$$

Keep picking new points $\mathbf{y}_n$ as long as you can. You must stop with some *finite* n; for otherwise you could pick an infinite sequence of points $\mathbf{y}_1, \mathbf{y}_2, \ldots$ that satisfied the inequalities (25). This sequence could not have a convergence subsequence, and this violates our assumption that Y is compact. The finite set $\mathbf{y}_1, \ldots, \mathbf{y}_n$ is ε-*dense* in Y: for every $\mathbf{y}$ in Y, we must have

$$|\mathbf{y}_i - \mathbf{y}| < \varepsilon \quad \text{for some } i = 1, \ldots, n; \tag{26}$$

otherwise we could increase n by defining $\mathbf{y}_{n+1} = \mathbf{y}$.

We now define the convex polytope

$$X_\varepsilon = \{\theta_1 \mathbf{y}_1 + \cdots + \theta_n \mathbf{y}_n : \textstyle\sum \theta_i = 1, \text{ all } \theta_i \geqslant 0\}. \tag{27}$$

This is a subset of X, since X is convex and X contains all the points $\mathbf{y}_i$ in the subset Y. (But X_ε need not lie in Y, which is not assumed convex.)

We will now map all of Y into the polytope X_ε by a continuous function $\mathbf{p}_\varepsilon(\mathbf{y})$ that approximates $\mathbf{y}$:

$$|\mathbf{p}_\varepsilon(\mathbf{y}) - \mathbf{y}| < \varepsilon \quad \text{for all } \mathbf{y} \text{ in } Y. \tag{28}$$

To construct the function $\mathbf{p}_\varepsilon(\mathbf{y})$, we must construct n continuous functions

$$\theta_i = \theta_i(\mathbf{y}) \geqslant 0, \text{ with } \sum_{i=1}^n \theta_1 = 1. \tag{29}$$

First we define, for $i = 1, \ldots, n$,

$$\varphi_i(\mathbf{y}) = \begin{cases} 0 \text{ if } |\mathbf{y}_i - \mathbf{y}| \geqslant \varepsilon \\ \varepsilon - |\mathbf{y}_i - \mathbf{y}| \text{ if } |\mathbf{y}_i - \mathbf{y}| < \varepsilon. \end{cases} \tag{30}$$

Each of these n function $\varphi_i(\mathbf{y})$ is continuous, and (26) guarantees $\varphi_i(\mathbf{y}) > 0$ for some $i = 1, \ldots, n$.

And now we construct the n continuous functions

$$\theta_i(\mathbf{y}) = \varphi_i(\mathbf{y})/s(\mathbf{y}) \qquad (i = 1, \ldots, n; \mathbf{y} \text{ in } Y) \tag{31}$$

where

$$s(\mathbf{y}) = \varphi_1(\mathbf{y}) + \cdots + \varphi_n(\mathbf{y}) > 0.$$

The functions $\theta_i(\mathbf{y})$ satisfy $\theta_i \geqslant 0$, $\sum \theta_i = 1$.

Finally, we construct the continuous function

$$\mathbf{p}_\varepsilon(\mathbf{y}) = \theta_1(\mathbf{y})\mathbf{y}_1 + \theta_2(\mathbf{y})\mathbf{y}_2 + \cdots + \theta_n(\mathbf{y})\mathbf{y}_n. \tag{32}$$

This function maps Y into the polytope X_ε. By (30), $\theta_i(\mathbf{y}) = 0$ unless $|\mathbf{y}_i - \mathbf{y}| < \varepsilon$. Therefore, $\mathbf{p}_\varepsilon(\mathbf{y})$ is a convex combination of just those points $\mathbf{y}_i$ for which $|\mathbf{y}_i - \mathbf{y}| < \varepsilon$; and so

$$\begin{aligned} |p_\varepsilon(\mathbf{y}) - \mathbf{y}| &= \left|\sum \theta_i(\mathbf{y})(\mathbf{y}_i - \mathbf{y})\right| \\ &\leqslant \sum \theta_i(\mathbf{y})|\mathbf{y}_i - \mathbf{y}| < \varepsilon. \end{aligned} \tag{33}$$

This established the approximating property (28).

Now we map the convex polytope X_ε continuously into itself by the function

$$\mathbf{f}_\varepsilon(\mathbf{x}) \equiv \mathbf{p}_\varepsilon(\mathbf{f}(\mathbf{x})) \qquad \text{for } \mathbf{x} \text{ in } X_\varepsilon. \tag{34}$$

Now a fixed point

$$\mathbf{x}_\varepsilon = \mathbf{f}_\varepsilon(\mathbf{x}_\varepsilon) \quad \text{in} \quad X_\varepsilon \tag{35}$$

must exist for this reason:

The polytope X_ε lies in the finite-dimensional linear subspace L spanned by the n points $\mathbf{y}_1, \ldots, \mathbf{y}_n$. If this subspace has dimension N, it can be put in one-to-one continuous correspondence with the familiar Euclidian vector space R^N. Explicitly, if $\mathbf{b}_1, \ldots, \mathbf{b}_N$ are a basis for the subspace L of the Banach space, we set up the correspondence

$$c_1\mathbf{b}_1 + \cdots + c_N\mathbf{b}_N \leftrightarrow \begin{pmatrix} c_1 \\ \vdots \\ c_N \end{pmatrix} \quad \text{in} \quad R^N.$$

Now the polytope X_ε in the Banach space corresponds bicontinuously to the polytope

$$\langle \mathbf{z}^1, \mathbf{z}^2, \ldots, \mathbf{z}^n \rangle \quad \text{in} \quad R^N \tag{36}$$

where

$$\mathbf{y}_1 \leftrightarrow \mathbf{z}^1, \ldots, \mathbf{y}_n \leftrightarrow \mathbf{z}^n \tag{37}$$

and

$$\mathbf{x} = \theta_1\mathbf{y}_1 + \cdots + \theta_n\mathbf{y}_n \leftrightarrow \theta_1\mathbf{z}^1 + \cdots + \theta_n\mathbf{z}^n.$$

The continuous mapping $\mathbf{f}_\varepsilon$ of X_ε into itself corresponds to a continuous mapping $\mathbf{g}_\varepsilon$ of the Euclidian polytope (36) into itself. A polytope in R^N is a closed, bounded, convex set; therefore it is topologically equivalent to a single point or to a ball in R^M for some $M \leqslant N$. (This was proved in the Appendix to Section 2.) Now the Brouwer fixed-point theorem guarantees a fixed point

$$\mathbf{z}^\varepsilon = \mathbf{g}_\varepsilon(\mathbf{z}^\varepsilon) \quad \text{in} \quad R^N.$$

The corresponding point is a fixed point in the Banach space:

$$\mathbf{x}_\varepsilon = \mathbf{f}_\varepsilon(\mathbf{x}_\varepsilon) \quad \text{in} \quad X_\varepsilon.$$

(Perhaps I have labored this point unnecessarily; perhaps without argument you would have believed that the Brouwer theorem guarantees the fixed point $\mathbf{x}_\varepsilon$ in the Banach space. But I needed the argument to convince myself, since we proved the Brouwer theorem only for convex bodies in R^N.)

Now we will cautiously take a limit as $\varepsilon \to 0$. Set $\mathbf{y}_\varepsilon = \mathbf{f}(\mathbf{x}_\varepsilon)$. Since Y is compact, we may let $\varepsilon \to 0$ through some sequence $\varepsilon_1, \varepsilon_2, \ldots$ for which $\mathbf{y}_\varepsilon$ converges to a limit in Y:

$$\mathbf{f}(\mathbf{x}_\varepsilon) = \mathbf{y}_\varepsilon \to \mathbf{y}^* \quad \text{as} \quad \varepsilon = \varepsilon_k \to 0. \tag{38}$$

We now write

$$\mathbf{x}_\varepsilon = \mathbf{f}_\varepsilon(\mathbf{x}_\varepsilon) \equiv \mathbf{p}_\varepsilon(\mathbf{f}(\mathbf{x}_\varepsilon)) = \mathbf{p}_\varepsilon(\mathbf{y}_\varepsilon),$$

$$\mathbf{x}_\varepsilon = \mathbf{y}_\varepsilon + [p_\varepsilon(\mathbf{y}_\varepsilon) - \mathbf{y}_\varepsilon].$$

But we have $|p_\varepsilon(\mathbf{y}) - \mathbf{y}| < \varepsilon$ for all $\mathbf{y}$, so (38) implies

$$\mathbf{x}_\varepsilon \to \mathbf{y}^* \quad \text{as} \quad \varepsilon = \varepsilon_k \to 0. \tag{39}$$

Now, since $\mathbf{f}$ is continuous, (38) yields the fixed point:

$$\mathbf{f}(\mathbf{y}^*) = \mathbf{y}^*. \tag{40}$$

Appendix. The Arzelà-Ascoli theorem: For $0 \leqslant t \leqslant 1$ let the sequence $y_1(t), y_2(t), \ldots$ *satisfy*

$$|y_n(t)| \leqslant M; \text{ and } |y_n(s) - y_n(t)| < \varepsilon \text{ if } |s - t| < \delta(\varepsilon).$$

Then the sequence has a uniformly convergent subsequence.

PROOF. Let $r_1, r_2, \ldots$ be the rational numbers in $[0,1]$. Let the bounded sequence $y_n(r_1)$ converge if n goes to infinity through the set

$$N_1 : n_{11} < n_{12} < n_{13} < \cdots.$$

Choose the subset $N_2 \subset N_1$ so that $y_n(r_2)$ converges if $n \to \infty$ through the set

$$N_2 : n_{21} < n_{22} < n_{23} < \cdots.$$

In general, choose $N_k \subset N_{k-1}$ so that $y_n(r_k)$ converges if $n \to \infty$ through the set

$$N_k : n_{k1} < n_{k2} < n_{k3} < \cdots.$$

Now define the diagonal set:

$$D: n_{11} < n_{22} < n_{33} < \cdots .$$

Since $n_{kk} \in N_j$ for all $k \geq j$, we have limits

$$y_n(r_j) \to \lambda_j \quad \text{as} \quad N = n_{kk} \to \infty .$$

If t lies in $[0,1]$, for $\varepsilon > 0$ we have a $\delta(\varepsilon)$ such that, for all n,

$$|y_n(r) - y_n(t)| < \varepsilon \quad \text{if} \quad |r - t| < \delta(\varepsilon).$$

Then

$$|y_n(t) - y_m(t)| \leq |y_n(t) - y_n(r)| + |y_n(r) - y_m(r)| + |y_m(r) - y_m(t)|$$

$$\leq \varepsilon + \varepsilon + \varepsilon$$

if n and m are sufficiently large in the diagonal set D. Given ε, we may let r be one of the numbers $0, 1/q, 2/q, \ldots, 1$ if $q > 1/\delta(\varepsilon)$. Thus, given $\varepsilon > 0$, we can find a number $M(\varepsilon)$ such that

$$|y_n(t) - y_m(t)| \leq 3\varepsilon \qquad \text{if } n, m \geq M(\varepsilon) \text{ and } n, m \text{ are in } D.$$

This proves the uniform convergence of $y_n(t)$ as n tends to infinity in D.

References

1. J. Schauder, Der Fixpunktsatz in Funktionalräumen, *Studia Math.* Vol. 2 (1930) pp. 171–180.
2. G. Pólya, *How to Solve It*, Princeton Univ. Press., 1948.
3. H. Brezis and F. E. Browder, Existence theorems for nonlinear integral equations of Hammerstein type, *Bull. Amer. Math. Soc.*, Vol. 81 (1975) pp. 73–78.

PROBLEMS

1. For $0 \leq t \leq 1$ let Y be the set of differentiable functions $y(t)$ that satisfy $|y(t)| \leq 1732$, $|y'(t)| \leq 1756$. Prove that every sequence $y_n(t) \in Y$ has a uniformly convergent subsequence. (Use the Arzelà-Ascoli theorem.)

2. Let $g(t,x)$ be continuous for $t \geq 0$ and $|x| \leq 1$, with $|g(t,x)| \leq M$. Let $\mathbb{B}$ be the Banach space of continuous functions $x(t)$ for $0 \leq t \leq t_0$, with $|x(t)| \leq 1$. How small must the positive number t_0 be so that the equation

$$y(t) = \int_0^t g(s,x(s))\, ds \qquad (0 \leq t \leq t_0)$$

maps $\mathbb{B}$ into a subset $Y \subset \mathbb{B}$? (Answer: t_0 must be $\leq 1/M$.) Show that the mapping is continuous in the maximum norm. Show that the subset Y is compact.

3. (Continuation.) Now you are ready to prove a famous theorem of Peano: *Assume that the function $g(t,x)$ is continuous for $0 \leq t < t_1$ and $|x| \leq 1$. Then the initial-value problem*

$$\frac{dx(t)}{dt} = g(t,x(t)) \qquad (0 \leq t \leq t_0)$$

$$x(0) = 0$$

has a solution $x(t)$ *if the positive number* t_0 *is small enough.* (Do not assume a Lipschitz condition! Don't try to prove uniqueness, because it isn't true. Example: $x' = \sqrt{x}$, $x(0) = 0$ has *two* solutions: $x_1 \equiv 0$ and $x_2 = t^2/4$.)

*4. (Continuation.) When I was a student, I proved a generalization of Peano's theorem for functional differential equations like this one:

$$\frac{dx(t)}{dt} = g(t,x(t),x(\omega(t))),$$

where $\omega(t)$ is a given continuous function satisfying $\omega(t) \leqslant t$. My proof was long and clumsy because I did not know Schauder's theorem. You can prove my theorem in a few lines. Assume $-a \leqslant \omega(t) \leqslant t$ for $0 \leqslant t \leqslant t_1$, and give the initial condition

$$x(t) = \phi(t) \quad \text{for} \quad -a \leqslant t \leqslant 0.$$

Assume the given functions g, ω, and ϕ are continuous. Now prove that a solution $x(t)$ exists for $0 \leqslant t \leqslant t_0$ if the positive number t_0 is small enough. (Reference: *Proc. Amer. Math. Soc.*, Vol. 5 (1954) pp. 363–369.)

5. First verify that the integral

$$u(x) = \int_0^1 G(x,y)\psi(y)\,dy$$

solves the boundary-value problem

$$-u''(x) = \psi(x) \qquad (0 \leqslant x \leqslant 1)$$
$$u(0) = u(1) = 0$$

if G is the Green's function

$$G(x,y) = \begin{cases} (1-x)y & \text{for} \quad y \leqslant x \\ (1-y)x & \text{for} \quad x \leqslant y \end{cases}.$$

Now use Schauder's theorem to prove the existence of a solution to the nonlinear boundary-value problem

$$-u''(x) = e^{-u(x)} \qquad (0 \leqslant x \leqslant 1)$$
$$u(0) = u(1) = 0.$$

*6. For **y** in a 3-dimensional bounded solid D, suppose that the function $G(\mathbf{x},\mathbf{y})$ is positive and integrable, and suppose that the integral

$$\int_D G(\mathbf{x},\mathbf{y})\,dy$$

is a bounded, continuous function of **x** in D. Use the Schauder theorem to establish the existence of a solution to the nonlinear integral equation

$$u(\mathbf{x}) = \int_D G(\mathbf{x},\mathbf{y})e^{-u(\mathbf{y})}\,dy,$$

where dy stands for $dy_1\,dy_2\,dy_3$. (That's how you prove a solution exists to the nonlinear boundary-value problem $-\nabla^2 u = e^{-u}$, $u = 0$ on ∂D.)

*7. From Walras to Debreu, economists have talked about *equilibrium*. First, the economy is described by a state variable **x** in an appropriate mathematical space.

When something happens in the economy, the state $\mathbf{x}$ goes to a state $\mathbf{f}(\mathbf{x})$. An equilibrium is a state that stays fixed: $\mathbf{x} = \mathbf{f}(\mathbf{x})$. Use Schauder's theorem to give general conditions for the existence of economic equilibria. Give economic examples or interpretations of these terms: *Banach space, norm, boundedness, continuity, convexity, compactness.*

8. Prove that this boundary-value problem has a solution:

$$-u''(x) + u(x) = x \sin(u(x)) \qquad (0 \leqslant x \leqslant 1)$$
$$u(0) = 5, \quad u(1) = 7.$$

Method: First get an integral equation.

9. Let X be a closed set in a normed space. Let Y be compact subset of X. Let $\mathbf{g}(\mathbf{x})$ be a contraction mapping such that $\mathbf{y} + \mathbf{g}(\mathbf{x})$ lies in X for $\mathbf{y} \in Y$ and $\mathbf{x} \in X$. Let the equation

$$\mathbf{x} = \mathbf{y} + \mathbf{g}(\mathbf{x})$$

have the solution $\mathbf{x} = \mathbf{h}(\mathbf{y})$. Prove that $\mathbf{h}(\mathbf{y})$ maps Y continuously into a compact subset of X.

10. (Continuation.) Now you can prove Krasnoselskii's theorem: Consider the fixed-point equation

$$\mathbf{x} = \mathbf{f}(\mathbf{x}) + \mathbf{g}(\mathbf{x})$$

for $\mathbf{x}$ in a Banach space $\mathbb{B}$. Let X be a non-empty closed convex set in $\mathbb{B}$. Let $\mathbf{f}(\mathbf{x})$ map X continuously into a compact subset $Y \subset X$. Let $\mathbf{g}(\mathbf{x})$ be a contraction mapping on X; do not assume that the range of $\mathbf{g}$ is compact. Assume $\mathbf{y} + \mathbf{g}(\mathbf{x}) \in X$ for $\mathbf{y} \in Y$ and $\mathbf{x} \in X$. Now prove there is a fixed point $\mathbf{x} = \mathbf{f}(\mathbf{x}) + \mathbf{g}(\mathbf{x})$.

11. (Continuation.) Prove the existence of a solution to the equation

$$x(t) = \frac{1}{3}\cos(x(t)) + \frac{2}{3}\int_0^1 e^{-st}\cos(7x(s))\,ds \qquad (0 \leqslant t \leqslant 1)$$

Note that the mapping $x(t) \mapsto \cos(x(t))$ is *not* compact on the Banach space of continuous functions. Use Krasnoselskii's theorem.

12. Let $\psi(x)$ be a given continuous function, and consider the linear boundary-value problem

$$-(1 + x\psi^2(x))u''(x) + u(x) = 0 \qquad (0 \leqslant x \leqslant 1)$$
$$u(0) = 0, \quad u(1) = 1.$$

This linear problem is known to have a unique solution. Show that the solution $u(x)$ must satisfy the bounds

$$0 \leqslant u(x) \leqslant 1, \quad 0 \leqslant u'(x) \leqslant 1$$

regardless of $\psi(x)$. Now prove that a solution exists to the nonlinear boundary-value problem

$$-(1 + xu^2(x))u''(x) + u(x) = 0$$
$$u(0) = 0, \quad u(1) = 1.$$

Method: Look for a fixed point of the mapping $\psi \mapsto u$.

6 Kakutani's Fixed-Point Theorem and Nash's Theorem for *n*-Person Games

Many theoretical economists have quoted Kakutani's fixed-point theorem. But even if no one quoted it, mathematicians would still study it because of its novelty. It talks about a novel kind of function $Y = F(\mathbf{x})$: if $\mathbf{x}$ equals a point in the set X, then Y *equals a subset* of X. Yes, I said *equals* a subset.

Here is a homely example of such a function. Let X be the set of all men. If $\mathbf{x}$ is a man, let $F(\mathbf{x})$ equal the subset of men whose names are known to the man $\mathbf{x}$.

Kakutani's theorem talks about the relationship

$$\mathbf{x} \in F(\mathbf{x}), \tag{1}$$

which says that $\mathbf{x}$ is a member of the subset $F(\mathbf{x})$. In our example a man $\mathbf{x}$ lies in $F(\mathbf{x})$ if he knows his own name. In other words, $\mathbf{x} \in F(\mathbf{x})$ unless $\mathbf{x}$ has amnesia.

The inclusion $\mathbf{x} \in F(\mathbf{x})$ is a generalization of the equation for a fixed point:

$$\mathbf{x} = \mathbf{f}(\mathbf{x}). \tag{2}$$

To see this, let each subset $Y = F(\mathbf{x})$ contain only the single member $\mathbf{y} = \mathbf{f}(\mathbf{x})$. Then "$\mathbf{x} \in F(\mathbf{x})$" means "$\mathbf{x} = \mathbf{f}(\mathbf{x})$."

Kakutani's theorem follows from the Brouwer fixed-point theorem. We will prove it by using the technique of barycentric subdivision. Then we will give a famous application to economics: the Nash equilibrium theorem for *n*-person games.

Kakutani's Theorem. *Let X be a closed, bounded, convex set in the real N-dimensional space R^N. For every $\mathbf{x} \in X$ let $F(\mathbf{x})$ equal a non-empty convex subset $Y \subset X$. Assume that the graph*

$$\{\mathbf{x}, \mathbf{y} \colon \mathbf{y} \in F(\mathbf{x})\} \text{ is closed.} \tag{3}$$

Then some point $\mathbf{x}^*$ lies in $F(\mathbf{x}^*)$.

Before the proof, here are a few remarks:

1. The condition (3) means this: Suppose a sequence $\mathbf{x}^n$ has a limit $\mathbf{x}^0$, and suppose that

$$\mathbf{y}^n \in F(\mathbf{x}^n) \qquad (n = 1, 2, 3, \ldots). \tag{4}$$

Suppose also that $\mathbf{y}^n$ tends to some limit $\mathbf{y}^0$. Then (3) requires that the limits satisfy

$$\mathbf{y}^0 \in F(\mathbf{x}^0). \tag{5}$$

All that says is this: Draw the graph of all points $\mathbf{x}$ and $\mathbf{y}$ for which $\mathbf{x}$ lies in X while $\mathbf{y}$ lies in the subset $Y = F(\mathbf{x})$; then this graph is a closed set in the

$2N$-dimensional space of points with the $2N$ real coordinates

$$x_1, \ldots, x_N, y_1, \ldots, y_N.$$

(Some authors express the *closedness of the graph* by writing: $F(x)$ is *upper semicontinuous*.)

The closedness of the graph (3) is a generalization of ordinary continuity. Suppose each set $Y = F(\mathbf{x})$ contains only the single point $\mathbf{y} = \mathbf{f}(\mathbf{x})$ in the closed, bounded set X. If $\mathbf{f}(\mathbf{x})$ is continuous, then the graph

$$\{\mathbf{x}, \mathbf{y} : \mathbf{y} = \mathbf{f}(\mathbf{x})\} \text{ is closed.} \tag{6}$$

Conversely, suppose that (6) holds; let's show that $\mathbf{f}(\mathbf{x})$ is continuous.

Suppose that $\mathbf{x}^n \to \mathbf{x}^0$. Then $\mathbf{x}^0$ lies in X because we assume that X is closed. Let $\mathbf{y}^0 = \mathbf{f}(\mathbf{x}^0)$ and let $\mathbf{y}^n = \mathbf{f}(\mathbf{x}^n)$ for $n = 1, 2, 3, \ldots$. We want to show that $\mathbf{y}^n \to \mathbf{y}^0$. Since the sequence $\mathbf{y}^n$ lies in the bounded set X, some subsequence converges:

$$\mathbf{y}^n \to \mathbf{y}^* \quad \text{for} \quad n = n_s \to \infty. \tag{7}$$

Now the closeness of the graph (6) implies

$$\mathbf{y}^* = \mathbf{f}(\mathbf{x}^0), \tag{8}$$

that is, $\mathbf{y}^* = \mathbf{y}^0$. Likewise, if $\mathbf{y}'$ is the limit of some other subsequence of the bounded sequence $\mathbf{y}^n$, then the closedness (6) implies $\mathbf{y}' = \mathbf{y}^0 = \mathbf{y}^*$. Since all convergent subsequences of the sequence $\mathbf{y}^n$ have the same limit, $\mathbf{y}^0$, the whole sequence $\mathbf{y}^n$ converges to $\mathbf{y}^0$. Thus, (6) implies $\mathbf{f}(\mathbf{x})$ is continuous.

(Here we have leaned heavily on the boundedness of the set X. If X is unbounded, then the graph may be closed while $\mathbf{f}(\mathbf{x})$ is discontinuous. For example, let X be the set of all the real numbers. Define $f(x) = 1/x$ if $x \neq 0$; define $f(0) = 17$. The graph is closed, but the function is discontinuous.)

2. In the statement of Kakutani's theorem the subset $Y = F(\mathbf{x})$ is assumed convex. Why? Otherwise the theorem would be false. Let X be the interval $-1 \leqslant x \leqslant 1$. Define

$$F(x) = \{\tfrac{1}{2}\} \qquad \text{for} \quad -1 \leqslant x < 0$$
$$F(0) = \{\tfrac{1}{2}, -\tfrac{1}{2}\}$$
$$F(x) = \{-\tfrac{1}{2}\} \qquad \text{for} \quad 0 < x \leqslant 1.$$

Here $F(x) \subset X$, and the graph of $[x, F(x)]$ is closed. But no point in X satisfies $x \in F(x)$. That is because the subset $F(0)$, which contains exactly two points, is not convex.

3. The Brouwer fixed-point theorem is a special case of Kakutani's theorem. If $F(\mathbf{x}) = \{\mathbf{f}(\mathbf{x})\}$, where $\mathbf{f}(\mathbf{x})$ is a single point in X, then $\mathbf{f}(\mathbf{x})$ is continuous if and only if the graph $[\mathbf{x}, \mathbf{f}(\mathbf{x})]$ is closed; we proved this in remark No. 1. And now $\mathbf{x}^* \in F(\mathbf{x}^*)$ means $\mathbf{x}^* = \mathbf{f}(\mathbf{x}^*)$.

4. The assumption that the convex body X has an interior point $\mathbf{a}$ in R^N is unnecessary; it appears in the following proof only for convenience. As

we showed before[1], if a convex body in R^N has no interior point, and if the body has more than one point, then the body does have an interior point relative to some M-dimensional hyperplane that contains the body. Now the proof can be carried out in R^M.

5. You may wish to review the definitions of these terms: *nondegenerate simplex, barycentric coordinates, nth barycentric subdivision, cell* (in the subdivision).

PROOF OF KAKUTANI'S THEOREM. First we say this: We may assume that X is a nondegenerate simplex in R^N.

Otherwise, let S be a nondegenerate simplex that contains X, as in Figure 1. We will map S continuously into X as follows:

(i) If $s \in X$, just let $x(s) = s$.

(ii) Let a be an interior point of X (see the preceding Remark No. 4). Suppose that $s \in S$ but $s \notin X$ (see Figure 1); now define $x(s)$ to be the unique boundary point of X that lies on the segment joining a to s. (This boundary point is unique because a is an interior point.)

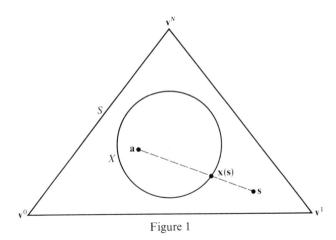

Figure 1

For each $s \in S$ we now define the subset

$$G(s) = F(x(s)) \subset X \subset S. \tag{9}$$

The subset $G = F$ is convex. And the graph $[s, G(s)]$ is closed; for if

$$s \to s^0 \quad \text{and} \quad y \in G(s) \quad \text{and} \quad y \to y^0, \tag{10}$$

then

$$x(s) \to x(s^0) \quad \text{and} \quad y \in F(x(s)) \quad \text{and} \quad y \to y^0, \tag{11}$$

and therefore

$$y^0 \in F(x(s^0)) = G(s^0). \tag{12}$$

---

[1] See the appendix to Section 2.

Now the assumptions of our theorem hold for the function $G(\mathbf{s})$ for $\mathbf{s} \in S$. If the theorem holds for simplexes, then some point in the simplex S satisfies

$$\mathbf{s}^* \in G(\mathbf{s}^*). \tag{13}$$

But we defined $G(\mathbf{s}) = F(\mathbf{x}(\mathbf{s})) \subset X$, and so (13) implies $\mathbf{s}^* \in X$. Then $\mathbf{s}^* = \mathbf{x}(\mathbf{s}^*)$, and (13) says

$$\mathbf{x}^* \in F(\mathbf{x}^*) \quad \text{with} \quad \mathbf{x}^* \equiv \mathbf{s}^* = \mathbf{x}(\mathbf{s}^*) \in X. \tag{14}$$

Thus, the theorem for simplexes implies the theorem for arbitrary convex bodies X.

From now on, assume X is the nondegenerate simplex

$$X = \langle \mathbf{v}^0, \mathbf{v}^1, \ldots, \mathbf{v}^N \rangle. \tag{15}$$

Form the nth barycentric subdivision of X. Define a continuous function $\mathbf{f}^n(\mathbf{x})$ as follows: If $\mathbf{x}$ is a vertex of any cell in the subdivision, let $\mathbf{f}^n(\mathbf{x})$ equal *some* point $\mathbf{y} \in F(\mathbf{x})$. If $\mathbf{x}$ is a general point in a cell, then define $\mathbf{f}^n(\mathbf{x})$ by linear interpolation from the values at the $N + 1$ vertices of the cell that contains $\mathbf{x}$. Explicitly,

$$\text{if } \mathbf{x} \in \text{the cell } \langle \mathbf{x}^0, \mathbf{x}^1, \ldots, \mathbf{x}^N \rangle,$$

$$\text{define } \mathbf{f}^n(\mathbf{x}) = \sum_{j=0}^{N} \theta_j \mathbf{f}^n(\mathbf{x}^j) \text{ if} \tag{16}$$

$$\mathbf{x} = \sum_{j=0}^{N} \theta_j \mathbf{x}^j, \quad \theta_j \geqslant 0, \quad \sum \theta_j = 1. \tag{17}$$

Note that if $\mathbf{x}$ lies on an $(N - 1)$-dimensional face common to two cells, then the two definitions of $\mathbf{f}^n(\mathbf{x})$ on the common face are consistent.

The function $\mathbf{f}^n(\mathbf{x})$ maps the body X continuously into itself. Now the Brouwer theorem yields a fixed point

$$\mathbf{x}^n = \mathbf{f}^n(\mathbf{x}^n). \tag{18}$$

If, by chance, $\mathbf{x}^n$ is a vertex of the subdivision, we're through, because we picked $\mathbf{f}^n(\mathbf{x}) \in F(\mathbf{x})$ at all vertices $\mathbf{x}$. But if $\mathbf{x}^n$ is not a vertex, we have more work to do.

Suppose that $\mathbf{x}^n$ lies in the cell

$$\langle \mathbf{x}^{n0}, \mathbf{x}^{n1}, \ldots, \mathbf{x}^{nN} \rangle. \tag{19}$$

As in (17), let $\theta_0, \ldots, \theta_N$ be barycentric coordinates relative to the cell. If

$$\mathbf{x}^n = \theta_{n0} \mathbf{x}^{n0} + \theta_{n1} \mathbf{x}^{n1} + \cdots + \theta_{nN} \mathbf{x}^{nN}, \tag{20}$$

then (18) implies

$$\mathbf{x}^n = \mathbf{f}^n(\mathbf{x}^n) = \theta_{n0} \mathbf{y}^{n0} + \theta_{n1} \mathbf{y}^{n1} + \cdots + \theta_{nN} \mathbf{y}^{nN}, \tag{21}$$

where

$$\mathbf{y}^{nj} = \mathbf{f}^n(\mathbf{x}^{nj}) \in F(\mathbf{x}^{nj}) \quad (j = 0, \ldots, N). \tag{22}$$

We now use the Bolzano-Weierstrass theorem to pick a subsequence $n_s \to \infty$ that makes everything in sight converge. We require these limits as $n = n_s \to \infty$:

$$\mathbf{x}^n \to \mathbf{x}^*$$
$$\theta_{nj} \to \theta_j \qquad (j = 0, \ldots, N) \tag{23}$$
$$\mathbf{y}^{nj} \to \mathbf{y}^j \qquad (j = 0, \ldots, N).$$

Since the cells shrink to points as $n \to \infty$, the first limit (23) implies the same limit for the cell vertices:

$$\mathbf{x}^{nj} \to \mathbf{x}^* \quad \text{as} \quad n_s \to \infty \qquad (j = 0, \ldots, N). \tag{24}$$

Now the fixed-point equation (21) gives

$$\mathbf{x}^* = \theta_0 \mathbf{y}^0 + \theta_1 \mathbf{y}^1 + \cdots + \theta_N \mathbf{y}^N. \tag{25}$$

Where are the limit points $\mathbf{y}^j$? If we apply the *closedness* assumption (3) to (22), we locate the limits:

$$\mathbf{y}^j \in F(\mathbf{x}^*) \qquad (j = 0, \ldots, N). \tag{26}$$

Ah! Now we recall the assumption: *each subset F is convex*. All the points $\mathbf{y}^j$ in the convex combination (25) lie in the same convex set $F(\mathbf{x}^*)$. So (25) yields the result:

$$\mathbf{x}^* \in F(\mathbf{x}^*). \tag{27}$$

In the theory of many-person games, the point $\mathbf{x}^*$ gives optimal strategies for all the players.

Application to n-person games. We will now deduce the Nash equilibrium theorem for n-person games. This is one of those mathematical topics in which the ideas are simple but the notation is complex. Subscripts beget sub-subscripts; superscripts grow supersuperscripts; and the simple ideas get lost. We don't need that kind of trouble.

So, with no loss of conceptional generality, we will fix $n = 3$. We have exactly three players; their names are Able, Baker, and Charlie. Each has a finite number of possible moves—called *pure strategies*:

$$\text{Able has pure strategies } i = 1, 2, \ldots, i_0$$
$$\text{Baker has pure strategies } j = 1, 2, \ldots, j_0 \tag{28}$$
$$\text{Charlie has pure strategies } k = 1, 2, \ldots, k_0.$$

If Able plays i while Baker plays j and Charlie plays k, the players get *payoffs*: Able get a_{ijk}; Baker gets b_{ijk}; Charlie get c_{ijk}.

Mixed strategies. As we know from the study of zero-sum two-person games, we should allow the players to choose their moves at random. We will assume:

$$\text{Able plays } i \text{ with probability } p_i$$
$$\text{Baker plays } j \text{ with probability } q_j \tag{29}$$
$$\text{Charlie plays } k \text{ with probability } r_k,$$

where $p_i \geqslant 0$, $q_j \geqslant 0$, $r_k \geqslant 0$, and

$$\sum p_i = \sum q_j = \sum r_k = 1. \tag{30}$$

We assume i, j, k are independent random variables. Now the players have more freedom. Instead of choosing pure strategies i, j, k, they may choose mixed-strategy vectors $\mathbf{p}, \mathbf{q}, \mathbf{r}$.

(Pure strategies are special cases of mixed strategies. For instance, if Able wants to choose the pure strategy $i = 2$, he chooses the mixed strategy $\mathbf{p}$ with component $p_2 = 1$ and all other $p_i = 0$.)

Now the payoffs are *expected values*. If our players play the mixed strategies $\mathbf{p}, \mathbf{q}, \mathbf{r}$, the payoff to Able is the expected value

$$a(\mathbf{p,q,r}) = \sum_{i,j,k} a_{ijk} p_i q_j r_k; \tag{31}$$

the payoffs to Baker and to Charlie are the analogous sums $b(\mathbf{p,q,r})$ and $c(\mathbf{p,q,r})$.

Let's look at the game through Able's eyes. He doesn't know exactly which moves Baker and Charlie will make, but we assume he does know their probability vectors $\mathbf{q}$ and $\mathbf{r}$. For instance, Able doesn't know which move Charlie will make, but Able does know the probability r_k that Charlie will make move k.

If Able knows Baker's $\mathbf{q}$ and Charlie's $\mathbf{r}$, how can Able best choose his $\mathbf{p}$? *Able will choose his $\mathbf{p}$ to maximize his payoff*:

$$a(\mathbf{p,q,r}) \geqslant a(\mathbf{p',q,r}) \qquad \text{for all } \mathbf{p'}, \tag{32}$$

where $\mathbf{p'}$ ranges over probability vectors. The maximum property (32) defines a set of solutions

$$\mathbf{p} \in P(\mathbf{q,r}). \tag{33}$$

Here P is a *subset* of the probability vectors with i_0 components.

Indeed, we can see just what P is if we look at the definition (31). As a function of the variable vector $\mathbf{p'}$, the payoff is linear:

$$a(\mathbf{p',q,r}) = \sum_i a_i p_i', \tag{34}$$

where

$$a_i = \sum_{j,k} a_{ijk} q_j r_k. \tag{35}$$

If $\mathbf{q}$ and $\mathbf{r}$ are given, then the coefficients a_i are *constants*.

How do you maximize a linear form (34)? For instance, how would you maximize

$$2p_1' + 7p_2' + 4p_3' + 7p_4' + 7p_5' \tag{36}$$

over probability vectors $\mathbf{p'}$? That's easy. You would let $\mathbf{p'}$ equal any $\mathbf{p}$ that averaged only the *maximum* coefficients. In the example (36), we see max $a_\mu = 7$ and

$$a_1 < 7 \quad \text{and} \quad a_3 < 7, \tag{37}$$

and so we require that **p** lie in the set

$$P = \{\mathbf{p}: p_i \geqslant 0, \sum p_i = 1, p_1 = p_3 = 0\}. \tag{38}$$

The maximum value 7 is attained if and only if **p′** lies in P.

In general, to maximize the linear form (34), we require that **p′** lie in the set

$$P = \left\{\mathbf{p}: p_i \geqslant 0, \sum p_i = 1, p_i = 0 \text{ if } a_i < \max_\mu a_\mu\right\}. \tag{39}$$

This is a closed, bounded convex set. If the coefficients $a_1, a_2, \ldots$ are functions of **q** and **r**, then the convex body P is a function of **q** and **r**. Then we write $P = P(\mathbf{q},\mathbf{r})$, as we did in formula (33). *The convex body $P(\mathbf{q},\mathbf{r})$ is the set of Able's optimal mixed strategies* **p**.

Now pretend you are Baker. Then you know your enemies' strategies **p** and **r**. And so you will choose your strategy **q** to maximize your payoff:

$$b(\mathbf{p},\mathbf{q},\mathbf{r}) \geqslant b(\mathbf{p},\mathbf{q}',\mathbf{r}) \text{ for all } \mathbf{q}'. \tag{40}$$

This holds for all **q** *in a convex body* $Q(p,r)$*, which is the set of Baker's optimal mixed strategies* **q**.

Analogously, Charlie knows **p** and **q**. He chooses **r** in the *convex body* $R(\mathbf{p},\mathbf{q})$ defined by the maximization

$$c(\mathbf{p},\mathbf{q},\mathbf{r}) \geqslant c(\mathbf{p},\mathbf{q},\mathbf{r}') \qquad \text{for all } \mathbf{r}'. \tag{41}$$

Nash's solution. We say that **p,q,r** *solve* the game if

$$\mathbf{p} \in P(\mathbf{q},\mathbf{r}), \ \mathbf{q} \in Q(\mathbf{p},\mathbf{r}), \text{ and } \mathbf{r} \in R(\mathbf{p},\mathbf{q}). \tag{42}$$

Then *no player has any incentive to change his mixed strategy as long as his enemies don't change theirs.* For instance, look at Baker. Why should he change his **q**? Since $\mathbf{q} \in Q(\mathbf{p},\mathbf{r})$, Baker is already getting as much as he can—as long as Able and Charlie don't change **p** and **r**.

Nash's Theorem. *Mixed strategies exist that solve the game.*

PROOF. Given the arrays $a_{ijk}, b_{ijk}, c_{ijk}$, we must show that mixed strategies **p, q, r** exist that solve (15).

We set up the composite vector

$$\mathbf{x} = \begin{pmatrix} \mathbf{p} \\ \mathbf{q} \\ \mathbf{r} \end{pmatrix}. \tag{43}$$

This vector has N real components where (1) gives $N = i_0 + j_0 + k_0$. The vector **x** lies in the closed, bounded, convex set X defined by (30).

For each $\mathbf{x} \in X$ we define the following subset of X:

$$F(\mathbf{x}) = \begin{bmatrix} P(\mathbf{p},\mathbf{r}) \\ Q(\mathbf{p},\mathbf{r}) \\ R(\mathbf{p},\mathbf{q}) \end{bmatrix}. \tag{44}$$

Here P, Q, and R are the convex bodies defined by (32), (40), and (41). Nash's theorem says just this: *Some point* $\mathbf{x}^*$ *lies in its own* $F(\mathbf{x}^*)$. That means: $\mathbf{p}^*$ lies in $P(\mathbf{q}^*,\mathbf{r}^*)$; $\mathbf{q}^*$ lies in $Q(\mathbf{p}^*,\mathbf{r}^*)$; $\mathbf{r}^*$ lies in $R(\mathbf{p}^*,\mathbf{q}^*)$.

This statement begs us to use Kakutani's theorem. All we have to do is to check these hypotheses:

(i) each subset F is convex in X;
(ii) the graph $[\mathbf{x}, F(\mathbf{x})]$ is closed.

Hypothesis (i) holds because the component subsets P, Q, R are convex. So all we have to do is to check hypothesis (ii).

Suppose $\mathbf{x}$ and $\mathbf{y}$ satisfy

$$\mathbf{x} \in X, \quad \mathbf{y} \in F(\mathbf{x}), \tag{45}$$

and suppose these points tend to limits in the closed set X:

$$\mathbf{x} \to \mathbf{x}^0, \quad \mathbf{y} \to \mathbf{y}^0. \tag{46}$$

Then we must show that these limits satisfy

$$\mathbf{y}^0 \in F(\mathbf{x}^0). \tag{47}$$

Formula (43) says $\mathbf{x}$ has three parts: $\mathbf{p}, \mathbf{q}, \mathbf{r}$. Similarly, $\mathbf{y}$ has three parts: $\mathbf{u}, \mathbf{v}, \mathbf{w}$. Then (45) says:

$$\mathbf{u} \in P(\mathbf{q},\mathbf{r}), \quad \mathbf{v} \in Q(\mathbf{p},\mathbf{r}), \quad \mathbf{w} \in R(\mathbf{p},\mathbf{q}). \tag{48}$$

These three statements mean the following: For all probability vectors $\mathbf{p}', \mathbf{q}', \mathbf{r}'$, we have

$$a(\mathbf{u},\mathbf{q},\mathbf{r}) \geqslant a(\mathbf{p}',\mathbf{q},\mathbf{r})$$
$$b(\mathbf{p},\mathbf{v},\mathbf{r}) \geqslant b(\mathbf{p},\mathbf{q}',\mathbf{r}) \tag{49}$$
$$c(\mathbf{p},\mathbf{q},\mathbf{w}) \geqslant c(\mathbf{p},\mathbf{q},\mathbf{r}').$$

As $\mathbf{x}$ and $\mathbf{y}$ tend to limits, their parts $\mathbf{p}, \mathbf{q}, \mathbf{r}$ and $\mathbf{u}, \mathbf{v}, \mathbf{w}$ tend to limits. Since the functions a, b, c are continuous, the inequalities (49) hold for the limits; and that means $\mathbf{y}^0 \in F(\mathbf{x}^0)$.

We have now verified the hypotheses of Kakutani's theorem. And so the game has a solution:

$$\mathbf{x}^* \in F(\mathbf{x}^*). \tag{50}$$

If you agree that we lost no conceptual generality be setting $n = 3$, then we have proved Nash's theorem for n-person games.

References

1. S. Kakutani, A generalization of Brouwer's fixed point theorem, *Duke Math. J.* Vol. 8 (1941) pp. 457–458.
2. J. F. Nash, Equilibrium points in n-person games, *Proc. Nat. Academy of Sciences*, Vol. 36 (1950) pp. 48–49.

PROBLEMS

1. Let X be the interval $-1 \leqslant x \leqslant 1$. Let $F(x)$ be the set of numbers y satisfying $x^2 + y^2 \geqslant \frac{1}{4}$. Draw the graph

$$G = \{(x,y): x \in X, y \in F(x)\}.$$

Show that G is a closed set in the plane. Draw the sets $F(-1)$, $F(0)$, $F(\frac{1}{3})$, $F(\frac{1}{2})$, $F(\frac{3}{4})$. Which of them are convex?

2. For $0 \leqslant x \leqslant 1$ define $f(0) = 17$, $f(x) = 1/x$ if $x > 0$. Draw the graph

$$G = \{(x,y): 0 \leqslant x \leqslant 1, y = f(x)\}.$$

Show that G is a closed set in the plane, although the function $f(x)$ is discontinuous. Is G convex?

3. For the function $f(x)$ in problem 2, define the set-valued function $F(x) = \{y: 0 \leqslant y \leqslant f(x)\}$. Draw the graph

$$G_1 = \{(x,y): 0 \leqslant x \leqslant 1, y \in F(x)\}.$$

Is the graph G_1 convex? Is it closed? Is the set $F(x)$ convex? Is it closed?

4. Using Nash's theorem, prove von Neumann's theorem for zero-sum, two-person games: Given an $m \times n$ matrix A, prove that there are mixed strategies $\mathbf{x}^0$ and $\mathbf{y}^0$ such that

$$\mathbf{x} \cdot A\mathbf{y}^0 \leqslant \mathbf{x}^0 \cdot A\mathbf{y}^0 \leqslant \mathbf{x}^0 \cdot A\mathbf{y}$$

for all mixed strategies $\mathbf{x}$ and $\mathbf{y}$.

5. Earlier, we discussed the nonzero-sum game *disarmament* (Ch. I, Sec. 14). I said that both countries *arm* in a Nash equilibrium; please verify that now. I also said that this equilibrium was *stable*, meaning that the optimal mixed strategies don't change if the payoffs change slightly. Is that true? Are all Nash equilibria stable?

6. Suppose Able, Baker, and Charlie play a game. Each writes an integer from 1 to 10. If Able writes i, Baker j, and Charlie k, these are the payoffs: $|i - j|$ to Able, $|j - k|$ to Baker, and $|k - i|$ to Charlie. Find the Nash equilibrium.

7. Majority wins: Each of three players shouts *Red!* or *Black!* If one player shouts one color while the other two players shout the other color, the one player must pay a dollar to each of the other two players. Show that this is a zero-sum game, and find a Nash solution. How is this solution upset if two of the players collude? Write the payoff matrix of the zero-sum two-person game in which Able plays against a coalition of Baker and Charlie. Assume Baker and Charlie always shout the same color. Show that Able must expect to lose, on the average, a dollar a game.

8. In the statement of Kakutani's theorem the subset $F(\mathbf{x})$ is not assumed closed. Show that the closed-graph assumption (3) *implies* $F(\mathbf{x})$ is closed.

9. Here is a quick false proof of Kakutani's theorem: The assumptions imply there must be a continuous point-valued function $\mathbf{f}(\mathbf{x}) \in F(\mathbf{x})$; now Brouwer's theorem guarantees a fixed point $\mathbf{x}^* = \mathbf{f}(\mathbf{x}^*)$. Construct a counterexample that shows this proof is false.

*10. In Kakutani's theorem drop the assumption that all the sets $F(\mathbf{x})$ are convex. Then prove some point $\mathbf{x}^*$ lies in the *convex hull* of $F(\mathbf{x}^*)$. (Definition: The convex hull of a set Y is the intersection of all convex sets that include Y. For $Y \subset R^N$ the convex hull is the set of all convex combinations

$$\theta_0 \mathbf{y}^0 + \theta_1 \mathbf{y}^1 + \cdots + \theta_N \mathbf{y}^N \quad \text{with} \quad \theta_i \geqslant 0, \ \Sigma \theta_i = 1,$$

where $\mathbf{y}^0, \ldots, \mathbf{y}^N$ lie in Y.)

*11. Let X be a closed, bounded, convex set in R^N. Let $\mathbf{f}(\mathbf{x})$ maps X into itself, but do not assume that $\mathbf{f}(\mathbf{x})$ is continuous. Let $F(\mathbf{x})$ be the convex hull of the set of limit points of $\mathbf{f}(\mathbf{z})$ for $\mathbf{z} \to \mathbf{x}$ (with $\mathbf{z} \neq \mathbf{x}$). Then show that some point $\mathbf{x}^*$ lies in the set $F(\mathbf{x}^*)$. Show that this result is just Brouwer's theorem if $\mathbf{f}(\mathbf{x})$ is continuous. Illustrate the result if $f(x)$ is the discontinuous function

$$f(x) = \begin{cases} 0.5 & \text{for} \quad -1 \leqslant x < 0 \\ 0.6 & \text{for} \quad x = 0 \\ -0.7 & \text{for} \quad 0 < x \leqslant 1 \end{cases}.$$

What are the two limit points of $f(z)$ as $z \to 0$? What is the set $F(0)$? What is x^*?

Index

Undergraduate Texts in Mathematics

Apostol: Introduction to Analytic
Number Theory.
1976. xii, 370 pages. 24 illus.

Childs: A Concrete Introduction to
Higher Algebra.
1979. xiv, 338 pages. 8 illus.

Chung: Elementary Probability Theory
with Stochastic Processes. Third Edition
1979. 336 pages.

Croom: Basic Concepts of Algebraic
Topology.
1978. x. 177 pages. 46 illus.

Fleming: Functions of Several Variables.
Second edition.
1977. xi. 411 pages. 96 illus.

Halmos: Finite-Dimensional Vector
Spaces. Second edition.
1974. viii. 200 pages.

Franklin: Methods of Mathematical Economics.
Linear and Nonlinear Programming,
Fixed-Point Theorems.
1980. x, 297 pages. 38 illus.

Halmos: Naive Set Theory.
1974. vii, 104 pages.

Kemeny/Snell: Finite Markov Chains.
1976. ix, 210 pages.

Lax/Burstein/Lax: Calculus with
Applications and Computing.
Volume 1.
1976. xi, 513 pages. 170 illus.

LeCuyer: College Mathematics with
A Programming Language.
1978. xii, 420 pages. 126 illus. 64 diagrams.

Malitz: Introduction to Mathematical
Logic.
Set Theory - Computable Functions -
Model Theory.
1979. 255 pages. 2 illus.

Prenowitz/Jantosciak: The Theory of
Join Spaces.
A Contemporary Approach to Convex
Sets and Linear Geometry.
1979. 534 pages. 404 illus.

Priestley: Calculus: An Historical
Approach.
1979. 441 pages. 300 illus.

Ross: Elementary Analysis
A Theory of Calculus
1980. viii, 264 pages.

Protter/Morrey: A First Course in Real
Analysis.
1977. xii, 507 pages. 135 illus.

Sigler: Algebra.
1976. xi, 419 pages. 32 illus.

Singer/Thorpe: Lecture Notes on
Elementary Topology and Geometry.
1976. viii, 232 pages. 109 illus.

Smith: Linear Algebra
1978. vii, 280 pages. 21 illus.

Thorpe: Elementary Topics in
Differential Geometry.
1979. 253 pages. 126 illus.

Whyburn/Duda: Dynamic Topology.
1979. 152 pages. 20 illus.

Wilson: Much Ado About Calculus.
A Modern Treatment with Applications
Prepared for Use with the Computer.
1979. 788 pages. 145 illus.

Instructor's Manual
vi, 165 pages.